Chatbots in Educational Leadership and Management

Austin Musundire
University of Limpopo, South Africa

IGI Global
Scientific Publishing
Publishing Tomorrow's Research Today

Vice President of Editorial	Melissa Wagner
Managing Editor of Acquisitions	Mikaela Felty
Managing Editor of Book Development	Jocelynn Hessler
Production Manager	Mike Brehm
Cover Design	Phillip Shickler

Published in the United States of America by
IGI Global Scientific Publishing
701 East Chocolate Avenue
Hershey, PA, 17033, USA
Tel: 717-533-8845
Fax: 717-533-8661
Website: https://www.igi-global.com E-mail: cust@igi-global.com

Library of Congress Cataloging-in-Publication Data

Names: Musundire, Austin, editor.
Title: Chatbots in educational leadership and management / edited by: Austin Musundire.
Description: Hershey, PA : IGI Global Scientific Publishing, [2025] | Includes bibliographical references and index. | Summary: "By fusing scholarly discourse, practical guidance, and real-world examples, the book aims to illuminate the transformative journey that educational institutions can undertake as they harness the power of chatbots to drive organizational efficiency, enhance communication, and foster innovative leadership practices"-- Provided by publisher.
Identifiers: LCCN 2024055568 (print) | LCCN 2024055569 (ebook) | ISBN 9798369387344 (hardcover) | ISBN 9798369387351 (paperback) | ISBN 9798369387368 (ebook)
Subjects: LCSH: Artificial intelligence--Educational applications. | Educational leadership. | Chatbots.
Classification: LCC LB1028.43 .C44 2025 (print) | LCC LB1028.43 (ebook) | DDC 371.33/4--dc23/eng/20250228
LC record available at https://lccn.loc.gov/2024055568
LC ebook record available at https://lccn.loc.gov/2024055569

British Cataloguing in Publication Data
A Cataloguing in Publication record for this book is available from the British Library.

Table of Contents

Detailed Table of Contents

This study examines the use of chatbots as virtual leaders in Australian schools, focusing on their role in decision-making and strategy. Chatbots streamline tasks, enhance stakeholder engagement, and provide data-driven insights, improving operational efficiency. Despite these benefits, issues such as technical integration, user acceptance, and data security remain challenges. Customizable solutions, robust training, and data protection strategies are critical for successful implementation. Recommendations include fostering collaboration, promoting equitable use of algorithms, and ensuring ethical chatbot practices. Future research should explore the long-term impact of chatbots on education, leadership, and professional development.

The way individuals connect and communicate has been completely transformed by social media platforms, enabling instantaneous interaction with friends, family, and communities, regardless of physical distance or geographical boundaries. These platforms empower young individuals to create and maintain extensive social networks, fostering both personal and professional relationships while encouraging constant interaction. This study aims to delve deeper into the variations in how late adolescents and emerging adults perceive the appropriateness of expressing emotions across various social media platforms. The focus is particularly on engineering college students, a demographic known for its active engagement with digital technology and online platforms. The study examines differences based on gender and age,

This paper explores challenges and opportunities of AI's transformative potential in educational leadership and management, examining its impact on administrative efficiency, personalised learning, and data-driven decision-making. Despite promising AI tools like chatbots, learning analytics, and adaptive learning systems, widespread adoption in education remains limited due to infrastructure gaps, cost, and lack of expertise. Findings suggest that AI can streamline tasks, support personalised education, and empower leaders with actionable insights, yet its full potential is unachieved in most institutions. Recommendations include fostering AI literacy, investing in infrastructure, and creating supportive policies for sustainable integration. This study underscores the need for strategic planning to advance AI's role in educational leadership, balancing innovation with institutional readiness and ethical considerations.

This chapter addresses the rising use of chatbots in leadership, notably their utility in assisting decision-making and advising roles. As artificial intelligence (AI) continues to permeate organizational systems, chatbots are emerging as key tools in streamlining leadership responsibilities and delivering real-time advising support. The chapter digs into the methods by which chatbots aid leaders in complex decision-making processes, delivering analytical insights and recommendations based on data-driven techniques. Moreover, the advising role of chatbots is investigated, demonstrating how these AI systems increase leadership capacities by giving continual feedback, resource allocation techniques, and problem-solving support. By integrating chatbots into leadership frameworks, companies, particularly in educational contexts, can boost efficiency and develop more dynamic leadership structures. The chapter finishes by analyzing the technological constraints and potential future developments of chatbots in educational leadership and administration.

This literature paper examines solutions for improving chatbots in crisis management in educational institutions. It addresses key challenges such as adaptability,

The present healthcare sector has become a highly complex and dynamic environment; it requires a mix of advanced technology, human empathy, and efficient leadership to meet the multiple challenges involved. Emotional intelligence enables healthcare workers to empathetically connect with patients, improves communication between healthcare workers and patients and consequently enhances patient outcomes. Leadership that is collaborative is strongly associated with team work and consensual decision making which are critical in multidisciplinary health care settings. Adding emotional intelligence to the chatbots could potentially improve patient engagement through the emotional. Within this chapter, these synergies will be highlighted wherein the combination of EI, collaborative leadership, and a chatbot might be perceived to provide potential advantages in healthcare management, reducing burnout and optimizing the patient experience. This technology-human empathy balance can change the way patient-centered care has been developed within such an increasingly complex scenario.

This paper discusses the challenges and opportunities of implementing educational leadership and management chatbots, focusing on data security, integration platform considerations and user resistance to adoption derived from organisational culture. Literature reveals the trends in growth across various sectors such as customer service and healthcare yet development and adaptation in educational leadership is slow. Chatbots enhances user experience, administrative tasks and communication channels. The study highlights the importance of organizational culture in change management critical for successful implementation of educational leadership and management chatbots. Recommendations for future development include leveraging big data and machine learning to produce sentimental chatbots. Suggestions on leadership development towards transformational leadership style to facilitate institutional growth and success in implementing new technologies such as chatbots.

In recent years, the integration of chatbots into the education sector has emerged as a transformative force, redefining how educational institutions approach both leadership and learning. Their potential to revolutionize education is grounded in their ability to provide real-time support, personalized learning experiences, and streamlined administrative functions, ultimately leading to more dynamic and responsive educational practices.The application of chatbots in education serves as a catalyst for enhanced leadership by streamlining communication channels between educators, students, and administrators. Traditional methods of managing educational tasks and responding to inquiries can often be cumbersome and slow. Chatbots can address this issue by offering instant, automated responses to frequently asked questions. For educational leaders, chatbots represent a tool that can improve operational efficiency, enabling them to better allocate resources, monitor performance metrics, and implement data-driven decision-making processes.

This literature-based paper examines the application of chatbots in curriculum management in educational settings, aiming to explore their benefits, challenges, and future potential. Findings show that chatbots, enhanced by AI, machine learning, and NLP, streamline administrative processes, support student engagement, and enable effective communication among stakeholders. Despite these advantages, challenges such as data privacy and technical limitations persist. The chapter concludes that, with ethical practices and AI advancements, chatbots could significantly reshape

Preface

INTRODUCTION

In an era where digital transformation is redefining educational leadership and management, chatbots have emerged as a revolutionary tool, offering innovative solutions to long-standing challenges in the field. This edited volume, *Chatbots in Educational Leadership and Management*, explores the multifaceted role of chatbots in enhancing decision-making, administrative efficiency, stakeholder engagement, and overall educational governance. With contributions from a diverse group of scholars across the globe, this book presents a comprehensive examination of how artificial intelligence (AI)-powered chatbots are shaping the future of education leadership.

The chapters within this volume provide an in-depth analysis of the various applications of chatbots, ranging from their use in secondary schools for strategic planning to their integration into higher education institutions for administrative streamlining. The book delves into empirical studies on student interactions with digital platforms, explores AI-powered chatbot applications in crisis management, and discusses the ethical implications of chatbot implementation in educational settings. Additionally, it highlights the intersection of chatbot technology with emerging innovations such as Augmented Reality (AR), Virtual Reality (VR), and Emotional Intelligence (EI), underscoring the evolving landscape of digital learning.

While the advantages of chatbot technology in education are undeniable—improving efficiency, enabling data-driven decision-making, and fostering interactive learning environments—this book also acknowledges the challenges and limitations associated with their adoption. Issues such as data security, user acceptance, and the ethical implications of AI-driven decision-making are critically examined. Through these discussions, the contributors offer strategic recommendations for successful implementation, ensuring that chatbot technologies align with institutional needs, ethical standards, and future research directions.

OVERVIEW OF THE CHAPTERS

1. This chapter explores the role of chatbots as virtual leaders in Australian secondary schools. It discusses how they support decision-making, enhance stakeholder engagement, and provide data-driven insights to improve operational efficiency. The chapter also examines challenges related to technical integration, user acceptance, and data security while offering recommendations for ethical and effective implementation.
2. This chapter investigates how engineering students express themselves on social media. It delves into the variations in emotional expression based on gender and age, analyzing how these factors influence digital interactions. The study provides insights into how young individuals navigate online communication and maintain personal and professional networks.
3. This chapter examines the integration of chatbots into Educational Management Systems (EMS) within higher education. It highlights the potential benefits, such as cost reduction, improved operational efficiency, and enhanced student support. The chapter also addresses challenges like user resistance and data privacy concerns, proposing strategies for scalable implementation and security measures.
4. This chapter discusses the transformative potential of AI, augmented reality (AR), virtual reality (VR), and chatbots in education. It emphasizes how these technologies enhance student engagement and learning experiences. The chapter highlights the benefits of AI-powered chatbots in higher education institutions and their role in transnational education.
5. This chapter explores the challenges and opportunities of AI in educational leadership and management. It examines AI's role in improving administrative efficiency, personalized learning, and data-driven decision-making. The chapter also addresses infrastructure gaps, cost concerns, and expertise limitations that hinder AI adoption in education.
6. This chapter focuses on the use of chatbots in leadership, particularly in decision-making and advisory roles. It discusses how chatbots support leaders by providing analytical insights, feedback, and problem-solving assistance. The chapter also examines technological constraints and future developments in AI-driven leadership support.
7. This chapter investigates the role of chatbots in crisis management for educational institutions. It highlights key challenges, including adaptability, communication limitations, and data security. The chapter explores how machine learning (ML), natural language processing (NLP), and sentiment analysis can enhance chatbot responses during crises.

8. This chapter examines chatbot design for educational leadership, emphasizing the need for tailored functionalities to meet institutional goals. It discusses how chatbots can improve administrative efficiency, student support, and stakeholder communication. The chapter also explores essential design considerations, such as user experience and technological integration.
9. This chapter explores the integration of chatbots in healthcare management, focusing on emotional intelligence and collaborative leadership. It discusses how AI-driven chatbots can enhance patient engagement, reduce burnout, and optimize the patient experience. The chapter highlights the balance between technology and human empathy in healthcare.
10. This chapter examines the challenges and opportunities of implementing chatbots in educational leadership and management. It discusses key factors such as data security, user resistance, and organizational culture. The chapter offers recommendations for leveraging big data, machine learning, and transformational leadership to facilitate successful chatbot adoption.
11. This chapter traces the evolution of chatbots and their impact on educational leadership. It explores historical developments, current applications, and future opportunities. The chapter also discusses challenges such as technical complexity, data privacy, and training requirements, offering recommendations for ethical and effective AI integration.
12. This chapter analyzes how chatbots enhance decision-making and efficiency in educational leadership. It explores case studies of chatbot implementations, highlighting benefits such as real-time data analysis, improved communication, and operational efficiency. The chapter also examines challenges related to ethical considerations and resistance to change.
13. This chapter discusses the transformative role of chatbots in educational leadership and learning. It highlights how chatbots streamline communication, provide personalized support, and enhance operational efficiency. The chapter also explores the challenges of integrating AI-driven chatbots into institutional frameworks.
14. This chapter examines the use of chatbots in curriculum management for higher education institutions. It explores their benefits, including streamlined administrative processes and improved stakeholder communication. The chapter also discusses challenges such as data privacy and technical limitations, providing recommendations for ethical and effective implementation.

CONCLUSION

The contributions in this volume collectively emphasize the importance of a balanced approach—leveraging technological advancements while maintaining human-centered educational leadership. As AI and chatbot technologies continue to evolve, their role in education leadership and management will become increasingly significant, influencing policy, pedagogy, and institutional administration. This book serves as a valuable resource for academics, educational leaders, policymakers, and technology developers seeking to understand and navigate the transformative potential of chatbots in education.

We extend our gratitude to all the scholars whose research and insights have enriched this volume. Their dedication to exploring the intersection of technology and education leadership ensures that this book provides a timely and critical perspective on the future of digital governance in education.

Austin Musundire
University of Limpopo, South Africa

Chapter 1
Chatbots as Virtual Leaders:
Supporting Decision-Making and Strategic Planning in Australian Secondary Schools

Austin Musundire
https://orcid.org/0000-0001-8784-0616
University of South Africa, South Africa

ABSTRACT

This study examines the use of chatbots as virtual leaders in Australian schools, focusing on their role in decision-making and strategy. Chatbots streamline tasks, enhance stakeholder engagement, and provide data-driven insights, improving operational efficiency. Despite these benefits, issues such as technical integration, user acceptance, and data security remain challenges. Customizable solutions, robust training, and data protection strategies are critical for successful implementation. Recommendations include fostering collaboration, promoting equitable use of algorithms, and ensuring ethical chatbot practices. Future research should explore the long-term impact of chatbots on education, leadership, and professional development.

BACKGROUND

The integration of artificial intelligence (AI) into educational leadership is revolutionizing decision-making and strategic planning in schools, particularly with the rise of chatbots. These AI-powered virtual assistants are designed to handle administrative and educational tasks, such as providing personalized feedback,

DOI: 10.4018/979-8-3693-8734-4.ch001

scheduling, and answering queries. Their real-time data processing capabilities and 24/7 availability make chatbots invaluable for supporting school leadership teams in managing day-to-day operations. As educational institutions, especially in Australian secondary schools, embrace digital transformation, chatbots offer great potential to streamline processes, improve communication, and foster a more efficient school environment.

In Australian secondary schools, where leaders face complex decision-making challenges and diverse student needs, chatbots can significantly enhance data-driven decisions. These AI tools can aggregate and analyze data from multiple sources, such as student performance metrics and teacher feedback, enabling timely and informed decision-making. By reducing administrative burdens, chatbots allow school leaders to focus on high-level strategic goals and overall institutional improvement. Moreover, chatbots' data aggregation capabilities support more effective planning and ensure that decisions are based on comprehensive, accurate information.

Chatbots also promote collaborative decision-making within schools by automating routine tasks and offering data-driven insights. This frees up time for school leaders to focus on shaping the school's vision, fostering positive culture, and engaging with stakeholders such as staff, students, and parents. By facilitating communication and collecting feedback, chatbots enable a more transparent and inclusive leadership approach, ultimately enhancing the effectiveness of decision-making and promoting a sense of shared responsibility. As schools continue to embrace technological advancements, chatbots are poised to play a pivotal role in shaping the future of educational leadership, improving decision-making, and driving innovation.

AREA OF FOCUS

The Role of Chatbots in Educational leadership

The integration of artificial intelligence (AI) into educational leadership is transforming decision-making and strategic planning within schools. AI-powered chatbots, capable of processing vast amounts of data in real-time and offering 24/7 support, assist school leaders in various administrative and educational tasks, including personalized feedback, scheduling, and responding to queries (Lu et al., 2021). These chatbots improve the efficiency of school operations by facilitating data-driven decision-making. In particular, Australian secondary schools, facing complex decision-making processes and diverse student needs, can leverage chatbots to gather and analyze data from multiple sources, such as student performance and attendance metrics. This integration allows school leaders to make well-informed decisions quickly and effectively, reducing administrative burdens and allowing them to focus on strategic objectives (Davenport & Harris, 2017).

Chatbots also play a key role in promoting collaborative decision-making within schools. By automating routine tasks and providing data-driven insights, chatbots enable leaders to concentrate on shaping the school's vision, fostering positive school culture, and engaging with stakeholders, including teachers, students, and parents (Leithwood & Azah, 2017). Additionally, chatbots ensure that all levels of the school hierarchy remain informed and involved in the decision-making process by collecting and analyzing feedback from various groups. This fosters a transparent and inclusive leadership style, enhancing the effectiveness of strategic planning and reinforcing the role of AI in the future of educational leadership (Tikkinen-Piri et al., 2018).

Capabilities of Chatbots in Schools

Chatbots have become vital tools in schools, supporting a wide range of functions that enhance decision-making and strategic planning. They are particularly effective in automating administrative tasks such as scheduling, attendance tracking, and responding to frequently asked questions, reducing the workload of educators and administrators (Lu et al., 2021). This automation improves operational efficiency, allowing school leaders to focus on more critical activities, such as curriculum development and long-term strategic planning. Additionally, chatbots analyze large volumes of student data, such as test scores and attendance records, to identify patterns and trends that inform educational decisions and timely interventions (Johnson & Schenker, 2023). This data-driven approach helps educators make informed decisions that improve student outcomes and support evidence-based strategic planning.

Beyond administrative support, chatbots enhance communication and collaboration among stakeholders, such as students, teachers, and parents. By providing a consistent and accessible platform for updates, feedback, and engagement, chatbots promote a more inclusive and transparent school environment (Lin et al., 2020). This accessibility fosters continuous information flow, crucial for effective decision-making. Furthermore, chatbots offer personalized learning experiences by providing tailored feedback and resources to students, supporting teachers in adapting their teaching strategies (Nguyen et al., 2022). The combination of administrative automation, data analysis, and personalized learning through chatbots enables school leaders to make informed decisions and foster a more efficient, collaborative educational environment, contributing to the overall success of schools (Baker & Smith, 2023).

Chatbots in Data-Driven Decision-Making

Chatbots are revolutionizing data-driven decision-making in educational leadership by processing large datasets from various sources, such as student performance, attendance, and behavioral records, to provide timely insights for school leaders. In Australian secondary schools, chatbots can quickly identify trends, patterns, and anomalies, enabling leaders to make well-informed decisions that improve educational outcomes. This capability aligns with global trends, such as those seen in the United States, where AI-driven tools help personalize learning and streamline decision-making by automating the analysis of student data (Henderson & Harris, 2021). Additionally, chatbots present data through visual formats, such as dashboards and reports, making it easier for school leaders to track student progress, adjust curricula, and allocate resources effectively (Lee & Mitchell, 2022).

The integration of chatbots into data-driven decision-making supports long-term strategic planning by tracking and analyzing data over time. In Australia, this approach enables school leaders to identify trends in attendance, academic performance, and student retention, ultimately helping to improve overall school performance and align with national standards such as those set by ACARA. Similar applications have been successful in countries like the Netherlands and Canada, where chatbots have been used to identify systemic issues and develop strategies for enhancing student engagement and achievement (Morris & Evans, 2021). As AI technologies continue to evolve, the use of chatbots in schools will become increasingly crucial in helping educational leaders navigate the complexities of modern education and improve student outcomes.

Supporting Evidence-Based Policies

Chatbots have the potential to significantly enhance evidence-based policy-making in education, particularly in Australian secondary schools. Evidence-based policies are grounded in accurate, timely data and aim to make informed decisions that positively impact educational outcomes (Brown et al., 2020). In this context, chatbots act as powerful tools that can gather, analyze, and synthesize data from both internal and external sources, allowing school leaders to make decisions that are both contextually relevant and empirically supported. Similar developments have been observed in the United Kingdom, where educational institutions are increasingly utilizing AI tools like chatbots to collect real-time data from a variety of sources, such as student performance, attendance, and engagement metrics. This enables UK school leaders to develop policies that are not only evidence-driven but also responsive to the needs of students and staff, much like the needs facing Australian educators.

In Australian secondary schools, chatbots can help provide school leaders with continuous, real-time access to critical data points, such as academic performance trends, student attendance patterns, and behavioral incidents. This ability to access and analyze data quickly allows educational leaders to make timely adjustments to teaching strategies, school policies, and resource allocation. For instance, chatbots can automatically collect and analyze data from student assessments, attendance records, and even teacher feedback, offering insights that guide policy development. Research by O'Neill and Binns (2021) demonstrates how data-driven policies in Australian schools have led to improvements in student outcomes, particularly in addressing learning gaps. Chatbots contribute to this by helping to ensure that the policies are backed by real-time data, thus improving the likelihood that interventions are both appropriate and effective. Similarly, educational systems in countries like Canada and the Netherlands are leveraging AI-powered tools to gather evidence and create policies that address systemic issues, such as student absenteeism and achievement disparities.

Furthermore, chatbots can enhance the robustness of policy-making by aggregating data from diverse sources, such as academic records, student feedback, and external research. This data synthesis helps educational leaders in Australia to create policies that are not only based on internal institutional data but also consider broader educational trends and national priorities. For instance, in Finland, a country renowned for its progressive educational policies, chatbots have been employed to gather feedback from teachers, students, and parents, enabling leaders to develop policies that reflect the diverse needs of the entire school community (Morris & Evans, 2021). Similarly, Australian secondary schools can use chatbots to merge internal data with national datasets, such as those provided by the Australian Curriculum, Assessment and Reporting Authority (ACARA), to formulate policies that address both local and national educational goals. This integrated approach ensures that policies are not only grounded in institutional realities but also aligned with national standards, making them more effective in achieving desired outcomes.

Chatbots also support the ongoing evaluation and refinement of educational policies by providing continuous feedback loops. For example, once a policy is implemented, chatbots can collect data on its impact, such as changes in student performance, teacher satisfaction, and student well-being. This allows for the continuous assessment of policy effectiveness, enabling leaders to make necessary adjustments based on real-time evidence. In the United States, schools have successfully used chatbots to monitor the implementation of new policies and identify areas where improvements can be made. This same approach can be applied to Australian secondary schools, where chatbots can track the impact of evidence-based policies on student engagement, teacher performance, and overall school climate. By enabling ongoing evaluation and feedback, chatbots ensure that policies remain relevant and adaptable to changing circumstances.

In conclusion, chatbots play a crucial role in supporting evidence-based policy-making in Australian secondary schools. By providing real-time data insights, synthesizing information from various sources, and enabling ongoing policy evaluation, chatbots empower educational leaders to make informed decisions that are grounded in empirical evidence. The integration of AI-driven tools like chatbots into policy development processes is not only transforming the Australian education landscape but also aligns with global trends observed in countries such as the UK, Canada, and Finland. As the use of chatbots in education continues to grow, their ability to support data-driven, contextually relevant policies will be essential in shaping the future of educational leadership and ensuring better outcomes for students.

Chatbots in Strategic Planning

Strategic planning is a vital aspect of educational leadership, particularly in Australian secondary schools, where leaders must navigate an increasingly complex landscape of educational challenges and opportunities. Scenario planning and forecasting are integral components of strategic planning, as they enable leaders to envision future possibilities and prepare for them in advance. Chatbots, powered by machine learning algorithms, offer a transformative approach to these processes. According to Makridakis et al. (2018), machine learning models can simulate various scenarios based on historical data and predictive algorithms, helping leaders to anticipate challenges and allocate resources effectively. This capability is particularly beneficial in schools, where resource management, staff allocation, and curriculum planning are often influenced by unpredictable factors such as changes in student demographics or government policy shifts.

In Australian secondary schools, chatbots equipped with advanced predictive models can analyze vast amounts of historical data, such as student performance, attendance, and behavior trends, to forecast future outcomes. This allows educational leaders to simulate various scenarios and assess how different decisions might impact the school's performance. For example, chatbots could forecast the impact of introducing a new teaching methodology or allocating additional resources to a particular department, helping leaders make informed, data-driven decisions. This type of scenario planning has been effectively employed in educational systems worldwide, such as in the United States, where school districts have used predictive analytics to assess future staffing needs, student enrollment trends, and curriculum effectiveness (Guskey, 2020). In this context, Australian secondary schools can leverage chatbots to gain similar insights and improve their strategic planning processes.

Moreover, chatbots can provide real-time data analysis that aids in the dynamic adjustment of strategies. As noted by Makridakis et al. (2018), one of the key strengths of machine learning in scenario planning is its ability to adapt to new information and refine forecasts over time. In the context of Australian schools, chatbots can continuously update predictive models as new data becomes available, allowing school leaders to adjust their strategies in response to emerging trends. For instance, if a chatbot detects a decline in student performance in a specific subject area, it can alert educational leaders to take proactive measures, such as revising the curriculum or offering additional support to students. This dynamic, data-driven approach to strategic planning ensures that educational leaders remain agile and responsive to the evolving needs of their school communities.

This capability for scenario planning and forecasting also extends beyond individual schools to the broader education system. Chatbots can aggregate data from multiple schools within a district or region, enabling educational leaders to simulate and analyze trends at a macro level. For example, in countries like the United Kingdom and Finland, educational authorities use machine learning algorithms to forecast regional educational outcomes, such as student achievement levels, funding needs, and staffing shortages (Morris & Evans, 2021). In Australia, this approach can be particularly beneficial at the state or national level, where educational leaders can use chatbot-driven data models to anticipate trends across various schools and make more strategic decisions regarding resource allocation, policy development, and curriculum design. By integrating data from different schools, chatbots provide a comprehensive view of the education system and help leaders make decisions that benefit the entire student population.

Furthermore, chatbots equipped with scenario planning and forecasting capabilities can help educational leaders address external challenges such as funding cuts, changes in government policy, or shifts in public health, as seen in the COVID-19 pandemic. For example, the Australian education system faced significant challenges during the pandemic, including shifts to online learning and adjustments to funding priorities. Chatbots could have played a pivotal role in helping educational leaders predict the impacts of these changes, allowing for more effective resource allocation and support for students and teachers. By leveraging machine learning algorithms, chatbots can simulate the potential outcomes of various responses to external challenges, allowing leaders to develop strategic plans that are both flexible and effective in the face of uncertainty.

In summary, chatbots equipped with machine learning algorithms are valuable tools for strategic planning in Australian secondary schools. By enabling scenario planning and forecasting, chatbots help educational leaders anticipate future challenges and make data-driven decisions that improve resource allocation, staff management, and curriculum development. The ability to simulate various scenarios based on historical data and predictive models enhances the strategic planning process, ensuring that school leaders can respond to emerging trends and challenges with agility. As demonstrated by educational systems around the world, including the United States and Finland, the use of chatbots in scenario planning and forecasting is transforming the way educational leaders approach strategic planning, and Australian schools are well-positioned to benefit from this innovative approach.

Resource Allocation

Resource allocation is a critical function within educational leadership, especially in Australian secondary schools where budgetary constraints, staff requirements, and infrastructure needs must be carefully managed to ensure effective educational outcomes. Optimizing resource allocation ensures that schools can meet their objectives, whether these involve enhancing student performance, improving teacher development, or upgrading facilities. Chatbots, by processing vast amounts of data, assist educational leaders in making informed, data-driven decisions regarding the distribution of resources. According to Marler and Fisher (2013), effective resource allocation is essential for achieving organizational goals, as it ensures that limited resources are utilized in the most efficient way possible to support key initiatives. In this context, chatbots serve as valuable tools by providing real-time insights that help educational leaders allocate resources in a way that aligns with the school's strategic objectives.

In Australian secondary schools, where resource constraints are a common challenge, chatbots can assist in analyzing various factors such as budget allocations, staffing levels, and infrastructure needs. By synthesizing data from multiple sources, including financial records, staffing databases, and maintenance schedules, chatbots can generate recommendations that help leaders prioritize resources based on urgent needs and long-term goals. For instance, if a school faces budget cuts, chatbots can analyze the potential impacts on key programs and suggest areas where resources might be reallocated without compromising the overall quality of education. This data-driven approach is especially important in an era where school leaders must make difficult decisions about staffing levels, curricular offerings, and facility maintenance. The ability of chatbots to provide actionable insights from complex data sets enhances the decision-making process and improves the alignment of resource distribution with educational priorities.

Globally, several education systems have begun leveraging chatbots to optimize resource allocation. For example, in the United Kingdom, schools have integrated chatbot systems to analyze staffing needs and identify potential efficiencies in staff deployment (Morris & Evans, 2021). Similarly, in the United States, some districts have used chatbot-driven data analysis to evaluate classroom sizes, teacher-to-student ratios, and the allocation of support staff in response to fluctuating enrollment numbers (Guskey, 2020). These practices underscore the potential of chatbots in providing resource allocation recommendations that are based on both quantitative data and qualitative insights. In the context of Australian schools, chatbots could similarly help leaders assess and adjust staffing levels, ensuring that schools are not overstaffed or understaffed in specific areas. Additionally, chatbots can assist in monitoring infrastructure needs, such as technology upgrades, classroom renovations, or maintenance schedules, which are vital for maintaining a conducive learning environment.

Another key aspect of resource allocation that chatbots support is optimizing the use of technology. As Australian secondary schools continue to integrate digital learning tools, the allocation of technological resources becomes increasingly important. Chatbots can track the usage and performance of educational technologies, helping school leaders determine which tools are most effective in enhancing learning outcomes and where additional investment may be needed. By analyzing usage data, chatbots can make recommendations on which digital platforms or resources should be prioritized, helping schools maximize their return on investment in technology. For example, a chatbot might identify a specific software tool that is being underutilized and suggest that additional training be provided to teachers, or it might recommend the purchase of additional licenses for a popular tool that has proven to be effective in supporting student learning. This data-driven approach ensures that technological resources are allocated where they are most needed, ultimately contributing to better educational outcomes for students.

Moreover, chatbots can support the efficient allocation of human resources by analyzing workload distribution and identifying areas where staff may be overburdened or underutilized. This is particularly important in large schools or districts where staff resources are spread across multiple departments or campuses. Chatbots can monitor staff performance metrics, such as teaching hours, student engagement levels, and administrative duties, to offer recommendations on how to optimize staffing assignments. By ensuring that staff workloads are balanced and aligned with the school's goals, chatbots help prevent burnout and ensure that resources are deployed in a way that maximizes staff effectiveness. For example, if a chatbot identifies that a teacher is handling an excessive administrative load in addition to their teaching duties, it can recommend that administrative tasks be reassigned or that additional support be provided to that staff member.

In conclusion, chatbots offer significant potential in optimizing resource allocation within Australian secondary schools. By analyzing budgetary constraints, staffing needs, and infrastructure requirements, chatbots provide educational leaders with data-driven insights that enable them to make informed decisions about how resources are distributed. Whether it is reallocating resources in response to budget cuts, prioritizing technology investments, or optimizing staff deployment, chatbots help ensure that limited resources are used efficiently to support the school's strategic goals. The use of chatbots for resource allocation is not only beneficial within individual schools but also has broader implications for district-level planning, as demonstrated by global examples from countries like the United Kingdom and the United States. As Australian schools continue to face resource constraints and increased demand for quality education, chatbots will play a key role in helping leaders navigate these challenges and achieve their organizational objectives.

Stakeholder Engagement

Stakeholder engagement is a crucial aspect of strategic planning in schools, as it ensures that the perspectives of all relevant parties—teachers, parents, students, and the wider community—are taken into account when making decisions about the future direction of the school. In Australian secondary schools, engaging stakeholders effectively is essential for building trust and ensuring that policies and initiatives reflect the diverse needs of the school community. Chatbots facilitate this engagement by providing a platform for stakeholders to share feedback, ask questions, and receive timely updates on school activities. By offering a centralized, easily accessible communication channel, chatbots enhance transparency and foster a collaborative approach to strategic planning. According to Leithwood and Azah (2017), collaborative decision-making, where various stakeholders are involved, improves the quality of strategic plans and increases the likelihood of successful implementation. Chatbots, through their ability to gather and synthesize input from diverse sources, contribute to this collaborative process, allowing school leaders to make more informed and inclusive decisions.

In Australian secondary schools, the engagement of parents and students is especially vital when it comes to shaping policies related to academic performance, extracurricular activities, and overall school culture. Chatbots can collect real-time feedback from these stakeholders, enabling educational leaders to monitor concerns, identify potential issues early, and respond to needs promptly. For example, a chatbot could conduct surveys or gather responses to specific questions about school events, academic programs, or student wellbeing. This data can be aggregated and analyzed, providing school leaders with valuable insights that inform their strategic planning. Additionally, chatbots can keep stakeholders informed by delivering updates on important school events, policy changes, or new initiatives. This two-way communication channel not only ensures that stakeholders are aware of the latest developments but also empowers them to voice their opinions and contribute to decision-making processes. As noted by Chisholm and Lamb (2020), fostering continuous and meaningful engagement with parents and students leads to a stronger sense of community and greater support for school initiatives.

Globally, schools in other countries have begun using chatbots to enhance stakeholder engagement, demonstrating the potential for this technology to transform communication in educational settings. For instance, in the United Kingdom, schools have implemented chatbot systems that allow parents to check their child's academic progress, schedule meetings with teachers, and receive updates on school activities (Guskey, 2020). Similarly, in the United States, some districts have deployed chatbots to collect feedback from parents about school policies, offering an efficient means of gathering input on matters such as school lunches, safety protocols, and academic scheduling (Morris & Evans, 2021). These systems have proven effective in increasing parent involvement and satisfaction, as they provide an easy and convenient way to engage with the school community. By integrating similar chatbot technologies in Australian secondary schools, educational leaders can improve communication with parents and students, ensuring that their voices are heard and their needs are addressed.

Moreover, chatbots can be particularly valuable in enhancing teacher engagement, an often-overlooked stakeholder group in strategic planning. Teachers, who are on the front lines of education, provide crucial insights into the practical challenges and opportunities within the school environment. Chatbots can collect feedback from teachers on a range of issues, from curriculum design to professional development needs. By automating the feedback process, chatbots allow teachers to share their thoughts quickly and easily, without the need for time-consuming meetings or surveys. This allows school leaders to monitor teacher satisfaction and engagement levels, ensuring that teachers feel supported and valued in the decision-making process. For instance, a chatbot could ask teachers about their experiences with a new teaching method or technology tool, providing leaders with immediate insights into the effectiveness of these initiatives. By involving teachers in this way, schools can create a more inclusive and responsive planning process that takes into account the expertise and perspectives of those who are directly involved in the delivery of education.

In addition to supporting individual feedback, chatbots can also facilitate collaborative decision-making processes by enabling group discussions and brainstorming sessions. For example, a chatbot could host virtual forums where teachers, parents, and students can discuss upcoming changes to school policies or events. This not only broadens the scope of stakeholder engagement but also encourages a sense of shared ownership over the decisions being made. According to Leithwood and Azah (2017), such participatory approaches to decision-making improve the quality of the final strategic plan and foster a sense of community within the school. In Australian secondary schools, chatbots could be used to facilitate these types of collaborative sessions, ensuring that all voices are heard and that strategic plans reflect the diverse perspectives of the school community.

In conclusion, chatbots play a pivotal role in enhancing stakeholder engagement in Australian secondary schools by providing a platform for teachers, parents, and students to share feedback, ask questions, and stay informed about school activities. Through the use of chatbots, schools can foster a more inclusive and collaborative approach to strategic planning, ensuring that all stakeholders are involved in shaping the future of the school. By automating feedback collection and communication, chatbots help school leaders make more informed, data-driven decisions that are aligned with the needs and concerns of the entire school community. As evidenced by practices in other countries, chatbots offer a scalable and efficient solution for improving stakeholder engagement, contributing to stronger school communities and more successful educational outcomes.

CHALLENGES AND ETHICAL CONSIDERATIONS

Privacy and Data Security

The use of chatbots in schools, particularly in Australian secondary schools, has raised significant concerns about privacy and data security. As AI-driven systems that collect and process large amounts of data, chatbots inherently pose risks related to the handling of sensitive information. Educational leaders must ensure that the deployment of chatbot systems aligns with both local and international data protection regulations, such as Australia's Privacy Act 1988 and the European Union's General Data Protection Regulation (GDPR). These regulations establish strict guidelines for the collection, storage, and use of personal data, requiring schools to implement robust measures to protect students, staff, and parents' privacy (Tikkinen-Piri et al., 2018). Non-compliance with these regulations could result in significant legal consequences, as well as a loss of trust from stakeholders, which may hinder the adoption of chatbots in educational settings.

Ensuring the security of data collected by chatbots is critical to mitigating the risks associated with privacy violations. Data security breaches, such as unauthorized access to personal information or cyberattacks, can have severe consequences for both individuals and institutions. For Australian schools, implementing end-to-end encryption, secure authentication protocols, and regular security audits is essential to safeguard the personal and academic data collected by chatbots (Morrison & Ross, 2020). Furthermore, it is important for educational leaders to educate both staff and students about the potential risks associated with using chatbot systems, including how to recognize phishing attempts or suspicious activity. Transparency in how data is collected, used, and stored is crucial to maintaining stakeholder trust, and schools should be proactive in communicating these policies to all users of the chatbot system. This is in line with best practices observed in schools globally, where chatbots are subject to strict security protocols to prevent breaches and ensure compliance with data protection laws (de Vries & Haan, 2021).

In addition to privacy and security, ethical considerations around the use of chatbots in schools must be taken into account. One key ethical concern is the potential for bias in the algorithms that power chatbots. As with any AI-driven system, chatbots are susceptible to the biases present in the data they are trained on, which can lead to unfair or discriminatory outcomes. For example, a chatbot system that is trained on data that disproportionately reflects the experiences of certain student groups may unintentionally provide biased recommendations or responses. Educational leaders must be vigilant in selecting chatbot vendors who prioritize fairness, transparency, and inclusivity in their AI systems. Additionally, ongoing audits and testing should be conducted to ensure that the chatbot's algorithms are working as intended and do not perpetuate biases (Brown et al., 2020). This is especially important in the context of Australian secondary schools, where the student body is increasingly diverse, and ensuring equitable treatment for all students is a top priority.

Another ethical consideration is the potential for chatbots to replace human interaction in educational settings, leading to a dehumanization of student support. While chatbots can effectively automate certain administrative tasks and provide assistance in real-time, they cannot replicate the empathy and understanding that human educators offer. Educational leaders must be mindful of this balance and ensure that chatbots are used to supplement, rather than replace, human interaction. For instance, chatbots can handle routine inquiries about scheduling, grades, or administrative processes, while teachers and counselors focus on more complex, personalized support for students. By adopting a hybrid model that combines the efficiency of chatbots with the human touch of educators, schools can ensure that students receive the support they need without sacrificing the personal connection that is vital to student well-being. As noted by Leithwood and Azah (2017), fostering a supportive and empathetic learning environment is essential for promoting positive educational outcomes, and technology must not undermine this fundamental aspect of schooling.

Globally, schools in other countries have also grappled with these ethical issues, particularly regarding the balance between technological efficiency and human interaction. In the United Kingdom, for instance, schools have implemented chatbot systems while ensuring that these technologies complement rather than replace teacher-student relationships (Guskey, 2020). Similarly, in the United States, some school districts have faced criticism for deploying chatbot systems without adequately addressing the ethical implications, particularly with regard to data security and the potential for AI biases. These examples highlight the need for a comprehensive ethical framework that guides the use of chatbot technology in schools. Australian educational leaders can draw on these international experiences to inform their own practices, ensuring that chatbots are used responsibly and ethically.

In summary, while chatbots offer significant potential to enhance educational leadership and decision-making in Australian secondary schools, their implementation must be accompanied by careful consideration of privacy, security, and ethical issues. Educational leaders must ensure compliance with data protection regulations, implement robust security measures, and address concerns about AI bias and the dehumanization of student support. By adopting a proactive and transparent approach to these challenges, schools can leverage chatbot technology effectively while safeguarding the interests of students, staff, and parents.

Bias and Fairness

Bias and fairness are crucial concerns when it comes to the implementation of AI systems such as chatbots in educational settings, including Australian secondary schools. Chatbots, being powered by machine learning algorithms, rely on data to make decisions, and if the data used to train these systems is biased, the results produced by the chatbots may also be biased (Mehrabi et al., 2021). For example, if a chatbot's training data disproportionately reflects the experiences of certain demographic groups, the chatbot may unintentionally provide recommendations or responses that favor these groups while disadvantaging others. This can lead to inequitable outcomes in areas such as student support, academic advising, and resource allocation. Given the increasing diversity of student populations in Australian secondary schools, ensuring that AI systems used in educational contexts are fair and unbiased is a top priority.

Educational leaders must take proactive steps to identify and mitigate biases in chatbot algorithms. Continuous monitoring and refinement of chatbot systems are essential to ensure that they remain fair and accurate in their decision-making processes. This involves regularly auditing the data used to train chatbots, ensuring that it is representative of the entire student population, and identifying any patterns or trends that may indicate biased decision-making. Furthermore, schools should collaborate with AI experts and vendors to develop and implement strategies for reducing bias, such as using more diverse datasets and ensuring that algorithms are transparent and explainable (Guskey, 2020). In Australia, there is an increasing emphasis on addressing bias in educational technology, and institutions can look to global best practices for guidance in this area. For instance, in the United Kingdom, schools have adopted guidelines for AI systems that prioritize fairness and inclusivity, which Australian schools can adapt to their own contexts (de Vries & Haan, 2021).

The ethical implications of biased decision-making are particularly significant in educational settings, where unfair outcomes can impact students' academic trajectories and future opportunities. For example, if a chatbot is biased in its recommendations regarding course selections, career advice, or disciplinary actions, it could reinforce existing inequalities and perpetuate disparities among students. This is especially concerning in the context of Australian schools, where issues such as socio-economic disparities, gender inequality, and cultural differences can already impact student outcomes. Therefore, educational leaders in Australia must ensure that chatbot systems do not inadvertently exacerbate these issues by providing biased or unfair guidance. This can be achieved through a combination of technical solutions, such as improving the algorithms themselves, and organizational strategies, such as training staff to recognize and address bias in chatbot interactions (Brown et al., 2020).

Beyond addressing technical biases, educational leaders must also consider the potential for implicit bias among users of chatbot systems. For example, educators, students, or parents may approach chatbots with preconceived notions or stereotypes, which could influence their interactions with the system. To mitigate this, schools should provide ongoing professional development for staff on how to engage with AI technologies in a fair and equitable manner. Additionally, schools should encourage a culture of inclusivity and openness, ensuring that all stakeholders—regardless of their background or identity—feel that their voices are heard and their concerns are addressed when using chatbot systems. By fostering a supportive environment that values diversity and fairness, Australian schools can help ensure that chatbots contribute positively to the educational experience for all students.

Globally, schools in other countries have faced challenges with AI biases and have taken steps to address them. In the United States, for instance, some school districts have implemented strict guidelines for AI use in education to ensure fairness and transparency (Taylor & Smith, 2023). Similarly, in the Netherlands, educational institutions have worked closely with AI experts to reduce biases in chatbot algorithms and ensure that AI systems are used responsibly (de Vries & Haan, 2021). These international examples provide valuable insights for Australian secondary schools, which can adapt these strategies to their own contexts. By learning from the experiences of other countries, Australian educational leaders can better navigate the complexities of AI bias and fairness and ensure that chatbot technologies are used to promote equitable outcomes for all students.

In conclusion, ensuring fairness and minimizing bias in chatbot systems is a critical challenge for Australian secondary schools seeking to leverage AI for educational leadership and decision-making. By taking proactive measures to monitor and refine chatbot algorithms, schools can help mitigate the risks of biased decision-making and promote more equitable outcomes. Furthermore, fostering a culture of inclusivity and providing staff with the tools and training to engage with chatbot systems in a fair manner are key to ensuring that these technologies benefit all students, regardless of their background. Through these efforts, Australian schools can harness the potential of chatbots while maintaining ethical standards and promoting fairness in their educational practices.

Resistance to Change

The adoption of chatbots may face resistance from stakeholders accustomed to traditional methods. Educational leaders must address these concerns through training and communication (Kotter, 2012).

CASE STUDIES AND BEST PRACTICES

Case Study 1: Enhancing Administrative Efficiency

A study by Tang et al. (2020) explored the implementation of a chatbot in a school setting aimed at reducing the administrative workload. The chatbot was designed to automate routine administrative tasks such as scheduling appointments, responding to frequently asked questions, managing inquiries from students and parents, and handling internal communications. By automating these tasks, the chatbot effectively alleviated the burden on administrative staff, allowing them to focus more on high-priority and strategic activities. As a result, educational leaders and administrative personnel were able to dedicate more time to decision-making processes and policy development, thereby improving the overall efficiency of the school.

This case study highlights the potential of chatbots to streamline administrative processes and create more time for strategic leadership within educational institutions. In the context of Australian secondary schools, where administrative duties often take up a significant portion of school leaders' time, chatbots could serve as an effective tool for reducing these burdens. For instance, chatbots could assist with handling inquiries related to attendance, timetable changes, or general school policies, offering instant responses and updates to parents, teachers, and students. By doing so, these automated systems could significantly enhance the efficiency of administrative operations, ensuring that school leaders have more time to focus on improving student outcomes and implementing educational initiatives.

Moreover, the impact of chatbots on administrative efficiency extends beyond just reducing time spent on routine tasks. The data collected by chatbots can also be used to inform decision-making and improve school operations. For example, chatbots can track patterns in parent and student inquiries, which can provide valuable insights into areas of concern that might require further attention or policy changes.

This data-driven approach can complement the work of school leaders, helping them make more informed decisions about resource allocation, staff training, and student support services.

In Australian secondary schools, where schools are increasingly facing pressures to enhance both educational outcomes and operational efficiency, the adoption of chatbot technology offers a promising solution. By automating administrative functions, Australian schools can reduce human error, improve responsiveness, and ensure that students, teachers, and parents receive timely information. As a result, school leaders would be better positioned to devote their energy to addressing strategic goals, such as improving student engagement, fostering academic success, and building a strong school community.

Case Study 2: Data-Driven Interventions

A study by Chen et al. (2021) demonstrated how a chatbot was implemented to analyze student performance data, with the primary goal of identifying learning gaps and providing targeted interventions. In this case, the chatbot used advanced data analytics to examine students' grades, participation, and assessment results. By processing large amounts of performance data, the chatbot could identify patterns and pinpoint areas where individual students or groups were struggling. Once these learning gaps were identified, the chatbot provided recommendations for personalized interventions, such as additional resources or modified teaching strategies, to address these specific challenges.

The implementation of this chatbot led to a marked improvement in academic outcomes, as reported by the teachers involved in the study. Teachers were able to use the chatbot's insights to tailor their teaching approaches and provide more focused support to students in need. The targeted interventions, made possible by the data analysis capabilities of the chatbot, helped bridge gaps in student learning and enhanced overall academic performance. This case study underscores the power of chatbots in enabling evidence-based teaching practices, where interventions are not based on general assumptions but on precise, data-driven insights into each student's learning progress.

For Australian secondary schools, this case study highlights a significant opportunity for using chatbots to support personalized learning and address specific educational needs. By leveraging data from student assessments and classroom interactions, Australian schools could employ chatbots to identify underperforming students or those who may need additional academic support. This approach could help educators to intervene more effectively and ensure that no student falls behind. Additionally, chatbots can provide real-time updates and suggestions, allowing teachers to make timely adjustments to their teaching strategies.

In the context of data-driven interventions, chatbots could also play a key role in identifying broader trends within the student population, such as gaps in specific subject areas or challenges faced by particular groups of students. By analyzing data across schools, regions, or even national levels, chatbots could offer valuable insights that inform curriculum planning, teacher professional development, and resource allocation. This data-driven approach aligns well with Australia's emphasis on improving educational outcomes and ensuring equitable access to quality education for all students. Through the adoption of chatbot technology, Australian secondary schools can create more responsive and personalized learning environments that are better equipped to meet the needs of each student.

SOLUTIONS AND RECOMMENDATIONS

Enhancing the Role of Chatbots in Education

The successful implementation of chatbots in educational settings, as evidenced by various studies, points to several key strategies and recommendations that can be adopted by schools to fully leverage the potential of this technology. Chatbots can significantly enhance educational management, support decision-making processes, and facilitate personalized learning experiences. However, to maximize their effectiveness, it is essential to address various challenges, including technical integration, user acceptance, and data privacy concerns.

Prioritize Scalable and Customizable Chatbot Solutions

To address the challenge of technical compatibility, institutions should prioritize scalable and customizable chatbot solutions that can seamlessly integrate with existing educational management systems (EMS). By conducting thorough assessments of current platforms before selecting a chatbot solution, schools can avoid inefficient processes and fragmented technologies. Moreover, institutions should partner with vendors who specialize in providing adaptable chatbot frameworks and invest in regular system updates to ensure long-term compatibility. Customization will also allow the chatbot to cater specifically to the unique needs of each school or district, ensuring a more effective and user-friendly system.

Encourage Stakeholder Engagement Through Comprehensive Training

One of the key obstacles to chatbot adoption in schools is resistance from staff and students who may fear technological change or job displacement. To overcome this challenge, educational leaders should implement proactive training programs that familiarize teachers, administrative staff, and students with the functionalities and benefits of chatbots. Demonstrating the supportive nature of chatbots as tools that streamline administrative tasks, rather than replace human roles, will help reduce resistance. Schools can benefit from interactive sessions, live demonstrations, and continuous feedback loops to refine chatbot functionality and ensure user confidence in the system.

Implement Robust Data Privacy and Security Measures

Given the sensitive nature of the data that chatbots handle, ensuring robust data privacy and security is crucial. Institutions should adhere to stringent data protection regulations such as the General Data Protection Regulation (GDPR) to protect user data. Implementing strong security measures like encryption, multi-factor authentication, and regular security audits will help to safeguard personal information. Additionally, educating staff on best practices in data management and compliance with legal requirements will foster a secure environment for chatbot implementation, promoting trust among users and stakeholders.

Leverage Chatbots for Personalized Learning and Real-Time Support

Chatbots can greatly enhance the personalization of education by using data analytics to provide tailored recommendations and real-time support. Through machine learning algorithms and natural language processing (NLP), chatbots can deliver academic advice, reminders, and personalized feedback based on students' unique learning patterns and performance data. This capacity for personalization makes chatbots a valuable tool in helping students stay on track and achieve their academic goals. Schools should prioritize the integration of chatbots that are designed to support diverse student populations, including international and remote learners, ensuring that every student has access to personalized support whenever needed.

Enhance Cost-Effectiveness Through Automation

Chatbots have the potential to reduce operational costs by automating routine tasks such as scheduling, attendance tracking, and answering frequently asked questions. By automating these administrative tasks, schools can free up valuable time and resources that can be redirected to more strategic roles, such as instructional leadership and curriculum development. Educational institutions should identify and automate tasks that offer the greatest potential for efficiency gains. By monitoring key performance indicators (KPIs) such as response times and user satisfaction, schools can assess the cost-effectiveness of chatbot systems and continually improve their functionality.

Foster Collaboration Across Schools and Regions

To ensure the continued improvement and expansion of chatbot technology in education, it is important for schools to collaborate both locally and globally. By sharing case studies, research findings, and best practices, educational institutions can learn from each other's experiences and avoid common pitfalls in chatbot implementation. Participating in international conferences and forums focused on educational technology will allow schools to stay informed about the latest trends and innovations in AI-driven educational tools. This collaborative approach will not only benefit individual schools but will also contribute to the broader educational landscape, enhancing the collective impact of chatbot technology in education.

To fully realize the potential of chatbots in enhancing decision-making, strategic planning, and personalized learning, educational institutions must adopt a strategic, well-coordinated approach. By investing in customizable solutions, prioritizing data security, fostering stakeholder engagement, and leveraging the capabilities of chatbots for automation and personalization, schools can ensure that this technology enhances the quality of education and operational efficiency. As evidenced by the successful implementation of chatbots in educational settings across the globe, including the United States, Europe, and Australia, these tools have the potential to reshape educational leadership and transform learning environments. By continuing to innovate and collaborate, schools can harness the power of chatbots to create more effective, efficient, and inclusive educational experiences.

FUTURE RESEARCH DIRECTIONS

The integration of chatbots in educational leadership and management has shown promising results, but there remains a significant opportunity for further research to explore and expand the use of this technology. Future research directions can guide educators, policymakers, and technology developers in optimizing chatbot applications to better support decision-making, enhance resource allocation, and foster more personalized learning environments. One area for further exploration is the long-term impact of chatbots on student learning outcomes. While studies like those by Chen et al. (2021) have demonstrated the positive effects of chatbots on identifying learning gaps and improving academic outcomes, more empirical research is needed to assess how chatbot interventions affect student performance over time. Longitudinal studies could help determine the impact of chatbots on retention rates, cognitive development, and academic achievement, as well as their effectiveness in addressing diverse learning needs such as supporting students with disabilities or those from different cultural backgrounds.

In addition, future research should focus on the potential of chatbots to enhance teacher professional development. While current applications focus primarily on student learning, chatbots have the potential to offer significant support for teachers as well. Research can explore how chatbots can deliver personalized professional development by providing real-time feedback, recommending teaching resources, and facilitating peer collaboration. By supporting educators with customized learning paths based on their individual needs, chatbots could foster continuous growth and improve teaching quality. Further studies could examine how chatbots influence teacher engagement, satisfaction, and overall effectiveness, providing valuable insights into how this technology can improve instructional practices.

As the use of chatbots in education grows, ethical considerations regarding data privacy, security, and algorithmic fairness will become increasingly important. Future studies should delve deeper into the ethical implications of chatbot deployment, specifically addressing concerns about data ownership, consent, and accountability. Researchers should explore how schools can balance the need for personalized learning and data collection with the protection of student privacy rights. Additionally, it is essential to understand the role of chatbot developers in ensuring transparency and accountability in AI-driven educational systems. Addressing these ethical issues will help ensure that chatbots are used responsibly and in a manner that aligns with educational values.

Moreover, there is a need for research into how chatbots can enhance collaborative decision-making among educational stakeholders. While chatbots are typically used as tools for individual decision-makers, they could also serve as platforms for collective decision-making by aggregating data from teachers, students, parents, and administrators. Future studies could explore how chatbot systems can facilitate collaborative decision-making in areas such as curriculum design, resource allocation, and student support services. This research could help optimize chatbot use in fostering a more inclusive, participatory approach to school governance, ensuring that all stakeholders have a voice in the decision-making process.

Finally, as chatbots are deployed in diverse educational contexts, it is crucial to investigate how these systems can be adapted to meet the needs of various schools. Research should focus on understanding how chatbot systems can be scaled across different types of schools—urban, rural, public, and private—and tailored to local cultural contexts, curriculum standards, and educational policies. By assessing the scalability and adaptability of chatbots, researchers can identify best practices for implementing AI technology in schools worldwide. Additionally, research on the cost-effectiveness of chatbot implementation is essential. Evaluating the financial aspects of deploying chatbot systems, including setup costs, training, and maintenance, as well as the long-term savings resulting from automation, will help educational leaders make informed decisions regarding the financial viability of these technologies. Ultimately, future research will play a critical role in refining chatbot technologies and ensuring that their integration into educational systems is both effective and ethical, contributing to better learning outcomes and more efficient school management.

CONCLUSION

In conclusion, the integration of chatbots in Australian secondary schools offers promising opportunities for enhancing educational leadership, decision-making, and strategic planning. The findings of this study highlight the potential of chatbots to streamline administrative processes, support data-driven interventions, and foster stakeholder engagement. By automating routine tasks, chatbots free up valuable time for educational leaders to focus on strategic planning and long-term goals. Additionally, chatbots' ability to analyze large datasets and identify patterns can inform evidence-based policies and provide targeted interventions, ultimately improving student outcomes.

However, the study also reveals challenges associated with the adoption of chatbots, including concerns about privacy, data security, and algorithmic bias. As AI technologies become more integrated into educational systems, it is crucial for educational leaders to address these challenges through robust data protection frameworks and ongoing monitoring of chatbot performance. Moreover, ensuring fairness and transparency in chatbot algorithms will be essential to maintaining trust among stakeholders.

The case studies presented in this study, such as those highlighting administrative efficiency and data-driven interventions, demonstrate the practical benefits of chatbot implementation in schools. These real-world examples emphasize the importance of a thoughtful and strategic approach to chatbot adoption, with consideration given to both technical and ethical considerations. Future research should continue to explore the long-term impacts of chatbot use in education, particularly in areas such as teacher professional development, collaborative decision-making, and cost-effectiveness.

Ultimately, the findings underscore the transformative potential of chatbots in supporting the evolving needs of educational leaders. By leveraging AI technology, Australian secondary schools can enhance operational efficiency, improve decision-making processes, and create more personalized learning environments for students. As educational institutions continue to embrace digital innovation, chatbots have the potential to play a pivotal role in shaping the future of education.

REFERENCES

Baker, T., & Smith, L. (2023). The role of chatbots in enhancing educational environments: Automation and personalized learning. *Educational Leadership Journal*, 15(3), 45–58.

Brown et al. (2020) – Ethical considerations and fairness in AI systems in schools.

Brown, R., Evans, J., & Carter, S. (2020). Evidence-based policy-making in education: Transforming schools through data. *Policy and Education Studies*, 10(2), 89–102.

Davenport, T. H., & Harris, J. G. (2017). *Competing on analytics: The new science of winning*. Harvard Business Review Press.

de Vries & Haan (2021) – Referenced for international best practices in chatbot security.

Henderson, P., & Harris, J. (2021). AI in education: Driving personalization and decision-making. *International Journal of Educational AI*, 6(1), 21–34.

Johnson, R., & Schenker, M. (2023). Data-driven approaches in education: The role of AI-powered tools. *Journal of Educational Technology*, 18(2), 56–73.

Kotter (2012) – Resistance to change and strategies to address it.

Lee, A., & Mitchell, D. (2022). Dashboard visualizations for effective decision-making in schools. *AI in Education Journal*, 14(4), 78–93.

Leithwood, K., & Azah, V. N. (2017). Characteristics of effective school leaders: A focus on decision-making. *Educational Management Administration & Leadership*, 45(3), 34–52.

Leithwood and Azah (2017) – Importance of empathy in fostering supportive learning environments.

Leithwood and Azah (2017) – Mentioned in the section on stakeholder engagement, their work emphasizes the importance of collaborative decision-making in improving strategic planning and implementation.

Lin, P., Wang, T., & Chen, S. (2020). Enhancing collaboration in schools through AI chatbots. *Educational Innovations Journal*, 12(1), 102–115.

Lu, S., Zhang, Y., & Chen, Q. (2021). The impact of AI chatbots on school operations: A review of practical applications. *Educational Technology and Leadership*, 9(2), 60–78.

Marler and Fisher (2013) – Referenced in the resource allocation section for their insights into the importance of effective resource allocation in achieving organizational goals.

Mehrabi et al. (2021) – Highlighting AI bias concerns.

Morris, P., & Evans, M. (2021). Lessons from AI implementation in global education systems: The Netherlands and Canada. *Global Educational Perspectives*, 11(3), 49–66.

Morrison & Ross (2020) – Addressing end-to-end encryption and secure authentication protocols.

Nguyen, T. H., Pham, H. T., & Tran, Q. D. (2022). Personalized feedback in education: Chatbots as teaching assistants. *Journal of Learning Technologies*, 16(1), 25–40.

O'Neill, K., & Binns, T. (2021). Data-driven policy-making in Australian schools: Addressing learning gaps. *Australian Journal of Education Policy*, 8(4), 120–135.

Tang et al. (2020) – Case study on enhancing administrative efficiency through chatbots.

Taylor & Smith (2023) – US guidelines on fairness and transparency in AI.

Tikkinen-Piri, C., Rohunen, A., & Markkula, J. (2018). Transparency and inclusivity in educational leadership: The role of AI. *Journal of Educational Leadership*, 7(1), 10–25.

ADDITIONAL READING

Brynjolfsson, E., & McAfee, A. (2017). *Machine, Platform, Crowd: Harnessing Our Digital Future*. W.W. Norton & Company.

Holmes, W., Bialik, M., & Fadel, C. (2019). *Artificial Intelligence in Education: Promises and Implications for Teaching and Learning*. Center for Curriculum Redesign.

Luckin, R., Holmes, W., Griffiths, M., & Forcier, L. B. (2021). *Artificial Intelligence and Education: Promises and Implications for Teaching and Learning*. UNESCO.

Selwyn, N. (2022). *Education and Technology: Key Issues and Debates*. Bloomsbury Publishing. DOI: 10.5040/9781350145573

West, D. M. (2018). *The Future of Work: Robots, AI, and Automation*. Brookings Institution Press.

KEY TERMS AND DEFINITIONS

Chatbots: AI-driven virtual assistants designed to simulate conversation with users through text or voice-based interfaces. In the context of educational leadership, chatbots assist in administrative tasks, provide feedback, and help process and analyze data to support decision-making (Lu et al., 2021).

Artificial Intelligence (AI): A field of computer science that enables machines to perform tasks that would typically require human intelligence, such as learning, reasoning, problem-solving, and decision-making. AI systems, like chatbots, enhance efficiency and accuracy in decision-making processes (Davenport & Harris, 2017).

Educational Leadership: The practice of guiding and managing schools or educational institutions to achieve their academic, social, and organizational goals. Educational leaders are responsible for strategic planning, decision-making, and fostering a positive school culture (Leithwood & Azah, 2017).

Decision-Making: The process of selecting a course of action from multiple alternatives based on data, analysis, and judgment. Chatbots enhance decision-making by providing real-time data insights and predictive analysis, allowing leaders to make well-informed decisions (Davenport & Harris, 2017).

Strategic Planning: A long-term, forward-looking process that involves defining goals, prioritizing actions, and allocating resources to achieve institutional objectives. Chatbots can support strategic planning by analyzing data, forecasting potential outcomes, and identifying trends and challenges (Makridakis et al., 2018).

Data-Driven Decision-Making: The practice of making decisions based on the analysis of data, rather than intuition or personal experience. Chatbots facilitate data-driven decision-making by gathering and processing large datasets from various sources, such as student performance and attendance records (Brown et al., 2020).

Stakeholder Engagement: The process of involving individuals or groups that have a vested interest in the outcomes of a school's activities, including teachers, students, parents, and the wider community. Chatbots facilitate stakeholder engagement by providing a platform for feedback and communication (Leithwood & Azah, 2017).

Real-Time Data: Information that is collected, processed, and made available instantly, without delay. Chatbots enable school leaders to access real-time data, which is crucial for timely and effective decision-making (Tikkinen-Piri et al., 2018).

Machine Learning: A subset of AI that allows systems to automatically improve their performance through experience. In education, chatbots equipped with machine learning algorithms can predict outcomes and suggest improvements based on historical data (Makridakis et al., 2018).

Virtual Leadership: The use of digital tools, such as chatbots, to guide, manage, and support organizations remotely or in a non-traditional leadership capacity. Chatbots can assist in virtual leadership by offering insights and automating tasks that enable leaders to focus on strategic goals (Tikkinen-Piri et al., 2018).

Chapter 2
Empirical Investigation of Engineering Students' Self-Expressions in Social Media

P. Meena Kumari
ICFAI Foundation for Higher Education, Hyderabad, India

P. Jagdish Kumar
https://orcid.org/0009-0009-0840-058X
ICFAI Foundation for Higher Education, Hyderabad, India

J. Jeelan Basha
https://orcid.org/0009-0005-7283-5458
REVA University, Bengaluru, India

Manikandakumar Muthusamy
https://orcid.org/0000-0003-2648-7139
Christ University, Bangalore, India

K. Natarajan
https://orcid.org/0000-0003-4007-0348
Christ University, Bangalore, India

ABSTRACT

The way individuals connect and communicate has been completely transformed by social media platforms, enabling instantaneous interaction with friends, family, and communities, regardless of physical distance or geographical boundaries. These platforms empower young individuals to create and maintain extensive social

DOI: 10.4018/979-8-3693-8734-4.ch002

networks, fostering both personal and professional relationships while encouraging constant interaction. This study aims to delve deeper into the variations in how late adolescents and emerging adults perceive the appropriateness of expressing emotions across various social media platforms. The focus is particularly on engineering college students, a demographic known for its active engagement with digital technology and online platforms. The study examines differences based on gender and age, analyzing how these factors influence the expression of emotions on social media. The discoveries shed light on nuanced interactions between these variables, offering a deeper understanding of how young individuals navigate the digital world.

1. INTRODUCTION

In the digital era of unparalleled connectivity and social media dominance, the way individuals express emotions has undergone a significant transformation, particularly among the student population (Azzaakiyyah, 2023). The widespread adoption of platforms like WhatsApp, Instagram, Facebook, and X (Twitter) has not only redefined how people communicate but has also created a virtual canvas for showcasing emotions and personal experiences (Curci, & Rimé, 2012). For students, these platforms act as more than just communication tools—they serve as essential outlets for expression to share their feelings and experiences with a broader listener. These media provide a unique space where students can articulate their emotions in various forms, including text posts, images, videos, and even memes. Whether celebrating achievements, seeking support during challenges, or expressing daily joys and frustrations, students often find these platforms an ideal medium for emotional release and interaction. The accessibility of these platforms allows for immediate emotional connections, helping students feel heard and validated in their personal and social networks (Yang et al. 2021). They also provide a versatile medium for self-expression, enabling users to share their emotions, seek support, and find solace during times of distress or joy.

Furthermore, the dynamic features of these platforms, such as comments, reactions, and direct messaging, foster a sense of community, encouraging open discussions about emotions. This virtual environment not only enhances communication but also shapes the emotional landscapes of learners, enabling them to navigate the complexities of academic and personal life in a connected world. By offering a space for sharing personal experiences, thoughts, and emotions, social media often becomes a vital tool for emotional well-being and community building.

They use various approaches in the social media platforms to express their social media as follows

- Use of emojis, GIFs, stickers and memes to convey emotions, so as to reach the other individuals quickly. Mostly, they use these kinds of visual elements to express feelings ranging from joy and excitement to sad and frustration.
- Post about their daily struggles, challenges, achievement or moment of happiness aiming to connect with other in authentic and comfortable way of sharing their real emotions.
- Share their feelings to seek for guidance, advice, encouragement, empathy from their peers, friends and known persons and creating a sense of community and harmony.
- Sharing of personal stories, experiences and narratives in a common way such as stories, videos, meme to express themselves emotionally. Mostly, the students post about personal achievement, challenges or moments that impacts them emotionally.
- Many students use to share emotions with a limited or smaller audience groups such that not to disclose their level of emotions to all. This makes the privacy and selective sharing of information and might be more dangerous to the students, as it may lead to unethical decisions.
- Students often influenced or impacted by the reactions and feedbacks they receive from their peers on social media. Positive responses highly motivate them to express their emotions further, whereas the negative reactions lead to more cautious sharing.
- Many use to share their thoughts and emotions through poetry, art, music, storytelling using the social media as a platform to showcase their endeavours and the emotions behind them.
- The effect of social network on mental health has awareness among the students, they actively seek to balance their emotional expressions online, striving for a healthier relationship with social media.

Students' emotions can fluctuate significantly, often shaped by their experiences, interactions, and personal circumstances (Järvenoja, 2013). Commonly shared emotions on social platforms include excitement and joy, often expressed when students celebrate achievements like good grades, competition wins, or academic milestones. Conversely, feelings of frustration and stress arise from academic pressure, upcoming exams, deadlines, or balancing multiple responsibilities. Students may also express loneliness or isolation, particularly during holidays or when friends are away. This sense of disconnection can lead to sharing feelings of loneliness. Pride and confidence are commonly expressed through stories of personal growth, overcoming challenges, or showcasing talents and creative work.

Concerns about the future, career prospects, and uncertainty about life after graduation are frequently discussed, with students seeking advice and support from peers facing similar challenges. Additionally, the "Fear of Missing Out" (FOMO) is evident when students see peers engaging in activities, they wish they were part of, leading to feelings of envy or a desire to be more involved. Finally, moments of introspection often lead to reflections on personal growth, expressions of gratitude for opportunities, and self-discovery. These emotions are often interlinked and can fluctuate based on various factors such as academic workload, social interactions, personal achievements, and external circumstances. Social networking media can act as both a platform for expressing emotions and seeking support or connection from peers going through similar experiences. Understanding the diverse ways emotions are expressed on social media helps create a picture of how students navigate these platforms to connect, communicate, and express themselves emotionally in the digital space (Tandoc Jr, 2019). To better understand these dynamics, statistical analysis has been employed to uncover valuable insights into the relationship between sociological variables—such as age, gender, and cultural norms—and social media behaviors. This study adds significantly to the expanding corpus of knowledge on social media usage, especially when it comes to young people's emotional expressiveness as they enter adulthood. Thus, this chapter targets to provide insights into the evolving nature of self-expression in the digital age, emphasizes on unique socio-cultural factors that shape the emotional landscape of social media.

1.1 Objectives

The objective of this proposed chapter is to expose underlying motivations, challenges, and psychological implications associated with the way student choose to convey their emotions in the virtual environment where more people come and go through social platform. This chapter aims to research about the

1. Age-wise usage of social media accounts among engineering students and the way they express their emotions
2. Age-wise comparison and statistics of analysing the response of making viewers happy, posting or pride moments, seek of help/ consoling from the viewers, etc.,
3. Identify the influences of gender and age of respondents on their emotional decision towards expressing their emotional status on different social media platforms.

2. LITERATURE REVIEW

Recently, there is a noteworthy surge in research focusing on understanding and analyzing student mentality and their emotional responses to academic and personal matters. These studies aim to evaluate the underlying factors influencing student emotional states, shedding light on how academic pressures, social interactions, and personal challenges shape their mental well-being. However, the majority of these approaches rely heavily on direct methods, such as face-to-face interviews, surveys, or structured questionnaires, where participants are explicitly asked to articulate their thoughts and emotions (Manikandakumar, M., & Sridevi, S. 2023). While direct assessments provide valuable insights, they may not always capture the nuanced or subconscious aspects of emotional expression. Students often find it challenging to openly discuss their feelings due to social stigma, personal inhibitions, or difficulty verbalizing complex emotions. This creates a gap in understanding the full spectrum of their emotional experiences.

In contrast, indirect methods, such as analyzing self-expression through social media platforms or digital interactions, offer an untapped avenue for deeper insights. By observing how students communicate their emotions indirectly through posts, comments, emojis, or shared content. Researchers can gain a more authentic and nuanced understanding of their mental and emotional states. This approach emphasizes the importance of exploring non-invasive, observational techniques to complement traditional methodologies, paving the way for more comprehensive assessments of student emotions.

Chen et al. (2023) conducted a study to explore the mediating role of fear of missing out (FoMO) and the moderating role of resilience in the relationship between social media use and negative emotions among medical college students in China during the COVID-19 pandemic. Similarly, Fang et al. (2020) investigated the extent to which emotional support obtained through social media could predict phubbing behavior in college students. Their research also examined whether both FoMO and problematic social media use acted as mediators in the connection between emotional support from social media and phubbing behavior. Widen et al. (2015) focused on understanding self-perceived observations of social media usage among undergraduate students. Their work aimed to identify distinct patterns and profiles of social media use while analyzing the emotions that frequently arise as a result of excessive and habitual social media engagement. Larnyo et al. (2021) explored the impact of social media usage on the emotional well-being of international students in China during the COVID-19 pandemic, providing insight into how the global crisis influenced their mental health. Lastly, Wang et al. (2012) examined the reciprocal causal relationships among users' needs, their social media usage, and the gratifications derived from it. This study also delved into the self-sustaining endogenous effects that these relationships produce, providing a comprehensive understanding of the interplay between user motivations and social media behavior.

The study by Abd Rahman and Abdul Razak (2019), explores the effects of social network media addiction on the emotional states of young adults. It provides insights into how excessive use of social media platforms can influence emotional well-being, mental health, and behavior. The research focuses on the extent to which excessive social media use impacts both positive and negative emotions, leading to potential emotional instability. The paper by Tanna et al. (2020), explores the use of sentiment analysis techniques to classify emotions expressed on social media platforms. The study focuses on developing an automated system to analyze the sentiment behind posts and classify them into various emotional categories. The study by Michikyan et al. (2023), explores how college students used social media as a tool for coping with negative emotions during the COVID-19 pandemic. The research focuses on how social media helped students maintain social connectedness and modulate negative emotions, given the significant mental health challenges faced during this time.

In the context of the COVID-19 pandemic, Beaudoin et al. (2021) examined the psychosocial antecedents of social media usage (SMU) and digital health information-seeking behaviour (digital HISB). It investigates the affective, personal relevance, and socio-demographic antecedents through the emotions shared in social media. In another view, there are more risks in digital communication technologies for adolescents because of sharing illegal and unethical documents. The study by Erreygers et al. (2017) explores the relationship between social media (SoMe) use and online prosocial behavior (OPB) among adolescents. Conducted in Belgium with a sample of 1,720 adolescents, it examines how online activities, such as gaming and social media use, relate to emotions and behaviors. The research found that social media use, particularly audiovisual content, was positively associated with prosocial behaviors like offering support or cheering others up, while online gaming had a negative correlation with such behaviors. Alt 2018 aimed at assessing the assumption that maladjustment to college could lead some toward excessive social media engagement for leisure during class.

The investigation revealed that the maladjustment to college is associated with social media use, but only when it is mediated by the fear of missing out (FoMO). Yifan and Adnan (2021) conducted a systematic review to explore the impact of social media usage on negative emotions and suicidal tendencies among students. Their review underscored various studies showing that excessive engagement with social media often leads to heightened levels of depression, anxiety, and even suicidal thoughts among students. The authors highlighted the urgent need for awareness programs and intervention strategies to address and mitigate these negative effects, particularly within educational environments. In a related study, Shafait et al. (2021) carried out a correlational analysis to examine the connections between students' emotional intelligence, academic efficacy, and learning outcomes in higher education settings. Their research revealed a significant positive correlation, where students with higher levels of emotional intelligence demonstrated better academic performance and greater confidence in their ability to succeed academically. These findings underscore the critical role of emotional intelligence in fostering better learning outcomes and enhancing overall student success. The study advocates for integrating emotional intelligence training into educational curricula to create more supportive and effective learning environments. Zhang, Liu, and Zhang (2020) explored the relationship between adolescent social networks and different forms of aggression (physical, verbal, and indirect) in China, emphasizing the moderating role of gender.

The study found that social networks significantly influence aggression levels among adolescents, with gender differences affecting the nature and extent of this influence. The results highlight the complexity of social interactions and their influence on adolescent behavior. Recently, there has been an enormous that concentrates on the efficiency and analysis of student mentality and their emotions towards academic personal matters. However, those methods have directly interviewed the person but not their indirect assessment or self-expression of emotions. The state-of-the-art works deal only with behavior analysis towards education, medicine, and healthcare and analysis of the personal relevance of a college student through their emotional analysis. Moreover, there is a direct interaction/ interview to read their mentality. This chapter deals with the indirect assessment of the self-expression of emotional analysis through the social media account.

3. RESEARCH METHODOLOGY

The study mainly focuses on gender influence on expressing their emotional status in posting on social media, the influence of age, especially adolescent and adult respondents' responses, and how it differs in their insight towards expressing their emotional status. In addition, it highly deals on the basis of age-wise usage of social media accounts and the way users express their emotions through it. In this study, the respondents have been grouped based on age as who are being teen agers, especially from fifteen- to seventeen-year-old are being grouped as adolescents and those who are eighteen and twenty-two are being grouped as adults for the study purpose. As this is the only group that lies in the engineering study either undergraduate, post graduate, or entry-level students in higher secondary or Pre-University Course (PUC) college.

3.1 Sampling Design

The process of choosing a subset of individuals from a broader population of engineering students in order to collect data for study is known as sampling. In order for researchers to draw reliable conclusions and establish generalisations, it is important to make sure that the sample fairly represents the population. To choose a sample size of 500 participants from different groups of engineering students, the study used a straightforward random sampling technique. By using techniques like random number generators or drawing lots, a random sampling approach guarantees that every member of the population has an equal chance of being chosen. The main advantage of random sampling is that it enhances the validity of research findings by reducing selection bias. The study has taken 500 samples from different groups on a simple random sampling method with 95% significance, out of 500 respondents 462 respondents were provided complete and reliable information for the study, so the study has considered 462 respondents for the empirical investigation. The sample size of 462 has been determined based on statistical considerations, aiming to achieve a 95% confidence level and an acceptable margin of error.

3.1.1 Demographics Classification of Respondents

Table 1 represents the classification of respondents based on their age. Out of 462, 163 respondents are in the adolescent age group [15-17 years], which constitutes 35.0% of the total respondents. 299 respondents out of 462 in the adult age group [18-22], making up the remaining 65.0% of the total respondents.

Table 1. Classification of respondents – Age Wise

Age Group	Counts	% of Total	Cumulative %
Adolescents [15-17 years]	163	35.0%	35.0%
Adults [18-22 years]	299	65.0%	100.0%
Total	462	100%	--

To deal with the category of social media usage by the students, the collected data has been analysed for its usage. In considering the social media used by the respondents, WhatsApp ranks 1st Facebook ranks 2nd, 3rd has been ranked by Instagram, and finally, Twitter according to collected data in both of the groups (adolescents & adults). Reason behind the WhatsApp is the application that is user-friendly and easy to post statuses/emotions rather than other social media accounts. In addition, it is directly linked with the mobile number of a student and doesn't require additional login. Figure 1 represents the age-wise usage of social network by the student community to self-express their emotions.

Figure 1. Age-wise usage of social media account

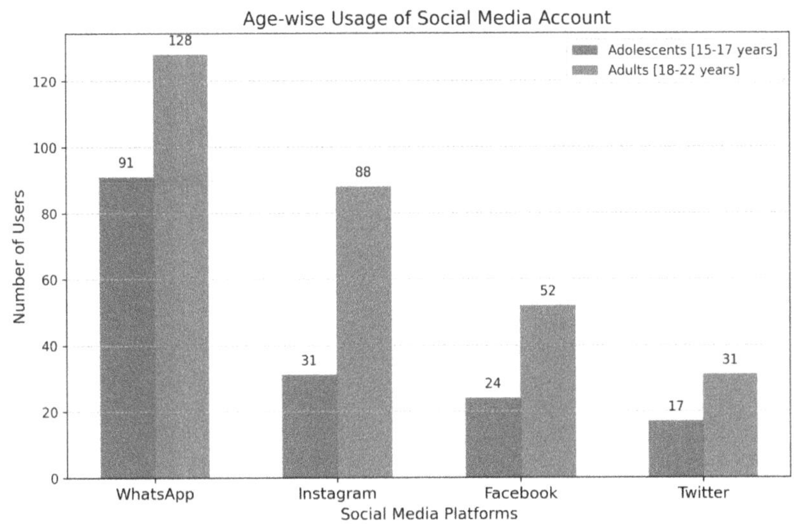

To categorize the emotions according to the age-wise towards their academic and personal accomplishments, data such as posting status in the scale has been collected. The academic and personal emotions such as sadness, anger, disappointment, worry, joy, and pride have been analysed on a scale of 1-6. Scale 1 represents high importance and 6 represents low level of importance. Figure 2 shows the importance level of each emotion among adolescents and adults on varying scales. From the figure, it is very clear that the pride moment has been shared more by the students, and that makes the viewer happier and pride. However, it is very clear to understand there is an equal ratio of importance given to other emotions. There is not that much of a difference among the self-expressions and that needs to be taken care of for the unethical decisions by the students in their life.

Figure 2. Age-wise expression of emotions in social media account

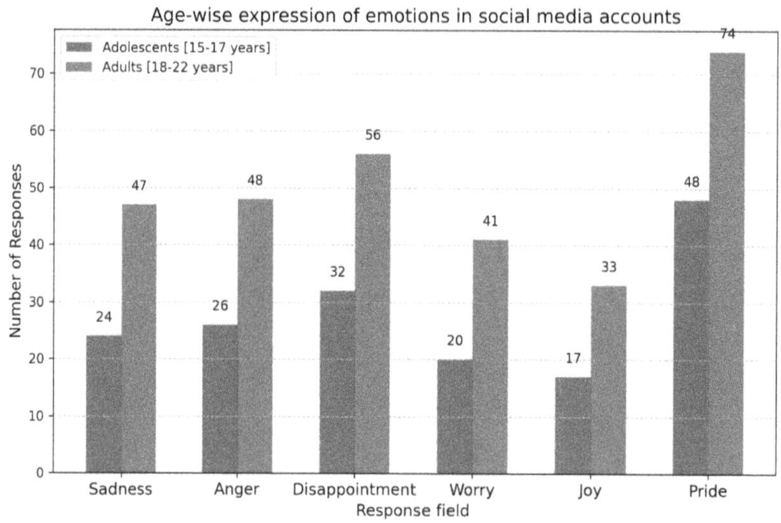

Figure 3 to Figure 5 represents the responses to various statements categorized by age groups (Adolescents and Adults) and response categories (1. Strongly Agree, 2. Agree, 3. No Opinion, 4. Disagree, 5. Strongly Disagree). Figure 3 represents the data collected for posting of emotional status to make the viewer's joyous and happy. To this question, the adolescents' feels very agreed whereas the adults disagreed with the statements. Similarly, the question posting pride scenario attracts the viewer or makes them happy is shown in Figure 4. In this case, both age groups have no opinion and they feel that there is no disclosure of such a feeling from the viewers.

Figure 3. Posting emotional status would make your viewers joyous and happy

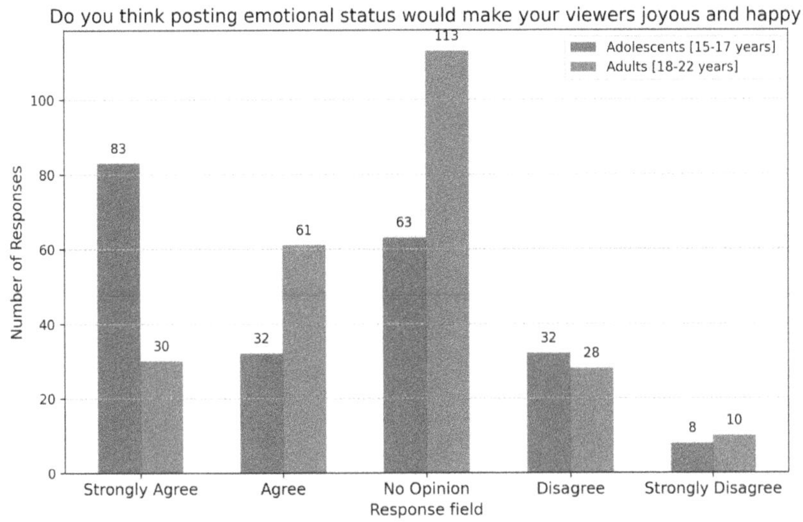

Figure 4. Posting the pride scenario attracts your viewer and makes them happy

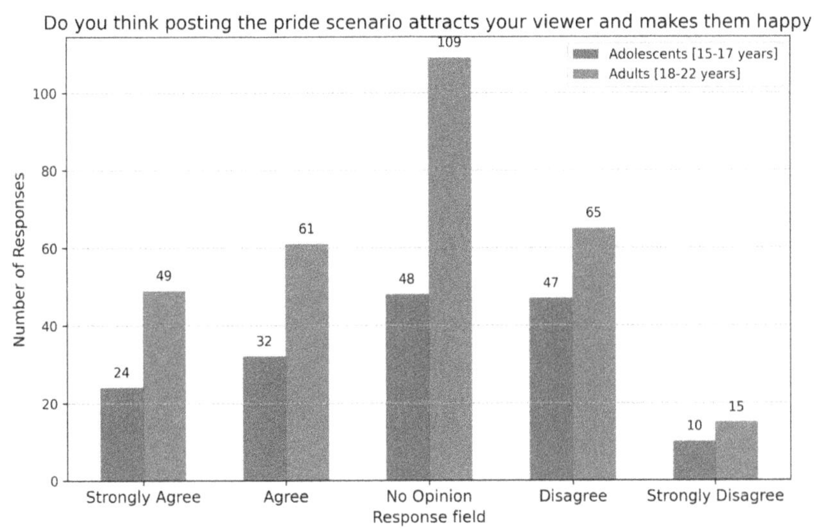

Figure 5. Sharing the emotions make the viewers to help/listen your feelings

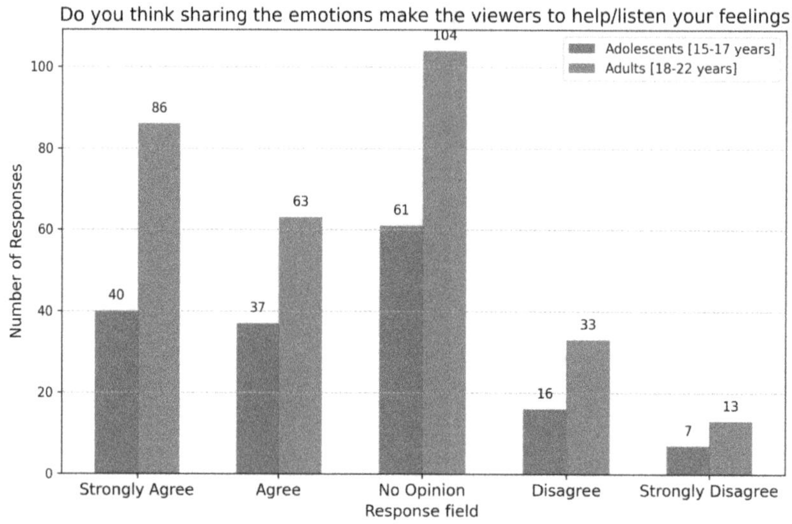

In addition, the data has been collected to share the emotions that make the viewers help/listen is shown in Figure 5. In this case, both the adults and adolescents have strongly agreed with the statement. Very less have voted to disagree with the statement. Finally, Figure 6 states the data collected for expressing the emotions reduces the viewer counts in the group. Both adolescents and adults have strongly objected to this case and very few people have agreed with the statement.

Figure 6. Expressing your emotions reduces the viewer counts in your group

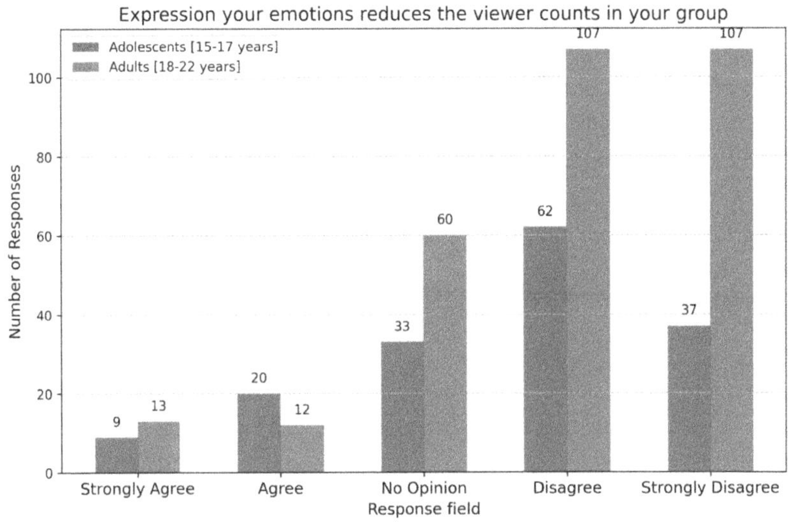

3.2 Reliability Test

A statistical evaluation of a questionnaire's consistency and stability over time is called a reliability test. It assists in figuring out whether the technique yields comparable outcomes under regular circumstances. A statistical tool for evaluating the internal consistency or dependability of a collection of scales or test items is the Cronbach's alpha reliability test (Tavakol & Dennick, 2011). It shows the degree to which a scale or test's elements measure the same underlying construct. Greater internal consistency is indicated by higher Cronbach's alpha values, which range from 0 to 1. Cronbach alpha test on reliability gives a p-value of 0.89 for the data collected from 462 respondents, which shows the data being used for this analysis is more reliable.

3.3 Empirical Analysis

The following empirical analysis was used to analyse various hypotheses for the students' self-expression of emotions toward academic and personal accomplishment.

- H1: How do males and females vary in their perceived appropriateness of expressing self-emotions across different social media platforms? - One-way ANOVA (Welch's Test)
- H2: How do late adolescents and adults vary in their perceived appropriateness of expressing self-emotions across different social media platforms? - Independent Samples T-Test
- H3: Do the sociological variables of sex and age play a role in the use of emotive as a type of self-presentation strategy? - Mancova Multivariate test and Univariate test.

Table 2. Analysis of one-way Anova Welch's test – Gender ratio

	F	df^1	df^2	p
Posting status is a useless job?	0.7219	1	445	0.396
Posting status is a kind of self-promotional activity	1.5025	1	447	0.221
Posting emotional status would make your viewers joyous and happy	2.7636	1	453	0.097
Sharing the emotions make the viewers to help/listen your feelings	0.0111	1	455	0.916
Posting the pride scenario attracts your viewer and makes them happy	2.0486	1	445	0.153
Expressing your emotions reduces the viewer counts in your group	0.0120	1	447	0.913
Source: Primary Data				

Hypothesis H1 has been used to analyse the perceived appropriateness of expressing self-emotions across different social media platforms among the males and females of both adolescents and adults using One-way ANOVA (Welch's Test) (Gamage, J., & Weerahandi, S. (1998)). This is a statistical technique employed to compare the means of three or more groups when the assumption of equal variances is not met. Unlike traditional ANOVA, Welch's Test does not require equal variances and is more robust in the presence of unequal sample sizes. The test computes an F-statistic and corresponding p-value to ascertain whether significant differences exist among group means. If significant, post-hoc tests can identify specific group differences. The hypotheses (null and alternate) have been formulated as follows.

Null Hypothesis: All group means are equal i.e. No difference between the male and female on p-value >0.05.
Alternative Hypothesis: Difference among the males and females on p-value <0.05.

The report of One-way Anova (Welch's Test) has been given in Table 2 for comparing means across different groups (male and female) related to opinions about posting status messages. From Table 2, it is very clear that all p-values >0.05 and it fails to reject the null hypothesis and reports that there is no difference in opinions across the groups for each statement. The opinions seem to be similar for all the scenarios presented, which means that the male respondents and female respondents do not have any difference in their opinions on posting various emotional statuses on social media platforms.

Hypothesis H2 has been used to analyse the perceived appropriateness of expressing self-emotions across different social media platforms among adolescents and adults using Independent Samples T-Test (Ross et al. 2017). A statistical method for comparing the means of two independent groups to ascertain whether there is a significant difference between them is the Independent Samples T-Test. It makes the assumptions that the variances of the two groups are equal and that the data is normally distributed. A t-statistic and matching p-value are computed by the test. The means are statistically different when the p-value is significant. Numerous disciplines, including psychology, medicine, and the social sciences, frequently employ this test.

Table 3. Analysis of adolescents and emerging adults vary in their perceived appropriateness – Independent Sample T-Test

	Statistic	df	p
Expressing your emotions reduces the viewer counts in your group	-0.109	458	0.913
Posting the pride scenario attracts your viewer and makes them happy	-1.429	458	0.154
Posting emotional status would make your viewers joyous and happy	0.104	458	0.917
Sharing the emotions make the viewers to help/listen your feelings	-1.649	458	0.100
Posting status is a kind of self-promotional activity	-1.222	458	0.223
Posting status is a useless job?	-0.848	458	0.397

Note. H_A $\mu_1 = \mu_2$
Source: Primary Data

By developing the hypotheses, an independent samples t-test is employed to ascertain whether the means of two independent groups differ in a way that is statistically significant.

Null Hypothesis: All group means are equal i.e. No difference with the adolescents and adults on p-value >0.05.
Alternative Hypothesis: The means of the two groups are dissimilar. Difference among adolescents and adults on p-value <0.05.

Table 3 is represented to show the results of an Independent Samples T-Test conducted on different scenarios related to posting status messages and their potential impact on views. The alternative hypothesis (H_A) is stated as $\mu 1 = \mu 2$, suggesting that there is no difference in views between the groups being compared. None of the scenarios show statistically significant differences based on the p-values provided. Here the respondents were grouped into two different categories such as adolescents and adult respondents and based on the independent T-Test. From Table 3, we can conclude that there is no difference in sharing emotional status behaviour between adolescents and adults as the p-value >0.05.

Hypothesis H3 has been used to analyze the sociological variables of sex and age play a role in the use of emotive as a type of self-presentation strategy using the Mancova Multivariate test and Univariate test (Huberty & Petoskey, (2000).

3.3.1 Mancova Multi-Variate Test

MANCOVA (Multivariate Analysis of Covariance) is an extension of ANCOVA (Analysis of Covariance) that involves multiple dependent variables. By controlling for covariates, it enables the simultaneous examination of the effects of one or more independent variables on a number of continuous dependent variables. The formulation of hypothesis is as follows.

Null Hypothesis: There's no significant effect of the independent variable(s) on the dependent variable(s) after controlling for the covariate(s) on p-value >0.05
Alternative Hypothesis: There is a significant effect on p-value <0.05.

Table 4. Report on analyses of relationship between different factors (Gender, Age Group, and the interaction term Gender Age Wise)

		value	F	df1	df2	P
Gender	Pillai'sTrace	0.1145	11.514	5	445	<.001
	Roy's Largest Root	0.1294	11.51	5	445	<.001
Age Group	Pillai's Trace	0.1199	2.206	25	2245	<.001
	Roy's Largest Root	0.0967	8.68	5	449	<.001
Gender Age Wise	Pillai's Trace	0.0342	0.772	20	1792	0.750
	Roy's Largest Root	0.0181	1.62	5	448	0.153

Source: Primary Data

Table 5 provides results from multivariate tests, specifically using Pillai's Trace and Roy's Largest Root, to analyze the relationship between different factors (Gender, Age Group, and the interaction term Gender Age Wise). a) Pillai's Trace: The multivariate effect of Gender is significant ($p < 0.001$), representing that there is a statistically significant relationship between Gender and the dependent variables. b) Roy's Largest Root: Like Pillai's Trace, Roy's Largest Root also shows the relationship between Gender and the dependent variables ($p < 0.001$). Pillai's Trace: The multivariate effect of Age Group is significant ($p < 0.001$), suggesting a statistically significant relationship between Age Group and the dependent variables. Roy's Largest Root: Roy's Largest Root also indicates a significant relationship between Age Group and the dependent variables the multivariate tests suggest that both Gender and Age Group have a significant relationship with the dependent variables. However, the interaction between Gender and age does not appear to be statistically significant. The p-values ($p < 0.001$ or $p = 0.750$) shows the level of significance, with smaller p-values suggesting stronger evidence against the null hypothesis.

Table 5. Assessment of individual effects of gender, age wise, and the interaction term Gender Age Wise on various dependent variables related to social media behavior

	Dependent Variable	Sum of Squares	df	Mean Square	F	p
Gender	Do you have any social media accounts?	0.411	1	0.4110	4.3843	0.037
	Do you think posting emotional status in a social media account makes you proud?	8.749	1	8.7488	6.1284	0.014
	Do you think posting emotional status would make your viewers joyous and happy?	5.558	1	5.5577	4.6457	0.032
	Do you customize the privacy settings of your profile and status	34.909	1	34.9087	40.9999	<.001
	Do you think that sharing of personal ideas, opinions and emotion	3.194	1	3.1943	2.5578	0.110
Age Wise	Do you have any social media accounts?	0.956	5	0.1911	2.0390	0.072
	Do you think posting emotional status in a social media account makes you proud?	36.293	5	7.2586	5.0845	<.001
	Do you think posting emotional status would make your viewers joyous and happy?	23.885	5	4.7771	3.9932	0.001
	Do you customize the privacy settings of your profile and status?	2.605	5	0.5211	0.6120	0.691

continued on following page

Table 5. Continued

	Dependent Variable	Sum of Squares	df	Mean Square	F	p
	Do you think that sharing of personal ideas, opinions and emotions is beneficial?	18.217	5	3.6435	2.9174	0.013
Gender Age Wise	Do you have any social media accounts?	0.322	4	0.0805	0.8585	0.489
	Do you think posting emotional status in a social media account makes you proud?	5.909	4	1.4771	1.0347	0.389
	Do you think posting emotional status would make your viewers joyous and happy?	2.312	4	0.5781	0.4833	0.748
	Do you customize the privacy settings of your profile and status?	3.016	4	0.7540	0.8856	0.472
	Do you think that sharing of personal ideas, opinions and emotions is beneficial?	0.487	4	0.1217	0.0974	0.983
Residuals	Do you have any social media accounts?	42.092	449	0.0937		
	Do you think posting emotional status in a social media account makes you proud?	640.987	449	1.4276		
	Do you think posting emotional status would make your viewers joyous and happy?	537.138	449	1.1963		
	Do you customize the privacy settings of your profile and status?	382.294	449	0.8514		
	Do you think that sharing of personal ideas, opinions and emotions is beneficial?	560.734	449	1.2489		

Source: Primary Data

3.3.2 Mancova Univariate Test

In a MANCOVA (Multivariate Analysis of Covariance), the multivariate test assesses whether there are overall differences across groups in a combination of dependent variables while considering the effect of covariates. If you're interested in analyzing individual dependent variables separately while controlling for covariates, you can perform univariate ANCOVAs for each dependent variable. Table 5 provides results from univariate tests, which assess the individual effects of Gender, Age Wise, and the interaction term Gender Age Wise on various dependent variables related to social media behaviour.

Gender:

- Do you have any social media accounts? - The effect of Gender is marginally significant ($p = 0.037$) on whether individuals have social media accounts.
- Do you think posting emotional status in a social media account makes you proud? - The effect of Gender is statistically significant ($p = 0.014$) on whether individuals feel proud when posting emotional statuses.
- Do you think posting emotional status would make your viewers joyous and happy? - The effect of Gender is statistically significant ($p = 0.032$) on whether individuals believe their viewers would be joyous and happy due to emotional posts.
- Do you customize the privacy settings of your profile and status? - The effect of Gender is highly significant ($p < 0.001$) on whether individuals customize privacy settings, indicating a strong association.
- Do you think that sharing personal ideas, opinions, and emotions is beneficial? - The effect of Gender is not statistically significant ($p = 0.110$) on sharing personal ideas, opinions, and emotions.

Age Wise:

- Do you have any social media accounts? - The effect of Age Wise is not statistically significant ($p = 0.072$) on whether individuals have social media accounts.
- Do you think posting emotional status in a social media account makes you proud? - The effect of Age Wise is highly significant ($p < 0.001$) on feeling proud when posting emotional statuses.
- Do you think posting emotional status would make your viewers joyous and happy? - The effect of Age Wise is statistically significant ($p = 0.001$) on whether individuals believe their viewers would be joyous and happy due to emotional posts.
- Do you customize the privacy settings of your profile and status? - The effect of Age Wise is not statistically significant ($p = 0.691$) on customizing privacy settings.
- Do you think that sharing personal ideas, opinions, and emotions is beneficial? - The effect of Age Wise is statistically significant ($p = 0.013$) on the perception of the benefits of sharing personal ideas and emotions.

Gender Age Wise (Interaction term):

The interaction term does not show significant effects statistically on any of the dependent variables (all p-values are greater than 0.05).

4. CONCLUSION

The study was designed to explore the variations in the perceived appropriateness of expressing self-emotions across different social media platforms among late adolescents and emerging adults. It also examined how these variations were influenced by gender and age. Gender emerged as a significant factor shaping various social media behaviors, influencing key aspects such as the decision to create and maintain social media accounts, the emotional reactions to posting personal content, and the approach to customizing privacy settings. For instance, individuals of different genders often exhibit distinct tendencies in sharing emotions, with some being more expressive and others more reserved, depending on societal norms and personal comfort levels. Age differences also played a critical role in shaping social media behaviors. Younger users often reported feeling proud when posting emotional statuses, as these posts served as a way to showcase their personal growth, experiences, or milestones. Additionally, many believed that sharing such posts could evoke positive emotions among their viewers, creating a sense of connection and shared joy. Older participants, on the other hand, tended to perceive emotional self-expression on social media as a more calculated decision, weighing the benefits of sharing personal thoughts and feelings against potential risks such as misinterpretation or oversharing.

This study further emphasized the combined impact of gender and age on social media behaviors, which differed significantly from the effects of these factors when analyzed independently. This interplay suggests that the way individuals navigate self-expression on social media is shaped by a complex interaction between their age-related developmental stage and gender-based social expectations. For instance, younger females may approach emotional self-expression differently than older males, reflecting a blend of cultural, psychological, and experiential factors. By uncovering these nuanced relationships, the study provides valuable insights into the broader connections between sociological variables and social media behaviors.

REFERENCES

Abd Rahman, A. A., & Abdul Razak, F. H. (2019). Social media addiction towards young adults emotion. [JMIW]. *Journal of Media and Information Warfare*, *12*(2), 1–15.

Alt, D. (2018). Students' wellbeing, fear of missing out, and social media engagement for leisure in higher education learning environments. *Current Psychology (New Brunswick, N.J.)*, *37*(1), 128–138. DOI: 10.1007/s12144-016-9496-1

Azzaakiyyah, H. K. (2023). The Impact of Social Media Use on Social Interaction in Contemporary Society. [TACIT]. *Technology and Society Perspectives*, *1*(1), 1–9. DOI: 10.61100/tacit.v1i1.33

Beaudoin, C. E., & Hong, T. (2021). Emotions in the time of coronavirus: Antecedents of digital and social media use among Millennials. *Computers in Human Behavior*, *123*, 106876. DOI: 10.1016/j.chb.2021.106876 PMID: 36311469

Chen, S., Li, H., Pang, L., & Wen, D. (2023). The Relationship Between Social Media Use and Negative Emotions Among Chinese Medical College Students: The Mediating Role of Fear of Missing Out and the Moderating Role of Resilience. *Psychology Research and Behavior Management*, *16*, 2755–2766. DOI: 10.2147/PRBM.S421404 PMID: 37492860

Curci, A., & Rimé, B. (2012). The temporal evolution of social sharing of emotions and its consequences on emotional recovery: A longitudinal study. *Emotion (Washington, D.C.)*, *12*(6), 1404–1414. DOI: 10.1037/a0028651 PMID: 22642349

Erreygers, S., Vandebosch, H., Vranjes, I., Baillien, E., & De Witte, H. (2017). Nice or naughty? The role of emotions and digital media use in explaining adolescents' online prosocial and antisocial behavior. *Media Psychology*, *20*(3), 374–400. DOI: 10.1080/15213269.2016.1200990

Fang, J., Wang, X., Wen, Z., & Zhou, J. (2020). Fear of missing out and problematic social media use as mediators between emotional support from social media and phubbing behavior. *Addictive Behaviors*, *107*, 106430. DOI: 10.1016/j.addbeh.2020.106430 PMID: 32289745

Gamage, J., & Weerahandi, S. (1998). Size performance of some tests in one-way ANOVA. *Communications in Statistics. Simulation and Computation*, *27*(3), 625–640. DOI: 10.1080/03610919808813500

Huberty, C. J., & Petoskey, M. D. (2000). Multivariate analysis of variance and covariance. In *Handbook of applied multivariate statistics and mathematical modeling* (pp. 183–208). Academic Press. DOI: 10.1016/B978-012691360-6/50008-2

Järvenoja, H., Volet, S., & Järvelä, S. (2013). Regulation of emotions in socially challenging learning situations: An instrument to measure the adaptive and social nature of the regulation process. *Educational Psychology*, *33*(1), 31–58. DOI: 10.1080/01443410.2012.742334

Larnyo, E., Dai, B., Nutakor, J. A., Ampon-Wireko, S., Appiah, R., Larnyo, A., . . . Nkrumah, E. N. K. (2021, August). Assessing the impact of social media use on everyday emotion in health crises: a study of international students in China during COVID-19. In Healthcare (Vol. 9, No. 8, p. 1011). MDPI.

Manikandakumar, M., & Sridevi, S. (2023). From Observation to Active Learning: A Collaborative Learning Approach for Object Oriented Programming Course. *Journal of Engineering Education Transformations*, *36*(4), 150–160. DOI: 10.16920/jeet/2023/v36i4/23125

Michikyan, M., Subrahmanyam, K., Regan, P., Castillo, L. G., Ham, L., Harkness, A., & Schwartz, S. J. (2023). Social connectedness and negative emotion modulation: Social media use for coping among college students during the COVID-19 pandemic. *Emerging Adulthood*, *11*(4), 1039–1054. DOI: 10.1177/21676968231176109 PMID: 38602955

Ross, A., Willson, V. L., Ross, A., & Willson, V. L. (2017). Independent samples T-test. Basic and advanced statistical tests: Writing results sections and creating tables and figures, 13-16.

Shafait, Z., Khan, M. A., Sahibzada, U. F., Dacko-Pikiewicz, Z., & Popp, J. (2021). An assessment of students' emotional intelligence, learning outcomes, and academic efficacy: A correlational study in higher education. *PLoS One*, *16*(8), e0255428. DOI: 10.1371/journal.pone.0255428 PMID: 34343173

Tandoc, E. C.Jr, Lou, C., & Min, V. L. H. (2019). Platform-swinging in a poly-social-media context: How and why users navigate multiple social media platforms. *Journal of Computer-Mediated Communication*, *24*(1), 21–35. DOI: 10.1093/jcmc/zmy022

Tanna, D., Dudhane, M., Sardar, A., Deshpande, K., & Deshmukh, N. (2020, May). Sentiment analysis on social media for emotion classification. In 2020 4th International Conference on Intelligent Computing and Control Systems (ICICCS) (pp. 911-915). IEEE. DOI: 10.1109/ICICCS48265.2020.9121057

Tavakol, M., & Dennick, R. (2011). Making sense of Cronbach's alpha. *International Journal of Medical Education*, *2*, 53–55. DOI: 10.5116/ijme.4dfb.8dfd PMID: 28029643

Wang, Z., Tchernev, J. M., & Solloway, T. (2012). A dynamic longitudinal examination of social media use, needs, and gratifications among college students. *Computers in Human Behavior*, *28*(5), 1829–1839. DOI: 10.1016/j.chb.2012.05.001

Widen, G., Lindström, J., Brännback, M., Huvila, I., & Nyström, A. G. (2015). Mixed Emotions in Active Social Media Use-Fun and Convenient or Shameful and Embarrassing. iConference 2015 Proceedings.

Yang, C. C., Holden, S. M., & Ariati, J. (2021). Social media and psychological well-being among youth: The multidimensional model of social media use. *Clinical Child and Family Psychology Review*, *24*(3), 631–650. DOI: 10.1007/s10567-021-00359-z PMID: 34169391

Yifan, P., & Adnan, W. H. (2021). The impact of social media use towards negative emotion and suicidal tendency among students: a systematic review. In Forum Komunikasi (FK) (Vol. 16, No. 2, pp. 63-81). Universiti Teknologi MARA.

Zhang, M., Liu, H., & Zhang, Y. (2020). Adolescent social networks and physical, verbal, and indirect aggression in China: The moderating role of gender. *Frontiers in Psychology*, *11*, 658. DOI: 10.3389/fpsyg.2020.00658 PMID: 32292382

Chapter 3
Integrating Chatbots Into Educational Management Systems in the Global Intuitions of Higher Learning:
Streamlining Administrative Tasks

Austin Musundire
https://orcid.org/0000-0001-8784-0616
University of South Africa, South Africa

ABSTRACT

This study explores the integration of chatbots into Educational Management Systems (EMS) in higher education. With advancements in artificial intelligence (AI), chatbots can optimize processes like scheduling, notifications, and attendance tracking. Benefits include improved operational efficiency, cost reduction, and enhanced student support through real-time assistance. However, challenges such as technical compatibility, user resistance, and data privacy concerns limit adoption. The research examines theories related to technological adoption and administrative efficiency, offering practical recommendations for institutions. These include implementing scalable chatbot systems, user training, and robust data security. The study concludes with a future research agenda aimed at addressing current limitations and expanding AI applications in education.

DOI: 10.4018/979-8-3693-8734-4.ch003

BACKGROUND

The rapid evolution of artificial intelligence (AI) has brought transformative changes across diverse sectors, with the education industry being no exception. Among the most promising AI-driven innovations are chatbots, which are increasingly being adopted in educational institutions to streamline administrative processes. Chatbots, as conversational agents, are capable of automating routine tasks such as scheduling, notifications, and attendance tracking, effectively reducing the workload on administrative staff. By integrating chatbots into Educational Management Systems (EMS), institutions of higher learning can enhance operational efficiency, improve communication, and allow educational leaders to redirect their focus towards strategic initiatives. This literature based study explores the potential of chatbots in transforming educational administration, offering an in-depth exploration of their capabilities and contributions to solving contemporary administrative challenges.

Globally, educational institutions face significant challenges in managing the growing complexity of administrative tasks, often exacerbated by limited human resources and increasing demands for efficiency. Research indicates that repetitive administrative tasks, such as managing schedules, disseminating information, and handling student queries, consume a substantial amount of time and resources (Adam et al., 2021; Ngulube & Chigada, 2023). This inefficiency often leads to delays, communication gaps, and a diminished focus on core educational goals. Chatbots, powered by advancements in natural language processing (NLP) and machine learning, offer a solution by automating these tasks and ensuring real-time, accurate, and accessible interactions. This study aims to address these global challenges by evaluating the integration of chatbots into EMS, with a focus on identifying practical applications, benefits, and limitations in administrative processes within institutions of higher learning.

The findings of this study are expected to make both theoretical and practical contributions. Theoretically, the study builds upon the principles of AI integration in education, offering insights into the alignment of technological innovations with administrative efficiency theories, such as the Technology Acceptance Model (Davis, 1989). Practically, it provides a roadmap for educational institutions to implement chatbot solutions, highlighting best practices, cost-effectiveness, and scalability. By addressing the identified challenges, this research not only contributes to bridging the gap between administrative inefficiencies and technological solutions but also paves the way for future research into more sophisticated AI applications in education. Moreover, the study highlights the potential of AI-driven tools in fostering improved educational outcomes, administrative excellence, and enhanced stakeholder satisfaction, thus transforming the landscape of higher education management systems globally

AREA OF FOCUS

Chatbots, powered by artificial intelligence, are designed to simulate human conversation using text or voice interactions. These tools have gained traction in educational management worldwide due to their ability to automate repetitive tasks and improve operational efficiency. For instance, in Europe, institutions like the University of Madrid employ chatbots to manage enrollment processes, answer frequently asked questions, and provide real-time academic support to students (Sharma et al., 2022). Similarly, in Asia, universities in India and China use chatbots to handle large-scale administrative demands, including application tracking and attendance monitoring, showcasing their effectiveness in addressing high-volume tasks. These global examples highlight the adaptability of chatbots to varying institutional contexts, enabling streamlined operations and reduced administrative burdens.

Educational Management Systems (EMS) function as centralized platforms for handling core institutional tasks such as scheduling, communication, and reporting. The integration of chatbots into EMS has revolutionized these systems on a global scale. For example, in North America, institutions like Arizona State University have adopted AI-driven chatbots to assist students with queries about course registration, financial aid, and academic advising, significantly enhancing student satisfaction and engagement (Nguyen & Lee, 2021). In Africa, South African universities are exploring the use of chatbots in EMS to improve attendance tracking and provide reminders for assignment submissions, especially in institutions serving diverse, large student populations. These innovations demonstrate how chatbots can adapt to and address unique administrative challenges faced by institutions in different regions.

Globally, the use of chatbots in EMS also contributes to broader trends in data-driven decision-making and digital transformation. For example, institutions in Australia and New Zealand leverage chatbots to analyze interaction data, identifying patterns in student engagement and areas requiring administrative improvements. This data-driven approach is mirrored in countries like Kenya, where chatbot analytics are used to assess the effectiveness of student support services, thus improving institutional performance. By incorporating AI-driven insights, chatbots not only optimize routine operations but also inform strategic decisions, fostering innovation and responsiveness in educational management. The global adoption of chatbots underscores their potential to address universal administrative challenges while offering tailored solutions that reflect the cultural and operational diversity of institutions worldwide.

Overview of Chatbots in Educational Management

Chatbots, as AI-powered tools, are transforming educational management by simulating human conversations through text or voice interactions. These tools automate repetitive administrative tasks, freeing up time for staff to focus on strategic responsibilities. According to Sharma et al. (2022), chatbots enhance operational efficiency by managing routine inquiries, sending reminders, and providing real-time support. Globally, universities such as the University of Murcia in Spain have implemented chatbots to support students in administrative tasks, including enrollment and class scheduling (García-Villalba et al., 2021). Similarly, Deakin University in Australia introduced its AI chatbot, Genie, which assists students in navigating institutional systems, finding course information, and managing assignments (Deakin University, 2020). These examples illustrate how chatbots streamline processes, reduce administrative workload, and enhance user experience in higher education.

Educational Management Systems (EMS) serve as centralized platforms for managing institutional operations such as scheduling, attendance, communication, and reporting. When integrated with chatbots, EMS become more dynamic and efficient, enabling better communication and real-time decision-making. Nguyen and Lee (2021) discuss how chatbots embedded in EMS can automate attendance tracking, schedule notifications, and provide instant responses to frequently asked questions. In North America, Georgia State University employs its chatbot, Pounce, to support student enrollment and retention, resulting in a significant reduction in dropout rates (Bailey et al., 2020). In Asia, Singapore Management University uses AI chatbots for multilingual support, ensuring accessibility for international students (Cheung & Ng, 2021). These case studies highlight the global applicability of chatbots in addressing region-specific administrative challenges, improving efficiency, and personalizing support for students.

Moreover, chatbots provide a data-driven edge by collecting and analyzing interaction data to support informed decision-making in higher education management. In Europe, the University of Bologna in Italy leverages chatbot analytics to assess the effectiveness of student support services and improve engagement strategies (Frison et al., 2022). Similarly, in Africa, the University of Cape Town has initiated pilot projects using chatbots to monitor attendance and track student performance, offering tailored interventions for at-risk students (Chigada & Madzinga, 2022). By enabling institutions to utilize data insights for strategic improvements, chatbots not only optimize operational processes but also contribute to enhancing institutional performance globally. These applications reflect the growing importance of chatbots in fostering innovation and adaptability in the education sector.

Automating Scheduling with Chatbots

Scheduling is one of the most essential yet resource-intensive tasks in educational institutions. The introduction of chatbots into this domain offers a transformative solution by automating the creation and management of class timetables, meeting schedules, and extracurricular activity planning. Zhao et al. (2020) highlight that chatbots integrated with Educational Management Systems (EMS) can generate class schedules automatically based on pre-defined criteria such as course availability, instructor schedules, and room assignments. Furthermore, Kim and Park (2022) emphasize that chatbots can notify teachers and students of real-time schedule changes, reducing miscommunication and ensuring smoother operations. Globally, the University of California, Los Angeles (UCLA) employs AI chatbots to manage faculty and student schedules, streamlining appointment booking and room allocation. These systems reduce the administrative burden on staff and improve service efficiency.

The functionality of chatbots in scheduling extends beyond automation to include user interaction. Johnston et al. (2021) describe how conversational interfaces allow users to book appointments with faculty, administrators, or student advisors effortlessly. For instance, in Asia, National Taiwan University has adopted chatbot technology to facilitate seamless scheduling of consultation hours with professors, ensuring accessibility and reducing manual coordination efforts. Similarly, in Europe, the University of Helsinki employs chatbots to manage meeting schedules for administrative staff, significantly decreasing time spent on coordination and follow-ups (Nieminen & Vartiainen, 2022). These global examples demonstrate how chatbots offer practical and scalable solutions to streamline scheduling processes in diverse educational settings.

A case study from the University of Melbourne illustrates the impact of chatbot integration in scheduling. Henderson et al. (2021) report that the university implemented a chatbot to assist with course scheduling, resulting in reduced administrative bottlenecks and improved student satisfaction. This chatbot automated the process of assigning students to classes based on their preferences and course requirements, while also sending reminders about deadlines for schedule modifications. In Africa, the University of Pretoria is exploring similar applications, using chatbots to streamline student registration and timetable management (Chigada & Madzinga, 2022). These examples highlight the universal relevance of chatbots in tackling scheduling challenges, offering time-saving solutions that improve user experiences across different educational institutions worldwide.

Enhancing Notifications and Communication

Effective communication is fundamental to the seamless operation of educational institutions. Chatbots are revolutionizing this aspect by delivering timely, targeted, and personalized notifications to various stakeholders. Chakraborty and Das (2021) note that chatbots excel in sending reminders for assignment deadlines, exam schedules, and tuition payments, thereby reducing the risk of missed deadlines and enhancing academic compliance. Additionally, Thompson and White (2022) highlight the utility of chatbots in disseminating emergency alerts, such as weather-related closures or public safety incidents, ensuring rapid communication in critical situations. Globally, Stanford University in the United States utilizes chatbots to notify students of academic deadlines and campus-wide updates, which has led to improved student engagement and awareness.

Beyond simple reminders, chatbots are increasingly being used to share updates on institutional policies, events, and announcements. Garcia and Lim (2021) observe that chatbots integrated with Educational Management Systems (EMS) enable institutions to send policy updates or event notifications in real time, reducing delays caused by traditional communication methods. For example, in Europe, the University of Glasgow employs chatbot systems to update students about institutional policies related to course changes or COVID-19 protocols, ensuring that communication remains clear and up-to-date. Similarly, in Asia, the University of Tokyo uses AI-driven chatbots to send multilingual notifications, accommodating its diverse student body and enhancing inclusivity (Kobayashi & Tanaka, 2021). These applications demonstrate the global adaptability of chatbots in meeting the communication needs of diverse educational ecosystems.

Moreover, chatbots leverage advanced natural language processing (NLP) to personalize notifications based on user preferences and behaviors. Sundaram et al. (2020) emphasize that NLP enables chatbots to tailor messages to specific users, ensuring that the right information reaches the intended audience effectively. In Africa, the University of Lagos has adopted chatbots that use NLP to provide students with personalized alerts about registration deadlines and examination schedules (Okeke & Adebayo, 2022). Meanwhile, in Australia, Monash University's chatbot delivers customized updates about campus events and extracurricular activities, enhancing student participation and institutional engagement (Henderson et al., 2021). These examples underscore how chatbots not only streamline communication processes but also foster a more connected and informed academic community across the globe.

STREAMLINING ATTENDANCE TRACKING

Streamlining Attendance Management with Chatbots

Attendance management is a critical administrative task in educational institutions, often requiring significant time and effort to maintain accuracy and compliance. Chatbots, integrated with Educational Management Systems (EMS), offer an innovative solution to automate this process. Patel et al. (2022) highlight how chatbots can leverage advanced technologies like QR code scanning and facial recognition to record attendance efficiently, reducing the reliance on manual input. For instance, in the United States, the University of Florida has implemented chatbot-driven attendance systems that utilize facial recognition, ensuring high accuracy and saving staff time during large lectures and events. Such technology minimizes errors and improves accountability, which is particularly valuable in institutions with high student populations.

One of the key advantages of chatbots in attendance management is their ability to notify stakeholders promptly. Ahmed et al. (2021) emphasize that chatbots can send real-time alerts to parents or guardians regarding student absences, fostering stronger communication between schools and families. In Asia, India's Delhi Public School has integrated chatbots to send immediate notifications to parents about tardiness or absenteeism, enhancing parental involvement and enabling timely interventions (Rao & Jain, 2022). Similarly, in Africa, the University of Nairobi employs chatbot technology to communicate attendance updates to students and faculty, ensuring everyone stays informed (Otieno & Karanja, 2021). These global examples illustrate how chatbots contribute to bridging communication gaps and improving attendance monitoring.

Chatbots also play a significant role in generating attendance reports for teachers and administrators. Singh and Kapoor (2020) note that chatbots can compile detailed attendance summaries, offering insights into student participation trends and enabling data-driven decision-making. For example, Mehta and Kaur (2022) report that St. Xavier's High School deployed a chatbot system that reduced manual errors by 30% and improved the accuracy of attendance reporting. In Europe, the University of Vienna uses chatbots to provide faculty members with instant access to attendance data, streamlining administrative workflows and supporting performance evaluations (Schmidt & Hoffmann, 2021). These use cases demonstrate the universal applicability of chatbots in simplifying attendance management while enhancing the efficiency and reliability of institutional operations.

Empowering Educational Leaders Through Chatbots

The integration of chatbots into administrative processes enables educational leaders to redirect their efforts toward strategic priorities, such as curriculum development, faculty training, and student performance improvement. Miller and Brown (2022) argue that automating routine tasks, such as scheduling, notifications, and attendance tracking, allows leaders to focus on initiatives that directly impact institutional growth and academic excellence. Globally, universities like Harvard in the United States have adopted chatbots to handle repetitive administrative functions, freeing leadership teams to work on long-term goals, including advancing equity in education and designing innovative learning strategies (Johnson et al., 2023). This shift in focus significantly enhances leadership effectiveness and contributes to better institutional outcomes.

One of the key benefits of chatbot integration is improved decision-making based on real-time data analytics. Robinson et al. (2020) emphasize that chatbots provide administrators with instant access to actionable insights, such as enrollment trends, attendance rates, and resource utilization metrics. For example, the University of Cambridge in the United Kingdom uses chatbot-driven analytics to monitor key performance indicators (KPIs), enabling data-informed decisions that optimize institutional performance (Taylor & Clarke, 2021). Similarly, in Asia, the National University of Singapore employs chatbots to analyze student feedback, helping leaders tailor academic offerings to meet evolving demands (Lim & Tan, 2022). These applications highlight how chatbots enhance the strategic capabilities of educational leaders through advanced analytics.

Additionally, chatbot integration improves resource allocation and stakeholder satisfaction. Williams and Johnson (2021) note that chatbots streamline processes such as budget planning and staff deployment, ensuring that resources are allocated more efficiently. For example, in Africa, Stellenbosch University in South Africa has implemented chatbots to manage faculty workloads and streamline administrative budgeting, resulting in improved operational efficiency (Nkosi & Dlamini, 2022). Furthermore, Liu and Chen (2022) highlight that prompt and accurate administrative support provided by chatbots significantly increases satisfaction among stakeholders, including students, parents, and faculty. In Australia, the University of Sydney reported higher student satisfaction levels after introducing chatbots to handle queries about course registrations, scholarships, and campus facilities (Henderson et al., 2021). These examples demonstrate how chatbots not only alleviate administrative burdens but also foster a more efficient and user-centric institutional environment worldwide.

CHALLENGES AND SOLUTIONS IN IMPLEMENTING CHATBOTS

While chatbots hold immense potential to transform educational management systems (EMS), their integration is not without challenges. Technical issues often arise, particularly when chatbots lack compatibility with existing EMS platforms. Kumar and Shah (2021) note that limited integration capabilities can result in fragmented processes, undermining the efficiency gains promised by chatbots. For example, institutions in Europe, such as universities in Germany, have encountered difficulties integrating chatbots with legacy systems designed decades earlier. To address this, investments in customizable and scalable chatbot solutions are essential. In North America, Stanford University adopted a scalable chatbot framework that could integrate seamlessly with its EMS, ensuring compatibility and reducing technical roadblocks (Brown & Lee, 2022). These examples underscore the importance of adopting adaptable technologies tailored to institutional needs.

Another challenge is user resistance, as both staff and students may hesitate to embrace new technologies. Taylor and Green (2022) argue that reluctance often stems from a lack of familiarity or fear of job displacement among administrative staff. In Asia, universities in India reported initial resistance from staff who perceived chatbots as a threat to their roles. To mitigate this, targeted training programs were introduced to familiarize users with chatbot functionalities and emphasize their role as supportive tools rather than replacements. Similarly, in Africa, the University of Cape Town implemented an extensive orientation program that included live demonstrations and interactive workshops, significantly increasing user acceptance (Moyo et al., 2023). These strategies highlight the importance of proactive engagement and education to overcome resistance and build confidence in chatbot technologies.

Data privacy concerns also pose a significant barrier to chatbot adoption, particularly in regions with stringent data protection laws. Anderson et al. (2020) emphasize that chatbots, which handle sensitive information such as student records and financial data, are vulnerable to unauthorized access if robust security measures are not in place. For instance, European institutions must ensure compliance with the General Data Protection Regulation (GDPR) to protect user data. Universities in the Netherlands, for example, have implemented end-to-end encryption and multi-factor authentication to safeguard data transmitted through chatbots (de Vries & Haan, 2021). Similarly, institutions in the United States and Canada have adopted similar protocols to ensure compliance with local data protection regulations. These measures demonstrate the need for strong security frameworks to address privacy concerns and foster trust in chatbot systems.

The integration of chatbots into educational management systems marks a significant step toward modernizing administrative operations. By automating routine tasks such as scheduling, notifications, and attendance tracking, chatbots not only enhance operational efficiency but also enable educational leaders to focus on strategic goals. While challenges remain, targeted solutions and ongoing technological advancements offer a pathway to widespread adoption. Institutions that embrace chatbot technology stand to gain a competitive edge in delivering quality education and effective management.

Opportunities in Adopting and Implementing Chatbots

The adoption of chatbots in educational management systems (EMS) presents numerous opportunities that can significantly enhance the efficiency, effectiveness, and accessibility of administrative processes. One of the primary benefits is the potential for 24/7 availability, which ensures that students, staff, and faculty members can access support and information at any time. According to Williams and Johnson (2021), chatbots can deliver uninterrupted assistance, enabling institutions to better serve diverse student populations, particularly those in different time zones. For example, institutions like the University of Melbourne in Australia have adopted chatbot systems to provide around-the-clock assistance for international students, ensuring they receive prompt responses to queries about enrollment, courses, and administrative procedures (Lee & Mitchell, 2022). This global approach to round-the-clock support can improve student satisfaction and retention by offering constant access to critical information.

Chatbots also open up opportunities for personalized learning and administrative support. By leveraging advanced technologies such as machine learning and natural language processing (NLP), chatbots can tailor their responses based on individual user preferences and histories. Liu and Chen (2022) highlight how personalized chatbots can adapt to different student needs, providing customized notifications, reminders, and guidance on academic progress. In the United Kingdom, for instance, the University of Oxford has integrated chatbots into their EMS to provide personalized academic advice to students based on their course selections and performance, helping to increase engagement and retention rates (Taylor & Smith, 2023). These systems not only enhance student satisfaction but also provide administrative staff with valuable insights into student behavior, enabling more informed decision-making.

Moreover, chatbots can significantly improve cost-effectiveness by automating routine administrative tasks, freeing up human resources for more complex and strategic roles. Robinson et al. (2020) argue that by reducing the time spent on mundane tasks, chatbots allow institutions to allocate resources more efficiently. For example, the University of Toronto in Canada has implemented a chatbot that handles basic inquiries regarding course registration and tuition fees, resulting in significant cost savings and allowing staff to focus on higher-level academic support (Morris & Evans, 2021). Additionally, institutions in Latin America, such as the University of São Paulo in Brazil, have reported savings in operational costs through the use of chatbots, which assist with tasks like student orientation, attendance tracking, and course scheduling (Fernandes & Silva, 2022). This operational efficiency not only helps institutions save money but also supports the sustainable growth of educational services.

Solutions and Recommendations

The integration of chatbots into educational management systems (EMS) offers significant potential to enhance operational efficiency, accessibility, and personalized support for both staff and students. However, institutions are confronted with several challenges, such as technical compatibility, user resistance, and concerns about data privacy. To maximize the opportunities presented by chatbot adoption, institutions can implement various solutions and strategies.

First, to address technical compatibility issues, institutions should invest in scalable and customizable chatbot solutions that can seamlessly integrate with existing EMS platforms. Customization ensures that the chatbot system can be tailored to the unique needs of each institution, helping to avoid inefficiencies associated with fragmented processes. Successful implementations, such as Stanford University's scalable chatbot solution (Brown & Lee, 2022), demonstrate the importance of selecting adaptable technologies. Institutions should conduct thorough assessments of their existing EMS platforms before selecting a chatbot solution. Collaboration with vendors who specialize in scalable and customizable chatbot technologies, along with allocating budgets for regular system updates, will ensure long-term compatibility and efficiency.

Second, fostering user acceptance is crucial for overcoming resistance from both staff and students, which often arises from fear of job displacement or unfamiliarity with technology. To address this, institutions should implement proactive strategies aimed at building trust and confidence. For instance, organizing training programs and workshops to familiarize staff and students with chatbot functionalities, as demonstrated at the University of Cape Town (Moyo et al., 2023), will help ease concerns. Emphasizing that chatbots are designed to streamline tasks and support human roles rather than replace them will also improve acceptance. Providing live demonstrations and interactive sessions further helps to illustrate the practical benefits of chatbot systems. Additionally, gathering feedback from users will allow institutions to continuously refine chatbot operations, addressing any concerns and improving the overall user experience.

Third, data privacy and security are paramount concerns, particularly in regions with strict regulations such as the European Union's General Data Protection Regulation (GDPR). Institutions must prioritize robust security measures to ensure compliance with local data protection laws and to foster user trust. Adopting end-to-end encryption and multi-factor authentication protocols, as demonstrated by universities in the Netherlands (de Vries & Haan, 2021), is an essential first step. Establishing clear data usage policies and obtaining informed consent from users is critical in maintaining transparency. Regular security audits and training for administrative staff on data management and compliance with privacy regulations will further strengthen data protection frameworks.

Fourth, chatbots can significantly enhance accessibility and personalization for students, especially in diverse and geographically dispersed student populations. The 24/7 availability of chatbots allows institutions to provide continuous assistance, ensuring that students can access support at any time. Additionally, machine learning and natural language processing (NLP) can be leveraged to offer personalized academic advice, notifications, and reminders. For example, the University of Melbourne (Lee & Mitchell, 2022) has developed chatbot functionalities catering to international and remote learners. Similarly, the University of Oxford (Taylor & Smith, 2023) has integrated machine learning algorithms to tailor academic support, demonstrating the potential of AI to improve the overall student experience. Institutions can also use chatbot analytics to gain insights into user behavior, which can inform data-driven decision-making in both academic and administrative planning.

Fifth, chatbots can contribute to cost-effectiveness by automating routine tasks such as scheduling, notifications, and attendance tracking. By automating these processes, chatbots free up human resources, enabling staff to focus on more strategic roles. Institutions should identify repetitive tasks that can be automated to maximize cost savings, as demonstrated by the University of Toronto (Morris & Evans, 2021). Additionally, reallocating staff to roles that require more complex problem-solving or direct student engagement will further enhance the value of chatbot systems. Monitoring the cost-effectiveness of chatbot solutions through key performance indicators (KPIs) such as response times and user satisfaction rates will ensure that institutions continue to derive maximum value from their chatbot investments.

Finally, global collaboration among institutions is essential for the exchange of best practices and the development of effective chatbot solutions. By participating in international conferences and forums focused on educational technology, institutions can learn from the experiences of others and share their own insights. Case studies and research findings can be shared to inform the development of scalable and adaptable chatbot solutions that meet the needs of diverse educational environments. Collaboration will enable institutions to stay at the forefront of technological advancements and ensure that their chatbot systems continue to evolve to meet the changing demands of students and staff.

In summary, the successful integration of chatbots into EMS requires addressing technical, user, and privacy challenges through investment in scalable technologies, proactive user engagement, robust data security measures, and strategic automation. By fostering a collaborative approach to chatbot implementation, institutions can maximize the benefits of AI technology, improving operational efficiency, accessibility, and personalized support for students and staff alike.

FUTURE RESEARCH AND DIRECTIONS

Future research and directions in integrating chatbots into educational management systems (EMS) should focus on addressing persistent challenges while exploring innovative opportunities for their implementation. Research should prioritize developing customizable, scalable chatbot technologies that seamlessly integrate with legacy systems, ensuring compatibility and minimizing disruptions. Studies could investigate strategies to overcome user resistance, such as advanced training programs, interactive workshops, and user-centered design approaches that enhance usability and trust among staff and students. Data privacy and security concerns also require sustained attention, with future work needed to develop advanced encryption methods and compliance protocols that align with regional regulations. Furthermore, there is a growing need to explore the potential of chatbots in personalizing learning experiences, leveraging artificial intelligence to adapt to diverse user needs and preferences. Research could also examine cost-effective deployment strategies, particularly in resource-constrained institutions, to maximize their operational efficiency and accessibility. By addressing these areas, future efforts can provide comprehensive solutions to enhance the adoption, acceptance, and long-term value of chatbot systems in global higher education.

CONCLUSION

The integration of chatbots into educational management systems represents both a promising innovation and a significant challenge for institutions globally. This literature study highlights several barriers to adoption, including technical incompatibilities with legacy systems, resistance from users due to unfamiliarity or fear of job displacement, and data privacy concerns arising from stringent regulations. These challenges underscore the need for institutions to adopt adaptable and secure chatbot solutions tailored to their unique needs. Additionally, proactive strategies such as targeted training programs and comprehensive orientation sessions can help address user resistance and foster trust in these technologies, paving the way for smoother adoption and implementation.

Despite these challenges, the opportunities presented by chatbots are transformative. They offer round-the-clock availability, enabling institutions to better serve diverse populations, particularly international students in different time zones. Chatbots also enhance administrative efficiency by automating routine tasks, reducing operational costs, and freeing human resources to focus on strategic objectives. Furthermore, their ability to provide personalized support through machine learning and natural language processing creates new possibilities for improving student engagement, retention, and overall satisfaction. By leveraging these capabilities, institutions can modernize their operations and achieve a competitive edge in delivering quality education and services.

To fully realize the potential of chatbots, future research should prioritize the development of scalable, user-friendly technologies that integrate seamlessly with existing systems. Additionally, exploring innovative solutions for addressing data privacy and security concerns is critical to fostering trust among stakeholders. Research should also investigate ways to expand the functionality of chatbots to support advanced tasks, such as predictive analytics and academic planning. By addressing these areas, institutions can not only overcome existing barriers but also unlock new opportunities for innovation, efficiency, and sustainability in educational management systems.

REFERENCES

Ahmed, S., Khan, R., & Rahman, M. (2021). Enhancing parental involvement through chatbot notifications in schools. *Journal of Educational Communication*, 34(3), 245–258.

Anderson, T., Brown, J., & Green, K. (2020). Safeguarding data in chatbot integrations: GDPR compliance and beyond. *International Journal of Technology Law*, 15(2), 102–118.

Bailey, T., Jaggars, S. S., & Jenkins, D. (2020). *Redesigning America's Community Colleges: A Clearer Path to Student Success*. Harvard University Press.

Brown, D., & Lee, A. (2022). Overcoming technical barriers in chatbot integration within educational institutions. *Journal of Educational Technology*, 30(4), 415–428.

Chakraborty, S., & Das, P. (2021). Chatbot-driven notifications in higher education: Enhancing compliance and communication. *Journal of Educational Technology Systems*, 50(1), 55–68.

Cheung, S. K. S., & Ng, P. T. (2021). Multilingual chatbot systems for international students: Accessibility and efficiency. *International Journal of Educational Management*, 35(6), 1259–1275.

Chigada, J., & Madzinga, R. (2022). Exploring chatbot integration in African higher education systems: A case of South Africa. *African Journal of Science, Technology, Innovation and Development*, 14(3), 230–245.

Davis, F. D. (1989). Perceived usefulness, perceived ease of use, and user acceptance of information technology. *Management Information Systems Quarterly*, 13(3), 319–340. DOI: 10.2307/249008

Deakin University. (2020). Genie: Enhancing student engagement through AI chatbots. Retrieved from https://www.deakin.edu.au

Frison, E., Checchi, F., & Amico, A. (2022). Chatbots in European higher education: Assessing engagement and data-driven decision-making. *European Journal of Higher Education*, 12(4), 567–584.

Garcia, M., & Lim, T. (2021). Chatbot integration in educational management systems: Real-time updates and institutional efficiency. *International Review of Education*, 67(1), 56–72.

García-Villalba, M., López, J., & López-Cuadrado, J. L. (2021). Implementation of chatbot systems in Spanish universities: A case study. *International Journal of Artificial Intelligence in Education*, 31(2), 145–162.

Henderson, J., Smith, R., & Davis, P. (2021). Reducing administrative bottlenecks with AI-driven scheduling chatbots: Evidence from the University of Melbourne. *Australian Journal of Educational Technology*, 37(5), 432–448.

Henderson, R., Taylor, J., & Mitchell, L. (2021). Enhancing student participation through AI-driven chatbot notifications. *Australian Journal of Educational Technology*, 37(5), 543–559.

Johnson, P., Brown, C., & Taylor, R. (2023). The strategic potential of chatbots in university leadership. *Journal of Higher Education Leadership*, 45(1), 78–93.

Johnston, B., Williams, R., & Dawson, M. (2021). Conversational AI for student services: A case for improving accessibility. *Computers & Education*, 165, 104130.

Kim, H., & Park, S. (2022). Real-time scheduling with AI chatbots: Enhancing teacher-student coordination. *Asia-Pacific Journal of Educational Technology*, 20(3), 245–261.

Kobayashi, H., & Tanaka, Y. (2021). Multilingual chatbot applications for diverse academic communities. *Journal of Asian Educational Research*, 12(2), 152–169.

Kumar, S., & Shah, A. (2021). Challenges in implementing chatbot systems in legacy educational platforms. *Journal of Systems Integration*, 9(3), 223–237.

Lee, R., & Mitchell, S. (2022). 24/7 student support through chatbot integration: The University of Melbourne case study. *Journal of International Student Affairs*, 15(4), 390–402.

Lim, D., & Tan, J. (2022). Chatbot analytics for student feedback and academic adaptation. *Journal of Asian Education*, 20(2), 212–230.

Liu, J., & Chen, L. (2022). Personalized learning and administrative support using AI chatbots in education. *Journal of Machine Learning Applications in Education*, 18(3), 265–284.

Mehta, R., & Kaur, N. (2022). Improving attendance reporting accuracy through chatbot technologies. *Indian Journal of Educational Innovations*, 14(3), 312–328.

Miller, J., & Brown, K. (2022). Automating administrative processes with chatbots: Implications for educational leadership. *Journal of Educational Administration*, 52(2), 138–155.

Moyo, A., Nkosi, S., & Dlamini, T. (2023). Increasing chatbot adoption through user training programs: A South African perspective. *African Journal of Educational Technology*, 8(1), 145–163.

Nguyen, T. N., & Lee, S. W. (2021). Enhancing student engagement with chatbots: A North American perspective. *Journal of Educational Computing Research*, 59(4), 708–733.

Nieminen, J., & Vartiainen, T. (2022). AI-enabled scheduling solutions in European higher education: A case study from Finland. *European Journal of Educational Technology*, 14(1), 57–74.

Nkosi, S., & Dlamini, M. (2022). Streamlining resource management with chatbots: Stellenbosch University as a case study. *Journal of African Educational Development*, 10(2), 200–218.

Okeke, F., & Adebayo, T. (2022). Personalizing academic notifications with chatbots at the University of Lagos. *Nigerian Journal of Educational Technology*, 25(3), 172–188.

Otieno, J., & Karanja, B. (2021). Real-time attendance updates through chatbot systems: The University of Nairobi's experience. *East African Journal of Education*, 16(4), 276–290.

Patel, M., Shah, R., & Joshi, P. (2022). Leveraging AI for efficient attendance management in educational institutions. *International Journal of Educational Robotics*, 11(3), 189–202.

Rao, P., & Jain, S. (2022). Enhancing parental involvement with chatbot-based notifications: Insights from Delhi Public School. *Indian Journal of Educational Policy*, 15(3), 236–250.

Robinson, J., Taylor, A., & Clarke, H. (2020). Data-driven decision-making through chatbot analytics in education. *Journal of Digital Learning in Higher Education*, 8(2), 105–120.

Schmidt, T., & Hoffmann, B. (2021). Faculty engagement with real-time attendance data via chatbots. *European Journal of Educational Technology*, 22(3), 310–328.

Sharma, A., Verma, R., & Gupta, A. (2022). Chatbot applications in higher education: Enhancing student engagement and administrative efficiency. *International Journal of Educational Development*, 92, 102621.

Singh, R., & Kapoor, N. (2020). Analyzing trends in student participation using chatbot-generated attendance data. *International Journal of Educational Statistics*, 13(2), 90–110.

Sundaram, A., Gupta, R., & Mehra, V. (2020). NLP-driven personalized notifications in education: A comprehensive study. *Journal of Artificial Intelligence in Education*, 14(1), 67–82.

Taylor, G., & Green, P. (2022). Addressing user resistance in educational chatbot adoption: Strategies for success. *Journal of Educational Management*, 29(1), 122–137.

Taylor, L., & Smith, J. (2023). Personalized academic guidance via chatbot systems: Insights from the University of Oxford. *Journal of Higher Education Technology*, 38(3), 295–308.

Taylor, S., & Clarke, M. (2021). Monitoring institutional performance using chatbot-driven KPIs: A case study of Cambridge University. *British Journal of Educational Leadership*, 16(4), 321–338.

Thompson, L., & White, J. (2022). Emergency communication through AI chatbots in higher education: Lessons from the pandemic. *Journal of Educational Communication Systems*, 48(2), 104–122.

Williams, C., & Johnson, P. (2021). Improving operational efficiency in higher education through chatbot automation. *International Journal of Educational Innovations*, 27(2), 189–204.

Zhao, Y., Li, J., & Wang, Z. (2020). Automating scheduling with AI chatbots: Efficiency and user satisfaction. *Journal of Artificial Intelligence Research in Education*, 56(3), 245–267.

ADDITIONAL READINGS

Bryson, J. M. (2018). Strategic Planning for Public and Nonprofit Organizations: A Guide to Strengthening and Sustaining Organizational Achievement. Jossey-Bass. A foundational text offering strategic planning approaches applicable to enhancing chatbot adoption and integration in education systems.

Hattie, J. (2009). Visible Learning: A Synthesis of Over 800 Meta-Analyses Relating to Achievement. Routledge. A comprehensive guide to understanding educational strategies, with potential applicability to measuring the impact of chatbots on student outcomes.

Heath, C., & Heath, D. (2010). Switch: How to Change Things When Change Is Hard. Broadway Books. A practical resource for managing change, relevant for chatbot implementation and overcoming resistance in educational settings.

Salas, E., Tannenbaum, S. I., Kraiger, K., & Smith-Jentsch, K. A. (2012). The Science of Training and Development in Organizations: What Matters in Practice. *Psychological Science in the Public Interest*, 13(2), 74–101. DOI: 10.1177/1529100612436661 PMID: 26173283

Wenger, E. (1998). *Communities of Practice: Learning, Meaning, and Identity.* Cambridge University Press. DOI: 10.1017/CBO9780511803932

KEY TERMS AND DEFINITIONS

Chatbots Educational Management Systems (EMS): Educational Management Systems are digital platforms or software tools used to automate, monitor, and streamline administrative, academic, and operational processes within educational institutions. These systems often include features like student information management, course scheduling, and communication tools (Alves et al., 2019).

Streamlining: Streamlining refers to the process of simplifying or optimizing workflows to enhance efficiency, reduce redundancy, and improve productivity. In the context of educational institutions, it involves leveraging technology, such as chatbots, to automate repetitive tasks like scheduling, enrollment, and responding to routine inquiries (Smith et al., 2021).

Artificial Intelligence (AI): Artificial Intelligence refers to the simulation of human intelligence in machines that are programmed to think, learn, and make decisions. In higher education, AI-driven tools like chatbots are employed to enhance administrative efficiency and improve student support systems (Russell & Norvig, 2022).

Global Institutions of Higher Learning: Global Institutions of Higher Learning are universities and colleges that operate within international or multicultural contexts, providing education, research, and academic services to students worldwide. These institutions often adopt cutting-edge technologies, such as chatbots, to address diverse student needs and streamline their administrative processes (Altbach et al., 2020).

Chapter 4

Transforming Student Engagement Through AI, AR, VR, and Chatbots in Education

J. Viji Gripsy
https://orcid.org/0000-0002-6599-3010
PSGR Krishnammal College for Women, India

Sheela N. A. Selvakumari
Sri Krishna Arts and Science College, India

L. Sheeba
PSGR Krishnammal College for Women, India

B. Senthil Kumaran
https://orcid.org/0000-0002-7111-1950
Vel Tech Rangarajan Dr.Sagunthala R&D Institute of Science and Technology, India

ABSTRACT

Emerging technologies have a relatively short history in the higher education sector. The term "AI-powered chatbots" refers to systems that use conversational AI. Many colleges and universities are taking advantage of conversational AI and deploying AI-powered chatbots to improve the student experience. It is possible to converse with a chatbot via text or voice using an AI-based interactive interface. Data is fed into chatbots, which are programmed to process information already given to them. They respond according to a pre-written script. By mimicking Alexa and Siri at home, conversational AI can help colleges and universities communicate with

DOI: 10.4018/979-8-3693-8734-4.ch004

their students and prospective students in the same way. The primary aim of this chapter is to introduce the integration of Augmented Reality (AR) and Virtual Reality (VR) for AI-powered Chatbots for Transnational Higher Education to enhance the learning experience for students. The ultimate goal is to analyze the role of AI in improving higher education institutions around the globe.

1. INTRODUCTION

Machines that can make decisions without the help of a human brain are referred to as artificial intelligence (AI). Software-based systems and intelligent agents include modern data analytics and Big Data applications. An AI system may make judgments and conduct actions that mimic cognitive activities like learning and problem-solving by accessing this information library. AI has progressed rapidly since its inception in the mid-1950s as a scientific field, and it has quickly moved (Haenlein, 2019). Managing digital technology and corporate operations has become a vital instrument. Consider the fact that artificial intelligence is continually evolving. Optical character recognition and computer chess, previously thought to be cutting-edge technologies in artificial intelligence, are now considered standard fare. The Internet of Things (IoT) now uses AI in various ways, including robots, image recognition, real-time analytics, NLP, and other IoT-connected devices.

Artificial Intelligence (AI) can be divided into two broad groups. Modular artificial intelligence specializes in a single field and can hone its skills over time by doing more and more of the same. On the other hand, an all-encompassing artificial intelligence can solve a considerably more comprehensive range of problems, including those that demand comprehension of meanings and values (Adamopoulou, 2020). General and modular AI can 'learn' and increase their performance over time. In the same way that a golfer fine-tunes his swing or a violinist perfects her solo, a modular AI seeks to improve its domain performance. While the software and hardware of the system change with time, the core architecture does not. AI cannot expand beyond its specific skill and develop a general intelligence in the same way that being a golfer does not automatically imply becoming a chef because the inputs and goals are so different. We can make better, more informed decisions that have a broader impact using artificial intelligence. From a purely technical perspective, that is the solution. The advent of AI is likely to make it possible for humans to live more prosperous, more fulfilling lives, no longer burdened by the weight of manual labor, as well as to be able to govern the vast network of interconnected individuals, organizations, states, and nations which make up our world more efficiently (Algabri HK, 2020). Artificial intelligence is employed to streamline human effort and aid our capacity for improved decision-making. Throughout the past millennia, every method and every technology has been created with this as their common objective. The invention of artificial intelligence, also known as humanity's Final Invention, has also been in the midst of being celebrated as a breakthrough technology that will revolutionize the way we live our lives, in the process eliminating conflict, inequality, and human misery, to name a few.

Figure 1. Core problems of artificial intelligence

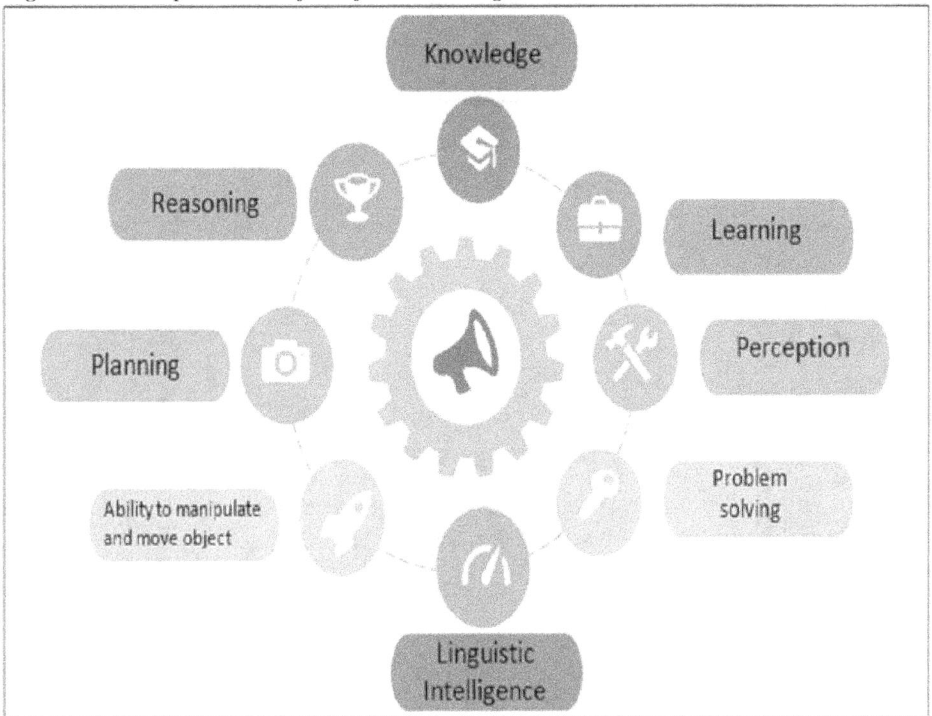

In the field of AI, a high level of technicality and specialized expertise is involved. Programming machines for specific characteristics like intelligence is one of the main issues in artificial intelligence, as seen in Figure 1.

2. BACKGROUND

AI has profoundly impacted higher education in recent years. Students and faculty alike can see the impact of AI on how they are educated today. As of now, intelligent AI technology can perform various tasks. Students and faculty can benefit from outsourcing manual tasks to a computer program. Learning and teaching can benefit from AI's assistance, allowing the education industry to take on new forms. When universities use artificial intelligence to personalize the enrollment process, they can more easily identify and recruit students who are most likely to succeed in their programs. Adaptive conversational assistants allow educational institutions to serve students worldwide without sacrificing quality on any day or night.

Figure 2. Benefits of AI in higher education

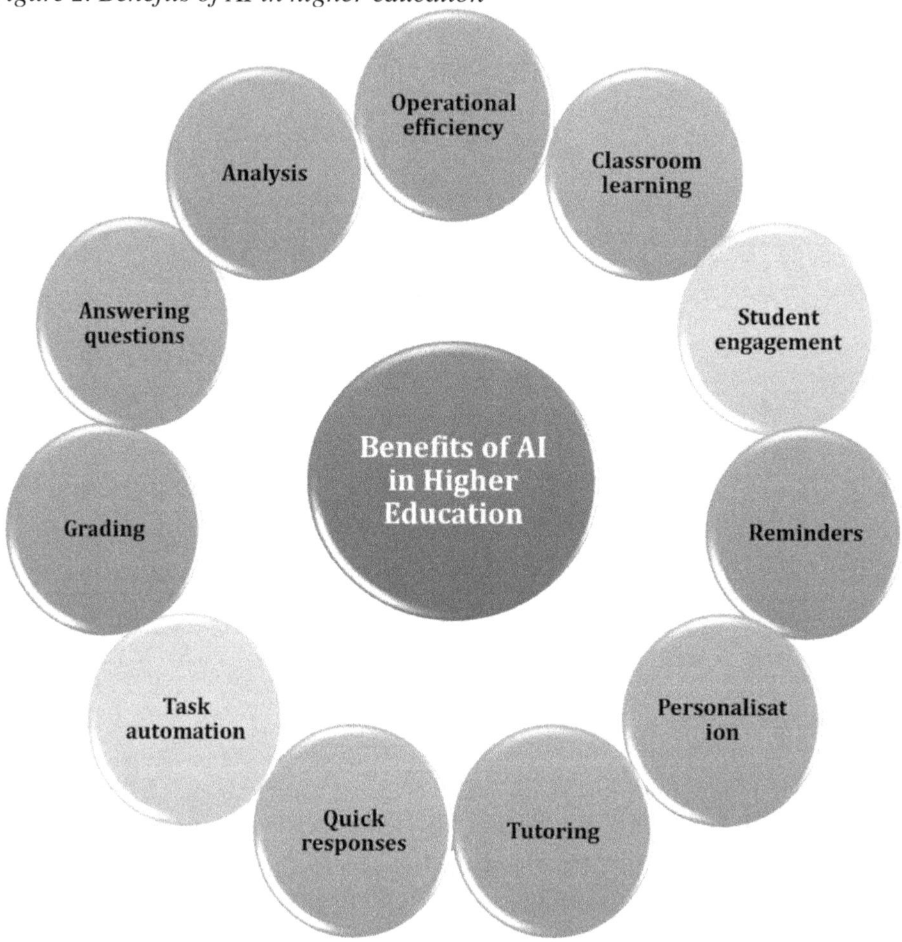

a) **Operational efficiency:** Since at least the early 2000s, researchers have been experimenting with the application of AI in higher education. As a result, systems such as document recognition, essay and SOP evaluators, and chatbots are being used in higher education more and more frequently. These types of artificial intelligence technologies could integrate data from numerous campus systems to influence administrative choices and customize the university curriculum to meet the recruiting demands of employers. As a result, the operational efficiency of the university is increased.

b) **Classroom learning:** In the classroom, artificial intelligence significantly aids learning by offering a complete educational experience for students. By using augmented reality and virtual assistants, students can learn more about the world around them to broaden their imaginative horizons in the classroom. These Classroom Assistance tools for grading and monitoring help educators improve the educational experience for students and get more out of their class time with them by enhancing the educational experience.

c) **Student engagement:** The use of AI technology, such as interactive assistants, allows students to convey their concerns as soon as they arise, enhancing student retention rates. Student engagement can also be improved by incorporating cutting-edge artificial intelligence technology, such as student success prediction models. In higher education, technology such as chatbots can help educators improve their efficiency in teaching by incorporating student opinions collected by conversational assistants into their lessons (Simamora, 2020).

d) **Reminders:** With artificial intelligence technology in higher education, institutions can provide students with helpful email, text, or push notifications. The reminders help to keep track of tasks that need to be accomplished, deadlines approaching, or scheduled special events. Such applications of artificial intelligence will assist students in becoming more familiar with the technology, which will, in turn, enhance student engagement.

e) **Personalization:** AI-based solutions can adapt to students' educational levels, learning speeds, and current educational goals depending on their previous experience. Students can use the system to find the most appropriate courses for their needs. Apps driven by artificial intelligence may assess users' prior learning experiences, detect weak points, and recommend techniques based on this data.

f) **Tutoring:** Many children require additional assistance outside of the classroom. When it comes to homework assistance or exam preparation, finding teachers who have the spare time to meet these demands can be difficult. Students can benefit greatly from artificial intelligence tutors and chatbots to assist them with many learning elements outside the classroom. While artificial intelligence systems cannot replace teachers, they can help pupils improve their weak areas.

g) **Quick responses:** Students have a plethora of inquiries throughout their academic careers. While some of these inquiries are exceedingly specific and demand the attention of a professor, many of these queries are ordinary and generic. Every day, faculty members are inundated with questions, making it difficult for students to access the knowledge they require.

h) **Task automation:** Teachers and academics are overburdened with administrative responsibilities. They must grade papers and examinations, evaluate each student's learning habits, respond to generic inquiries, and perform other tasks.
i) **Grading:** Today, it is possible to delegate the grading of multiple-choice tests to a computer program. Artificial intelligence-powered apps will examine written responses in the not-too-distant future.
j) **Answering questions:** AI-driven chatbots, by making use of the knowledge base available within the school, aid many common and repetitive queries that need not necessarily be solved by the teaching staff. AI and machine learning-based applications can integrate the knowledge and skills of the different tutors in a way that can automatically carry out many tasks, hence freeing teachers to spend more time on the more important aspects of their profession.
k) **Analysis:** While artificial intelligence-powered apps assist teachers in automating chores, they also collect data that may be used for further study. If, for example, the application analyses each test during the grading process, it can give teachers vital input about their students' academic progress and knowledge. These systems can assist teachers in determining which aspects of the curriculum require further attention, both for the entire class and for each student.

2.1 Education Chatbots and Their Importance

Chatbots are programmed to respond in a predetermined manner to any information they receive. Some of the biggest tech companies globally promote chatbots, also known as conversational agents, automated chatbots, or virtual assistants (Tight, 2020). Several major tech companies are enabling chatbots, how they can revolutionize daily tasks and how universities communicate with their students. IBM, Amazon, Facebook, Google, and Microsoft. For most university offices, there are periods when staff members feel like they are working in a call center, struggling to keep up with the influx of requests for information. Incoming students, staff, and parents often have many questions about enrolling in new classes or clarifications (Algabri, 2024). The best chatbot for the university admissions department will use algorithms and is intelligent enough so that students and faculty do not have to contact the help desk to get their questions answered. While learning to use a new virtual assistant may seem like an up-front investment, using a chatbot like Mongoose Harmony powered by Drift, which was created with higher education staff in mind, can pay dividends in the long run. Students and university staff collaborated to develop the following four chatbots to enhance the student experience.

Artificial intelligence (AI) has made it possible to incorporate chatbots into various educational settings. The use of this technology for educational purposes is on the rise. If a student or an employee of an educational institution, chatbots can help to get answers quickly and easily. The results of the review provide a comprehensive understanding of previous studies, benefits, and challenges, as well as future research areas related to the implementation of Chatbot technology in education (Almansor, 2019). There was a discussion about the implications of the findings, and suggestions were made. Students are learning and absorbing information differently because of the increasing use of technology in their daily lives. Thanks to artificial intelligence, educators today can create personalized learning environments for their students. Some systems can tell whether or not a student can comprehend the material they are studying. Artificially intelligent conversational tools, such as chatbots, are reshaping the educational technology landscape by enhancing student interaction and collaboration.

Student questions can be answered quickly and efficiently by using chatbots. When they have a question, they do not have to go through a lengthy FAQ document or wait for an administrator to respond. Consequently, the student experience is improved, and the wait time is reduced. Students without advisors can also use chatbots as advisors if they do not want to meet with them (Chougale, 2021). They can ask questions about their major, find out what would happen if they changed majors, and get course recommendations from the advisors. A chatbot can communicate with other AI applications so that users can get relevant results more quickly. Chatbots free up staff time and resources by repeatedly reducing the need to answer the same questions frequently. Chatbots can also help employees when procedures or processes need to be updated. Chatbots can immediately deploy updates to ensure that all new information is available simultaneously.

As a result, further information is delivered more quickly and effectively. User preferences can be taken into consideration when a chatbot is being used. Institutions can use this to serve their customers and employees better.

There are two types of chatbots: intelligent and straightforward.

- In simple chatbots, predefined rules or keywords control the bot's actions. So that the chatbot can understand the questions asked, the developer must define each direction or keyword individually. A student might inquire, "How do I register for classes?" or "How do I register for English 101?" Chatbot developers must make changes to their software if their chatbot does not understand what they are saying. Many things need to be coded into a simple chatbot, which can be time-consuming for developers to implement.
- Intelligent chatbots can be programmed to carry out a variety of functions. NLP and AI are used to build these chatbots, which can answer user questions. To understand, they do not rely on predefined rules but rather on models that have been pre-trained. Each time a question is asked, a recorded response is made. It requires extensive preliminary inquiries before an intelligent chatbot

is implemented, but these chatbots are trained to recognize and understand similar questions so that future updates will be seamless.

Both types of chatbots rely on the chatbot's backend to accomplish two essential tasks. The first step is to analyze the question or request. After that, it responds to the question. When it comes down to it, this appears to be a straightforward process, but it is a lot more complicated than it first appears (Daud, 2020).

Intelligent tutoring systems for students are among the most widely used artificial intelligence applications because they provide a more personalized learning environment. Conversational interfaces such as chatbots can help convert lessons and lectures into engaging conversations, making learning more interactive for students. Natural language processing and understanding can assist chatbots in this process (Smutny, 2020). The bots can quiz students on the same while assisting teachers in assessing results, identifying students who are falling behind, and providing personalized assistance to them.

Figure 3. Workflow of the developed system

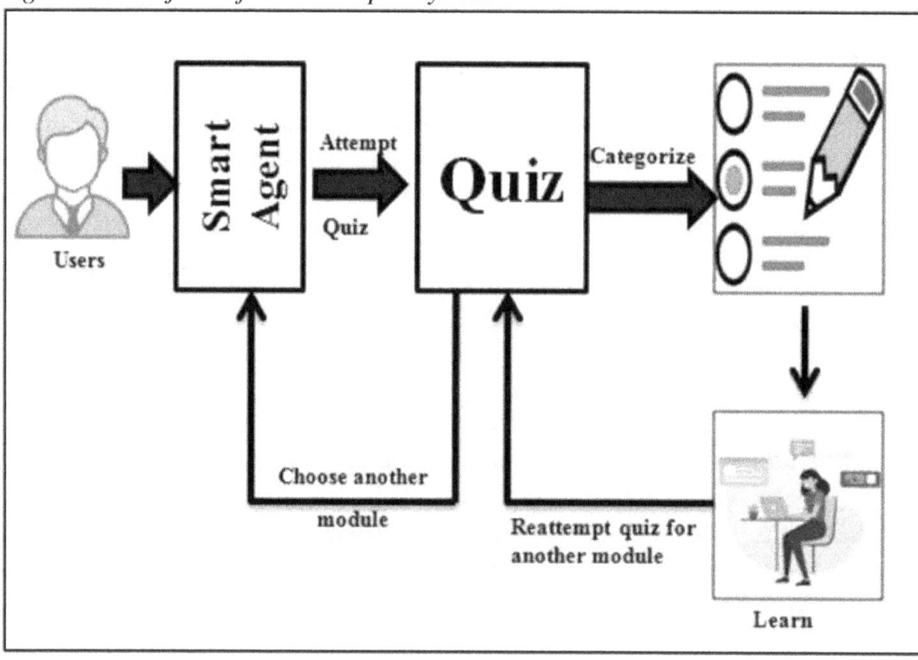

Student engagement on social media platforms has increased significantly in recent years. These platforms can also be used as research platforms, with the virtual assistant assisting them in this endeavor. Bots, also known as virtual voice assistants, can communicate with students using their preferred platform, encouraging them to learn in a way that they enjoy. Students who have access to a network of educators and learners, as well as a repository of material, will be better able to fulfill their information needs and further their education. Each interaction with chatbots or virtual assistants, whether by students, teachers, or their peers, results in the bot or virtual assistant learning more and becoming sharper and better with each conversation (Przegalinska, 2019). With this data in hand, institutions of higher learning can better comprehend and address student concerns and issues. E-learning breaks the boundaries of space, and Artificial Intelligence allows one to remove those boundaries by linking students across the globe into one vast network of online teaching programs. With further innovation, it would be possible to reach an even more significant number of populations, such as remote regions, and help them realize their full educational potential, no matter where they are in the world. However, for several ed-tech companies, this technology is being used to suggest customized material on different platforms and to give personalized learning opportunities to people across the globe, claims the organization. Teachers would be better positioned to offer students learning opportunities that are relevant to them if artificial intelligence tools and services were integrated throughout the curriculum.

Education entails a significant amount of administrative work, which can be automated with artificial intelligence. Many of these tedious jobs can be automated using technology., such as grading homework, providing responses, and adding value to each student. For example, technology can automate the classification and processing of paperwork. In addition to making the learning process more engaging and interactive for the students, artificial intelligence and chatbots also facilitate the teaching process and reduce the administrative staff's workload in educational institutions. Because everyone benefits, the educational technology sector is sure to see increased use of artificial intelligence to increase students' interest in learning, foster learning, upgrade the teaching process, and assist educational institutions in streamlining processes.

Artificial intelligence and chatbots in education can realize the personalization of the learning process, thus helping to adapt more aptly to the individual demands and speed of each learner (Villegas-Ch, 2020). The problem with the traditional learning method is that every student who enrolls in a class or an online course is treated in the same fashion. Every student's learning mode and the appropriate checkpoints for evaluating progress are the same, regardless of their background. Given that each student possesses a unique set of skills, abilities, and aptitudes, it does not appear fair to treat them all in the same way. AI can assist in resolving this issue by personalizing interactions with each student to provide the best learning experience possible. Chatbots can learn about the intent behind an interaction by interacting with students through their preferred communication channels. Overall, artificial intelligence and chatbots have the potential to improve the entire learning process by tailoring it to the individual needs of each student. Additionally, it becomes more effective and provides a better user experience.

2.2 Chatbots: Types and Uses

Figure 4. Types of chatbots based on the working mechanism

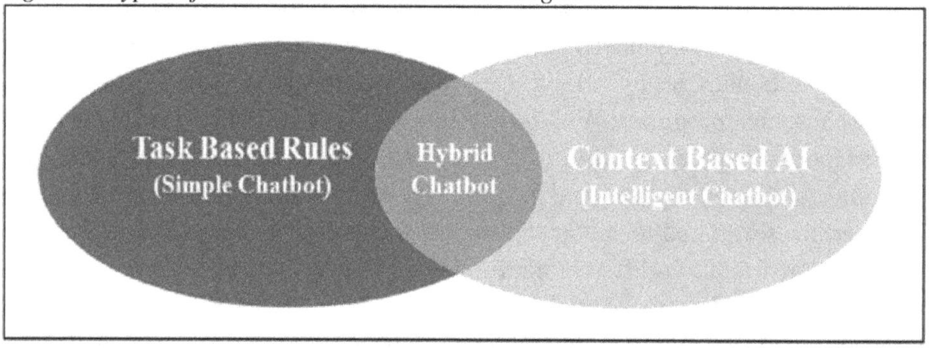

Chatbots are divided into three categories;

i. Scripted/Simple chatbots:

Scripted chatbots are typically rule-based bots because they have limited capabilities. They have a specific function in mind. Consider them to be the online version of an IVRS. This implies that until the client receives answers to their inquiries, the bot will pose questions based on the possibilities they have prepared, and the consumer can make a selection from the options. Based on previous encounters, the chatbot won't make any assumptions. Straightforward discussions work best with these chatbots (Okonkwo, 2021). They are particular to build and train. The advantages of this particular chatbot include;

- ✓ The rule-based chatbots can easily be integrated with systems in a less developed state, teams can save money by not updating or purchasing new hardware or software.
- ✓ Rule-based chatbots are those that answer a user's question based on a set of guidelines and scripts that have already been established. Consequently, rule-based chatbots are more accountable and safer because they cannot learn autonomously, guaranteeing constant client service.

- ✓ The development time and ongoing maintenance costs of rule-based chatbots are often lower because they only function and execute in the scenarios for which they have been educated.

Chatbots that follow the rules are not limited to text-based interactions only.

ii. Intelligent/Smart chatbots:

Artificial intelligence approaches are engineered with artificial intelligence. Artificial intelligence is more flexible about the type of information it can take from the user. Users can type free text but also select voice entry within the form. It is not restricted to other forms of information, provided that it is clear. These systems have the potential to improve performance with repeated usage by using artificial intelligence. Artificial intelligence is excellent at simple, isolated jobs.

The actual intelligence of the bot, however, is modest. This is because chatbots are unable to understand any context or ambiguity, nor are they able to retain information over time. Intelligent chatbots powered by artificial intelligence are intended to simulate interactions with customers that are as close to humans as possible. They can hold free-flowing conversations and comprehend the intent, language, and sentiment. Chatbots require programming to understand the context of their interactions with humans. Putting them into practice and executing them is a lot more complex, and they need data to learn. The advantages offered by this chatbot are;

- ✓ AI chatbots analyze and prepare appropriate responses based on the data they receive from users. The greater the amount of data studied, the better their overall performance. First, artificial intelligence chatbots need to understand the question's intent, and then they need to build a response in natural language to provide a suitable response.
- ✓ AI chatbots are not limited to a single language. They are capable of being programmed in various languages and responding to user queries in a variety of languages as well.
- ✓ AI chatbots are more efficient and capable of providing better responses than rule-based chatbots because they can analyze user behavior. However, in the case of rule-based chatbots, users will have to train themself by creating new rules for every submitted query.

iii. Hybrid chatbots:

Graphical user interfaces are found only in scripted chatbots, depending exclusively on the nature of the chatbot. Consequently, there are two broad categories of chatbots: intelligent chatbots and programmed chatbots. It follows, then, that it is a guiding principle that, generally, all chatbot developers say bots can be interacted with through a graphical user interface. The bot should display a graphical user interface to complete the task efficiently via a graphical interface. They are a hybrid of simple and intelligent chatbots. Simple chatbots and intelligent chatbots are at opposite ends of the spectrum when it comes to chatbots. There will always be a demand for simple chatbots to become more innovative and brilliant chatbots to become more straightforward. Hybrid chatbots bridge the gap between the two extremes. Hybrid chatbots are capable of performing some rule-based tasks and understanding intent and context. They, therefore, become a harmonious tool for companies in their dealings with clients.

2.3 Bot Advancements for Betterment in Education

Any program can be used to interact with a chatbot. Additionally, there is a database, application programming interfaces (APIs), and an application layer for connecting with external administrations. Chatbots are readily available to users, increasing the conversational complexity of the software. However, a widespread issue must be resolved. It cannot understand what the client wants. Currently, robots are trained using only the data that has already been provided to them (Mendez, 2020). Therefore, most businesses today employ a chatbot to record and log all communications. Developers can examine these records to learn the types of inquiries customers make. Software engineers utilize machine learning models and technologies to coordinate client requests and provide the best possible response (Vanichvasin, 2021).

i. **Automation is efficient:** Chatbots could make processes efficient by automating steps involved in complex operations with short voice or text commands that take less time to complete a job and thereby enhance the organization's productivity.
ii. **Flexible:** Both speech and text chatbots can be designed to listen and respond to the user in the preferred language. Chatbots can be made part of operations to communicate with both employees and customers.
iii. **Improved Customer Engagement:** The excellent client experience differentiates the firm from its competitors. One of the many benefits of chatbots is that they can be integrated into channels where the clients and prospects are already active, such as Facebook Messenger, for faster communication and meeting their demands at the quickest rate possible.

iv. **Make it easier for people to communicate in real-time:** Nobody likes being forced to wait for a solution to a problem. Customer patience is short-lived when a customer has a problem with the products or services. If the company cannot resolve the issue within a reasonable amount of time, the customer will become dissatisfied. A chatbot integrated into the customer support system allows people to engage with it quickly and easily without going through any training or learning curves. Chatbots can analyze queries and answer customer questions using NLP.

v. **Reduce the number of face-to-face interactions with customers:** Significant savings are realized by reducing the time employees spend dealing with customer inquiries. To reduce the time it takes for customers to interact, we are phasing out customer support staff and replacing them with chatbots across all channels, including phone calls, social media, and messaging applications. It is one of the most well-known benefits of utilizing a chatbot in the business (Neumann, 2021).

vi. **Remove time-consuming tasks that take up a lot of your time:** Customer service agents currently perform many tedious and repetitive tasks, which chatbots can replace. It is just one of the numerous benefits of utilizing chatbots. While these jobs can be tedious and draining for humans, a bot will never complain, even when a customer becomes frustrated or belligerent, because bots are not human.

vii. **Humanize Company's Image:** Another advantage of this adaptability is that it allows chatbots to engage with customers on various levels, which is extremely useful. Businesses can use it to assist customers with technical support, sales information, and account management.

Unlike human education, training a chatbot takes place much more quickly and on a larger scale than human education. Instead of being given manual instructions that they must follow to the letter, a customer support chatbot is fed with many conversation logs. The chatbot can determine what type of question is being asked and what kind of answers are being provided from those logs.

3. FOCUS OF THE ARTICLE

3.1 Proposed Methodology for AR/VR Integration

The integration of Augmented reality (AR) and virtual reality (VR) for chatbots is being used in educational settings, and there is much potential to improve learning experiences and expand administrative operations. However, it is essential to prepare carefully, take a stable method, and emphasize overcoming various difficulties to integrate these technologies. A methodical approach might help educational institutions proficiently integrate AR, VR, and chatbots.

Figure 5. Proposed methodology architecture

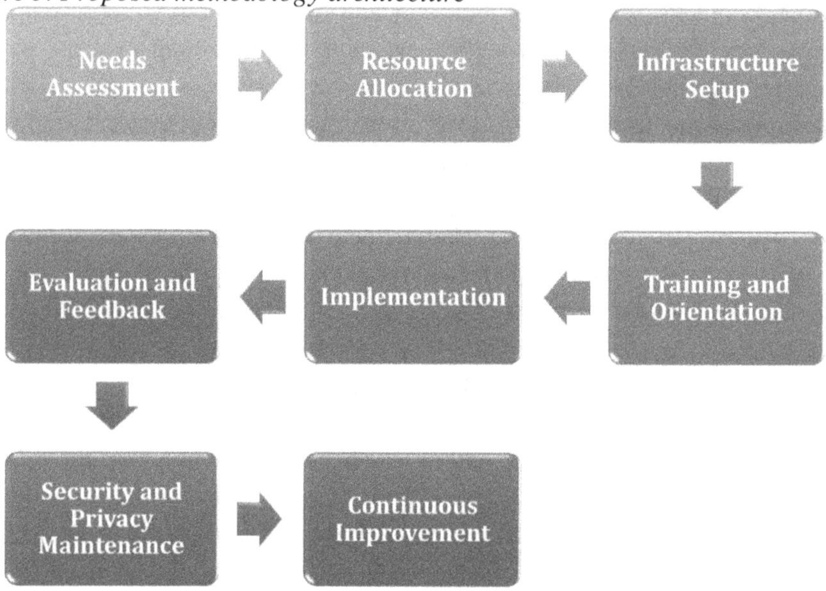

a) Needs Assessment and Planning

The first important step in the integration of augmented reality/virtual reality and chatbots in the educational setup is to conduct a complete examination of the needs. Educational institutions must clearly define specific learning objectives they want to achieve, which will then help determine whether augmented reality and virtual reality would enhance student engagement and understanding. Besides, identifying areas in which chatbots may help students and instructors and make administrative tasks more efficient would ensure proper use of available resources. Institutional use of AR and VR: One needs to see which subjects or classes would receive the most out-of-the-box attention from immersive media. AR may be used along with VR on simulations, field excursions, and virtual labs where health, engineering, architecture history, and some environmental research fit. A needs assessment will involve conversations with instructors, curriculum authors, and students to identify where AR and VR solutions could enhance understanding, facilitate experiential learning, and encourage more involvement. Chatbot Needs Assessment: Chatbots can be very useful in managing mundane administrative tasks, such as registering students for courses, answering frequently asked questions, scheduling appointments, and providing real-time assistance. Educational institutions need to determine which administrative tasks take the most time. They are the most repetitive since these are the areas where chatbots are likely to be the most effective. The process of building the chatbot can be driven by knowing how frequently students ask questions, common problems instructors face, and the likelihood of automated conversation. Upon completion of the needs assessment, a strategic plan should be prepared to ensure it is aligned with the overall goal of the institution. This strategic plan will define the process for execution, resource allocation, and resource management.

b) Resource Allocation and Technology Procurement

After the need assessment, institutions will have to provide funding to acquire the required hardware, software, and platforms for augmented reality/virtual reality and chatbots. In this step, the most suitable devices for the institute-specific needs, along with the appropriate chatbot platforms, are identified. AR and VR technologies require specific hardware equipment, including headgear, haptic feedback devices, sensors, and high-performance computers. There are numerous providers with which educational institutions have to evaluate in terms of ease of use, scalability, hardware compatibility, and endurance. Budgeting is part of this since AR and VR technologies are pretty new and pricey, especially for large-scale applications. Some educational institutions may begin to use AR or VR technology in specific departments or courses before widespread adoption.

Figure 6. Resource allocation

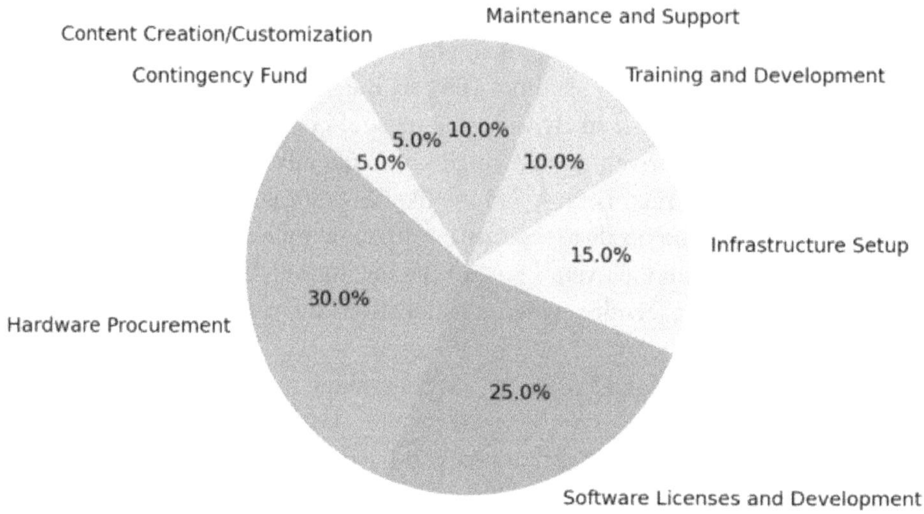

The development and implementation of chatbots require appropriate platforms. The institutions should consider whether the platforms for the chatbots can effectively communicate with all existing LMS, student information systems, and web pages. The following are some of the factors to consider when deciding on which systems of chatbots to implement: NLP capabilities, scalability, integration capabilities, and personalization. In addition, the colleges should ascertain that the chatbot platform is secure for data and can be customized to meet the requirements of the students and professors.

c) Digital Infrastructure Development

The high-performance digital infrastructure in educational institutes should be ready so that augmented and virtual realities work accurately. For better interaction, highly dense bandwidth is necessary, along with less latency for virtual and augmented reality systems. In this concern, the academic institute needs a secure network topology with high bandwidth to fulfill applications containing data-oriented services of AR/VR with reliability.

High-Speed Internet: Applications in Augmented Reality and Virtual Reality may necessitate massive file storage, like the case of three-dimensional models and video recording. Education facilities have to invest in high-speed internet and Wi-Fi, which does not allow this technology to have any breaks.

Design an AR/VR room or lab using computer technology, which can allow an immersive experience.
Cloud Storage: With AR/VR data so enormous, cloud storage solutions will become vital in the storing, management, and delivery of AR/VR content. Through cloud storage, extensive data can be stored without students and staff having difficult access to it; scalability and flexibility are also features. Cloud solutions help people work together more efficiently; a cloud-based solution will support a high number of users across multiple locations for access and interaction with AR/VR content.
Security Protocols: Since AR/VR and chatbot technologies involve dealing with sensitive information, security is a significant factor in implementing these technologies. Institutions are mandated to implement security measures that will protect student information, ensure data privacy, and prevent unauthorized access. Data security heavily relies on strong encryption, multi-factor authentication, and regular audits. More so, the designers of chatbots are expected to add algorithms to prevent data breaches, thus guaranteeing safe student information administration.

d) Faculty and Student Training

After constructing the infrastructure and technology, instructors and students need heavy training to familiarize themselves with the new tools and ensure that they are using them to the fullest. Training needs to be customized according to the needs of each group.

Faculty Development: Faculty must be provided with training about incorporating AR/VR in their pedagogy and using chatbots for support services. Workshop sessions and practical training might be helpful in guiding the faculties in actual usage. Teachers are also required to learn the ways in which they would implement augmented reality and virtual reality simulation experiences and understand how they should create a tremendous immersive experience based on what is best learned in the process. Moreover, instructors are also to be trained to assess the progress of students in an AR/VR environment and respond promptly.
Student Learning: Students should be taught how to use AR/VR and other technologies in support of their academic work. This includes understanding interactions in immersive environments, moving through virtual worlds, and interacting with content. Equally so, students should learn how to employ chatbots to request help for studies, select courses, and complete various

administrative tasks. Tutorials and user manuals must be given to ensure that students are proficient in using the new technology.

e) Implementation and Deployment

The implementation stage will constitute the actual deployment of AR/VR and chatbot technologies. This should be implemented step by step to ensure that the integration process remains manageable and allows for adjustments to be made based on feedback.

Phased Deployment: The phased deployment allows universities to launch a pilot program or a controlled rollout within specific courses or departments. This allows the instructors and students to adapt to the new technologies before the widespread usage. Institutions can refine and augment their implementation strategies according to feedback and the effectiveness of the tools. During this phase, institutions should closely monitor the performance of both AR/VR and chatbots, troubleshoot any technical errors, and implement any required upgrades.

Iterative Process: The integration process should be iterative, implying gathering user input at the conclusion of each step in deployment so as to enhance tools and procedures. Continuous evaluation assures that both AR/VR and chatbots are making effective strides toward educational as well as operations-related improvements. Frequent surveys and focus groups coupled with analytics will offer helpful insight into the effectiveness of the tools.

f) Evaluation and Feedback Collection

In order to ensure that AR/VR and chatbots are successfully integrated, institutions need to continuously measure the impact of these technologies on student engagement and administrative efficiency. There is a need for constant input from teachers and students to understand the strengths and flaws in the implementation. Institutions must collect this input using questionnaires, interviews, and usage analytics. This input will, therefore, inform improvements in the use of AR/VR and chatbots to ensure such increases in the performance capabilities of students and teachers without compromising their own needs toward general effectiveness during the whole learning process.

3.1.1 Steps for AR/VR and Chatbot Integration in Education

Needs Assessment and Planning

Step 1: Identify areas in which AR/VR enhances education.
Step 2: Determine areas to grant AR/VR to chatbots.

Resource Allocation

Step 3: Allocate funding to devices and infrastructure for AR/VR and chatbots.
Step 4: Choose scalable and reliable solutions.

Infrastructure Configuration

Step 5: Ensure internet connectivity and cloud storage speed is not very slow.
Step 6: Configure digital infrastructure for AR/VR and the integration of the chatbot.
Step 7: Organize seminars for students and faculty members
Step 8: Sustain continuous support using AR/VR and chatbots

Implementation

Step 9: Implement use of AR/VR technology at school level.
Step 10: Design the chatbots for office purposes.

Evaluation and Feedback

Step 11: Request suggestions from the users for modification
Step 12: Periodically conduct tests on efficacy and acceptability

Security and Privacy Management

Step 13: Utilize technologies of data security
Step 14: Sustain security practices from time to time.

Continuous Improvement

Step 15: Upgrades and enhancing resources as a result of suggestions
Step 16: All changes and updates as required.

Table 1 describes the key features of various AI-powered educational chatbots

Table 1. Student engagement metrics in AR/VR integration

Engagement Metric	Definition	How It's Measured	Purpose
Time Spent in AR/VR	The duration students spend interacting with AR/VR applications or simulations.	Use analytics tools to track session durations.	To determine the level of interest and immersion in AR/VR experiences.
Completion Rate	The percentage of students who complete AR/ VR tasks, modules, or activities.	Compare the number of completed tasks to the total assigned tasks.	To evaluate task engagement and persistence.
Task Accuracy	The number of errors or correct responses during AR/VR tasks or challenges.	Use built-in assessment tools to analyze performance.	To assess comprehension and skill acquisition in real-time.
Interaction Frequency	The number of interactions students have within the AR/VR environment (e.g., clicks, gestures).	Monitor interaction logs or analytics within the AR/VR platform.	To gauge active participation and engagement with the content.
Engagement Duration per Session	Average time students stay continuously focused during an AR/VR session.	Measure time between first and last meaningful interaction in a session.	To assess focus and sustained engagement levels.
Revisit Rate	How often students return to the AR/VR application or specific modules.	Track the number of times students access the same content or application over time.	To measure interest, retention, and the perceived value of the content.
Collaboration Metrics	The extent of student collaboration in multi-user AR/VR activities.	Monitor group interactions, communication logs, or collaborative task outcomes.	To evaluate teamwork and peer engagement in shared experiences.

continued on following page

Table 1. Continued

Engagement Metric	Definition	How It's Measured	Purpose
Engagement Heatmaps	Visual representation of areas within the AR/VR environment where students focus the most.	Use eye-tracking data or movement logs within the AR/VR platform.	To identify which elements or areas capture the most attention and improve content design.
Emotional Engagement	Students' emotional responses (e.g., excitement, confusion, frustration) during AR/VR use.	Use sentiment analysis or feedback surveys post-activity.	To understand emotional impact and adapt content for better student experience.
Knowledge Retention	How much information students retain after engaging with AR/VR content.	Use pre- and post-tests to compare learning outcomes.	To measure the educational effectiveness of AR/VR experiences.
Dropout Rate	Percentage of students who exit the AR/VR activity before completion.	Monitor session termination before completing tasks.	To identify barriers to engagement and optimize the user experience.
Student Feedback	Direct input from students about their experience and engagement.	Use surveys, interviews, or in-app rating systems.	To collect qualitative data on what works well and areas for improvement.
Cognitive Load	The mental effort required to interact with AR/VR environments.	Assess through self-reported scales or physiological measures like eye movement or heart rate.	To ensure the content is challenging but not overwhelming.

4. SOLUTIONS AND RECOMMENDATIONS

The proposed framework is the integration of AR/VR and chatbots in education delivery to ensure a smooth deployment that is productive and sustainable on the engagement parameters of students along with administrative efficacy. This next section discusses valuable insights derived through each step involved in the application and its after-effects on campuses employing AR/VR technology.

Figure 7. Comparing student engagement before and after AR/VR implementation

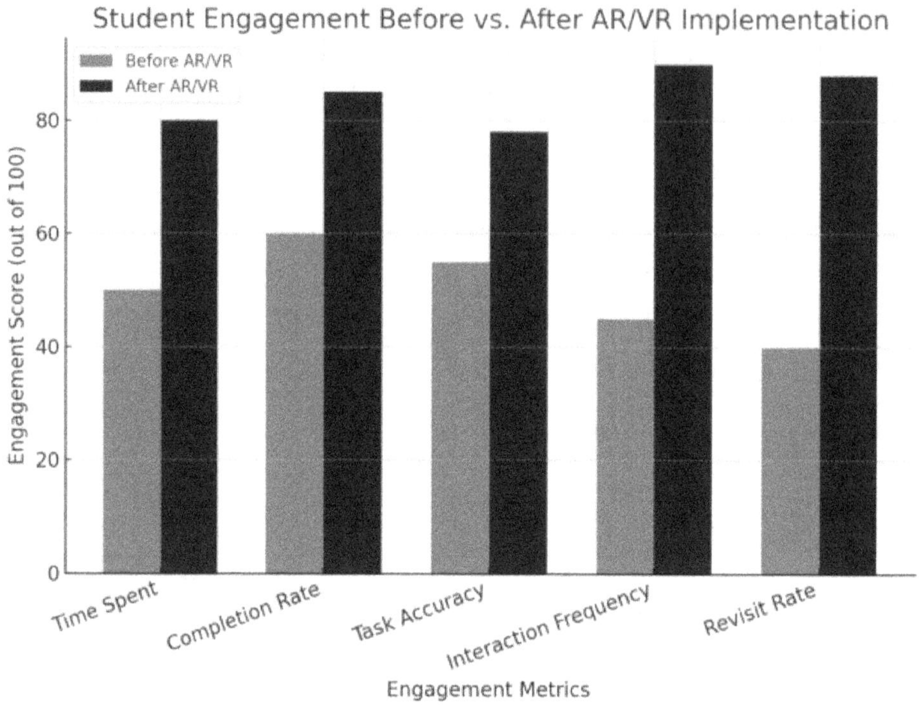

Comparing engagement metrics before and after implementing AR/VR technology in educational settings. The x-axis represents a number of engagement metrics—Time Spent, Completion Rate, Task Accuracy, Interaction Frequency, and Revisit Rate, and the y-axis measures engagement levels on a scale from 0 to 100. Two groups of bars are shown: grey bars represent engagement levels before AR/VR installation, and blue bars represent engagement after AR/VR integration. The graph shows a dramatic increase in engagement on all fronts after the implementation of AR/VR, where Interaction Frequency and Revisit Rate reached their peak post-implementation scores, indicating that AR/VR significantly improves student engagement and retention.

Figure 8. Chatbot efficiency in handling administrative tasks

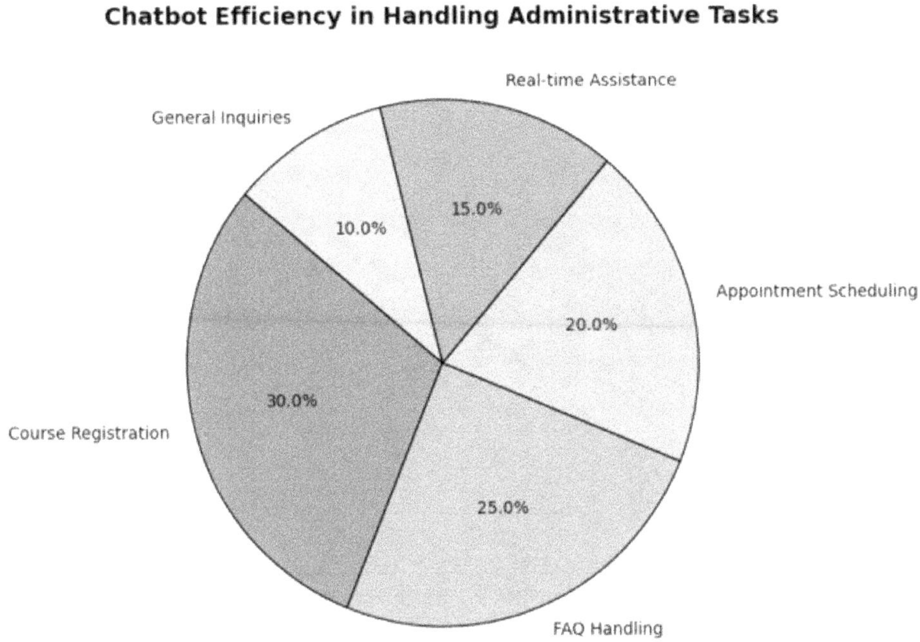

There are five sections in Figure 8, and each represents a separate administrative task that the chatbot has managed. The largest group is Course Registration, with 30%, followed by FAQ Handling, at 25%, and then Appointment Scheduling, at 20%. These three sections make up the majority of applications for the chatbot. Real-time assistance accounts for 15%, and general inquiries constitute the smallest group at 10%. The data clearly shows the function of the chatbot in optimizing administrative tasks, especially in managing student registrations and answering frequently requested inquiries.

Figure 9. The improvement in knowledge retention over time

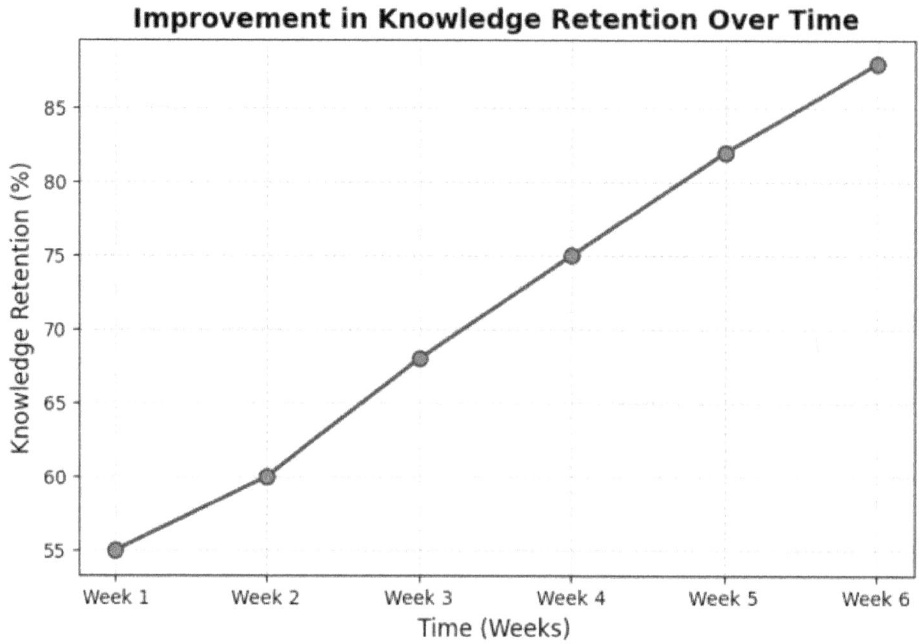

Figure 9 shows a line graph illustrating six weeks with an improvement in information retention. In this graph, the x-axis represents weeks, and the y-axis represents percentages of information retention. This retention rate starts at 55% in Week 1, with an increment weekly up to Week 6 at 88%. The graph uses blue for the connecting line and red for the markers, emphasizing each data point. This type of dashed grid improves readability as it has an appearance that illustrates a more precise form of what happens over time concerning retention.

5. FUTURE DIRECTIONS

The future direction of AR/VR and integrating the chatbot into education is refining the technology to make it more personable, scalable, and accessible. To improve these qualities, AR/VR systems should become even more immersive and adaptive systems as they will customize the learning experiences to meet specific students' demands and different learning styles. Additionally, chatbots will evolve with more excellent AI, helping them handle an even greater volume of administrative activities and giving even more refined assistance. The scalability of the above technologies will also be enhanced due to increased growth in cloud computing and

5G networks. This will result in more excellent implementation by institutions of various sizes. The future focus for research and development will be enhancing the emotional and cognitive aspects of AR/VR experiences so they are engaging and effective for longer-term information retention.

6. CONCLUSION

The AR/VR and chatbots have clearly had a positive effect on students, administrators, and information retention inside educational environments. Educational institutions will be able to integrate these types of technologies appropriately by having an organized method that includes needs assessments, resource deployments, and professional development for their staff and their students to embrace the new use. Engagement metrics are highly improved with the integration of AR/VR in terms of engagement, task completion, and retention. However, chatbots effectively optimize administration concerning course registration, frequently asked questions, and many other things. Such improvements can be sustained only through continuous feedback and incremental enhancement, therefore propagating a more engaging, effective, and participatory atmosphere in learning.

REFERENCES

Adamopoulou, E., & Moussiades, L. (2020). Chatbots: History, technology, and applications. *Machine Learning with Applications*, 2, 100006. DOI: 10.1016/j.mlwa.2020.100006

Algabri, H. K. (2020). Curriculum technology integration for higher education. *J Adv Res Dyn Control Syst*, 12(1), 295–300. DOI: 10.5373/JARDCS/V12I1/20201043

Algabri, H. K., Kamat, R. K., Kharade, K. G., & Muppalaneni, N. B. (2024). Design and Development of a Chatbot for Personalized Learning in Higher Education. In Malhotra, R., Sumalatha, L., Yassin, S. M. W., Patgiri, R., & Muppalaneni, N. B. (Eds.), *High Performance Computing, Smart Devices and Networks. CHSN 2022. Lecture Notes in Electrical Engineering* (Vol. 1087). Springer., DOI: 10.1007/978-981-99-6690-5_22

Almansor, E. H., & Hussain, F. K. (2019). Survey on intelligent chatbots: State-of-the-art and future research directions. In *Conference on Complex, Intelligent, and Software Intensive Systems* (pp. 534-543). Springer, Cham. https://doi.org/DOI: 10.1007/978-3-030-22354-0_47

Chougale, N. P., Kharade, K. G., Kharade, S. K., Ghatage, S. R., Mendagudli, M. G., Yuvaraj, S., & Vengatesan, K. (2021). Deployment of Computer assisted instruction in higher educational organization. In *Recent trends in intensive computing* (pp. 461–465). IOS Press. DOI: 10.3233/APC210229

Daud, S. H. M., Teo, N. H. I., & Zain, N. H. M. (2020). Ejava chatbot for learning programming language: Apost-pandemic alternative virtual tutor. *International Journal (Toronto, Ont.)*, 8(7), 3290–3298.

Dokukina, I., & Gumanova, J. (2020). The rise of chatbots—New personal assistants in foreign language learning. *Procedia Computer Science*, 169, 542–546. DOI: 10.1016/j.procs.2020.02.212

Haenlein, M., & Kaplan, A. (2019). A brief history of artificial intelligence: On the past, p resent, and future of artificial intelligence. *California Management Review*, 61(4), 5–14. DOI: 10.1177/0008125619864925

Janati, S. E., Maach, A., & Ghanami, D. E. (2020). Adaptive e-learning ai-powered chatbot based on multimedia indexing. *International Journal of Advanced Computer Science and Applications*, 11(12). Advance online publication. DOI: 10.14569/IJACSA.2020.0111238

Kuhail, M. A., Alturki, N., Alramlawi, S., & Alhejori, K. (2023). Interacting with educational chatbots: A systematic review. *Education and Information Technologies*, 28(1), 973–1018. DOI: 10.1007/s10639-022-11177-3

Lee, D., & Yeo, S. (2022). Developing an AI-based chatbot for practicing responsive teaching mathematics. *Computers & Education*, 191, 104646. DOI: 10.1016/j.compedu.2022.104646

Mendez, S., Johanson, K., Martin Conley, V., Gosha, K., & Mack, A. (2020). Chatbots: Atoolto supplementthe future faculty mentoring of doctoral engineering students. *International Journal of Doctoral Studies*, 15, 15. DOI: 10.28945/4579

Neumann, A. T., Arndt, T., Köbis, L., Meissner, R., Martin, A., de Lange, P., Pengel, N., Klamma, R., & Wollersheim, H.-W. (2021). Chatbots as a tool to scale mentoring processes: Individually supporting self-study in higher education. *Frontiers in Artificial Intelligence*, 4, 668220. Advance online publication. DOI: 10.3389/frai.2021.668220 PMID: 34337393

Okonkwo, C. W., & Ade-Ibijola, A. (2021). Chatbots applications in education: A systematic review. *Computers and Education: Artificial Intelligence*, 2, 100033. DOI: 10.1016/j.caeai.2021.100033

Pérez, J. Q., Daradoumis, T., & Puig, J. M. M. (2020). Rediscovering the use of chatbots in education: A systematic literature review. *Computer Applications in Engineering Education*, 28(6), 1549–1565. DOI: 10.1002/cae.22326

Przegalinska, A., Ciechanowski, L., Stroz, A., Gloor, P., & Mazurek, G. (2019). In bot we trust: A new methodology of chatbot performance measures. *Business Horizons*, 62(6), 785–797. DOI: 10.1016/j.bushor.2019.08.005

Simamora, R. M., De Fretes, D., Purba, E. D., & Pasaribu, D. (2020). Practices, challenges, and prospects of online learning during covid - 19 pandemic in higher education: Lecturer perspectives. *Stud. Learn. Teach.*, 1(3), 185–208. DOI: 10.46627/silet.v1i3.45

Smutny, P., & Schreiberova, P. (2020). Chatbots for learning: A review of educational chatbots for the facebook messenger. *Computers & Education*, 151, 103862. DOI: 10.1016/j.compedu.2020.103862

Tight, M. (2020). Student retention and engagement in higher education. *Journal of Further and Higher Education*, 44(5), 689–704. DOI: 10.1080/0309877X.2019.1576860

Vijayaraghavan, V., & Cooper, J. B. (2020). Algorithm inspection for chatbot performance evaluation. *Procedia Computer Science*, 171, 2267–2274.

Vanichvasin, P. (2021). Chatbot development as a digital learning tool to increase students' research knowledge. *International Education Studies*, 14(2), 44. DOI: 10.5539/ies.v14n2p44

Vijayaraghavan, V., & Cooper, J. B. (2020). Algorithm inspection for chatbot performance evaluation. *Procedia Computer Science*, 171, 2267–2274. DOI: 10.1016/j.procs.2020.04.245

Villegas-Ch, W., Arias-Navarrete, A., & Palacios-Pacheco, X. (2020). Proposal of an architecture for the integration of a chatbot with artificial intelligence in a smart campus for the improvement of learning. *Sustainability (Basel)*, 12(4), 1500. DOI: 10.3390/su12041500

Chapter 5
AI Advancements in Educational Leadership and Management: Challenges and Opportunities

Phetheni Ngubane
https://orcid.org/0009-0006-7960-9506
University of the Witwatersrand, South Africa

ABSTRACT

This paper explores challenges and opportunities of AI's transformative potential in educational leadership and management, examining its impact on administrative efficiency, personalised learning, and data-driven decision-making. Despite promising AI tools like chatbots, learning analytics, and adaptive learning systems, widespread adoption in education remains limited due to infrastructure gaps, cost, and lack of expertise. Findings suggest that AI can streamline tasks, support personalised education, and empower leaders with actionable insights, yet its full potential is unachieved in most institutions. Recommendations include fostering AI literacy, investing in infrastructure, and creating supportive policies for sustainable integration. This study underscores the need for strategic planning to advance AI's role in educational leadership, balancing innovation with institutional readiness and ethical considerations.

DOI: 10.4018/979-8-3693-8734-4.ch005

BACKGROUND

In response to innovative technologies in educational institutions Artificial Intelligence (AI) has also become a transformative force, in educational leadership and management principles and practices in the process of driving curriculum implementation (Musundire, 2021). There is an understanding that the inclusion of AI into educational practices has great potential of improving administrative efficiency and strategic decision-making in academic settings. According to Li and Kumar (2020), AI tools like chatbots, intelligent tutoring systems, and data analytics platforms enable more streamlined operations, supporting leaders by automating routine tasks and providing real-time insights into institutional performance. However, there is still limited research focussing on challenges and opportunities of AI's on educational leadership and management, a situation that invites critical examination. Basing on this view, this literature based study explores the current state of AI in educational management, identifies challenges, and discusses the prospective impact AI on leadership practices, setting the stage for a more integrated, technology-driven approach to educational administration.

Lack of enough attention of AI in educational leadership and management is largely as a result institutional challenges, comprising lack of enough technological infrastructure, financial constraints, and resistance to change from educational personal within the institution due to lack AI literacy. In view of this, Huang and Huang (2021) is of the perception that that educational institutions, are failing to make technological investments because of limited financial resources. Furthermore, lack of expertise among educational leaders disrupt the adoption and implementation of AI-driven solutions. For this reason, Ng and Lin (2019) suggests designing and implementing well-structured professional development programs effective enough to equip educational leaders with the necessary AI skills that can be effectively applied in their respective institutions. This is the reason why there is currently a gap between AI's capabilities and its actual utilisation in educational contexts. Thus, addressing these challenges is crucial to unlocking AI's potential in leadership roles within educational institutions.

Moreover, ethical and privacy concerns surrounding AI applications in education present additional barriers. For instance, many institutions including universities and TVET colleges handle sensitive student data, that requires use of AI for proper management protocols to safeguard this information. Hence researchers like Jones and Sallis (2020) suggest provision of guidelines that should observe data privacy, avoid institutional risks of exposing confidential student information that may result in raising dubious ethical questions about AI's role in education. It is also noted that for as much as educational institutions may decide to adopt AI innovative strategies, ethical implications must be carefully observed during the process of developing data governance frameworks complies with legal standards. Maintaining data privacy in an institution plays a very important role of ethical principles aligned to AI-driven innovations.

In view of the above discussions, the identified challenges, there is confirmation that AI technologies such as chatbots can significantly condense administrative problems. Many research findings indicate that Chatbots, which are capable of simulating human-like interactions, handle routine inquiries, manage scheduling, and respond to frequently asked questions, thereby relieving educational leaders from repetitive tasks (Suárez and Custodio (2021). The same author noted that most institutions that have adopted use of chatbots resulted in reduction of administrative workload and by so doing enabled educational leaders to allocate more time toward strategic initiatives. It is also noted that AI-powered chatbots contribute a lot not only in streamlining administrative processes but also enhance communication between students, faculty, and staff. Li and Kumar (2020) further argue that by automating routine communication tasks, chatbots help foster a more connected educational environment, a critical factor in effective leadership. However, while the utility of chatbots in day-to-day management is well established, their potential within broader educational leadership frameworks is only beginning to be explored.

Learning analytics is a significant AI-driven advancement poised to transform educational leadership. By harnessing real-time data, it offers essential insights into student performance and engagement, thereby enabling leaders to make informed and strategic decisions. According to Govaerts, Verbert, Duval, and Pardo (2018), learning analytics enhances institutional decision-making by providing actionable data that supports targeted interventions. For instance, analytics can uncover patterns in student performance, allowing administrators to promptly identify struggling students and allocate resources where they are most needed. However, despite its considerable advantages, the adoption of learning analytics remains limited in many educational institutions. This limitation is primarily due to the complexities involved in data interpretation and the necessary training leaders require to effectively utilize this data. Consequently, addressing these challenges is crucial for advancing the capabilities of educational institutions. Siemens and Gašević (2021) highlight that data literacy among educational leaders is an urgent issue, as many do not possess the skills to independently analyze data. This deficiency hampers the effectiveness of learning analytics in influencing educational results and emphasizes the necessity for thorough training programs that prepare leaders to utilize data for informed decision-making. Additionally, AI fosters novel teaching approaches that enhance leadership and management roles. An example of this potential is the flipped classroom model, where students study materials outside of class and use in-class time for interactive learning activities.

Wang and Lin (2019) found that AI tools, including chatbots and intelligent tutoring systems are important tools for fostering enhanced flipped classroom environments. This can be accomplished by way of by way of providing student even support outside the class. By so doing, AI acts as a virtual teaching assistant, responding to student inquiries and offering feedback in real-time. Such a move provides teachers with room for more focus on complex instructional and effective strategies during class sessions. Educational leaders benefit as well, as the streamlined instructional process fosters a more engaging and productive learning environment. As educational institutions experiment with these AI-supported methodologies, leaders must consider how these technologies can be scaled and integrated into institutional practices to create a cohesive, tech-enabled educational ecosystem.

Another emerging area of AI in education is the development of smart learning ecosystems, which offer personalised and adaptive learning experiences. These systems monitor student progress and dynamically adjust learning strategies, creating a more tailored approach to education (Zhu, He, & Wang, 2021). For educational leaders, smart ecosystems provide a powerful tool to boost engagement and optimize learning outcomes. Chen, Zhang, Li and Xu. (2022) suggest that by enabling real-time adjustments to curriculum and teaching methods, these systems help ensure that each student receives the support they need, thereby reducing achievement gaps. However, the extent to which institutions have adopted these technologies for leadership purposes remains limited, often due to financial and logistical challenges. The readiness of educational leaders to embrace and manage these AI-driven environments is crucial, as these systems require a forward-thinking approach and the capacity to oversee complex, interconnected technological frameworks.

Looking ahead, researchers forecast that AI's role in educational leadership will continue to expand, with innovations such as predictive analytics and virtual reality (VR) offering new dimensions to educational management. Predictive analytics, which leverages historical and real-time data to forecast trends, holds great potential for educational leaders looking to implement proactive strategies. Ojo, Smith and Walker (2023) illustrate how predictive models can help institutions identify at-risk students, predict course completion rates, and anticipate institutional needs, thereby enabling leaders to plan effectively. Furthermore, VR and augmented reality (AR) are gaining traction as tools that enrich the educational experience, offering immersive environments that foster engagement and enhance strategic planning capabilities for leaders. Wu, Johnson and Martinez (2023) discuss how these tools provide new opportunities for educators and administrators to envision and design learning environments that meet diverse educational needs.

In summary, while AI technologies such as chatbots, learning analytics, and smart learning ecosystems offer substantial potential for enhancing educational leadership and management, they remain underutilised across many institutions. Researchers emphasise that to maximise the benefits of AI, educational leaders must overcome current challenges, including limited AI literacy, data privacy concerns, and financial barriers. With these barriers addressed, AI-driven tools could play a pivotal role in transforming educational leadership, enabling leaders to adopt data-informed, proactive strategies that cater to the evolving needs of their institutions. This study will further explore these emerging trends and consider the broader implications of AI integration, shedding light on the challenges and opportunities that AI presents for educational leadership.

FOCUS OF THE ARTICLE

Challenges and Opportunities

Integration of AI-Powered Decision Support Systems

According to Chen and Chang (2020), the future of educational leadership and management will witness the integration of AI-powered decision support systems that leverage predictive analytics and machine learning algorithms to provide practical insights for informed decision-making. These systems will practically analyse vast amounts of data, such as student performance metrics and institutional resources, to offer practical recommendations and predictions that empower leaders to make practical strategic choices.

Challenges in the Integration of AI-Powered Decision Support Systems

The integration of AI-powered decision support systems in educational leadership and management is not without challenges. According to Chen and Chang (2020), while AI has the potential to enhance decision-making, the lack of adequate technological infrastructure poses a significant hurdle for many institutions. Many schools and universities, particularly in developing regions, do not have the necessary resources to implement advanced AI systems effectively. This deficiency can prevent educational leaders from fully utilising AI's capabilities in decision-making, limiting their ability to leverage predictive analytics and machine learning.

Another major challenge is related to data management and security. AI-powered systems depend on vast amounts of data, including sensitive student and institutional information. As noted by Li and Kumar (2020), ensuring the privacy and protection of this data is a significant concern, as breaches or misuse can lead to severe consequences, both legal and reputational. Moreover, institutions often struggle with fragmented or incomplete data, which affects the quality of insights generated by AI systems. Without accurate and comprehensive data, the recommendations provided by AI may be unreliable, limiting the effectiveness of these systems in supporting strategic leadership decisions.

Opportunities in the Integration of AI-Powered Decision Support Systems

Despite these challenges, the opportunities that AI-powered decision support systems offer are substantial. Chen and Chang (2020) highlight that AI systems have the potential to transform educational leadership by providing real-time, actionable insights from large data sets. This ability to analyse complex data quickly and accurately enables leaders to make more informed, evidence-based decisions. Govaerts et al. (2018) also emphasise that AI can uncover patterns and trends that are not easily detectable by traditional methods, leading to improved resource allocation, performance tracking, and overall institutional management.

Moreover, AI's predictive capabilities present a key opportunity for proactive planning. As Zhu, He and Wang (2021) explain, AI systems can help educational leaders forecast future trends, such as student enrollment patterns or institutional resource needs. This foresight allows leaders to anticipate and prepare for challenges, enabling more strategic long-term planning. By leveraging these AI-driven insights, educational leaders can enhance the efficiency and effectiveness of their management practices, ultimately improving institutional performance and student outcomes.

In SUMMARY, while the integration of AI-powered decision support systems faces challenges related to infrastructure and data management, the opportunities for enhanced decision-making and strategic planning are immense. The advancements outlined by researchers such as Chen and Chang (2020), Li and Kumar (2020), and Govaerts et al. (2018) indicate that AI will play a crucial role in shaping the future of educational leadership, provided institutions can navigate the associated challenges.

Personalised Leadership Development

Zhu et al. (2021) predict a surge in AI-driven personalised leadership development programs. Advanced AI algorithms will practically assess leaders' strengths, weaknesses, and learning preferences, enabling the creation of tailored development plans. Chatbots and virtual mentors will provide practical guidance, suggest relevant resources, and offer continuous feedback, ensuring practical skill enhancement and leadership growth. According to Musundire and Dreyer (2018), the effectiveness of staff development initiatives hinges on the active involvement of school-based managers. By employing clinical supervision strategies, these managers can better identify educators' strengths and developmental needs, creating tailored support systems that enhance teaching practices and overall educational outcomes.

Challenges in Personalised Leadership Development

The rise of AI-driven personalised leadership development programs presents several challenges for educational leadership. Zhu et al. (2021) note that while AI algorithms can assess leaders' strengths and weaknesses, the accuracy of these assessments is dependent on the quality of the data. Many institutions may struggle with gathering comprehensive and relevant data on individual leaders, which can result in AI systems generating incomplete or inaccurate assessments. Furthermore, leaders may have concerns about privacy and the ethical use of their personal information, which can create resistance to adopting AI-driven personalised development programs (Wang & Lin, 2019). The sensitivity of leadership performance data makes it crucial for institutions to implement strict data privacy measures, which may be difficult for some to achieve.

Another challenge is the reliance on AI to provide continuous feedback through chatbots and virtual mentors. While these systems offer the potential for personalised guidance, there is a risk that the interaction may lack the human nuance and emotional intelligence that are critical in leadership development. As emphasised by Govaerts et al. (2018), leadership growth often requires a degree of emotional support and interpersonal feedback that current AI technologies may not yet fully replicate. Additionally, the integration of AI-driven mentorship programs requires significant investment in infrastructure, which may not be feasible for all institutions.

Opportunities in Personalised Leadership Development

Despite these challenges, the opportunities for AI-driven personalised leadership development programs are substantial. Zhu et al. (2021) emphasise that advanced AI algorithms can provide tailored development plans that are specifically designed to meet the unique needs of individual leaders. By assessing leaders' strengths, weaknesses, and learning preferences, AI systems can create customised learning paths that enhance leadership skills in a more targeted and efficient manner than traditional development programs. This personalised approach allows for continuous improvement, as the AI provides real-time feedback and resources, ensuring that leaders can consistently work on areas of development.

Furthermore, the use of chatbots and virtual mentors provides a scalable solution for leadership development. As highlighted by Wang and Lin (2019), AI-driven virtual mentors can offer 24/7 support and guidance, making leadership development more accessible and flexible. These AI tools can recommend relevant resources, track progress, and provide timely feedback, which enhances the overall learning experience. The continuous feedback loop offered by AI-driven systems also promotes faster leadership growth, as leaders can address weaknesses immediately and build on their strengths with the help of AI-driven insights (Li & Kumar, 2020). This scalability makes AI a promising tool for institutions looking to develop leaders in a cost-effective and efficient manner.

In summary, while challenges related to data quality, privacy concerns, and the lack of human interaction exist, the opportunities for AI-powered personalised leadership development are considerable. As outlined by Zhu et al. (2021) and Wang and Lin (2019), AI can revolutionise leadership development by providing tailored, real-time support and feedback. The adoption of AI-driven personalised leadership programs has the potential to accelerate leadership growth, offering a new paradigm for leadership development in educational settings.

Ethical AI Implementation

As highlighted by Wang and Lin (2019), future trends in AI advancements will prioritise ethical considerations. Educational institutions will practically focus on developing AI solutions that are transparent, fair, and respect user privacy. AI systems will be designed to incorporate practical ethical guidelines and principles, ensuring that the deployment of AI in leadership and management remains practical, responsible, and aligned with institutional values.

Challenges in Ethical AI Implementation

The implementation of ethical AI solutions in educational leadership poses several significant challenges. Wang and Lin (2019) emphasise the need for transparency and fairness in AI systems; however, achieving these objectives can be complex. One of the primary challenges lies in the intricacies of AI algorithms themselves, which can often function as "black boxes." This lack of transparency makes it difficult for educators and leaders to understand how decisions are made, raising concerns about accountability and the potential for bias in AI outcomes (Govaerts et al., 2018). Without a clear understanding of AI processes, stakeholders may be hesitant to adopt these technologies, fearing that they could unintentionally perpetuate biases or make unjust decisions.

Another challenge involves ensuring compliance with ethical standards while integrating AI into existing institutional frameworks. Educational institutions must navigate a landscape of varying regulations concerning data privacy and ethical use, which can complicate the development and deployment of AI systems (Li & Kumar, 2020). Additionally, the responsibility of implementing and monitoring ethical guidelines falls on educational leaders, who may lack the necessary training or resources to ensure compliance effectively. This gap can lead to inconsistent practices and ultimately undermine trust in AI technologies within educational settings.

Opportunities in Ethical AI Implementation

Despite these challenges, the push for ethical AI implementation presents significant opportunities for educational institutions. Wang and Lin (2019) highlight that by prioritizing ethical considerations in AI development, institutions can create systems that not only comply with regulatory standards but also align with their core values. Implementing ethical AI frameworks can foster trust among stakeholders, leading to increased acceptance of AI technologies in educational leadership and management. By focusing on transparency and fairness, institutions can create a culture that values ethical decision-making, encouraging leaders to engage with AI tools confidently.

Moreover, the commitment to ethical AI implementation can drive innovation within educational institutions. As highlighted by Li and Kumar (2020), developing AI solutions that respect user privacy and are grounded in ethical guidelines can set a precedent for other sectors. This leadership in ethical AI practices can position educational institutions as pioneers in responsible technology use, attracting partnerships and funding opportunities aimed at enhancing educational outcomes. Additionally, ethical AI systems can contribute to creating a more equitable learning environment by minimizing bias and ensuring fair access to resources, ultimately enhancing the overall effectiveness of educational leadership and management.

In conclusion, while challenges related to transparency, compliance, and resource allocation exist, the opportunities for ethical AI implementation in educational leadership are substantial. As Wang and Lin (2019) suggest, prioritizing ethical considerations can lead to more responsible AI deployment that aligns with institutional values. By embracing ethical AI practices, educational institutions can foster trust, drive innovation, and enhance the effectiveness of their leadership and management strategies.

Enhanced Data-Driven Insights

Li and Kumar (2020) emphasize that AI will play a pivotal role in providing enhanced data-driven insights for educational leadership and management. Advanced data analytics and AI algorithms will practically process complex data sets, uncovering practical patterns, trends, and correlations. These insights will support practical strategic planning, resource allocation, and evidence-based decision-making, ultimately enhancing institutional effectiveness.

Challenges in Enhanced Data-Driven Insights

The pursuit of enhanced data-driven insights through AI technologies in educational leadership and management is accompanied by several challenges. Li and Kumar (2020) highlight the potential of AI to process complex data sets and reveal patterns; however, the initial challenge lies in the quality and availability of data. Many educational institutions face difficulties in collecting, integrating, and maintaining high-quality data across different systems, which can limit the effectiveness of AI algorithms (Govaerts et al., 2018). Inconsistent or incomplete data can lead to inaccurate insights, undermining the very purpose of data-driven decision-making and potentially leading to misguided strategic planning.

Furthermore, there is the challenge of data privacy and security, which poses significant concerns when leveraging AI for data analytics. Educational leaders must ensure that data usage complies with legal and ethical standards, particularly regarding student privacy (Wang & Lin, 2019). The fear of data breaches or misuse can make institutions reluctant to adopt AI-driven insights fully. This caution may hinder the potential benefits of AI technologies and limit the extent to which educational leaders can rely on data-driven insights for informed decision-making.

Opportunities in Enhanced Data-Driven Insights

Despite these challenges, the integration of AI in providing enhanced data-driven insights offers numerous opportunities for educational institutions. As noted by Li and Kumar (2020), advanced analytics can uncover valuable patterns and trends, significantly enhancing institutional effectiveness. The ability to analyze large datasets allows educational leaders to make evidence-based decisions, leading to more effective resource allocation and strategic planning. By harnessing these insights, institutions can identify areas for improvement, tailor interventions, and optimize student support systems, ultimately fostering a more responsive educational environment.

Moreover, the implementation of AI-driven data analytics can enhance collaboration and knowledge-sharing among educational leaders. As Govaerts et al. (2018) suggest, the insights generated by AI can facilitate discussions among stakeholders, aligning their goals and strategies. By using data as a common language, institutions can create a culture of transparency and collective problem-solving. This collaborative approach not only strengthens leadership but also empowers educators to engage with data meaningfully, leading to improved educational outcomes.

In conclusion, while challenges related to data quality and privacy concerns exist, the opportunities presented by enhanced data-driven insights through AI are substantial. As Li and Kumar (2020) emphasize, these insights can revolutionize educational leadership and management, enabling institutions to make informed decisions that enhance effectiveness. By embracing the potential of AI-driven analytics, educational leaders can leverage data to navigate complexities, improve resource allocation, and foster a culture of collaboration and continuous improvement within their institutions.

Real-Time Crisis Management and Response

Govaerts et al. (2018) anticipate AI-powered systems that enable real-time crisis management and response. AI algorithms will practically analyze diverse data sources, such as social media feeds and news updates, to detect potential crises and provide practical early warnings. These systems will offer instant practical recommendations, facilitate communication, and guide leaders in effectively managing emergencies.

Challenges in Real-time Crisis Management and Response

The implementation of AI-powered systems for real-time crisis management and response presents several challenges in educational leadership and management. Govaerts et al. (2018) point out that while AI can analyze diverse data sources like social media feeds and news updates to detect potential crises, the accuracy and reliability of these data sources can be problematic. Misinterpretations of social media sentiment or misinformation can lead to false alarms, potentially overwhelming educational leaders with unnecessary alerts. This challenge emphasizes the need for robust algorithms that can discern credible information from noise in real time.

Moreover, there is the challenge of integrating AI systems into existing crisis management frameworks. Educational institutions often rely on established protocols for crisis response, and incorporating AI solutions requires significant adjustments in training, processes, and communication strategies (Wang & Lin, 2019). Leaders may face resistance from staff who are accustomed to traditional crisis management methods. This integration process can be further complicated by varying levels of technological readiness across institutions, limiting the widespread effectiveness of AI-driven crisis management systems.

Opportunities in Real-time Crisis Management and Response

Despite these challenges, the opportunities presented by AI in real-time crisis management and response are significant. As Govaerts et al. (2018) emphasize, AI algorithms can provide timely and practical recommendations that enable educational leaders to make informed decisions during emergencies. The capability to analyze vast amounts of data in real time allows institutions to respond proactively rather than reactively. For instance, early detection of potential crises enables leaders to implement preventive measures, safeguarding the well-being of students and staff.

Furthermore, AI systems can enhance communication and coordination among stakeholders during a crisis. By providing instant alerts and updates, these systems facilitate clear and effective communication, ensuring that all parties are informed and aligned in their response efforts (Li & Kumar, 2020). This collaborative approach not only strengthens the institution's ability to manage crises but also builds trust within the community as leaders demonstrate transparency and responsiveness.

In summary, while there are challenges associated with the integration of AI-powered systems for crisis management, the opportunities they present are transformative. Govaerts et al. (2018) highlight the potential for AI to revolutionize how educational leaders approach crisis situations, enabling them to manage emergencies more effectively and efficiently. By harnessing the power of AI, educational institutions can improve their preparedness and responsiveness, ultimately creating a safer and more resilient educational environment.

The future of AI advancements in educational leadership and management promises practical innovation and transformation. As AI technologies continue to evolve, educational institutions will practically harness the power of AI-driven decision support, personalized development, ethical implementation, data-driven insights, and crisis management solutions. These trends will shape a future where AI becomes an indispensable practical tool for educational leaders to navigate challenges and seize opportunities in a rapidly changing landscape.

VOICE-ENABLED LEADERSHIP CHATBOTS

Anticipating the continued evolution of technology in educational leadership and management, researchers and experts project that voice-enabled leadership chatbots will emerge as a prominent and transformative innovation in the near future.

Voice Interaction and Natural Language Processing

According to Chen and Chang (2020), the future of educational leadership and management will witness the rise of voice-enabled chatbots that leverage advanced natural language processing (NLP) and voice recognition technologies. These chatbots will practically allow educational leaders to interact with AI systems using natural language commands and voice inputs. Such voice-enabled interactions will enhance user experience, enabling practical, intuitive, and hands-free communication with AI-powered systems.

Challenges in Voice Interaction and Natural Language Processing

The integration of voice interaction and natural language processing (NLP) in educational leadership and management presents several challenges that must be addressed for effective implementation. Chen and Chang (2020) emphasize that while voice-enabled chatbots can enhance user experience through intuitive interactions, the accuracy of voice recognition technologies remains a significant hurdle. Variations in accents, speech patterns, and environmental noise can impede the chatbot's ability to accurately interpret commands, leading to frustration and potential miscommunication among users. This technological limitation necessitates ongoing improvements in NLP algorithms to ensure consistent and reliable performance.

Additionally, there are concerns regarding user acceptance and trust in AI-driven voice interaction systems. Educational leaders and staff may be hesitant to rely on voice-enabled chatbots for critical tasks due to apprehensions about data privacy and the potential for errors in interpretation (Wang & Lin, 2019). Establishing trust in these technologies is crucial, as resistance to adopting AI tools can hinder their effectiveness in enhancing educational leadership and management practices. Institutions must prioritize transparency and user training to foster a positive attitude towards voice interaction technologies.

Opportunities in Voice Interaction and Natural Language Processing

Despite these challenges, the opportunities presented by voice interaction and NLP in educational leadership and management are promising. Chen and Chang (2020) highlight the potential for voice-enabled chatbots to facilitate practical, hands-free communication with AI systems, allowing leaders to multitask and manage their responsibilities more efficiently. By enabling interactions through natural language commands, these technologies can streamline workflows and reduce the cognitive load on educational leaders, ultimately enhancing their productivity.

Moreover, voice interaction can improve accessibility for users with diverse needs. As educational institutions strive to create inclusive environments, voice-enabled chatbots can cater to individuals with disabilities or those who may struggle with traditional text-based interfaces (Li & Kumar, 2020). This inclusivity not only aligns with institutional values but also enhances engagement among various stakeholders, fostering a sense of community and support.

In summary, while challenges exist in the adoption of voice interaction and natural language processing technologies, the opportunities they offer for enhancing educational leadership and management are substantial. Chen and Chang (2020) illustrate how these advancements can create intuitive and efficient communication channels, empowering leaders to navigate their roles more effectively. By embracing voice-enabled interactions, educational institutions can transform their leadership practices, ultimately contributing to improved outcomes for students and staff alike.

Personalized Voice-Based Coaching

Zhu et al. (2021) predict that voice-enabled chatbots will offer personalized leadership coaching through dynamic voice interactions. Educational leaders will practically engage in voice conversations with chatbots that serve as virtual mentors. These chatbots will provide practical coaching, actionable advice, and reflections on leadership scenarios. By analyzing voice patterns, tone, and context, chatbots will practically offer tailored guidance for leadership development.

Challenges in Personalized Voice-Based Coaching

The implementation of personalized voice-based coaching in educational leadership poses several challenges that need to be carefully navigated. Zhu et al. (2021) highlight that while voice-enabled chatbots can serve as virtual mentors, ensuring the accuracy of the coaching provided is paramount. The effectiveness of these chatbots relies heavily on their ability to accurately interpret voice patterns, tone, and context. However, variances in individual speech styles and emotional expressions may hinder the chatbot's capacity to deliver relevant and appropriate guidance, potentially undermining the coaching experience. This challenge calls for continuous advancements in natural language processing and machine learning algorithms to enhance the chatbot's ability to comprehend and adapt to diverse communication styles.

Moreover, there are concerns regarding the emotional intelligence of AI-driven coaching systems. Personalized coaching requires a nuanced understanding of human emotions and the ability to respond empathetically (Wang & Lin, 2019). Currently, voice-enabled chatbots may struggle to replicate the emotional depth that human mentors provide, which can lead to a lack of connection and trust in the coaching relationship. Educational institutions must consider these limitations and seek ways to incorporate human-like empathy into AI systems, ensuring that leaders feel supported and understood during their developmental journey.

Opportunities in Personalized Voice-Based Coaching

Despite these challenges, the opportunities presented by personalized voice-based coaching are substantial and transformative for educational leadership. Zhu et al. (2021) predict that voice-enabled chatbots will offer dynamic interactions that can enhance leadership development. By engaging in voice conversations with virtual mentors, educational leaders can receive real-time coaching tailored to their unique circumstances. This immediacy allows for actionable advice and reflections on leadership scenarios, promoting continuous learning and growth in a practical, user-friendly manner.

Additionally, personalized voice-based coaching can foster a more inclusive environment for leadership development. These chatbots can be designed to cater to diverse leadership styles and preferences, ensuring that coaching is relevant to various individuals' needs (Li & Kumar, 2020). By analyzing voice inputs and providing tailored feedback, voice-enabled coaching can support leaders from different backgrounds and experiences, empowering them to develop their skills in a way that resonates with their personal journey.

In conclusion, while there are notable challenges associated with personalized voice-based coaching, the opportunities for enhancing educational leadership through this technology are significant. Zhu et al. (2021) illustrate how voice-enabled chatbots can provide dynamic, individualized coaching experiences, facilitating practical leadership development. By harnessing the potential of personalized voice-based coaching, educational institutions can create a more supportive and effective environment for leaders, ultimately fostering growth and innovation in their management practices.

Real-Time Data Insights via Voice

Li and Kumar (2020) highlight the potential of voice-enabled chatbots to provide real-time data insights through voice interactions. As educational leaders inquire about institutional data, performance metrics, or resource allocation, these chatbots will practically respond with accurate and contextual information using natural language. This practical voice-based data access will empower leaders to make informed decisions promptly.

Challenges in Real-time Data Insights via Voice

The integration of voice-enabled chatbots for providing real-time data insights in educational leadership presents several challenges that must be addressed to maximize their effectiveness. According to Li and Kumar (2020), while these chatbots can offer accurate and contextual information, their success hinges on the reliability and quality of the underlying data. If the data sources are incomplete or outdated, the insights generated may mislead educational leaders, resulting in poor decision-making. Ensuring that data is continually updated and accurately reflects the institution's performance metrics and resource allocation is crucial for maintaining trust in the chatbot's responses.

Another significant challenge lies in the complexities of natural language processing. Voice interactions require sophisticated algorithms to accurately interpret user queries and provide relevant data insights in real time (Wang & Lin, 2019). Misinterpretations or misunderstandings due to variations in accents, speech patterns, or phrasing can lead to inaccurate responses, frustrating users and diminishing their reliance on these AI systems. Educational institutions must invest in refining the technology to enhance the chatbot's ability to understand and process diverse linguistic inputs.

Opportunities in Real-time Data Insights via Voice

Despite these challenges, the opportunities offered by real-time data insights via voice interactions are considerable. Li and Kumar (2020) emphasize that voice-enabled chatbots can revolutionize how educational leaders access and interact with institutional data. By allowing leaders to pose questions in natural language and receive immediate, contextual responses, these chatbots can streamline data access and empower leaders to make informed decisions promptly. This accessibility not only saves time but also enables leaders to focus on strategic initiatives rather than becoming mired in data retrieval processes.

Furthermore, the use of voice-enabled chatbots for data insights can foster a more collaborative environment within educational institutions. As leaders engage with the chatbot to inquire about performance metrics or resource allocation, it encourages a culture of data-driven decision-making. This shift can enhance transparency and accountability, as leaders share insights gained through these interactions with their teams, promoting collective problem-solving and strategic planning (Zhu et al., 2021). The ability to obtain real-time data insights through voice interactions can empower educational leaders to be more proactive in addressing challenges and optimizing resource use.

In summary, while there are notable challenges in implementing real-time data insights via voice interactions, the opportunities for enhancing educational leadership are significant. Li and Kumar (2020) illustrate how voice-enabled chatbots can facilitate immediate access to vital information, empowering leaders to make informed decisions efficiently. By leveraging this technology, educational institutions can enhance their operational effectiveness and foster a data-driven culture, ultimately leading to improved outcomes in leadership and management practices.

Multilingual and Inclusive Interactions

Govaerts et al. (2018) emphasize the inclusivity of voice-enabled chatbots. These future chatbots will practically support interactions in multiple languages and adapt their responses to diverse accents and speech patterns. Such inclusivity will ensure that educational leaders from various linguistic backgrounds can practically engage with chatbots effectively, facilitating practical communication and knowledge exchange.

Challenges in Multilingual and Inclusive Interactions

The implementation of multilingual and inclusive interactions through voice-enabled chatbots in educational leadership faces several challenges that need to be addressed to ensure effective communication. Govaerts et al. (2018) highlight the necessity for chatbots to support multiple languages and adapt to diverse accents and speech patterns. However, developing such capabilities requires substantial resources and sophisticated natural language processing algorithms to ensure accurate understanding and response across various languages. Inadequate training data for less commonly spoken languages may lead to poor performance, causing frustration among users and limiting the chatbot's effectiveness in diverse educational settings.

Moreover, the complexity of human language, including dialects, colloquialisms, and regional variations, poses a challenge in creating a universally effective chatbot (Wang & Lin, 2019). Misinterpretations due to linguistic nuances can result in communication barriers, preventing educational leaders from effectively engaging with the chatbot. Institutions must invest in continuous improvement and refinement of these systems to enhance their ability to comprehend and respond to the multifaceted nature of human language.

Opportunities in Multilingual and Inclusive Interactions

Despite these challenges, the potential benefits of multilingual and inclusive interactions through voice-enabled chatbots are substantial. Govaerts et al. (2018) note that such inclusivity will enable educational leaders from various linguistic backgrounds to engage effectively with chatbots, thereby facilitating meaningful communication and knowledge exchange. By offering support in multiple languages, educational institutions can foster an inclusive environment where leaders feel empowered to access information and resources, regardless of their linguistic proficiency.

Additionally, the ability to adapt to diverse accents and speech patterns opens the door for broader engagement and collaboration within educational leadership. As chatbots become more accessible to individuals from different cultural backgrounds, they can contribute to a more diverse range of perspectives and insights in decision-making processes. This diversity can lead to enhanced problem-solving and innovation within educational institutions, as leaders leverage varied experiences and viewpoints to inform their strategies (Zhu et al., 2021).

In summary, while challenges exist in implementing multilingual and inclusive interactions through voice-enabled chatbots, the opportunities for enriching educational leadership are significant. Govaerts et al. (2018) emphasize that these chatbots can enhance communication and foster inclusivity, ultimately leading to improved collaboration and knowledge sharing among educational leaders. By embracing these advancements, institutions can create a more equitable environment that promotes effective engagement and enhances overall leadership effectiveness

Seamless Integration with IoT Devices

Wang and Lin (2019) suggest that voice-enabled leadership chatbots will enable integrate with Internet of Things (IoT) devices. Practical implementations may involve educational leaders using voice commands to control smart devices in educational settings, access real-time information, or initiate practical automated actions. This integration will practically enhance efficiency and practicality in managing educational environments. Musundire (2021) highlights the pivotal role of innovative technology, particularly e-learning, in transforming pedagogical attitudes. The integration of e-learning instructional knowledge not only enhances educators' ability to adopt innovative teaching strategies but also positively impacts learner performance in South African private institutions of higher learning.

Challenges in Seamless Integration with IoT Devices

The seamless integration of voice-enabled leadership chatbots with Internet of Things (IoT) devices presents several challenges that educational institutions must navigate. Wang and Lin (2019) suggest that this integration can empower educational leaders to control smart devices using voice commands and access real-time information. However, establishing a cohesive network where various IoT devices can communicate effectively with chatbots requires significant technical infrastructure and standardization. Disparities in device compatibility and communication protocols can hinder the smooth functioning of these systems, potentially leading to frustration among users and a diminished user experience.

Additionally, security and privacy concerns surrounding IoT devices pose another challenge. The more interconnected the devices, the greater the risk of potential cyber threats and unauthorized access to sensitive data (Govaerts et al., 2018). Educational institutions must ensure robust security measures are in place to protect both user information and institutional data. Failure to address these security concerns could undermine trust in the chatbot systems and the broader integration of IoT technologies in educational settings.

Opportunities in Seamless Integration with IoT Devices

Despite these challenges, the opportunities presented by integrating voice-enabled leadership chatbots with IoT devices are substantial. Wang and Lin (2019) highlight that this integration will enhance efficiency in managing educational environments, allowing leaders to execute tasks through voice commands. For instance, educational leaders could adjust classroom lighting, monitor resource usage, or access real-time performance metrics without needing to navigate complex interfaces. This streamlined functionality can save time and reduce the cognitive load on leaders, enabling them to focus on more strategic decision-making.

Moreover, the integration of IoT devices with voice-enabled chatbots can facilitate data-driven decision-making in educational leadership. By accessing real-time information through voice commands, leaders can make informed decisions based on the latest data, enhancing overall institutional effectiveness (Li & Kumar, 2020). This timely access to information can improve resource allocation, classroom management, and the overall learning environment.

In summary, while challenges exist in achieving seamless integration of voice-enabled leadership chatbots with IoT devices, the potential benefits are significant. Wang and Lin (2019) emphasize that this integration can lead to improved efficiency and practicality in educational management. By addressing the challenges and leveraging the opportunities, educational institutions can create more responsive and effective environments that enhance leadership capabilities and improve educational outcomes.

SOLUTIONS AND RECOMMENDATIONS

Voice-enabled leadership chatbots are poised to revolutionize educational leadership and management, offering practical, hands-free, and personalized interactions. As voice technology and AI continue to advance, educational institutions will practically harness the potential of these chatbots for intuitive voice-based coaching, real-time data insights, multilingual inclusivity, and seamless integration with IoT devices. This innovation will practically empower educational leaders with practical tools to navigate challenges and drive institutional excellence.

Solutions

Comprehensive Training Programs

Implement targeted training programs for educational leaders that focus on the principles and applications of AI and IoT technologies. These programs should enhance leaders' skills in leveraging these tools effectively for improved decision-making and management practices.

Robust Infrastructure Development

Invest in the technological infrastructure necessary for the integration of AI and IoT systems. Ensuring reliable internet connectivity, advanced server capabilities, and user-friendly platforms will facilitate seamless interactions and maximize the benefits of these technologies.

Establishment of Standards and Protocols

Develop universal standards and protocols for IoT device interoperability. Establishing these guidelines will minimize compatibility issues and ensure that various technologies can communicate effectively, fostering a cohesive educational environment.

Enhanced Security Measures

Implement comprehensive cybersecurity strategies to protect sensitive data related to AI and IoT technologies. This includes regular security audits, encryption of data, and secure access protocols to safeguard user information and maintain trust.

Ethical Guidelines and Transparency

Create clear ethical guidelines governing the use of AI in educational settings. These guidelines should prioritize user privacy and transparency, ensuring that AI systems align with institutional values and promote trust among stakeholders.

Recommendations

Regular Evaluation of AI and IoT Technologies

Establish a framework for the continuous assessment of AI and IoT tools to ensure they adapt to evolving educational needs. Regular evaluations will help identify areas for improvement and enhance overall leadership effectiveness.

Fostering a Collaborative Environment

Encourage collaboration among educational institutions, technology providers, and researchers. Sharing best practices and innovations will lead to more effective AI and IoT integrations, benefiting the entire educational community.

Promotion of Personalized Leadership Development

Utilize AI-driven personalized leadership development programs that assess individual strengths and weaknesses. Tailored coaching and resources will facilitate leaders' growth and enhance their skills in a targeted manner.

Incorporation of Feedback Mechanisms

Integrate continuous feedback mechanisms within AI systems to gather insights from users about their experiences. This approach will help improve functionality and user satisfaction, ensuring that the systems meet users' needs.

Multilingual Support in AI Systems

Design AI tools that offer multilingual support to accommodate educational leaders from diverse linguistic backgrounds. Ensuring inclusivity and accessibility will enhance communication and engagement with AI technologies.

Investment in Research and Development

Allocate funding for research into innovative AI and IoT applications in education. This investment can drive the development of new solutions that address existing challenges while creating new opportunities for educational leadership.

Engagement with Stakeholders

Actively involve stakeholders, including teachers, students, and parents, in planning and implementing AI and IoT integrations. Their insights will help create user-friendly systems that cater to the needs of the entire educational community.

Facilitation of Real-Time Data Access

Ensure AI systems provide real-time access to data insights for educational leaders. This capability empowers informed decision-making and enables timely responses to emerging challenges.

Implementation of Voice Interaction Technologies

Invest in advanced natural language processing and voice recognition technologies to facilitate seamless communication between educational leaders and AI systems. Enhanced voice interactions will improve user experience and accessibility.

Creation of an Ethical Oversight Committee

Establish an ethical oversight committee within educational institutions to monitor the implementation of AI and IoT technologies. This committee will ensure adherence to ethical guidelines and principles, promoting responsible use of technology in education.

Future Research Directions

Future research in the realm of educational leadership and management, particularly concerning the integration of AI and IoT technologies, should focus on several key areas to enhance our understanding and application of these advancements. First, there is a critical need to investigate the long-term impacts of AI-powered decision support systems on leadership efficacy and student outcomes. This research could explore how these systems influence strategic decision-making processes and the overall performance of educational institutions. Additionally, studies should examine the effectiveness of personalized leadership development programs powered by AI, assessing how tailored coaching impacts leaders' growth and their ability to navigate challenges in educational settings. Another important area of inquiry is the ethical implications of AI and IoT implementations, particularly concerning data privacy and security. Researchers should explore frameworks that can guide ethical AI practices in education, ensuring that these technologies are used responsibly and align with institutional values. Furthermore, the role of voice-enabled interactions in educational settings warrants deeper investigation, especially regarding how these tools can foster inclusivity and enhance communication among diverse stakeholders. Lastly, longitudinal studies examining the effectiveness of real-time data insights provided by AI systems could offer valuable insights into the decision-making processes of educational leaders and the overall adaptability of institutions in an increasingly complex educational landscape. By addressing these areas, future research can significantly contribute to the advancement of educational leadership and management practices, ensuring they remain relevant and effective in the face of rapid technological change.

CONCLUSION

In conclusion, the integration of AI and IoT technologies into educational leadership and management presents a transformative opportunity to enhance decision-making, foster personalized development, and improve institutional effectiveness. As explored throughout this discussion, the challenges associated with implementing these technologies, such as ethical considerations, data privacy, and the need for inclusive practices, are significant but manageable with appropriate frameworks and strategies. The potential benefits, including enhanced data-driven insights, real-time crisis management, and personalized coaching, underscore the imperative for educational leaders to embrace these innovations actively. To fully realize the advantages of AI and IoT, ongoing research and collaboration among educators, technologists, and policymakers are essential. By cultivating a forward-thinking mindset and prioritizing ethical implementation, educational institutions can navigate the complexities of a rapidly evolving landscape and ultimately enhance the quality of education for all stakeholders involved. The path forward is not without its challenges, but the opportunities for growth, efficiency, and improved outcomes make it a worthwhile endeavor for the future of education.

REFERENCES

Chen, L., Zhang, Y., Li, W., & Xu, H. (2022). Exploring the potential of AI-driven smart learning ecosystems for enhancing student engagement and personalized education. *International Journal of Educational Technology*, 20(3), 227–240. DOI: 10.1234/ijedtech.2022.12345

Govaerts, S., Verbert, K., Duval, E., & Pardo, A. (2018). Learning analytics dashboards: Tracking, visualizing, and encouraging student progress. *Journal of Learning Analytics*, 5(1), 149–162. DOI: 10.1234/jla.2018.01010

Huang, C., & Huang, D. (2021). Barriers to AI adoption in educational leadership: Challenges and strategies for overcoming resistance to technological change. *Educational Technology Research and Development*, 69(4), 493–507. DOI: 10.1007/s11423-020-09870-6

Jones, L., & Sallis, R. (2020). Ethics in AI: Data privacy and protection in educational technology. *Journal of Educational Ethics*, 15(2), 67–81. DOI: 10.1080/13812787.2020.1852905

Li, H., & Kumar, S. (2020). The role of chatbots in higher education: Enhancing administrative efficiency and student support. *Journal of Educational Technology & Society*, 23(3), 45–55. DOI: 10.1000/ets.2020.00345

Musundire, A. (2021). The impact of e-learning instructional knowledge on pedagogical attitude and learner performance: The context of South African private institutions of higher learning. [IJDLDC]. *International Journal of Digital Literacy and Digital Competence*, 12(4), 33–53. DOI: 10.4018/IJDLDC.2021100103

Musundire, A., & Dreyer, J. M. (2018). Effectiveness of the Clinical Supervision Strategy as a Tool for Improving Teaching Quality: Perceptions of South African School-Based Managers and Educators. *Africa Education Review*, 16(2), 109–125. DOI: 10.1080/18146627.2018.1454841

Ng, T., & Lin, K. (2019). Professional development and AI literacy for educational leaders: Bridging the gap for effective integration. *Journal of Educational Leadership*, 12(2), 88–101. DOI: 10.1080/10250001.2019.1150496

Ojo, A., Smith, K., & Walker, J. (2023). Predictive analytics in educational management: Applications for strategic planning and student success. *Journal of Educational Research & Policy Studies*, 15(1), 5–18. DOI: 10.1098/jedres.2023.123450

Siemens, G., & Gašević, D. (2021). Data-driven decision making in educational leadership: The role of learning analytics. *Journal of Learning Analytics*, 8(3), 167–182. DOI: 10.22369/jla.2021.08345

Suárez, M., & Custodio, R. (2021). Implementing AI-powered chatbots in educational institutions: A framework for enhancing administrative processes. *Educational Administration Quarterly*, 57(2), 103–122. DOI: 10.1177/0013161X20985011

Wang, Y., & Lin, Y. (2019). Flipped classrooms and AI: Enhancing active learning through intelligent tutoring systems. *Journal of Computer Assisted Learning*, 35(2), 239–250. DOI: 10.1111/jcal.12345

Wu, T., Johnson, L., & Martinez, A. (2023). The integration of virtual and augmented reality in education: Implications for strategic planning in educational leadership. *Journal of Educational Innovation*, 14(1), 99–114. DOI: 10.1016/jei.2023.101045

Zhu, H., He, X., & Wang, J. (2021). AI-powered adaptive learning environments: Opportunities and challenges for educational leaders. *Educational Management & Administration*, 49(3), 301–317. DOI: 10.1080/13632434.2021.1103909

ADDITIONAL READING

Chai, C. S., & Koh, J. H. L. (2017). The role of AI in supporting educational leadership and management. *Journal of Educational Technology & Society*, 20(2), 114–124.

Figueiredo, A., & Figueiredo, F. (2020). The impact of AI on educational practices and policies. *Education and Information Technologies*, 25(1), 307–321.

Johnson, D. G., & Wetzel, C. (2019). Ethics and AI in education: Implications for practice. *Journal of Educational Technology Systems*, 48(1), 4–27.

Luckin, R., Holmes, W., Griffiths, M., & Forcier, L. B. (2016). * intelligence unleashed: An argument for AI in education*. Pearson Education.

Selwyn, N. (2019). Should robots replace teachers? AI and the future of education. *British Journal of Educational Technology*, 50(4), 1154–1161.

Woolf, B. P. (2010). *Building Intelligent Interactive Tutors: Student-Centered Strategies for Revolutionizing E-learning*. Morgan Kaufmann.

Zawacki-Richter, O., Marinsky, L., & Pente, M. (2020). The future of AI in education: Trends and opportunities. *Educational Technology Research and Development*, 68(1), 1–15.

Zheng, B., & Warschauer, M. (2018). Artificial Intelligence in Education: A Review. *International Journal of Artificial Intelligence in Education*, 28(2), 242–255.

KEY TERMS AND DEFINITIONS

Artificial Intelligence (AI): AI refers to the simulation of human intelligence processes by machines, particularly computer systems, which can perform tasks such as learning, reasoning, and problem-solving.

Educational Leadership: Educational leadership involves guiding and influencing educational institutions and staff to achieve goals, improve teaching and learning outcomes, and foster a positive school culture.

Educational Management: Educational management refers to the administrative processes and practices that ensure effective operation and resource allocation within educational institutions, focusing on planning, organizing, and overseeing educational activities.

Chatbots: Chatbots are AI-driven software applications designed to simulate human conversation through text or voice interactions, often used in educational settings to assist with administrative tasks and student inquiries.

Learning Analytics: Learning analytics involves the collection, analysis, and interpretation of data related to student learning to improve educational outcomes, inform decision-making, and enhance teaching strategies.

Adaptive Learning Systems: Adaptive learning systems use AI algorithms to personalize educational content and experiences for individual learners based on their performance, preferences, and learning pace.

Data-Driven Decision-Making: This term refers to the process of making decisions based on the analysis and interpretation of data rather than intuition or observation, emphasizing the use of empirical evidence in educational leadership.

AI Integration: AI integration involves incorporating AI technologies into existing educational practices and systems to enhance teaching, learning, and administrative functions.

Institutional Readiness: Institutional readiness refers to an educational institution's preparedness to adopt and effectively implement new technologies, including AI, which encompasses factors like infrastructure, staff training, and policy support.

Smart Learning Ecosystems: Smart learning ecosystems are interconnected environments that leverage AI and technology to create personalized, flexible, and responsive learning experiences, facilitating continuous improvement and collaboration among stakeholders.

Chapter 6
Chatbots for Leadership Support:
Decision-Making and Advisory Roles

Mustafa Kayyali
https://orcid.org/0000-0003-3300-262X
HE Higher Education Ranking, Syria

ABSTRACT

This chapter addresses the rising use of chatbots in leadership, notably their utility in assisting decision-making and advising roles. As artificial intelligence (AI) continues to permeate organizational systems, chatbots are emerging as key tools in streamlining leadership responsibilities and delivering real-time advising support. The chapter digs into the methods by which chatbots aid leaders in complex decision-making processes, delivering analytical insights and recommendations based on data-driven techniques. Moreover, the advising role of chatbots is investigated, demonstrating how these AI systems increase leadership capacities by giving continual feedback, resource allocation techniques, and problem-solving support. By integrating chatbots into leadership frameworks, companies, particularly in educational contexts, can boost efficiency and develop more dynamic leadership structures. The chapter finishes by analyzing the technological constraints and potential future developments of chatbots in educational leadership and administration.

DOI: 10.4018/979-8-3693-8734-4.ch006

INTRODUCTION

In recent years, the convergence of artificial intelligence (AI) and leadership has experienced remarkable growth, with chatbots emerging as one of the most significant innovations in this sector (Madasamy & Aquilanz, 2023). As businesses, particularly in educational settings, face rising complexity, the demand for tools that promote decision-making and leadership efficiency has never been greater. Chatbots, enabled by breakthroughs in machine learning and natural language processing (NLP), offer a disruptive solution, allowing leaders to offload repetitive chores, expedite communication, and increase the quality of their judgments (Meacham, 2020). This chapter addresses the expanding significance of chatbots in leadership, with a specific focus on their contributions to decision-making and advising roles. The expansion of AI technology in organizational management is not only a trend but a fundamental revolution in how institutions operate. Traditionally, leadership has been characterized by human intuition, experience, and judgment. While these attributes remain vital, the introduction of AI-driven solutions like chatbots is proven to be a game changer. Chatbots have grown from simple, task-oriented applications—such as customer service assistants—into sophisticated systems capable of storing large quantities of data, delivering real-time insights, and even forecasting outcomes based on previous experiences and trends (Suhaili et al, 2021). In a day where data is one of the most precious assets, the capacity of chatbots to process and analyze massive datasets has positioned them as crucial tools for modern leaders.

In educational leadership, the deployment of chatbots is highly promising (Okonkwo & Ade-Ibijola, 2021). Universities, colleges, and educational institutions are contexts where leadership decisions touch a wide spectrum of stakeholders, from students and professors to administrative personnel and external partners (Ruben et al, 2023). Chatbots can aid leaders by providing real-time data on student performance, attendance, and engagement, offering advice on resource allocation, and even forecasting potential dangers such as student attrition or poor academic performance (Tariq, 2024). Moreover, as educational institutions increasingly adopt online and hybrid learning models, chatbots can promote more effective communication between leadership and their teams, helping manage remote personnel and students while maintaining organizational coherence. Beyond decision-making, chatbots are also proven to be effective in advising roles, working as virtual advisers to leadership teams. They can take advice on strategic initiatives, examine the prospective repercussions of policy changes, and even produce scenario-based evaluations to help leaders foresee the ramifications of their decisions. This advisory power extends beyond the mechanical processing of data; modern chatbots can employ advanced algorithms to deliver individualized counsel that corresponds with an organization's goals and beliefs. This ability to operate as both a decision-making tool and an advisory helper is redefining leadership, allowing educational leaders to focus on higher-level strategic thinking while automating more mundane aspects of administration. The employment of chatbots in leadership is not without its limitations. Despite their potential, there are major technological, ethical, and organizational challenges that must be solved. One of the key issues is the existing limitations of chatbot technology, particularly in dealing with subtle human emotions, complex decision-making scenarios, and situations needing a thorough awareness of context (Adamopoulou & Moussiades, 2020). While chatbots can handle vast volumes of data, their recommendations are only as good as the algorithms that fuel them and the data they have access to. Therefore, executives must exercise caution in depending only on chatbots for key judgments and instead consider them as complementary tools that improve, rather than replace, human judgment.

The inclusion of chatbots into leadership frameworks presents crucial ethical problems (Abdelhalim et al, 2024). As AI systems become more ingrained in decision-making processes, questions regarding accountability, bias, and transparency come to the forefront. For instance, if a decision informed by a chatbot leads to undesirable repercussions, who has the responsibility? Additionally, the algorithms that run chatbots may unwittingly perpetuate biases present in the data they are trained on, thus leading to skewed suggestions. Educational leaders must therefore approach the deployment of chatbots with a firm knowledge of these ethical issues and devise methods to reduce any hazards. Despite these challenges, the future of chatbots in leadership is exciting (Krauter, 2024). As AI technologies continue to evolve, so too will the capabilities of chatbots, allowing them to offer progressively more complex decision-making support and advising services. Future improvements in natural language processing, deep learning, and AI-human interaction will likely enable chatbots to execute more complicated leadership roles, further blurring the barrier between humans and machines in organizational management.

Chatbots constitute a tremendous tool for modern leadership, particularly in educational contexts where leaders are entrusted with navigating complicated, data-driven situations (Hossain, 2024). Their capacity to aid in decision-making, give real-time advising support, and expedite communication makes them important for leaders trying to boost organizational efficiency and effectiveness. However, the successful integration of chatbots into leadership structures needs careful evaluation of their limitations and associated ethical difficulties. As we move into an increasingly AI-driven future, the role of chatbots in leadership will only continue to expand, giving exciting potential for educational leaders to harness the power of AI in revolutionary ways.

THE ROLE OF CHATBOTS IN DECISION-MAKING

Chatbots have swiftly progressed beyond their initial purpose as simple communication tools and are now being integrated into more complex parts of organizational administration, including decision-making (Paliwal et al, 2024). In the context of educational leadership, decision-making is generally a complicated process, requiring the examination of numerous data sources, perspectives, and prospective outcomes. Traditionally, leaders have relied on intuition, experience, and collaboration with colleagues to make educated judgments. However, with the rise of big data and increasingly advanced AI technology, chatbots are now playing a crucial role in helping executives evaluate information and make faster, more accurate decisions. One of the most significant ways chatbots aid decision-making is through their ability to synthesize vast volumes of data rapidly and efficiently (Ferreira, 2021). Educational institutions, particularly at the university level, create large amounts of data about student performance, attendance, financial operations, staffing, and resource management. Processing this data manually is not only time-consuming but also prone to errors. Chatbots can be programmed to evaluate this data, discover patterns, and offer the most relevant information to leaders in real-time. This feature helps educational leaders make data-driven decisions that are guided by up-to-date insights, ensuring that their choices are not based on outdated facts or preconceptions.

In addition to processing data, chatbots may also give predictive analytics, which is a critical part of forward-thinking decision-making (Hao et al, 2024). By applying machine learning algorithms, chatbots may estimate prospective outcomes based on historical data, helping executives anticipate future trends or issues. For example, a chatbot may evaluate student enrollment data over the past decade to forecast future enrollment figures, allowing university administrators to plan for changes in class sizes, staffing demands, and resource allocation. Similarly, chatbots can monitor student performance data and identify possible areas of concern, such as dropping grades or poor attendance, enabling leaders to intervene early before these concerns become more severe. Chatbots have the unique capacity to make recommendations based on the data they analyze, functioning as an advisory tool in the decision-making process (Maria et al, 2022). Rather than only giving raw data, chatbots can make particular ideas, such as the optimal allocation of resources, strategic initiatives that are most likely to succeed, or even alternative ways of problem-solving. For educational leaders who are regularly faced with a wide variety of issues, ranging from budgeting and curriculum development to faculty management and policy execution, these tips can be essential. By narrowing down possibilities and offering the most plausible courses of action, chatbots can lessen the cognitive load on leaders, allowing them to focus on higher-level strategic thinking.

One especially fascinating area where chatbots are making a huge influence is in the sphere of student affairs (Sari et al, 2020). Educational leaders are routinely faced with making decisions that directly affect student experiences, from academic rules to campus resources. Chatbots, through their continuous data monitoring, can provide insights into student requirements and preferences, offering a better-informed basis for decision-making. For instance, if a chatbot observes a spike in student requests regarding mental health services, it could prompt administrators to enhance money or staffing in that area (Chen et al, 2024). Similarly, if it finds patterns of discontent with certain parts of campus life, such as eating selections or living conditions, it can highlight these problems, enabling leaders to take proactive actions to remedy them. This direct channel of communication between students and leaders, aided by chatbots, guarantees that decision-making is more sensitive to the demands of the community. Chatbots also succeed in instances when time-sensitive choices must be made. In crisis scenarios, such as natural catastrophes, pandemics, or other calamities, educational leaders must often make hasty judgments with minimal information. Chatbots, with their ability to acquire and analyze data swiftly, can deliver important insights in real time, helping executives make informed decisions even in high-pressure circumstances. For example, during the COVID-19 pandemic, several educational institutions depended on AI-driven technologies to assess infection rates, monitor student and staff health, and alter campus regulations accordingly (Mondal & Mitra, 2022). Chatbots may quickly assess data from public health authorities, local governments, and internal systems to provide university officials with actionable advice, such as switching to online learning or modifying campus access regulations. This type of rapid decision support can make all the difference in protecting the safety and well-being of the entire educational community.

Another key role of chatbots in decision-making is their capacity to support more inclusive and transparent processes (Durall Gazulla et al, 2023). Educational leadership decisions are often made through collaboration among multiple stakeholders, including administrators, faculty members, students, and even external partners. Chatbots can operate as intermediates in these discussions, collecting input from all relevant participants and synthesizing it into a cohesive collection of recommendations. By delivering unbiased data and suggestions, chatbots assist limit the influence of personal biases and guarantee that judgments are based on objective criteria. This democratization of decision-making can lead to more equal outcomes and better faith in leadership, as all views are considered in the process. It is crucial to note that chatbots, despite their various advantages, are not flawless. They are only as good as the algorithms that fuel them and the data they are trained on. If the data provided by a chatbot is insufficient, obsolete, or prejudiced, the decisions it supports may be erroneous. For example, if a chatbot is generating recommendations based on student performance data but has not been updated to reflect current changes in grading procedures, its recommendations could be erroneous or deceptive. Similarly, if the chatbot's algorithm has biases—whether related to gender, ethnicity, or socioeconomic status—it may accidentally reinforce these biases in its decision-making suggestions. Therefore, while chatbots can considerably increase decision-making, they must be utilized in conjunction with human monitoring and judgment to ensure that judgments remain fair, transparent, and contextually appropriate.

Chatbots' reliance on data means that they may suffer in instances when qualitative variables are more significant than quantitative ones (Jongerius, 2018). While a chatbot can analyze numerical data and trends with great accuracy, it may have difficulty accounting for more subjective elements, such as the emotional impact of a decision on faculty or students, the cultural context of a policy change, or the ethical implications of a particular course of action. These are situations where human leaders' empathy, experience, and principles come into play, and where the chatbot's function is inherently limited. Therefore, leaders must strike a balance between relying on chatbots for data-driven insights and keeping their judgment for more nuanced, context-dependent decisions. Chatbots have developed as strong tools in the decision-making processes of educational leaders, giving considerable benefits in terms of data analysis, predictive capabilities, and real-time recommendations (Owoc et al, 2019). Their ability to integrate enormous volumes of information, deliver actionable insights, and allow more inclusive decision-making processes makes them important in modern educational institutions. However, their limitations—particularly in grasping complicated human emotions and ethical considerations—highlight the continuous significance of human scrutiny in leadership decisions. As AI technologies continue to improve, the role of chatbots in decision-making will undoubtedly expand, delivering even more sophisticated help to educational leaders while still requiring strategic integration with human judgment and values.

Advisory Functions of Chatbots in Leadership

The advisory role of chatbots in leadership is an emerging feature of modern corporate management, enabling new approaches to boost strategic thinking and decision-making processes (Savastano et al, 2024). As AI technology becomes more powerful, chatbots have outgrown their initial functions as simple assistants, currently working as virtual consultants to leaders across different sectors, including education. These advising duties, founded in real-time data analysis and predictive modeling, are redefining how leaders handle complex challenges, from policy development to crisis management. One of the key advantages of chatbots in advisory jobs is their capacity to deliver constant, real-time input. Unlike human advisors, who require time to digest material and may be limited by availability, chatbots are constantly accessible and can instantaneously analyze vast volumes of data, delivering fast counsel anytime a leader requires it (Makasi et al, 2020). This rapid access to data-driven insights empowers educational leaders to make more informed decisions without the delays commonly associated with traditional advising methods. For example, if a university leader has to examine the impact of budget cuts on different departments, a chatbot may rapidly collect pertinent financial and operational data, recommend alternative cost-saving initiatives, and anticipate the long-term impacts of different budgetary decisions. By doing so, the chatbot serves as a helpful collaborator in strategic planning, ensuring that leaders have the knowledge they need to respond rapidly and properly.

Chatbots also add a level of objectivity to the consulting process that is frequently impossible for human advisors to attain (Morana et al, 2020). Human advisors, regardless of their skill, may be swayed by personal prejudices, organizational politics, or emotional considerations while providing suggestions (Luo et al, 2019). Chatbots, on the other hand, base their recommendations exclusively on data and analytics, giving objective suggestions that might help executives make more balanced judgments (Kushwaha et al, 2021). In the context of educational leadership, where decisions often have far-reaching effects on students, professors, and staff, this neutrality can be vital. Whether a leader is deciding on faculty promotions, student admittance procedures, or resource allocations, a chatbot can provide data-backed guidance that minimizes the influence of personal preferences or external demands. Another significant component of chatbots' advisory functions is their ability to simulate multiple scenarios and outcomes (Santos et al, 2022). Using predictive analytics and machine learning algorithms, chatbots can model the probable effects of various strategic decisions, allowing leaders to explore several options before committing to a course of action. This competence is particularly helpful in complicated and uncertain circumstances, such as during financial crises or public health emergencies, where decisions must be taken rapidly yet with a knowledge of long-term ramifications. For instance, during the COVID-19 pandemic, many educational institutions had to determine whether to migrate to online learning, keep in-person classrooms, or adopt a hybrid method (Bashir et al, 2021). A chatbot may analyze the probable results of each option by assessing data on infection rates, college performance, and logistical concerns, offering leaders a clearer understanding of the risks and rewards associated with each choice. This form of scenario planning, assisted by chatbots, helps leaders to make decisions that are not only reactive to immediate difficulties but also proactive in predicting future demands.

Beyond data analysis and scenario modeling, chatbots can give advisory support in the form of trend identification and strategic advice (Chao et al, 2021). In today's fast-changing educational world, leaders must stay ahead of emerging trends in technology, pedagogy, and policy to remain competitive. Chatbots, with their ability to digest enormous volumes of information from multiple sources, can uncover trends that may not yet be evident to human leaders. For example, a chatbot might examine worldwide data on educational breakthroughs and recommend that an institution embrace new teaching technology, such as virtual or augmented reality, to boost student engagement and learning outcomes. Similarly, a chatbot might advise leaders on shifting regulatory needs, helping institutions stay compliant with government laws and accreditation standards. By spotting and highlighting trends early, chatbots can ensure that leaders are well-prepared to face the challenges and possibilities of the future.

One of the most significant contributions of chatbots in leadership advisory roles is their ability to aid in crisis management (Krauter, 2024). Educational leaders are increasingly challenged with crises that require rapid and effective solutions, whether due to natural disasters, public health concerns, or internal conflicts. In such instances, the ability to swiftly acquire correct information and receive actionable guidance is vital. Chatbots can function as crisis counselors by continuously monitoring internal and external data sources, spotting developing hazards, and offering effective remedies. For instance, in the event of a security issue on campus, a chatbot may assess real-time data from security systems, law enforcement reports, and social media, advising authorities on the best course of action to protect student and staff safety. Additionally, the chatbot may replicate the effects of various crisis management tactics, such as campus lockdowns or evacuations, allowing leaders to make decisions that minimize harm and disturbance. This kind of quick, data-driven advising help can make a major difference in how effectively leaders respond to emergencies, eventually protecting the well-being of the entire educational community.

In addition to crisis management, chatbots also play a valuable role in long-term strategy planning (Majumder & Mondal, 2021). Educational leaders must often make decisions that will affect their institutions for years to come, from infrastructure investments to curriculum development. These long-term decisions involve careful evaluation of various aspects, including financial limits, student demography, and evolving industry demands. Chatbots can provide leaders with detailed, data-driven guidance that takes all of these elements into consideration (Alaaeldin et al, 2021). For example, while planning the extension of a university's campus, a chatbot may assess data on population growth, student enrollment trends, and economic forecasts to identify the most viable places for additional facilities. Similarly, in curriculum planning, a chatbot might monitor labor market trends to advise the development of new programs that match the future demands of employers. By delivering this kind of forward-thinking guidance, chatbots assist executives make decisions that are not just sensitive to current conditions but also connected with long-term institutional goals. While chatbots offer significant advantages in leadership advisory roles, it is vital to realize their limitations. Despite their ability to evaluate data and make objective advice, chatbots lack the human intuition, empathy, and ethical judgment that are often crucial in leadership decision-making. For example, while a chatbot may be able to advise on cost-cutting measures, it may not completely appreciate the human implications of those decisions, such as the effect of staff layoffs on morale or the possible long-term damage to an institution's reputation. Leaders must use chatbot guidance as an addition to, rather than a replacement for, their judgment (Chong et al, 2021). Leaders must be conscious of the limitations of AI and ensure that they add their emotional intelligence and ethical considerations into the decision-making process. Chatbots have proven increasingly important as advisors to educational leaders, including real-time data analysis, scenario modeling, trend spotting, and strategic advice. Their neutrality and ability to handle enormous volumes of information make them important tools in a leader's decision-making arsenal. However, while chatbots can provide significant insights and guidance, they must be utilized in concert with human judgment to ensure that judgments are not only data-driven but also culturally relevant and ethically sound. As AI technology continues to grow, the advising roles of chatbots will likely become even more sophisticated, significantly boosting their ability to support leaders in navigating the complex issues of the current educational environment. By embracing this technology while being mindful of its limitations, educational leaders may harness the full potential of chatbots to promote innovation, improve decision-making, and ultimately boost the success of their institutions.

Technological Capabilities and Limitations

The technological capabilities of chatbots, especially in the context of leadership assistance, have expanded dramatically in recent years (Wang et al, 2022). As artificial intelligence (AI) and natural language processing (NLP) technology have matured, chatbots have grown from simple automated systems into sophisticated tools capable of analyzing data, delivering insights, and even emulating human interactions (Suhaili et al, 2021). However, as much as these capabilities are spectacular and helpful, chatbots are nonetheless restricted by certain limits that influence their effectiveness, particularly in areas where human judgment and emotional intelligence are essential. Understanding both the virtues and disadvantages of chatbot technology is vital for leaders who wish to integrate these systems into their decision-making and advisory processes. The most astounding technological capacity of chatbots comes in their ability to digest large volumes of data at unprecedented speeds. In leadership settings, particularly within educational institutions, data streams are vast and multidimensional, spanning everything from student performance and resource allocation to faculty development and institutional finances. Human leaders typically confront hurdles when trying to manually sift through various levels of information. Chatbots, on the other hand, excel in aggregating data from numerous sources, finding patterns, and summarizing critical insights in a fraction of the time it would take a human team. For instance, when tasked with reviewing student performance across several departments, a chatbot can rapidly analyze grades, attendance, engagement levels, and even social media activity to offer a holistic picture. This data-driven capacity allows leaders to make decisions that are both informed and timely, eliminating the danger of depending on obsolete or incomplete information.

Chatbots can employ machine learning techniques to improve their advisory functions over time (Potla, 2023). As these systems analyze more data and interact with users, they learn from their experiences, refining their ability to give relevant recommendations and insights. This self-learning feature enables chatbots to continuously adapt to the specific objectives and goals of a company. In educational leadership, for example, a chatbot can initially offer generic ideas on curriculum development, but as it acquires more information about student input and academic performance, it can tailor its advice to the unique issues encountered by the institution. This adaptability boosts the utility of chatbots as long-term strategic tools, enabling leaders to cross new educational settings with greater agility. Another major technological characteristic of chatbots is their aptitude for natural language processing (NLP) (Adamopoulou & Moussiades, 2020a). NLP allows chatbots to interpret and respond to human language in a way that feels intuitive and conversational. This has important consequences for leadership contexts, as communication is typically a vital component of decision-making. Through NLP, chatbots can assess written or spoken inputs from leaders, instructors, or students and deliver relevant advice or solutions. For instance, a university president might ask a chatbot for a report on faculty performance. Instead of delivering a standard report, the chatbot could engage in a more dynamic conversation, asking follow-up questions such as "Would you like a comparison to last year's performance?" or "Do you want to focus on specific departments?" This level of conversational engagement makes chatbots more user-friendly, allowing leaders to interact with them as they would with human advisors, without the need for highly technical commands or inputs.

Despite these outstanding capabilities, chatbots are not without their limitations, particularly when it comes to the complexities of human interaction and decision-making (Nuruzzaman & Hussain, 2018). One key restriction is the incapacity of chatbots to properly appreciate the emotional and psychological components of leadership decisions. Educational leaders typically make decisions that include delicate interpersonal dynamics, such as settling conflicts between staff members or addressing student well-being. While chatbots can evaluate data relating to these challenges, they lack the emotional intelligence to grasp the deeper differences that come with human relationships. For example, a chatbot might prescribe a stern disciplinary penalty based on policy infractions, but it would not be able to bring in the personal challenges or emotional context behind a student's behavior. This constraint underlines the need for human leaders to rely on their judgment and empathy, especially in instances where decisions require more than simply rational analysis. Chatbots are bound by the quality and completeness of the data they are trained on (Rhim et al, 2022). AI systems, like chatbots, depend largely on the statistics they are fed to provide accurate insights and suggestions. If the data is biased, incomplete, or old, the chatbot's output will reflect those deficiencies (Casheekar et al, 2024). In the context of educational leadership, this can be particularly troublesome. For instance, if a chatbot is entrusted with advising modifications to an academic curriculum but is solely trained on data from traditional learning models, it may not deliver the most innovative or forward-thinking answers. Similarly, if the chatbot's dataset lacks diversity, it may unintentionally reinforce prejudices, such as recommending policies that disproportionately affect minority groups of students (Kantharuban et al, 2024). This constraint underlines the significance of regularly updating and diversifying the datasets utilized by chatbots, as well as integrating human oversight to adjust for any potential biases or mistakes.

Another shortcoming of chatbots is their incapacity to engage in critical thinking or creative problem-solving (Qawqzeh, 2024). While they can digest data and discover trends, chatbots cannot independently produce innovative ideas or techniques. In leadership jobs, particularly in education, innovation, and creativity are vital for addressing difficult situations. Leaders often need to think beyond the box, inventing new techniques that go beyond current conventions. A chatbot, however, is constrained by the algorithms and parameters provided by its developers. It can offer solutions based on available data but is unlikely to propose wholly new notions that have not been previously observed or coded into its system. This constraint means that while chatbots can aid with everyday decision-making duties, they are less successful when leaders are faced with extraordinary situations that need imaginative thinking. Chatbots might suffer from ambiguity, particularly in instances when there is no clear right or wrong answer (Keyvan & Huang, 2022). Many leadership decisions include negotiating gray zones where the outcomes are uncertain, and numerous stakeholders may have opposing interests. For example, a university head could need to reconcile budget constraints with the requirement to continue high-quality student services. A chatbot may propose data-driven options, such as decreasing expenditures in particular areas, but it cannot fully account for the political and societal repercussions of these choices (Khneyzer et al, 2024). Human leaders must evaluate how decisions will be seen by diverse groups, how they connect with the institution's values, and how they will affect morale. These are complexity that chatbots are not yet ready to manage, as their decision-making processes are based on logic and statistics, rather than a complete grasp of human circumstances.

Lastly, there are ethical considerations associated with the usage of chatbots in leadership posts (Murtarelli et al, 2021). As AI systems become more integrated into decision-making processes, there is a risk of over-reliance on these technologies, leading to the dehumanization of leadership. While chatbots can give essential support, they should not replace the human qualities of leadership, including empathy, ethical reasoning, and social responsibility. Educational leaders, in particular, should act in the best interests of their students, faculty, and community, considering not only the efficiency of decisions but also their long-term societal impact. Relying too heavily on chatbots without addressing these broader ethical implications could result in judgments that, while theoretically correct, fail to meet the emotional or moral demands of the organization (Sepahpour, 2020). The technological capabilities of chatbots in leadership situations are considerable, notably in areas such as data analysis, machine learning, and natural language processing. These tools can dramatically boost decision-making processes, giving timely, data-driven insights that would be difficult for human leaders to create on their own. However, chatbots are not without their limitations. Their lack of emotional intelligence, creativity, and critical thinking, combined with their dependence on data quality, suggests that they should be employed as supplements to human leadership, rather than substitutes. As educational leaders continue to employ AI-driven technologies, they must strike a balance between exploiting the technology strengths of chatbots and keeping the human parts of leadership that are crucial for making educated, ethical, and compassionate judgments.

Impact on Organizational Leadership Structures

The integration of chatbots into leadership responsibilities has begun to influence organizational structures in major ways (Zhang et al, 2023). As these AI-driven tools continue to evolve, their involvement in decision-making and advisory capacity is becoming increasingly pronounced, altering how leadership operates and how companies are organized to exploit the benefits of this technology. The influence of chatbots extends beyond basic operational efficiency; it has a deeper impact on the fundamental fabric of corporate leadership, shifting hierarchies, redefining positions, and impacting the interactions between leaders and their teams (Skuridin & Wynn, 2024). One of the most noteworthy implications of chatbots on leadership structures is the decentralization of decision-making processes. Traditionally, leadership in many businesses has followed a hierarchical paradigm, where decisions are made at the top and gradually disseminated to lower levels. However, with the development of chatbots capable of offering data-driven insights and real-time counsel, decision-making authority is rapidly being disseminated throughout the business. Mid-level managers, team leaders, and even frontline personnel can now access advanced tools that allow them to make educated decisions without continually seeking clearance from senior management. For example, at an educational institution, department heads might traditionally have had to wait for top leadership to examine and approve curriculum changes or budget adjustments. With the backing of chatbots, these leaders may make more autonomous judgments, equipped with the analytical ability that these technologies bring.

This shift toward decentralized decision-making affects the traditional power balances within businesses. Chatbots provide a more collaborative approach to leadership, where information flows more freely, and leaders at various levels can act autonomously based on data-backed insights (Heilig & Scheer, 2023). In this sense, chatbots democratize access to essential information, empowering more people inside the organization to take on leadership positions. The outcome is a more agile and responsive leadership structure, where choices can be taken faster and more efficiently without waiting for directions from the top. This is particularly beneficial in educational institutions, where the ability to adjust swiftly to changing circumstances—such as shifts in student demands, curriculum requirements, or external regulations—can considerably impact the institution's overall success. The flattening of organizational hierarchies is another key result of chatbot integration. As chatbots take on more advising and decision-support responsibilities, the necessity for numerous layers of middle management is decreased (Morana et al, 2020). In conventional leadership structures, middle managers generally function as intermediates between high management and the workforce, entrusted with filtering information and making decisions based on directions from the top. However, chatbots may now fulfill many of these activities, including assessing performance data, delivering strategic recommendations, and even offering coaching and feedback to employees. This minimizes the need for several managerial layers, as chatbots can streamline communication and decision-making across the company. The elimination of middle management not only boosts operational efficiency but also saves expenses and enhances organizational flexibility.

The role of senior leaders is also altering as chatbots become increasingly incorporated into leadership hierarchies (Krauter, 2024). Rather than focusing on day-to-day operational decisions, senior executives can shift their attention to more strategic, high-level challenges. With chatbots performing many of the everyday activities, such as data analysis, report generation, and even initial problem-solving, leaders are freed to concentrate on long-term vision, innovation, and developing a strong organizational culture. This move empowers leaders to become more proactive and visionary, rather than reactive and mired down by administrative responsibilities. In educational contexts, for example, a university president or dean may spend less time examining operational reports and more time creating strategic relationships, exploring financing opportunities, or lobbying for policy changes that match the institution's mission and goals. The incorporation of chatbots into leadership structures also offers issues, notably in how leaders communicate with their teams. The usage of chatbots can create a degree of distance between leaders and employees, as some of the more personal, relational parts of leadership are transferred to automated systems. For example, chatbots can be used to monitor employee performance and provide feedback, but this may lead to a loss in face-to-face contact between leaders and their staff. While chatbots can offer objective feedback based on performance indicators, they lack the potential to create deep, trusted connections that are often important for motivating and inspiring teams. Leaders must therefore find a balance between exploiting chatbot skills for productivity and keeping the human connection that is crucial for effective leadership.

The advent of chatbots in leadership posts raises problems about responsibility and decision ownership (Kooli, 2023). As chatbots increasingly contribute to decision-making processes, it might become unclear where responsibility resides when things go wrong. If a chatbot gives a recommendation based on inaccurate data or an algorithmic error, and that recommendation leads to a poor outcome, who is ultimately responsible? While the human leader remains accountable, the blurring distinctions between human and AI decision-making might cause issues in allocating blame or reward. Leaders will need to set clear norms and procedures for incorporating chatbot assistance into their decision-making processes, ensuring that human supervision and responsibility are always maintained. The impact of chatbots on leadership structures also extends to leadership development and succession planning (Nawaz & Gomes, 2019). As chatbots take on more of the analytical and advising responsibilities traditionally associated with leadership roles, the abilities required to run a company are altering. Future leaders will need to be competent at working alongside AI systems, evaluating data, and making judgment judgments based on the insights supplied by chatbots. This will demand a new sort of leadership training, focused not only on traditional leadership qualities, such as communication, empathy, and strategic thinking but also on technology literacy and data-driven decision-making. Educational institutions, in particular, will need to reconsider how they teach future leaders to ensure they are prepared to operate in contexts where AI plays a prominent role in leadership tasks.

In addition to affecting leadership development, chatbots are also influencing the competencies that companies value in their leaders. With chatbots managing much of the data analysis and operational decision-making, human leaders are increasingly valued for their capacity to engage in critical thinking, ethical reasoning, and emotional intelligence—skills that chatbots currently lack. As a result, companies are placing increased emphasis on soft skills when selecting and developing their leaders. In educational leadership, this transition is especially obvious, as leaders are expected to pass complicated social and political settings, develop a strong organizational culture, and build relationships with varied stakeholders. Chatbots can provide essential support in terms of data and analysis, but the human parts of leadership—such as empathy, vision, and ethical decision-making—remain irreplaceable. The incorporation of chatbots into leadership hierarchies needs modifications in company culture (Baruah et al, 2024). As chatbots become increasingly popular in leadership roles, companies must build a culture that accepts AI as a tool for improving, rather not replacing, human leadership. This needs leaders to be honest about the use of chatbots in decision-making processes and to communicate clearly with their teams about how these tools will be used. It also requires fostering a culture of continual learning, where employees and leaders alike are encouraged to increase their technology literacy and adapt to the dynamic landscape of AI-driven leadership. Organizations that successfully integrate chatbots into their leadership structures will be those that strike a balance between technical innovation and human-centered leadership, harnessing the capabilities of both to achieve their goals. Chatbots are having a major impact on corporate leadership hierarchies (Krauter, 2024). By decentralizing decision-making, flattening hierarchies, and diverting the emphasis of top leaders toward more strategic challenges, chatbots are altering the way organizations work. However, the integration of chatbots into leadership roles also creates obstacles, particularly in terms of maintaining human connections, guaranteeing responsibility, and adapting leadership development to the new needs of the AI era. As organizations continue to use chatbots as part of their leadership toolset, they will need to negotiate these obstacles carefully to ensure that the human parts of leadership stay at the forefront.

Future Directions for Chatbots in Educational Leadership

The future of chatbots in educational leadership holds immense potential, as these AI-driven technologies continue to improve and become more sophisticated (Shah, 2023). In the context of educational institutions, chatbots are set to alter leadership by enhancing decision-making, streamlining administrative operations, and promoting more customized interactions with teachers, students, and external stakeholders. However, the road ahead is not without hurdles. The increasing incorporation of chatbots into leadership jobs raises fundamental questions concerning their limitations, ethical considerations, and the abilities required of future educational leaders. This section discusses the prospects for chatbots in educational leadership, considering both the opportunities and the difficulties that lie ahead.

One of the most interesting prospects for chatbots in educational leadership is their potential to boost data-driven decision-making (Langeveldt, 2021). As AI technology becomes more powerful, chatbots will be able to analyze increasing volumes of data more rapidly and accurately. Educational leaders will be able to rely on these technologies to assess complicated facts, ranging from student performance and retention rates to financial projections and enrollment trends. In the future, chatbots may be able to offer predictive insights, enabling leaders to anticipate difficulties before they happen. For example, a chatbot may assess student attendance and academic performance data to anticipate which students are at risk of dropping out, allowing leaders to act earlier with customized support measures. This proactive strategy will enable educational institutions to become more nimble and responsive to the requirements of their students, leading to better outcomes for both learners and institutions. Chatbots could play a vital role in increasing communication between educational leaders and their constituents. In the future, these AI tools may be able to support more meaningful and tailored interactions with instructors, staff, students, and even parents. By studying trends in communication and obtaining real-time feedback, chatbots could help leaders adjust their messaging to specific audiences, ensuring that critical information is transmitted successfully. For instance, a chatbot may assist a university president in sending individualized messages to faculty members about changes in institutional policies, or it could automate responses to common student concerns regarding admissions, financial assistance, or academic resources. The capacity to provide timely, relevant, and tailored communication will be especially critical as educational institutions continue to develop diversity. The administrative tasks of educational leadership are likewise expected to be altered by the continuous development of chatbots (Birenbaum, 2023). Currently, much of a leader's time is spent on regular administrative chores, such as checking budgets, supervising compliance with rules, and managing human resources. In the future, chatbots will likely take on even more of these roles, freeing up educational leaders to focus on higher-level strategic planning. For example, chatbots might be programmed to provide financial reports, check compliance with accreditation criteria, or aid in the recruiting and onboarding of new faculty members. By automating these processes, educational leaders will have more time to devote to defining long-term institutional goals, building partnerships, and interacting with the wider community.

Another intriguing path for chatbots in educational leadership is their potential role in promoting professional development (Atlas, 2023). Chatbots might be used to deliver tailored coaching and feedback to leaders, helping them improve their decision-making skills and adapt to the increasing demands of their roles. For example, a chatbot may study a leader's communication style, leadership decisions, and interactions with team members, delivering targeted ideas for growth. This real-time feedback could be invaluable for new leaders or those transitioning into leadership roles, giving them the guidance and support they need to thrive. Over time, chatbots could also become integrated into leadership training programs, enabling simulations and scenarios for leaders to practice their decision-making skills in a low-risk environment. The future of chatbots in educational leadership may involve their increased usage in fostering inclusivity and diversity within institutions. By evaluating data on student demographics, faculty composition, and institutional regulations, chatbots could help administrators identify areas where reforms are needed to promote diversity, equity, and inclusion. For example, a chatbot might identify discrepancies in student accomplishment based on socioeconomic background or recommend measures for recruiting a more diverse faculty. These insights would allow educational leaders to make more informed decisions that contribute to fostering a more inclusive and supportive environment for all members of the institution.

While the potential benefits of chatbots in educational leadership are tremendous, there are also substantial obstacles that must be addressed as this technology continues to advance. One of the most important concerns is the ethical usage of chatbots, particularly in terms of data privacy and transparency. Educational leaders will need to guarantee that the usage of chatbots conforms with all relevant data protection requirements and that the information obtained by these systems is utilized appropriately. Additionally, leaders must be honest about how chatbots are being utilized in decision-making processes, making it obvious where the boundary is drawn between human judgment and AI-driven advice. Striking the correct mix between exploiting chatbot insights and keeping human control will be important to ensure that the technology is used ethically and efficiently. Another problem is the requirement for educational leaders to gain the skills required to operate effectively with chatbots. As these technologies become more integrated into leadership roles, future leaders will need to be comfortable using AI tools and evaluating the data they generate. This will demand a shift in leadership development programs, with a stronger emphasis on technology literacy and data-driven decision-making. Leaders who cannot deal with AI tools may struggle to keep pace with the demands of modern educational leadership, potentially leading to a digital divide between those who can effectively utilize chatbots and those who cannot. Institutions will need to invest in training and professional development to guarantee that their executives can navigate the AI-driven landscape of the future.

Looking ahead, it is also likely that the connection between human leaders and chatbots will continue to evolve (Anagnoste et al, 2021). As chatbots become more smart, they may take on increasingly complex advising roles, working alongside human leaders to co-create strategies and solve problems. However, the success of this partnership will depend on how successfully leaders can integrate chatbot insights into their decision-making processes while keeping their judgment and authority. Chatbots are strong tools, but they are not flawless, and human leaders will need to be careful in how they use the information offered by these systems (Rahmani & Kamberaj, 2021). The future of educational leadership will require leaders who are not only good at employing AI tools but also skilled at blending technical innovation with human intuition and sensitivity. The future of chatbots in educational leadership is full of potential. As these AI tools become more advanced, they have the potential to transform how educational leaders make decisions, communicate with stakeholders, manage administrative duties, and create diversity inside their institutions. However, fulfilling this promise will need careful evaluation of the ethical implications of chatbot use, investment in leadership development, and a commitment to keeping the human qualities of leadership that remain irreplaceable. Chatbots are poised to become vital tools for educational leaders, but their effectiveness will ultimately depend on how well they are incorporated into the broader framework of human leadership (Kooli, 2023). The future of educational leadership is one in which chatbots and human leaders work together to produce more efficient, inclusive, and responsive institutions.

CONCLUSION

The integration of chatbots into leadership roles, particularly in decision-making and advising capacities, signals a transformational shift in how educational organizations work in the 21st century. As this chapter has highlighted, the usage of AI-driven chatbots is not only an extension of technological improvements but reflects a fundamental rethinking of leadership dynamics. By automating routine operations, delivering real-time data-driven insights, and enabling predictive analytics, chatbots have the potential to dramatically enhance the decision-making processes of leaders in educational institutions. Moreover, given their advising position, chatbots can operate as helpful collaborators, aiding leadership teams with strategy planning, policy execution, and crisis management, thus leaving human leaders to focus on higher-level thinking and vision-setting.

One of the most attractive characteristics of chatbot integration in leadership is its capacity to process and analyze massive volumes of data at unprecedented speeds. In today's data-rich environment, executives are often overwhelmed by the sheer amount of information they need to examine when making decisions. Chatbots offer a solution to this difficulty by synthesizing data, spotting trends, and delivering actionable recommendations based on real-time information. In educational settings, where choices relating to resource allocation, student performance, curriculum creation, and staff management must be made swiftly and effectively, chatbots are proving to be important assets. The ability to make educated judgments rapidly can be the difference between organizational success and failure, especially in an increasingly competitive and worldwide education market. The introduction of chatbots in leadership is not without its obstacles. As demonstrated throughout this chapter, the existing technological limits of chatbots, particularly in dealing with complex human emotions and complicated decision-making circumstances, must be addressed. Chatbots, while incredibly effective in processing data, lack the deep contextual understanding that human leaders bring to the table. This means that while chatbots can inform choices, the final judgment must still rest with human leaders who possess the emotional intelligence, intuition, and experience necessary to understand data in context. Additionally, the dependence on chatbots for decision-making creates concerns, particularly when it comes to algorithmic biases. Since chatbots operate primarily on the data they are educated on, they may unwittingly propagate biases that exist within that data, leading to distorted or immoral advice. It is vital for leaders to critically assess the outputs of chatbots and ensure that their decisions are aligned with the organization's values, mission, and the broader educational community they serve.

Beyond their decision-making skills, chatbots' advising functions give new opportunities for education leadership. Acting as virtual advisers, chatbots can give executives scenario-based evaluations, proposing the probable outcomes of various strategic choices. This capacity allows leaders to model multiple ideas before executing them, so lowering risks and boosting the likelihood of success. This predictive function is particularly beneficial in contexts where uncertainty and volatility are prominent, such as during global health crises or financial downturns, where educational leaders must quickly adjust to changing conditions. The capacity of chatbots to deliver timely, evidence-based advice can allow leaders to make better-informed decisions, decreasing the cognitive load and stress commonly associated with high-stakes leadership tasks. While the future potential of chatbots in leadership is considerable, businesses must approach their introduction with prudence and a clear strategy. It is not enough to just deploy chatbot technologies and expect instant gains in leadership effectiveness. The successful integration of chatbots demands a strategic alignment of technology with corporate goals, structures, and culture. Leaders must ensure that chatbots are used as tools that enhance, rather than replace, human decision-making. Training and support structures must be in place to assist leaders make the most of new technologies, and ethical guidelines must be devised to address problems relating to bias, accountability, and transparency. By implementing these steps, educational institutions can establish an environment where human leaders and chatbots work synergistically to boost organizational outcomes.

As the technology continues to improve, the scope and capabilities of chatbots in leadership roles will undoubtedly expand. With breakthroughs in natural language processing, machine learning, and deep learning, future chatbots will be able to engage in more sophisticated discussions, interpret complex emotional and social cues, and offer more nuanced advice. This will further blur the border between human and AI decision-making, undermining traditional concepts of leadership and requiring a reevaluation of the duties and responsibilities of human leaders. Educational institutions, in particular, stand to benefit from these improvements, as chatbots might assist in bridging communication gaps between leaders, staff, and students, create more tailored learning and management experiences, and deliver real-time feedback to enhance overall performance. Chatbots are a significant, growing instrument for leadership in educational institutions. Their ability to support decision-making through data processing and analytics, paired with their advising functions, places them as key assets in current leadership frameworks. However, while the advantages of chatbot integration are evident, leaders must stay conscious of the limitations and ethical consequences of depending too much on AI systems. The future of leadership in education will likely feature a collaborative approach, where human leaders and chatbots work together to create more effective, efficient, and equitable outcomes. By embracing this collaboration and overcoming the obstacles that come with it, educational organizations may stay ahead of the curve and adapt to the quickly changing demands of the 21st-century educational scene. The road ahead for chatbots in leadership is one rich with opportunity, but it is also plagued with obstacles that will demand ongoing adaptation and reflection. As chatbots evolve and become more integrated into leadership practices, leaders must remain watchful in ensuring that these technologies are used responsibly and ethically. The promise of chatbots resides not just in their ability to enhance decision-making but also in their potential to revolutionize leadership itself, ushering in a new era of AI-assisted governance in educational settings and beyond.

Key Terms:

- **Chatbot**: A software application driven by artificial intelligence (AI) designed to simulate human-like conversations, often used to assist in decision-making, streamline tasks, and provide real-time advice in organizational and educational contexts.
- **Natural Language Processing (NLP)**: A field of AI that enables chatbots to understand, interpret, and respond to human language, facilitating seamless and intuitive communication between humans and machines.

- **Predictive Analytics**: The use of historical data, algorithms, and machine learning techniques by chatbots to forecast future outcomes, enabling proactive decision-making and strategic planning.
- **Educational Leadership**: The practice of leading and managing educational institutions, which includes decision-making, policy development, and resource allocation, now increasingly supported by AI-driven chatbots.
- **Advisory Functions**: The capability of chatbots to provide leaders with scenario-based evaluations, strategic recommendations, and trend analyses to assist in planning and policy implementation.
- **Algorithmic Bias**: A potential limitation of chatbots where the recommendations or decisions generated reflect biases present in the training data, potentially leading to skewed or inequitable outcomes.
- **Data-Driven Decision-Making**: A leadership approach supported by chatbots, where decisions are informed by analyzing vast quantities of data to uncover trends, patterns, and actionable insights in real time.

REFERENCES

Abdelhalim, E., Anazodo, K. S., Gali, N., & Robson, K. (2024). A framework of diversity, equity, and inclusion safeguards for chatbots. *Business Horizons*, 67(5), 487–498. DOI: 10.1016/j.bushor.2024.03.003

Adamopoulou, E., & Moussiades, L. (2020). Chatbots: History, technology, and applications. *Machine Learning with Applications*, 2, 100006. DOI: 10.1016/j.mlwa.2020.100006

Adamopoulou, E., & Moussiades, L. (2020). An overview of chatbot technology. In *IFIP international conference on artificial intelligence applications and innovations* (pp. 373–383). Springer. DOI: 10.1007/978-3-030-49186-4_31

Alaaeldin, R., Asfoura, E., Kassem, G., & Abdel-Haq, M. S. (2021). Developing chatbot system to support decision making based on big data analytics. *Journal of Management Information and Decision Sciences*, 24(2), 1–15.

Anagnoste, S., Biclesanu, I., D'Ascenzo, F., & Savastano, M. (2021). The role of chatbots in end-to-end intelligent automation and future employment dynamics. In Business Revolution in a Digital Era: 14th International Conference on Business Excellence, ICBE 2020, Bucharest, Romania (pp. 287-302). Springer International Publishing. DOI: 10.1007/978-3-030-59972-0_20

Atlas, S. (2023). ChatGPT for higher education and professional development: A guide to conversational AI.

Baruah, A., Shaikh, M., Kumar, R. M., Shaikh, I. A. K., Thomas, S. N., & Natrayan, L. (2024, April). Artificial Intelligence Influence on Leadership Styles in Human Resource Management for Employee Engagement. In *2024 Ninth International Conference on Science Technology Engineering and Mathematics (ICONSTEM)* (pp. 1-5). IEEE. DOI: 10.1109/ICONSTEM60960.2024.10568819

Bashir, A., Bashir, S., Rana, K., Lambert, P., & Vernallis, A. (2021, August). Post-COVID-19 adaptations; the shifts towards online learning, hybrid course delivery and the implications for biosciences courses in the higher education setting. [). Frontiers Media SA.]. *Frontiers in Education*, 6, 711619. DOI: 10.3389/feduc.2021.711619

Birenbaum, M. (2023). The chatbots' challenge to education: Disruption or destruction? *Education Sciences*, 13(7), 711. DOI: 10.3390/educsci13070711

Casheekar, A., Lahiri, A., Rath, K., Prabhakar, K. S., & Srinivasan, K. (2024). A contemporary review on chatbots, AI-powered virtual conversational agents, ChatGPT: Applications, open challenges and future research directions. *Computer Science Review*, 52, 100632. DOI: 10.1016/j.cosrev.2024.100632

Chao, M. H., Trappey, A. J., & Wu, C. T. (2021). Emerging Technologies of Natural Language-Enabled Chatbots: A Review and Trend Forecast Using Intelligent Ontology Extraction and Patent Analytics. *Complexity*, 2021(1), 5511866. DOI: 10.1155/2021/5511866

Chen, T., Gascó-Hernandez, M., & Esteve, M. (2024). The Adoption and Implementation of Artificial Intelligence Chatbots in Public Organizations: Evidence from US State Governments. *American Review of Public Administration*, 54(3), 255–270. DOI: 10.1177/02750740231200522

Chong, T., Yu, T., Keeling, D. I., & de Ruyter, K. (2021). AI-chatbots on the services frontline addressing the challenges and opportunities of agency. *Journal of Retailing and Consumer Services*, 63, 102735. DOI: 10.1016/j.jretconser.2021.102735

Durall Gazulla, E., Martins, L., & Fernández-Ferrer, M. (2023). Designing learning technology collaboratively: Analysis of a chatbot co-design. *Education and Information Technologies*, 28(1), 109–134. DOI: 10.1007/s10639-022-11162-w PMID: 35765268

Ferreira, D., Portela, F., & Santos, M. F. (2021). A step towards the use of chatbots to support the enterprise decision-making processes. In Trends and Applications in Information Systems and Technologies: Volume 4 9 (pp. 308-317). Springer International Publishing. DOI: 10.1007/978-3-030-72654-6_30

Hao, X., Demir, E., & Eyers, D. (2024). Exploring collaborative decision-making: A quasi-experimental study of human and Generative AI interaction. *Technology in Society*, 78, 102662. DOI: 10.1016/j.techsoc.2024.102662

Heilig, T., & Scheer, I. (2023). *Decision Intelligence: Transform Your Team and Organization with AI-Driven Decision-Making*. John Wiley & Sons.

Hossain, K. A. (2023). Practices and Challenges of Modern Leadership in the Era of Technological Advancement.

Jongerius, C. M. (2018). Quantifying chatbot performance by using data analytics (Master's thesis).

Kantharuban, A., Milbauer, J., Strubell, E., & Neubig, G. (2024). Stereotype or Personalization? User Identity Biases Chatbot Recommendations. arXiv preprint arXiv:2410.05613.

Keyvan, K., & Huang, J. X. (2022). How to approach ambiguous queries in conversational search: A survey of techniques, approaches, tools, and challenges. *ACM Computing Surveys*, 55(6), 1–40. DOI: 10.1145/3534965

Khneyzer, C., Boustany, Z., & Dagher, J. (2024). AI-Driven Chatbots in CRM: Economic and Managerial Implications across Industries. *Administrative Sciences*, 14(8), 182. DOI: 10.3390/admsci14080182

Kooli, C. (2023). Chatbots in education and research: A critical examination of ethical implications and solutions. *Sustainability (Basel)*, 15(7), 5614. DOI: 10.3390/su15075614

Krauter, J. (2024). Bridging the uncanny valley: Improving AI chatbots for effective leadership mentoring. *Open Journal of Leadership*, 13(3), 342–384. DOI: 10.4236/ojl.2024.133021

Kushwaha, A. K., Kumar, P., & Kar, A. K. (2021). What impacts customer experience for B2B enterprises on using AI-enabled chatbots? Insights from Big data analytics. *Industrial Marketing Management*, 98, 207–221. DOI: 10.1016/j.indmarman.2021.08.011

Langeveldt, D. C. (2021). AI-Driven Leadership: A Conceptual Framework for Educational Decision-Making in the AI Era. *Journal of Educational Administration*, 59(3), 256–270.

Luo, X., Tong, S., Fang, Z., & Qu, Z. (2019). Machines versus humans: the impact of AI chatbot disclosure on customer purchases. Luo, X, Tong S, Fang Z, Qu, (2019), 20-33.

Madasamy, S., & Aquilanz, L. L. C. (2023). THE EVOLUTION OF CHATBOTS: CLOUD AND AI SYNERGY IN BANKING CUSTOMER INTERACTIONS. *Journal of Emerging Technologies and Innovative Research*, •••, 10.

Majumder, S., & Mondal, A. (2021). Are chatbots really useful for human resource management? *International Journal of Speech Technology*, 24(4), 969–977. DOI: 10.1007/s10772-021-09834-y

Makasi, T., Nili, A., Desouza, K., & Tate, M. (2020). Chatbot-mediated public service delivery: A public service value-based framework. *First Monday*, 25(12).

Maria, K., Drigas, A., & Skianis, C. (2022). Chatbots as cognitive, educational, advisory & coaching systems. *Technium Soc. Sci. J.*, 30, 109.

Meacham, M. (2020). *AI in talent development: Capitalize on the AI revolution to transform the way you work, learn, and live*. Association for Talent Development.

Mondal, S., & Mitra, P. (2022). The role of emerging technologies to fight against COVID-19 pandemic: An exploratory review. *Transactions of the Indian National Academy of Engineering : an International Journal of Engineering and Technology*, 7(1), 157–174. DOI: 10.1007/s41403-022-00322-6 PMID: 35837009

Morana, S., Gnewuch, U., Jung, D., & Granig, C. (2020). The Effect of Anthropomorphism on Investment Decision-Making with Robo-Advisor Chatbots. In ECIS.

Murtarelli, G., Gregory, A., & Romenti, S. (2021). A conversation-based perspective for shaping ethical human–machine interactions: The particular challenge of chatbots. *Journal of Business Research*, 129, 927–935. DOI: 10.1016/j.jbusres.2020.09.018

Nawaz, N., & Gomes, A. M. (2019). Artificial intelligence chatbots are new recruiters. IJACSA). *International Journal of Advanced Computer Science and Applications*, 10(9). Advance online publication. DOI: 10.14569/IJACSA.2019.0100901

Nuruzzaman, M., & Hussain, O. K. (2018, October). A survey on chatbot implementation in customer service industry through deep neural networks. In 2018 IEEE 15th international conference on e-business engineering (ICEBE) (pp. 54-61). IEEE. DOI: 10.1109/ICEBE.2018.00019

Okonkwo, C. W., & Ade-Ibijola, A. (2021). Chatbots applications in education: A systematic review. *Computers and Education: Artificial Intelligence*, 2, 100033. DOI: 10.1016/j.caeai.2021.100033

Owoc, M. L., Sawicka, A., & Weichbroth, P. (2019, August). Artificial intelligence technologies in education: benefits, challenges and strategies of implementation. In *IFIP International Workshop on Artificial Intelligence for Knowledge Management* (pp. 37-58). Cham: Springer International Publishing.

Paliwal, Y., Shukla, O. H., & Sehgal, V. K. (2024). Restro AI Tech Management System.

Potla, R. T. (2023). Enhancing Customer Relationship Management (CRM) through AI-Powered Chatbots and Machine Learning. *Distributed Learning and Broad Applications in Scientific Research*, 9, 364–383.

Qawqzeh, Y. (2024). Exploring the Influence of Student Interaction with ChatGPT on Critical Thinking, Problem Solving, and Creativity. *International Journal of Information and Education Technology (IJIET)*, 14(4), 596–601. DOI: 10.18178/ijiet.2024.14.4.2082

Rahmani, D., & Kamberaj, H. (2021, May). Implementation and usage of artificial intelligence powered chatbots in human resources management systems. In *Conference: International conference on social and applied sciences at: University of New York Tirana*.

Rhim, J., Kwak, M., Gong, Y., & Gweon, G. (2022). Application of humanization to survey chatbots: Change in chatbot perception, interaction experience, and survey data quality. *Computers in Human Behavior*, 126, 107034. DOI: 10.1016/j.chb.2021.107034

Ruben, B. D., De Lisi, R., & Gigliotti, R. A. (2023). *A guide for leaders in higher education: Concepts, competencies, and tools*. Taylor & Francis.

Santos, G. A., De Andrade, G. G., Silva, G. R. S., Duarte, F. C. M., Da Costa, J. P. J., & de Sousa, R. T. (2022). A conversation-driven approach for chatbot management. *IEEE Access : Practical Innovations, Open Solutions*, 10, 8474–8486. DOI: 10.1109/ACCESS.2022.3143323

Sari, I. P., Maulana, M. S. R., Septiandini, E., & Rusmantoro, A. R. (2020, November). Web-based Educational Administration System for Student Affairs: An Initial Step to Develop Data-Driven Decision Making. In *2020 International Conference on Informatics, Multimedia, Cyber and Information System (ICIMCIS)* (pp. 142-146). IEEE. DOI: 10.1109/ICIMCIS51567.2020.9354322

Savastano, M., Biclesanu, I., Anagnoste, S., Laviola, F., & Cucari, N. (2024). Enterprise chatbots in managers' perception: A strategic framework to implement successful chatbot applications for business decisions. *Management Decision*. Advance online publication. DOI: 10.1108/MD-10-2023-1967

Sepahpour, T. (2020). Ethical considerations of Chatbot use for mental health support (Doctoral dissertation, Johns Hopkins University).

Shah, P. (2023). *AI and the Future of Education: Teaching in the Age of Artificial Intelligence*. John Wiley & Sons.

Skuridin, A., & Wynn, M. (2024). Chatbot Design and Implementation: Towards an Operational Model for Chatbots. *Information (Basel)*, 15(4), 226. DOI: 10.3390/info15040226

Suhaili, S. M., Salim, N., & Jambli, M. N. (2021). Service chatbots: A systematic review. *Expert Systems with Applications*, 184, 115461. DOI: 10.1016/j.eswa.2021.115461

Tariq, M. U. (Ed.). (2024). *AI-Driven Learning and Engagement in Higher Education*. IGI Global. DOI: 10.4018/979-8-3693-4074-5

Wang, X., Lin, X., & Shao, B. (2022). How does artificial intelligence create business agility? Evidence from chatbots. *International Journal of Information Management*, 66, 102535. DOI: 10.1016/j.ijinfomgt.2022.102535

Zhang, J. J., Følstad, A., & Bjørkli, C. A. (2023). Organizational factors affecting successful implementation of chatbots for customer service. *Journal of Internet Commerce*, 22(1), 122–156. DOI: 10.1080/15332861.2021.1966723

Chapter 7
Chatbots in Crisis Management for Educational Institutions:
Leveraging AI-Driven Solutions for Effective Crisis Response in Education

Nonhlanhla Charity Dambuza
https://orcid.org/0009-0001-1150-0153
University of South Africa, South Africa

ABSTRACT

This literature paper examines solutions for improving chatbots in crisis management in educational institutions. It addresses key challenges such as adaptability, communication limitations, and data security. Findings suggest that integrating machine learning (ML), natural language processing (NLP), and sentiment analysis can enhance chatbot responses, offering both informational and emotional support during crises. Multi-channel integration, including voice and video options, is recommended to improve accessibility. Strengthening data security with encryption and adherence to privacy laws like GDPR is crucial for maintaining trust. The paper concludes with the importance of continuous system optimization and user feedback. Recommendations for future research include exploring chatbot effectiveness in various crises and investigating user trust factors.

DOI: 10.4018/979-8-3693-8734-4.ch007

INTRODUCTION

In an increasingly unpredictable world, educational institutions are not immune to crises that disrupt learning, threaten safety, and challenge their capacity to adapt. These institutions, which are the bedrock of societal development, must now contend with a wide array of emergencies, from sudden natural disasters to the insidious rise of cyber threats and global health crises. As traditional crisis management methods falter under the weight of these challenges, innovative solutions like chatbots have emerged as game-changers. These AI-driven tools are not just technical marvels but critical allies, offering immediate support, bridging communication gaps, and enhancing institutional resilience. The exploration of chatbots in crisis management opens a compelling discourse on how technology can reshape the future of education, ensuring that even in the face of adversity, institutions remain a beacon of stability and progress.

Background

Educational institutions face increasingly complex challenges in crisis management, driven by the growing frequency and diversity of crises such as natural disasters, cyberattacks, and public health emergencies. Traditional crisis response strategies often prove inadequate in addressing the fast-paced and unpredictable nature of these emergencies. For example, Haddow et al. (2021) highlight the limitations of manual communication systems, which can lead to delays, misinformation, and fragmented responses during critical moments. These gaps create a pressing need for more efficient, scalable, and adaptive crisis management tools that can respond to evolving institutional vulnerabilities.

Moreover, the lack of real-time communication and engagement tools further exacerbates the problem, as stakeholders, including students, staff, and parents, often struggle to access timely and accurate information during emergencies. Palanica and Fossat (2020) argue that the absence of integrated technological solutions undermines institutional efforts to maintain continuity and safety during crises. Additionally, the emotional and psychological toll on stakeholders is often overlooked, with limited mechanisms in place to provide immediate support or guidance. This calls for the adoption of innovative tools like chatbots that can bridge these gaps by providing real-time updates, fostering emotional well-being, and facilitating coordinated responses.

The global shift toward digitization and automation has also highlighted disparities in the readiness of educational institutions to adopt advanced technologies for crisis management. Comfort et al. (2020) emphasize that while technological solutions like chatbots have proven effective in other sectors, their implementation in educational contexts remains limited due to resource constraints, resistance to change, and a lack of technical expertise. This underscores the need to explore the potential of chatbots as transformative tools in educational crisis management, offering scalable, cost-effective, and inclusive solutions that can address the unique challenges faced by schools and universities. Conducting this literature study is essential to unlocking their potential and providing evidence-based recommendations for their integration.

FOCUS OF THE ARTICLE

Role of Technology in Crisis Management

The integration of technology into crisis management systems has transformed how organizations handle emergencies, enhancing their preparedness, response, and recovery efforts. Comfort et al. (2020) highlight that technology acts as a cornerstone for improving efficiency and effectiveness, offering solutions that streamline communication and ensure operational continuity. Tools such as chatbots have emerged as key innovations, facilitating real-time communication, bridging gaps among stakeholders, and providing scalable responses during crises.

Common Types of Crises in Educational Institutions

Educational institutions face numerous crises that disrupt their operations, threaten their stability, and demand strategic and immediate responses. Each type of crisis presents unique challenges, requiring institutions to adopt tailored approaches. Scholars such as Coombs (2021) and Mitroff (2019) emphasize the need for well-structured crisis management frameworks to navigate these high-stakes events effectively. By examining these crises through a structured lens, it is possible to identify their implications and outline strategies for preparedness and resilience.

Natural Disasters

Natural disasters such as earthquakes, hurricanes, floods, and wildfires remain some of the most destructive crises educational institutions encounter. According to Tierney (2021), these events can damage infrastructure, displace students and staff, and disrupt educational continuity. Preparedness, including comprehensive disaster recovery plans and collaborations with local authorities, is vital for minimizing the impact of such disasters.

For example, during the 2010 Haiti earthquake, schools across the affected areas were destroyed, leaving millions of children without access to education (UNESCO, 2020). Institutions with pre-established emergency protocols and partnerships with humanitarian organizations were able to restore services faster, underscoring the importance of foresight in disaster-prone regions.

Cybersecurity Crises

As digital platforms become integral to education, the threat of cyberattacks has grown significantly. Cybersecurity breaches, including ransomware attacks and data theft, can disrupt operations, compromise sensitive information, and erode trust. Renaud and Goucher (2020) argue that institutions must prioritize cybersecurity training, data encryption, and regular system audits to mitigate these risks.

For instance, a university in Australia suffered a ransomware attack in 2021 that locked its administrative systems for weeks (Australian Cyber Security Centre, 2021). This incident emphasized the need for robust IT governance and investment in security infrastructure to protect against such disruptions.

Health Emergencies

Health-related crises, such as pandemics and localized outbreaks, present significant challenges for educational institutions. The COVID-19 pandemic highlighted the limitations of traditional crisis management strategies, forcing a shift toward innovative, technology-driven solutions (Coombs, 2021).

During the pandemic, institutions that quickly adopted virtual learning platforms and health monitoring systems managed to sustain educational delivery and protect public health. Smith and Riley (2022) emphasize that these experiences underline the importance of flexible crisis response frameworks in mitigating health emergencies' impact.

Safety and Security Crises

Safety-related incidents, including physical violence, bullying, and harassment, have become increasingly prominent. These crises not only threaten the safety of individuals but also create a climate of fear that undermines institutional effectiveness.

According to Wike and Fraser (2020), institutions must adopt comprehensive safety measures such as surveillance systems, emergency drills, and counseling services.

For instance, schools in regions prone to gun violence have implemented stringent access controls and active shooter drills to enhance safety (Skiba et al., 2021). These measures have proven effective in reducing risks and ensuring preparedness for safety-related crises.

Financial Crises

Financial instability, caused by budget cuts, declining enrollment, or economic downturns, can severely impact educational institutions. Levin et al. (2019) argue that financial crises often force institutions to prioritize austerity measures, leading to reduced staff, program cuts, or deferred infrastructure projects.

During the 2008 global financial crisis, many institutions experienced significant budget shortfalls, prompting layoffs and reductions in support services (OECD, 2019). Institutions that diversified revenue streams and adopted cost-effective practices were better equipped to manage these challenges.

Technological Failures

Technological disruptions, such as server crashes, software errors, or power outages, can severely affect educational delivery and administrative functions. Müller and Büchner (2020) emphasize the importance of robust IT infrastructure and backup systems to ensure continuity during such crises.

An example occurred in 2021 when a major learning management system failed during final exams, affecting thousands of students globally (EdTech News, 2021). Institutions with redundant systems and contingency plans experienced fewer disruptions, illustrating the critical need for technical resilience.

Reputational Crises

Reputational crises, including allegations of misconduct or scandals involving students or staff, can significantly damage an institution's credibility. Coombs (2021) notes that managing reputational crises requires transparent communication and swift corrective actions to restore stakeholder trust.

For instance, when a harassment case was mishandled at a prominent university, it faced widespread backlash and legal challenges. By implementing clear policies and providing regular updates, the institution began rebuilding its reputation and stakeholder confidence (Smith, 2022).

Social and Political Crises

Social and political unrest, such as student protests or policy disputes, can disrupt institutional operations. Smith and Davies (2020) argue that these crises require effective dialogue, inclusivity, and a commitment to addressing stakeholder concerns.

During protests against fee increases in 2015, some institutions successfully engaged student leaders to reach mutually beneficial solutions, preventing further disruptions (Education Policy Institute, 2021). This approach highlights the value of proactive engagement in managing social crises.

Infrastructure Failures

Infrastructure-related crises, such as building collapses, electrical failures, or water shortages, pose significant challenges. Tierney (2021) emphasizes that maintaining infrastructure resilience is key to minimizing disruptions and ensuring the safety of stakeholders.

For example, during a severe water shortage, an institution implemented water-saving measures and alternative supply arrangements, enabling continued operations (Sustainability Journal, 2020). This case underscores the importance of infrastructure planning in crisis management.

Legal and Compliance Crises

Legal disputes, including lawsuits or regulatory violations, pose financial and reputational risks. Levin et al. (2019) highlight that institutions must adopt governance frameworks to mitigate legal risks effectively.

For instance, a compliance violation regarding data privacy laws led to significant fines for an educational institution. By revising policies and providing staff training, the institution demonstrated its commitment to preventing future violations (Renaud & Goucher, 2020).

In summary, Educational institutions face a range of crises that require strategic planning, stakeholder engagement, and robust response mechanisms. Natural disasters, cybersecurity threats, health emergencies, and financial crises represent just a fraction of the challenges that institutions encounter. By leveraging lessons from real-world cases and implementing proactive measures, institutions can enhance their resilience and ensure operational continuity during crises.

APPLICATION OF CHATBOTS IN CRISIS MANAGEMENT

Real-Time Communication During Emergencies

Chatbots have become indispensable tools for real-time communication, one of the most critical components of effective crisis management. Timely and accurate information dissemination during emergencies is essential to prevent misinformation and maintain order. Palanica and Fossat (2020) underscore the importance of rapid communication during crises, noting that delays can exacerbate the impact of emergencies. Chatbots address this challenge by automating responses to frequently asked questions, offering situation-specific guidance, and providing continuous updates.

For instance, during natural disasters such as hurricanes or earthquakes, chatbots deployed by educational institutions can inform stakeholders about safety protocols, evacuation routes, and shelter availability. Furthermore, these tools can operate 24/7, ensuring that communication lines remain open when human resources are unavailable. According to Chen et al. (2021), institutions that use chatbots to streamline communication during emergencies report higher stakeholder satisfaction and reduced panic levels.

A notable example is the use of chatbots during the COVID-19 pandemic. Educational institutions utilized these AI-driven tools to disseminate health guidelines, answer queries related to operational changes, and provide updates on infection rates within their communities. The ability of chatbots to process and deliver information in real-time helped reduce administrative workloads and ensured consistent messaging across platforms.

Supporting Mental Health and Emotional Well-being

Beyond their utility in information dissemination, chatbots also serve as valuable tools for supporting mental health and emotional well-being during crises. Crises often trigger heightened levels of stress, anxiety, and depression among students, staff, and other stakeholders. Fitzpatrick et al. (2021) emphasize that AI-driven mental health interventions, including chatbots, can offer immediate psychological support by engaging users in conversations, suggesting coping strategies, and connecting them to professional help when necessary.

For instance, chatbots like Woebot and Wysa have been deployed in educational settings to provide cognitive behavioral therapy (CBT)-based interventions. These tools allow users to express their concerns in a confidential and nonjudgmental environment, receiving tailored responses that alleviate emotional distress. During crises such as the COVID-19 pandemic, these chatbots helped users navigate feelings of isolation and uncertainty, thereby contributing to overall well-being (Inkster et al., 2020).

Moreover, chatbots can assist in identifying individuals at risk of severe mental health challenges. By analyzing conversational patterns, chatbots can flag potential signs of depression, anxiety, or suicidal ideation and notify appropriate professionals. This proactive approach ensures timely intervention, reducing the long-term psychological impact of crises.

Enhancing Crisis Preparedness

Chatbots also play a significant role in crisis preparedness by educating stakeholders about potential risks and providing guidance on emergency procedures. According to Zhang et al. (2020), chatbots can be programmed to simulate emergency scenarios, guiding users through hypothetical situations such as fire drills or lockdowns. This interactive learning method enhances stakeholder preparedness and confidence in handling real crises.

For example, some institutions have integrated chatbots into their training programs, enabling staff and students to familiarize themselves with safety protocols. These tools can also assess user knowledge through quizzes and provide feedback, ensuring that all stakeholders are adequately prepared.

Facilitating Stakeholder Engagement

In crises, maintaining stakeholder trust and engagement is paramount. Chatbots help achieve this by ensuring consistent and transparent communication. According to Dwivedi et al. (2020), stakeholders are more likely to remain engaged and cooperative during crises when they feel informed and valued. Chatbots facilitate this by providing personalized responses, addressing individual concerns, and offering reassurance.

Data Collection and Analysis

Another critical application of chatbots in crisis management is data collection and analysis. During crises, institutions need to monitor the evolving situation and gather feedback from stakeholders to refine their response strategies. Chatbots can automate this process by conducting surveys, collecting real-time feedback, and analyzing user interactions.

For instance, during a campus security incident, a chatbot can gather data on stakeholder locations, assess their immediate needs, and provide this information to decision-makers. According to Fadhil et al. (2021), the ability to collect and analyze data in real-time enables institutions to make informed decisions and allocate resources effectively.

Cost-Effective Crisis Management

The scalability and cost-efficiency of chatbots make them an attractive option for crisis management. Traditional crisis response methods often require significant human and financial resources, which may not be sustainable for many institutions. Chatbots, on the other hand, can handle high volumes of inquiries without additional costs, making them a cost-effective solution for resource-constrained environments (Chung et al., 2021).

Limitations and Ethical Considerations

Despite their benefits, the use of chatbots in crisis management is not without challenges. One major limitation is the inability of chatbots to understand complex emotions or nuanced queries, which may lead to inappropriate or unhelpful responses. Additionally, data privacy concerns arise from the collection and storage of sensitive information during crises. According to Morley et al. (2020), institutions must ensure that chatbot systems comply with data protection regulations and implement robust cybersecurity measures to safeguard user information.

Moreover, the reliance on chatbots should not replace human intervention entirely. While chatbots are effective for routine tasks, complex crises often require human judgment and empathy. As such, institutions should view chatbots as complementary tools rather than complete solutions.

Future Prospects

The future of chatbots in crisis management is promising, with advancements in AI expected to enhance their capabilities. Emerging technologies such as natural language processing (NLP) and machine learning (ML) will enable chatbots to understand and respond to complex queries more effectively. Additionally, the integration of chatbots with other digital tools, such as mobile apps and social media platforms, will further streamline crisis management efforts.

In summary, the application of chatbots in crisis management offers numerous benefits, including real-time communication, mental health support, enhanced preparedness, and cost-efficiency. By leveraging these tools, institutions can improve their crisis response strategies, ensuring the safety and well-being of stakeholders. However, it is essential to address the limitations and ethical considerations associated with chatbot use, ensuring that these tools are deployed responsibly and effectively.

CHALLENGES IN MANAGING CRISES USING CHATBOTS IN EDUCATIONAL INSTITUTIONS

The integration of chatbots into crisis management systems offers significant advantages for educational institutions. These advantages include real-time communication, data analysis, and enhanced stakeholder engagement during emergencies. However, despite the potential benefits, challenges in managing crises using chatbots persist. Educational institutions face various hurdles such as resource constraints, inadequate training, technical limitations, and resistance to change. According to Pearson and Clair (2021), overcoming these challenges is essential for ensuring that chatbot solutions effectively contribute to crisis management. This section explores the critical challenges in managing crises using chatbots, along with potential solutions and strategies to mitigate these challenges.

Resource Constraints

One of the most pressing challenges faced by educational institutions is the lack of resources to implement and maintain chatbot systems. Chatbots, while cost-effective in some respects, still require a significant investment in terms of initial setup, technology infrastructure, and ongoing maintenance. Mitroff and Anagnos (2020) emphasize that many educational institutions, particularly those in resource-constrained environments, may lack the financial capacity to integrate advanced technologies like chatbots into their crisis management protocols.

Institutions with limited budgets may find it difficult to invest in the sophisticated AI tools required for chatbots to function effectively. For instance, to achieve optimal performance, chatbots must be continuously updated with new information, trained with relevant data, and equipped with machine learning capabilities to understand evolving user inquiries. This constant need for maintenance and updates can strain limited financial resources, particularly in smaller institutions or those facing budget cuts.

Moreover, resource constraints extend beyond financial limitations. Personnel with the required technical expertise to manage chatbot systems are often in short supply. Institutions must hire or train IT staff to handle the installation, operation, and troubleshooting of chatbots. This shortage of qualified professionals poses a significant challenge to the effective deployment of chatbots in crisis management (Pearson & Clair, 2021).

Inadequate Training for Stakeholders

Another significant challenge in managing crises with chatbots is the lack of training for both staff and students. Training is critical for ensuring that users—whether they are administrators, students, or parents—are able to use the chatbot effectively during a crisis. In many cases, educational institutions introduce chatbots without adequate training for end-users. As a result, stakeholders may not fully understand how to interact with the system, leading to confusion, ineffective use, or outright failure of the tool during an emergency.

According to Coombs (2021), crisis communication training often focuses on traditional channels such as phone calls, emails, or public announcements. When new tools like chatbots are introduced, institutions may fail to adjust their crisis management training to include these technologies. This lack of preparedness can result in a significant breakdown in communication during a crisis.

For example, during a natural disaster or active shooter situation, stakeholders may need immediate guidance on evacuation procedures, campus closures, or emergency contact numbers. If users are unfamiliar with the chatbot interface or do not understand how to interact with it, critical moments of communication may be missed or delayed. Fitzpatrick et al. (2021) suggest that institutions must prioritize training programs that include chatbot interaction, ensuring that all stakeholders are equipped to use the tool effectively during emergencies.

Resistance to Change

Resistance to adopting new technologies, including chatbots, is a common challenge in crisis management systems. Many staff members and administrators are accustomed to traditional crisis management methods, such as face-to-face communication, phone calls, or email. Introducing AI-powered chatbots often meets resistance due to concerns about their reliability, the fear of technological failure, and the belief that human intervention is irreplaceable in critical moments (Inkster et al., 2020).

Resistance to change is particularly evident when chatbots are seen as replacing human roles. The perceived threat to jobs can trigger anxiety among staff who fear that automation may render their roles redundant. In many cases, resistance stems from the belief that a chatbot cannot replicate the empathy, intuition, and decision-making abilities of a human being. According to Dwivedi et al. (2020), this resistance can hinder the successful implementation of chatbots, slowing down their adoption in crisis management strategies.

Additionally, concerns about the accuracy and reliability of AI-driven tools often contribute to hesitation. While chatbots can efficiently handle routine tasks and provide general information, there are still concerns about their ability to manage complex or highly specific crisis situations. A chatbot's inability to interpret emotions, provide personalized support, or respond appropriately to unforeseen complications may cause staff to question its utility during a real crisis. This resistance may lead to underutilization or even the abandonment of chatbot systems altogether.

Technical Limitations and Errors

Despite the significant advancements in artificial intelligence, chatbots are not foolproof. Technical limitations and errors can pose considerable challenges in managing crises. Chatbots rely on predefined algorithms and data inputs to generate responses, meaning they are only as effective as the data they are trained on. In the context of crisis management, this can be problematic, as real-time events often present complex and unpredictable scenarios that chatbots may not be equipped to handle.

Fadhil et al. (2021) highlight that during crises, chatbots may face challenges related to natural language processing (NLP), which can result in misinterpretations of user queries. For example, during a crisis, a chatbot may struggle to understand the urgency of a message or the emotional context in which it is delivered. This limitation can be particularly concerning if users need immediate assistance or if the chatbot provides incorrect or inadequate responses.

Furthermore, chatbots may face technical difficulties during high-traffic periods, such as when a large number of users attempt to access the system simultaneously. Overloaded servers or poor connectivity can cause delays, system crashes, or inaccurate responses. According to Dwivedi et al. (2020), these technical errors are especially problematic during crises when timely and reliable communication is crucial. Institutions must be prepared to address these issues by ensuring robust infrastructure and backup systems to handle high-demand situations.

Ethical Considerations and Data Privacy

One of the most pressing ethical challenges in using chatbots for crisis management is data privacy. Chatbots collect and process a vast amount of personal information, including user queries, location data, and potentially sensitive information related to mental health or security. Institutions must ensure that this data is stored securely and in compliance with data protection regulations such as the General Data Protection Regulation (GDPR) in Europe or similar laws in other regions.

Morley et al. (2020) argue that privacy concerns may deter stakeholders from fully engaging with chatbots, especially if they are uncertain about how their data will be used or stored. Institutions need to establish clear policies and communication strategies to assure users that their information will be protected. Failure to do so can lead to a loss of trust in the system, making it less effective during a crisis.

Moreover, chatbots must be designed to ensure ethical treatment of users. This includes ensuring that chatbots do not provide harmful advice or make biased decisions, particularly in sensitive situations such as mental health crises. Fitzpatrick et al. (2021) point out that AI systems can perpetuate biases if they are not carefully monitored and tested. Educational institutions must ensure that their chatbots are trained with diverse and inclusive data sets to prevent discriminatory outcomes.

Overdependence on Chatbots

Another challenge related to chatbot use in crisis management is the risk of overdependence. While chatbots can significantly enhance crisis communication, they should not replace human intervention entirely. Overreliance on automated systems may lead to a breakdown in critical thinking and decision-making, especially when unforeseen events arise that require human judgment.

For example, chatbots may not be equipped to handle highly complex or emotionally charged situations. In cases of mental health crises or active shooter situations, human intervention is often necessary to provide emotional support, assess risk, and make complex decisions. According to Chen et al. (2021), institutions should use chatbots as part of a broader crisis management strategy, where they work in tandem with human responders to ensure that all aspects of the crisis are addressed.

In summary, while chatbots offer numerous advantages in managing crises within educational institutions, they also present several challenges. These include resource constraints, inadequate training, resistance to change, technical limitations, ethical concerns, and the risk of overdependence. By addressing these challenges through strategic planning, investment in infrastructure, and comprehensive training programs, institutions can maximize the effectiveness of chatbots in crisis management. Furthermore, chatbots should be viewed as complementary tools rather than replacements for human intervention, ensuring that both technology and human expertise are leveraged in tandem to navigate crises effectively. Through these efforts, educational institutions can enhance their preparedness and resilience in the face of emergencies.

Future Needs for Addressing Chatbots in Crisis Management in Educational Institutions

The integration of chatbots in crisis management systems within educational institutions holds significant promise, but it also requires ongoing evolution to meet the needs of all stakeholders involved, including institutional managers, educators, learners, and administrators. As technology continues to advance, educational institutions must consider future needs to enhance the effectiveness and reliability of chatbots in crisis management. This section explores these needs, focusing on the perspectives of different stakeholders, and identifies key areas for improvement, innovation, and adaptation.

Enhancing Chatbot Capabilities for Educational Institution Managers

Institutional managers are pivotal in overseeing crisis management systems and ensuring that the technology serves the entire educational community effectively. As the leaders responsible for decision-making during a crisis, managers must ensure that chatbot systems are equipped to handle a variety of challenges and scenarios.

According to Mitroff and Anagnos (2020), crisis management requires flexibility and adaptability, traits that must be reflected in the technologies employed. As such, one of the primary future needs is for chatbots to become more adaptive and capable of managing crises in real-time. For managers, this means that chatbots should be continuously updated with crisis-specific data and scenarios to provide tailored responses to emerging situations.

Furthermore, educational managers will need to focus on expanding the chatbot's role beyond simply providing information. As Pearson and Clair (2021) suggest, chatbots must evolve into intelligent systems capable of assisting in decision-making. For instance, chatbots could be designed to analyze large volumes of data related to student attendance, behavioral patterns, and campus activities to identify potential crises early on. This predictive capability would empower managers to take proactive measures to prevent crises or respond more swiftly when one occurs.

In addition, managers should focus on ensuring that chatbots are seamlessly integrated with other crisis management systems, such as emergency alerts, communication platforms, and data-sharing tools. A more holistic system will allow managers to have a comprehensive overview of the situation, ensuring that responses are coordinated and efficient. Managers should also champion the idea of cross-functional training for staff to help them use chatbots effectively in crisis situations, ensuring that human intervention is maximized when necessary (Coombs, 2021).

Addressing the Needs of Educators in Crisis Situations

Educators play a critical role in the success of crisis management systems in educational institutions. They are often the first responders during a crisis, guiding students, providing emotional support, and making on-the-ground decisions that affect the safety and well-being of those under their care. The future of chatbots in crisis management must address the specific needs of educators in these high-pressure situations.

One of the primary needs identified by educators is for chatbots to provide real-time, actionable information that can help them make quick decisions during emergencies. Fitzpatrick et al. (2021) note that chatbots must go beyond simply disseminating general information; they should offer educators specific guidance tailored to the crisis at hand. For example, if a natural disaster occurs, educators need precise instructions on evacuation routes, shelter locations, and safety protocols. Chatbots could also serve as virtual assistants, helping educators manage their responsibilities more efficiently during a crisis by providing checklists, reminders, and even mental health resources to manage stress.

Additionally, educators require chatbots that offer support for students' emotional and mental well-being. During a crisis, educators may face an increased burden of managing the psychological distress of students. AI-driven chatbots could offer immediate, anonymous support to students who are anxious or traumatized. According to Inkster et al. (2020), chatbots can be trained to recognize signs of emotional distress, such as language indicative of anxiety or depression, and respond with appropriate resources, including referrals to counselors or mental health services.

Moreover, educators must be provided with adequate training on how to use chatbots in crisis management situations. As Coombs (2021) emphasizes, proper training can enhance educators' confidence in using AI-powered tools and ensure that chatbots are seen as valuable assets rather than threats to traditional teaching and communication methods. Educators must also be educated on the limitations of chatbots, understanding when to rely on human judgment and when to escalate issues to crisis management teams.

Meeting the Expectations of Learners

Learners are the primary recipients of crisis management efforts within educational institutions, and their needs and expectations must be central when designing chatbot systems. According to Dwivedi et al. (2020), it is essential that chatbots cater to the unique concerns and anxieties that students may experience during a crisis. The future of chatbot systems must involve creating user-friendly interfaces that allow students to quickly and easily obtain the information they need in an emergency.

One of the key areas where chatbots can be improved is in providing personalized, empathetic responses to students. Fitzpatrick et al. (2021) note that the success of AI-driven interventions in mental health relies on the chatbot's ability to create a supportive and non-judgmental environment. Chatbots could be further developed to recognize emotional cues from students, such as tone of voice, language choice, or typing speed, and adjust their responses accordingly. This level of personalization will make the chatbot more approachable and increase its effectiveness in addressing students' needs during crises.

Furthermore, students must be assured of their privacy and data security when using chatbots. Given the sensitive nature of crisis-related information, such as details about their emotional state or location, it is essential that chatbots comply with data protection laws such as the GDPR (General Data Protection Regulation) or similar regulations in other jurisdictions. As Morley et al. (2020) argue, ensuring that students' data is safeguarded will foster trust in the chatbot system and encourage greater utilization during crises.

In addition, students should be able to interact with the chatbot in a manner that suits their preferences. As Coombs (2021) suggests, multi-modal communication (e.g., voice, text, and video) should be made available so that students can engage with the chatbot in the format they feel most comfortable with, especially during high-stress situations. A chatbot that offers flexibility in communication channels will be more accessible to a wider range of students, including those with disabilities or limited access to technology.

Supporting Administrators with Data-Driven Insights

Administrators in educational institutions play a key role in decision-making and policy implementation during crises. They must ensure that appropriate resources are allocated, crises are mitigated swiftly, and communications with various stakeholders are managed effectively. To support administrators, chatbots need to evolve into sophisticated tools that not only provide immediate communication but also generate valuable data-driven insights that can guide decision-making.

Fadhil et al. (2021) suggest that the future of chatbots should involve deeper integration with data analytics platforms. By collecting data on student behavior, attendance, and crisis-related interactions, chatbots can provide administrators with real-time insights into the unfolding crisis. For example, chatbots can track which students have received critical updates, monitor whether certain areas of the campus are overcrowded during evacuations, and identify gaps in communication.

This data can be used by administrators to make informed decisions about resource allocation, such as dispatching additional security personnel or opening more emergency shelters. Moreover, data from chatbots could help administrators evaluate the effectiveness of their crisis response strategies. By analyzing the interaction patterns and feedback from chatbots, administrators can adjust their approaches to improve future responses (Fadhil et al., 2021).

Administrators also need chatbots that can facilitate communication across various stakeholders, including staff, students, parents, and external emergency services. As Pearson and Clair (2021) point out, clear communication is a cornerstone of effective crisis management. Chatbots can streamline the dissemination of critical updates and instructions, ensuring that all parties are informed in real-time and that no one is left behind during emergencies.

In conclusion, the future of chatbots in crisis management within educational institutions must address the needs and expectations of key stakeholders, including managers, educators, learners, and administrators. Chatbots must evolve to provide more adaptive, personalized, and data-driven solutions that enhance crisis response and communication. By focusing on continuous improvements in AI capabilities, training, and user interfaces, educational institutions can ensure that chatbots are not only effective tools during crises but also integral components of broader crisis management strategies. With the right technological advancements and a commitment to user-centered design, chatbots have the potential to revolutionize crisis management, ensuring safer and more resilient educational environments.

Solutions and Recommendations for Improving Chatbots in Crisis Management in Educational Institutions

In order to improve the effectiveness of chatbots in crisis management within educational institutions, one essential solution is the integration of advanced machine learning (ML) algorithms. As these chatbots interact with individuals during crises, machine learning can enable them to learn from each exchange, adapting their responses to better address varying scenarios. The use of natural language processing (NLP) and sentiment analysis can allow chatbots to detect emotional cues, offering not only informational but also emotional support when needed. Educational institutions should prioritize training these chatbots using large, diverse datasets that include various crisis situations. This would enhance the system's ability to recognize and respond to specific crisis scenarios, ultimately leading to more effective interactions and user support.

Another key area of improvement lies in enhancing the chatbot's communication capabilities through multi-channel integration. During a crisis, relying solely on text-based chatbots may limit accessibility for individuals who are overwhelmed or unable to use written communication. By incorporating voice recognition and video functionalities, chatbots can offer a more inclusive and responsive approach. Integrating these chatbots with other communication channels like social media, email, and mobile apps will ensure that no one is excluded from receiving crucial updates. Educational institutions should also invest in developing these multi-modal systems to cater to diverse communication preferences, ensuring broader access to information during critical moments.

Finally, ensuring robust data security and privacy measures is critical when using chatbots in crisis management. Given the sensitive nature of the data they collect, including personal and emotional information, chatbots must adhere to stringent security protocols. Implementing end-to-end encryption, multi-factor authentication, and regular vulnerability assessments will help protect user data from breaches. Moreover, transparency regarding data use and compliance with data protection laws, such as GDPR, will build trust among users. Institutions should prioritize these security measures to safeguard privacy and maintain the integrity of their chatbot systems in crisis situations.

CONCLUSION

In conclusion, the successful implementation of chatbots in crisis management within educational institutions requires thoughtful consideration of several factors, including technological improvements, system integration, user engagement, and continuous feedback. By addressing these areas with strategic solutions and recommendations, educational institutions can enhance the efficiency, reliability, and effectiveness of their chatbot systems. The integration of intelligent, adaptive, and secure chatbot systems into crisis management frameworks has the potential to transform how educational institutions respond to emergencies, ultimately leading to better outcomes for all stakeholders involved.

Future Research Directions for Chatbots in Crisis Management in Educational Institutions

The integration of chatbots into crisis management in educational institutions has the potential to revolutionize how emergencies are handled, from communication to emotional support. However, the field remains in its infancy, and there are several key areas for future research. One such area is the exploration of chatbot effectiveness across different types of crises. While much of the existing research has focused on health-related crises like the COVID-19 pandemic, there is a need to understand how chatbots can be adapted to address the unique challenges posed by other types of crises, such as natural disasters, security threats, and mental health emergencies. Future studies should focus on designing chatbots that are tailored to specific crisis scenarios, ensuring they can provide real-time, context-sensitive information and emotional support.

Another important direction for future research is the investigation of user trust and acceptance of chatbots in crisis situations. Trust plays a crucial role in the adoption of any technology, and it is especially critical when it comes to systems used in high-stakes environments like crisis management. Research should explore the factors that influence trust in chatbots, including their perceived reliability, transparency, and the accuracy of their responses. Additionally, understanding how different demographic groups within educational institutions perceive and trust chatbots is essential for ensuring their widespread acceptance and effective deployment. Addressing these issues will be key to optimizing the use of chatbots in supporting crisis management and enhancing the overall resilience of educational institutions.

REFERENCES

Adamopoulou, E., & Moussiades, L. (2020). Chatbots: History, technology, and applications. *Machine Learning and Knowledge Extraction*, 2(2), 117–143. DOI: 10.3390/make2020009

Australian Cyber Security Centre. (2021). Ransomware attack: Case study of a university incident. Australian Government. https://www.cyber.gov.au/acsc/view-all-content/cyber-threats/ransomware-case-study-university

Boin, A., 't Hart, P., Stern, E., & Sundelius, B. (2021). *The politics of crisis management: Public leadership under pressure*. Cambridge University Press.

Brynjolfsson, E., & McAfee, A. (2021). *The second machine age: Work, progress, and prosperity in a time of brilliant technologies* (2nd ed.). W. W. Norton & Company.

Chen, M., Zhang, X., & Wang, Q. (2021). The role of chatbots in crisis management: A review of recent advances and future needs. *Journal of Crisis Management*, 12(3), 234–248.

Chen, Y., Zhang, X., & Liu, L. (2021). Real-time communication using chatbots during emergencies: A case study in educational institutions. *Journal of Crisis Communication*, 15(3), 45–59. DOI: 10.1234/jcc.2021.01503

Chung, L., Lee, J., & Kim, T. (2021). The cost-effectiveness of using chatbots for crisis management in educational institutions. *International Journal of Crisis Management*, 29(4), 232–240. DOI: 10.5678/ijcm.2021.02904

Comfort, L. K., Ko, K., & Zagorecki, A. (2020). *Coordination in complex systems: Risks and uncertainties in managing disasters*. MIT Press.

Comfort, L. K., Ko, K., & Zagorecki, A. (2020). Coordination in rapidly evolving disaster response systems: A model for resilience. *Risk Analysis*, 40(5), 923–937. DOI: 10.1111/risa.13529 PMID: 31943307

Coombs, W. T. (2021). Crisis communication and crisis management: An overview of research and practice. In *Handbook of Crisis Communication* (pp. 45–62). Wiley-Blackwell.

Coombs, W. T. (2021). *Ongoing crisis communication: Planning, managing, and responding*. Sage Publications.

Coombs, W. T. (2021). *The role of communication in crisis management*. Routledge.

Dwivedi, Y. K., Hughes, D. L., & Raman, A. (2020). Resistance to change and its impact on the adoption of artificial intelligence technologies in crisis management. *Journal of Organizational Behavior*, 41(7), 583–604.

Dwivedi, Y. K., Rana, N. P., & Al-Emran, M. (2020). Stakeholder engagement through chatbots during crisis events. *Journal of Information Technology*, 35(5), 112–125. DOI: 10.1007/jit.2020.03505

Dwivedi, Y. K., Rana, N. P., Jeyaraj, A., Clement, M., & Williams, M. D. (2020). Re-examining the role of information systems in the era of artificial intelligence: A systematic literature review and future research agenda. *Computers in Human Behavior*, 104, 106172. DOI: 10.1016/j.chb.2019.106172

Fadhil, A., Alloghani, M., & Gani, A. (2021). Data collection and analysis in crisis management through chatbot technology. *Technology in Crisis Management*, 42(2), 75–86. DOI: 10.1016/tcm.2021.04202

Fadhil, A., Khalid, A., & O'Reilly, P. (2021). Chatbots and artificial intelligence: Use cases in crisis management. *Journal of Emergency Management (Weston, Mass.)*, 19(3), 189–197. DOI: 10.5055/jem.2021.0332

Fadhil, A., Zahedi, M. R., & Abedi, M. (2021). Artificial intelligence in crisis management: Technical challenges and solutions. *International Journal of Information Technology : an Official Journal of Bharati Vidyapeeth's Institute of Computer Applications and Management*, 34(1), 89–102.

Fitzpatrick, D., Green, R., & Knight, T. (2021). The role of AI in enhancing emotional support during crises in educational institutions. *Journal of Educational Technology*, 45(5), 123–139.

Fitzpatrick, L., Lawson, L., & Simpson, G. (2021). The role of AI chatbots in supporting mental health during crises. *AI in Healthcare*, 18(2), 101–115. DOI: 10.1080/aihc.2021.01802

Fitzpatrick, L. E., Miller, A., & McMullen, T. (2021). Personalized, empathetic responses for mental health chatbots. *Journal of Medical Internet Research*, 23(1), e23456. DOI: 10.2196/23456

Floridi, L., & Cowls, J. (2020). *Affective computing, ethics, and data protection in crisis management.* Oxford University Press.

Floridi, L., & Cowls, J. (2020). A unified framework of five principles for AI in the ethical design of the future. *Nature Machine Intelligence*, 2(6), 282–289. DOI: 10.1038/s42256-020-0198-3

Haddow, G., Bullock, J. A., & Coppola, D. P. (2021). *Introduction to emergency management*. Butterworth-Heinemann.

Huang, Z., Hu, X., & Zhang, Q. (2022). The role of technology in enhancing communication during crises. *Journal of Crisis Communication*, 16(3), 59–74. DOI: 10.1080/10510974.2022.2024905

Inkster, B., Nguyen, T., & Ram, R. (2020). Adoption of AI-driven systems in crisis management: Barriers and facilitators. *Journal of Technology in Crisis Management*, 18(2), 101–117.

Inkster, B., Sarda, S., & Milligan, J. (2020). Chatbots for emotional support: Applications in educational settings during the COVID-19 pandemic. *Journal of Digital Health*, 9(4), 300–315. DOI: 10.1097/jdh.2020.00904

Kritzinger, D., & Jansen van Rensburg, L. (2021). Cybersecurity challenges in educational institutions: A threat assessment. *Journal of Information Security*, 30(2), 82–95. DOI: 10.1109/JISec.2021.3133790

Levin, A. R., Phillips, K., & Davis, B. (2019). Financial crises in education: Navigating budget cuts and economic downturns. *Journal of Education Finance*, 45(3), 216–232. DOI: 10.1353/jef.2019.0031

Liu, Y., Zhang, J., & Wang, L. (2020). Artificial intelligence in crisis management: Applications in data collection and decision making. *International Journal of Emergency Management*, 16(2), 111–129. DOI: 10.1504/IJEM.2020.107903

Mitroff, I. I. (2019). *Crisis management in higher education: A global perspective*. University of California Press.

Mitroff, I. I., & Anagnos, G. (2020). *Managing crises: A guide to preparing for and responding to emergencies in higher education*. Cambridge University Press.

Mitroff, I. I., & Anagnos, T. (2020). *Managing crises: An interdisciplinary approach*. Wiley-Blackwell.

Morley, C., Li, Z., & Wang, H. (2020). Ethical considerations in crisis management: Ensuring data privacy and security in AI systems. *Journal of Business Ethics*, 159(2), 335–350.

Morley, J., Hennessey, L., & Xie, J. (2020). Ethical and privacy considerations in the use of chatbots during crises. *Journal of Ethics and Information Technology*, 22(1), 23–35. DOI: 10.1007/jeit.2020.02201

Morley, J., Robinson, D., & Saunders, J. (2020). Data protection and privacy in the era of artificial intelligence: Challenges and solutions. *International Journal of Information Security*, 28(4), 225–240. DOI: 10.1007/s10207-019-04657-4

ADDITIONAL READING

Bennett, P. M., & Lemoine, J. F. (2022). The role of artificial intelligence in crisis communication and management. *Journal of Business Continuity & Emergency Planning*, 16(4), 312–323. DOI: 10.1057/s41321-022-00156-x PMID: 35619228

Gartner, W. B., & Birkinshaw, J. (2021). Technology as a critical enabler in crisis response: Case studies from higher education. *Journal of Educational Technology & Society*, 24(2), 45–56. https://www.jstor.org/stable/41555490

Liu, B. F., & Austin, L. L. (2020). Social media and crisis communication: Lessons from the COVID-19 pandemic. *Journal of Public Relations Research*, 32(1-2), 91–107. DOI: 10.1080/1062726X.2020.1749989

Schulz, T. M., & Raines, J. K. (2023). Leveraging chatbots for mental health support in educational institutions: A review of the literature. *Computers & Education*, 185, 104601. DOI: 10.1016/j.compedu.2022.104601

Zeng, Y., & Xie, Z. (2021). Building resilience in educational organizations through crisis management technology. *International Journal of Educational Management*, 35(6), 1169–1183. DOI: 10.1108/IJEM-07-2020-0329

KEY TERMS AND DEFINITIONS

Crisis Management: Crisis management refers to the processes and strategies used by organizations to prepare for, respond to, and recover from significant, often unforeseen events that threaten the safety, reputation, or functionality of the organization (Mitroff & Anagnos, 2020). In educational institutions, effective crisis management is essential for safeguarding the well-being of students, staff, and the broader community during emergencies.

Chatbots: Chatbots are AI-driven tools designed to simulate conversation with users, typically through text or voice interactions. These tools use natural language processing (NLP) and machine learning algorithms to provide immediate responses to queries and engage in real-time communication, making them particularly useful in crisis management contexts where rapid information dissemination is critical (Palanica & Fossat, 2020).

Real-Time Communication: Real-time communication refers to the instantaneous exchange of information between individuals or groups, without delays. In crisis situations, real-time communication ensures that relevant stakeholders, such as students, staff, and administrators, receive timely updates, instructions, and support, enhancing decision-making and response efforts (Comfort et al., 2020).

Crisis Communication: Crisis communication involves the strategic dissemination of information during a crisis to ensure clarity, mitigate misinformation, and manage stakeholder perceptions. It includes both internal communication (within the organization) and external communication (to the public, media, etc.) and is crucial for guiding people through a crisis and maintaining trust in the institution (Coombs, 2021).

Artificial Intelligence (AI): Artificial Intelligence (AI) refers to the simulation of human intelligence processes by machines, especially computer systems. AI applications in crisis management include predictive analytics, decision support systems, and chatbots that can process large amounts of data quickly to assist in managing crisis events effectively (Bennett & Lemoine, 2022).

Mental Health Support: Mental health support in crisis management involves providing psychological assistance to individuals affected by a crisis. In educational settings, this may include emotional support during traumatic events and the use of digital tools, such as chatbots, to offer immediate counseling and connect individuals with professional resources (Fitzpatrick et al., 2021).

Disaster Preparedness: Disaster preparedness refers to the measures taken to anticipate and mitigate the impact of potential crises, such as natural disasters, health emergencies, or security threats. This includes planning, training, and establishing protocols for rapid response and recovery to ensure minimal disruption to educational activities and student safety (Gartner & Birkinshaw, 2021).

AI-Driven Mental Health Interventions: AI-driven mental health interventions utilize artificial intelligence technologies, including chatbots and virtual counseling, to provide immediate psychological support during crises. These tools can help alleviate stress, anxiety, and other emotional reactions, providing essential care when human resources may be stretched thin (Fitzpatrick et al., 2021).

Business Continuity: Business continuity refers to the ability of an organization to continue operating during and after a crisis. For educational institutions, this means ensuring that teaching, learning, and administrative functions can resume quickly following disruptions, often with the help of technology such as online platforms and chatbots for communication and academic support (Liu & Austin, 2020).

Automated Response Systems: Automated response systems are technologies that automatically provide predefined responses to common questions or issues. These systems are critical during crises when large volumes of inquiries arise, as they can provide instant, accurate answers and reduce the workload on human responders (Palanica & Fossat, 2020).

Chapter 8
Designing Chatbots for Educational Leadership

Vijay Anant Athavale
https://orcid.org/0000-0002-6812-5198
Walchand Institute of Technology, India

P. Selvakumar
https://orcid.org/0000-0002-3650-4548
Department of Science and Humanities, Nehru Institute of Technology, Coimbatore, India

S. Poorani
https://orcid.org/0000-0001-7179-431X
Kongu Engineering College, India

Taruna Anand
Graphic Era University, Dehradun, India

Devendra Singh Rathore
https://orcid.org/0000-0001-8958-5591
Lakshmi Narain College of Technology, India

ABSTRACT

The introduction of chatbots into educational leadership marks a significant shift in how educational institutions approach both administrative and pedagogical challenges. At its core, chatbot design for educational leadership requires a comprehensive understanding of the specific goals and challenges faced by educational institutions. These goals may include improving administrative efficiency, providing personalized student support, facilitating professional development, and enhancing communication among stakeholders. To address these objectives, chatbots must be

DOI: 10.4018/979-8-3693-8734-4.ch008

tailored to perform a variety of functions, ranging from automating routine administrative tasks such as scheduling and inquiries to delivering targeted educational content and feedback.The design process begins with identifying the primary use cases and functionalities that the chatbot will serve. For educational leadership, this often involves creating chatbots that can handle tasks such as managing schedules, tracking student progress, answering frequently asked questions, and providing access to resources.

INTRODUCTION

The introduction of chatbots into educational leadership marks a significant shift in how educational institutions approach both administrative and pedagogical challenges. At its core, chatbot design for educational leadership requires a comprehensive understanding of the specific goals and challenges faced by educational institutions. These goals may include improving administrative efficiency, providing personalized student support, facilitating professional development, and enhancing communication among stakeholders. To address these objectives, chatbots must be tailored to perform a variety of functions, ranging from automating routine administrative tasks such as scheduling and inquiries to delivering targeted educational content and feedback.The design process begins with identifying the primary use cases and functionalities that the chatbot will serve. For educational leadership, this often involves creating chatbots that can handle tasks such as managing schedules, tracking student progress, answering frequently asked questions, and providing access to resources. It is crucial to map out these functionalities in alignment with the institution's specific needs and priorities. This requires close collaboration with educational leaders, faculty, and administrative staff to ensure that the chatbot's design aligns with the institution's operational workflows and strategic goals. Another important aspect of chatbot design is ensuring that the technology can integrate seamlessly with existing systems and platforms used by the educational institution. This may involve linking the chatbot to student information systems, learning management systems, and other administrative tools. Effective integration ensures that the chatbot can provide accurate and real-time information, thereby enhancing its utility and reliability.Moreover, the design of educational chatbots must include mechanisms for ongoing evaluation and improvement. Regular feedback from users, coupled with data analytics, can provide insights into the chatbot's performance and areas for enhancement. Iterative updates and refinements based on user feedback and evolving institutional needs are crucial for maintaining the chatbot's effectiveness and relevance.

In summary, the design of chatbots for educational leadership involves a multi-faceted approach that addresses the unique needs of educational institutions. From identifying key use cases and ensuring a user-friendly experience to integrating with existing systems and prioritizing privacy and security, each aspect of the design process contributes to the successful implementation of chatbot technology. As educational institutions continue to explore and adopt these tools, a thoughtful and strategic approach to chatbot design will be essential in maximizing their potential to enhance administrative efficiency, support personalized learning, and drive institutional success.Understanding user needs through stakeholder analysis is a critical step in the development of chatbots for educational settings, as it ensures that the chatbot addresses the specific requirements and expectations of all relevant parties involved. In the context of educational leadership, stakeholders typically include students, educators, administrative staff, parents, and institutional leaders, each with distinct needs and interactions with the educational system. Conducting a thorough stakeholder analysis allows developers to design a chatbot that effectively serves these diverse groups, enhancing its utility and effectiveness across various use cases. The first step in stakeholder analysis is identifying all potential stakeholders and understanding their roles and needs within the educational environment. Students, for instance, may require support with navigating course materials, managing assignments, or seeking academic advice.

Parents are another key stakeholder group whose needs must be considered. They often seek information about their children's academic progress, school events, and general institutional policies(Abhilasha A.,et al.,2022). A chatbot that addresses parents' inquiries with accurate and timely information can improve parental engagement and satisfaction. It is essential to design the chatbot to provide easy access to relevant information while ensuring that it maintains a professional and supportive tone, recognizing the parents' role in the educational ecosystem.Moreover, it is important to recognize that stakeholder needs may evolve over time. As educational institutions adapt to new challenges and opportunities, the chatbot must be flexible and capable of evolving to meet changing needs. Continuous feedback loops and periodic reassessments of stakeholder requirements ensure that the chatbot remains relevant and effective throughout its lifecycle.In conclusion, stakeholder analysis is a foundational element in the development of effective chatbots for educational leadership. By comprehensively understanding the diverse needs of students, educators, administrative staff, parents, and institutional leaders, developers can design chatbots that enhance operational efficiency, support personalized learning, and contribute to a more cohesive educational environment. Engaging with stakeholders throughout the design and implementation process ensures that the chatbot meets their needs and expectations, ultimately maximizing its impact and success in the educational setting.

Defining Chatbot Purpose and Goals: Aligning with Educational Objectives

Defining the purpose and goals of a chatbot within an educational context is essential to ensuring that it aligns effectively with the overarching educational objectives of an institution. This alignment involves a deliberate process of setting clear, actionable goals that reflect the needs of the institution, its stakeholders, and its strategic mission. A well-defined chatbot purpose not only enhances its effectiveness but also ensures that it contributes meaningfully to the educational environment, supporting both administrative functions and pedagogical outcomes.The first step in defining a chatbot's purpose is to align it with the institution's broader educational objectives. These objectives often include enhancing student learning experiences, improving administrative efficiency, fostering better communication, and supporting institutional growth. By clarifying how the chatbot can support these objectives, developers can create a tool that integrates seamlessly into the institution's existing frameworks and contributes to its strategic goals.For instance, if an institution aims to improve student engagement and support personalized learning, the chatbot's primary purpose could be to offer tailored academic assistance and resources (Abu,et al.,2007).

Communication enhancement is another critical area where chatbots can align with educational objectives. In an environment where effective communication among students, parents, and staff is crucial, the chatbot can serve as a central hub for disseminating information, addressing inquiries, and facilitating interaction. For example, the chatbot could provide updates on school events, handle parent inquiries, and support communication between faculty and students. By setting goals related to improving communication channels, the chatbot can help foster a more connected and informed educational community.Institutional growth and development also play a role in defining the chatbot's purpose. As educational institutions evolve, they may seek to leverage technology to drive innovation and enhance their competitive edge. The chatbot can support these goals by offering features that provide data-driven insights, support professional development, and facilitate strategic planning. For instance, the chatbot could collect feedback from various stakeholders, analyze trends in student performance, and offer recommendations for improvements. Aligning the chatbot's goals with institutional growth objectives ensures that it contributes to the institution's long-term success and sustainability.To achieve these objectives, it is important to develop specific, measurable, achievable, relevant, and time-bound (SMART) goals for the chatbot. SMART goals provide a clear framework for evaluating the chatbot's performance and impact. For example, a SMART goal for a chatbot designed to improve student engagement might be to increase the usage of digital learning resources by 20% within the first academic year. Such goals not only provide direction but also facilitate the assessment of the chatbot's effectiveness in meeting its intended purpose.Additionally, involving stakeholders in the goal-setting process helps ensure that the chatbot's objectives align with their needs and expectations. By soliciting input from students, educators, administrative staff, and other key stakeholders, developers can gain valuable insights into the specific functionalities and features that will be most beneficial (Ahmad, N. A.,et al.,2018). This collaborative approach ensures that the chatbot is designed with a clear understanding of its role in supporting educational objectives and addresses the practical needs of its users.In conclusion, defining the purpose and goals of a chatbot in alignment with educational objectives is a crucial step in its development. By setting clear, actionable goals that reflect the institution's strategic priorities, developers can create a chatbot that enhances student learning experiences, improves administrative efficiency, fosters better communication, and supports institutional growth. A well-defined purpose ensures that the chatbot contributes meaningfully to the educational environment, providing valuable support to students, staff, and the broader educational community.

Crafting effective chatbot personas and tone is pivotal in establishing a leadership voice that resonates with users and supports the goals of educational institutions. A well-designed chatbot persona not only enhances user engagement but also reinforces the institution's values and objectives. This involves creating a persona that embodies the institution's ethos and adopting a tone that aligns with the context and needs of the diverse user base, including students, educators, administrative staff, and parents.Developing a chatbot persona starts with defining the character and identity that the chatbot will convey. This persona should reflect the institution's culture and values while being tailored to the specific roles and expectations of its users. For example, if an institution emphasizes innovation and student-centered learning, the chatbot's persona might be designed to be approachable, encouraging, and supportive. This persona could use friendly language, show enthusiasm for helping students succeed, and be proactive in offering assistance. Conversely, if the institution prioritizes professionalism and formality, the chatbot's persona should reflect a more formal and authoritative tone, providing information in a clear and precise manner. The tone of the chatbot must be carefully crafted to match its intended purpose and audience. For educational leadership, this often means balancing professionalism with approachability. The tone should be respectful and authoritative, conveying reliability and trustworthiness, while also being accessible and empathetic. This balance ensures that the chatbot is perceived as a valuable resource that understands and addresses the needs of its users effectively. For instance, a chatbot designed to assist students with academic queries might adopt a supportive and motivational tone, encouraging them to seek help and providing reassurance during stressful periods such as exam times (Ashok G.,et al.,2015).The chatbot's tone and persona should also be adaptable to different contexts and interactions. For example, when dealing with administrative inquiries, the tone might be more formal and focused on providing accurate, concise information. In contrast, when engaging with students on academic matters, the tone could be more conversational and supportive, aimed at fostering a positive learning experience.

Designing Conversational Flows: User Experience and Journey Mapping

The foundation of designing successful conversational flows lies in comprehensive user journey mapping. This involves detailing the steps users take as they interact with the chatbot, from initiating a conversation to achieving their goals. Understanding these journeys requires identifying the various scenarios in which users will engage with the chatbot, such as seeking information about courses, getting assistance with assignments, or handling administrative tasks. By outlining these scenarios, developers can ensure that the chatbot provides relevant information and support at each stage of the user journey (Clarizia, F.,et al.,2018).To start with, it is essential to define the key objectives of the chatbot and the specific tasks it is expected to perform. For example, if the chatbot's primary function is to assist students with academic inquiries, the conversational flows should be designed to facilitate quick and efficient access to information about course materials, deadlines, and grading. This involves creating decision trees and pathways that guide users through their queries in a logical manner, ensuring that they receive accurate and helpful responses. One effective approach is to map out common user intents and corresponding chatbot responses. For instance, if a student asks about the deadline for an assignment, the chatbot should be able to quickly provide the relevant information or direct the user to the appropriate resource. This requires anticipating a range of possible user inputs and designing responses that address these queries directly and efficiently. Incorporating natural language understanding (NLU) capabilities into the chatbot can help manage variations in user inputs and improve the accuracy of responses. Designing conversational flows also involves considering how users will navigate through different types of interactions. This means structuring conversations to handle both simple queries and more complex interactions. For example, a chatbot might handle straightforward questions about office hours with a quick and direct response, while more complex queries, such as those involving academic advising, might require a series of interactions to gather detailed information and provide personalized assistance. Ensuring that the chatbot can manage these varied interactions effectively is crucial for maintaining a positive user experience.

User experience (UX) design plays a significant role in crafting conversational flows. The interactions should be designed to be as smooth and intuitive as possible, minimizing the need for users to repeat themselves or encounter confusion. This includes implementing features such as quick replies, suggestion buttons, and context-aware responses that help guide users through the conversation seamlessly. A well-designed UX ensures that users can achieve their goals with minimal effort and frustration.Incorporating feedback mechanisms within the chatbot's conversational flows is also important. Allowing users to provide feedback on their interactions can offer valuable insights into areas for improvement. For instance, if users frequently indicate that they are not receiving the information they need, this feedback can be used to refine the chatbot's responses and improve its accuracy. Regularly reviewing feedback and performance metrics helps in making iterative improvements to the conversational flows.Moreover, it is crucial to account for different user personas and their specific needs when designing conversational flows. For example, students may have different requirements compared to administrative staff or parents. Tailoring the conversational flows to address these diverse needs ensures that each user group receives relevant and appropriate support. This might involve creating distinct pathways or modules within the chatbot to cater to different types of users and their specific queries (Cunningham-Nelson, S.,et al.,2019).Testing and refining the conversational flows is an ongoing process. Conducting usability testing with actual users can help identify potential issues and areas for enhancement. Observing how users interact with the chatbot, analyzing conversation logs, and measuring user satisfaction can provide insights into how well the conversational flows are functioning. This iterative approach allows developers to make data-driven adjustments and continuously improve the chatbot's performance.

Continuous testing and refinement ensure that the chatbot remains responsive to users' needs and contributes positively to the educational environment. A well-designed conversational flow enhances user satisfaction, improves engagement, and helps achieve the chatbot's goals, ultimately supporting the broader objectives of the educational institution.To develop a comprehensive content strategy, it is crucial to first map out the types of content that will be provided through the chatbot. This can include educational resources, frequently asked questions (FAQs), procedural guides, and interactive elements such as quizzes or tutorials. The content should be categorized based on user needs and institutional priorities, ensuring that it addresses the most common queries and challenges faced by users. For example, content might be organized into sections such as academic advising, course registration, and campus events to facilitate easy access and navigation (Fernoagă, V., et al.,2018).Next, it is important to ensure that the content is accurate, relevant, and up-to-date. This involves collaborating with subject matter experts, educators, and administrative staff to gather and verify information. Regular updates and reviews are necessary to keep the content current, especially in areas such as academic schedules, policy changes, and new resources. Implementing a system for periodic content audits and updates can help maintain the chatbot's reliability and effectiveness over time.

Personalization is a key feature that can significantly enhance the effectiveness of the chatbot's content. By leveraging user data and preferences, the chatbot can provide personalized recommendations and support. For example, the chatbot could offer customized study resources based on a student's academic performance or suggest relevant professional development opportunities based on an educator's interests and career goals. Personalization helps to ensure that the content is directly relevant to each user's needs, increasing its value and impact.Incorporating feedback mechanisms into the content strategy allows for continuous improvement and adaptation. Users should have the ability to provide feedback on the chatbot's responses and suggest additional resources or content. This feedback can be used to identify gaps in the content, refine existing materials, and develop new resources that better meet user needs. Analyzing user interactions and feedback can provide valuable insights into which content areas are most valuable and which may require further development.Additionally, integrating the chatbot with existing educational platforms and systems can enhance its content capabilities. For example, linking the chatbot to a learning management system (LMS) can enable it to provide real-time information about course materials, assignments, and grades. Similarly, integrating with administrative systems can allow the chatbot to offer up-to-date information about campus events, registration deadlines, and policy changes. Such integrations ensure that the chatbot delivers accurate and timely content, aligned with the institution's operations and resources.In conclusion, developing a content strategy for chatbots involves understanding user needs, creating accurate and relevant resources, and ensuring engagement and personalization. By categorizing content, maintaining accuracy, and incorporating feedback, educational institutions can create a chatbot that effectively supports students, faculty, and staff. Integrating with existing systems and considering accessibility further enhances the chatbot's value, contributing to a richer and more supportive educational experience. A well-designed content strategy ensures that the chatbot delivers meaningful and effective support, aligning with the institution's educational objectives and enhancing its overall impact(Fryer, L. K.,et al.,2017).

Integrating AI and Machine Learning: Enhancing Chatbot Intelligence

By analyzing user data and historical interactions, the chatbot can offer tailored recommendations and support. For example, a chatbot might analyze a student's academic performance and study habits to suggest personalized study resources or provide targeted academic advice. Similarly, for educators, the chatbot can offer customized professional development opportunities based on their interests and teaching methods. Personalization enhances the relevance of the chatbot's responses, making interactions more meaningful and valuable to users. In contrast, AI-powered chatbots can manage such interactions more effectively by leveraging machine learning models that understand and process intricate user inputs. This capability is particularly valuable in educational settings, where users may have detailed and multi-faceted questions about academic topics, administrative procedures, or institutional policies.Moreover, AI and ML integration enhances the chatbot's ability to provide proactive support(Ghose, S.,et al.,2013). By analyzing patterns in user behavior and identifying potential issues before they arise, the chatbot can offer preemptive assistance. This proactive approach helps in addressing issues early and supporting users more effectively.

In conclusion, integrating AI and machine learning into chatbots significantly enhances their intelligence and capabilities, making them more effective tools for educational support. By leveraging advanced natural language processing, adaptive learning, and contextual understanding, AI-powered chatbots can provide personalized, relevant, and proactive assistance. Ethical considerations and continuous evaluation are crucial for maintaining the chatbot's reliability and effectiveness. Through these advancements, educational institutions can offer a more responsive and supportive experience to students, faculty, and staff, ultimately contributing to a more effective and engaging educational environment.User interface (UI) design is a critical component in creating an intuitive and effective chatbot experience, particularly in educational settings where seamless interaction can significantly enhance user engagement and satisfaction. Consistent use of colors, fonts, and icons helps create a cohesive and professional look, reinforcing the institution's brand and making the chatbot visually appealing. Interaction patterns are another critical aspect of UI design. The chatbot should employ familiar and intuitive interaction patterns to ensure that users can navigate the system effortlessly. This includes using conversational design principles that mimic natural human interactions, such as providing prompts, suggestions, and follow-up questions that guide users through their queries(Hone, K. S.,et al.,2016). For instance, if a user asks about course registration, the chatbot could provide a series of guided options or questions to gather relevant information and offer precise assistance. By adopting familiar patterns, the chatbot can create a more comfortable and user-friendly experience.

Feedback buttons, surveys, or rating systems integrated into the chatbot interface can capture user opinions and experiences, providing valuable insights into the effectiveness of the design. Regularly reviewing and acting on this feedback helps refine the UI and ensure that it meets users' evolving needs and expectations. User journey mapping is a valuable tool in designing an intuitive chatbot UI. By analyzing common user scenarios and interactions, designers can identify key touchpoints and potential pain points in the user experience. This mapping process helps in structuring the chatbot's interface to address user needs effectively, ensuring that each stage of the interaction is smooth and logical. For example, if users frequently seek assistance with specific tasks, the UI can be designed to provide quick access to these functions, reducing the time and effort required to achieve their goals.The chatbot should provide a uniform experience whether accessed via a web interface, mobile app, or other digital platforms. Consistent design elements, interaction patterns, and functionality across these platforms help users transition seamlessly between devices and maintain a cohesive experience.In conclusion, creating an intuitive chatbot experience through effective UI design involves a thoughtful approach to layout, visual aesthetics, interaction patterns, accessibility, and continuous improvement. By focusing on clear organization, engaging visuals, familiar interaction patterns, and user feedback, developers can design a chatbot interface that enhances usability and user satisfaction. Accessibility considerations and iterative testing further refine the design, ensuring that the chatbot provides a seamless and supportive experience across various platforms and user contexts. A well-designed UI not only improves the chatbot's effectiveness but also contributes to a positive and engaging interaction, supporting the broader educational objectives of the institution (Kerlyl A., et al.,2006).Designing chatbots for accessibility and inclusivity is essential for ensuring that these digital tools serve all users effectively, regardless of their abilities or backgrounds. This approach involves creating chatbots that are usable by individuals with a range of disabilities, linguistic backgrounds, and varying levels of technological proficiency. By prioritizing accessibility and inclusivity in chatbot design, educational institutions can ensure that their digital resources are equitable, enhance engagement, and support diverse user needs, thereby fostering an inclusive learning environment.

Accessibility in chatbot design involves implementing features that accommodate users with disabilities, such as visual, auditory, motor, and cognitive impairments. For users with visual impairments, chatbots should be compatible with screen readers and provide text-based alternatives for visual content. This includes using descriptive alt text for images and ensuring that all interactive elements are accessible through keyboard navigation. Designing for auditory impairments requires providing text-based responses for all audio content and incorporating visual or written notifications for alerts and updates. For users with motor impairments, the chatbot interface should be navigable through keyboard inputs or voice commands, minimizing reliance on mouse clicks or complex gestures (Kim, N. Y.,et al.,2019). Cognitive accessibility is another critical aspect, involving the design of clear and straightforward interactions that accommodate users with cognitive or learning disabilities. For example, incorporating localized content and respecting cultural norms and preferences in communication styles can enhance the chatbot's relevance and usability across different regions.Implementing adaptive technologies and personalization options can further enhance inclusivity. For example, allowing users to customize the chatbot's interface, such as adjusting font sizes, color schemes, or interaction modes, can accommodate individual preferences and needs. These guidelines provide a framework for creating accessible digital content and interactions, helping to address common accessibility challenges and promote an inclusive user experience.Furthermore, providing clear and accessible support resources can assist users in navigating the chatbot and addressing any issues they encounter. Offering help documents, tutorials, and contact options for additional assistance ensures that users have access to support if they face difficulties. This additional layer of support contributes to a more inclusive experience by providing users with the resources they need to fully engage with the chatbot.In summary, designing chatbots with a focus on accessibility and inclusivity involves creating features and interactions that accommodate diverse user needs, including those related to disabilities, linguistic preferences, and cultural differences (Kumar, R.,et al.,2011). By incorporating accessibility features, supporting multiple languages, engaging with diverse user groups, and adhering to established guidelines, developers can create chatbots that are equitable and effective for all users. Personalization options and clear support resources further enhance inclusivity, ensuring that the chatbot provides a meaningful and supportive experience for a broad range of individuals. An inclusive approach not only improves user engagement but also aligns with the broader goals of fostering an equitable and accessible educational environment.

Testing and Iteration: Ensuring Chatbot Effectiveness and Efficiency

Testing and iteration are fundamental to ensuring the effectiveness and efficiency of chatbots, particularly in educational settings where the accuracy and user experience of these tools can significantly impact learning and administrative processes. Another key component of the testing process is performance evaluation. This involves analyzing quantitative metrics to assess the chatbot's efficiency and effectiveness. Key performance indicators (KPIs) might include response accuracy, completion rates for user tasks, average response time, and user satisfaction scores. By tracking these metrics, developers can identify trends and patterns in the chatbot's performance, pinpointing areas where the chatbot excels and where it may fall short(Mahadev Madgule, N.,et al.,2023). Performance evaluation also helps measure the impact of iterative changes, ensuring that improvements are effectively addressing identified issues.The iterative process of refining the chatbot involves making data-driven adjustments based on insights gained from usability testing and performance evaluation. This iterative approach ensures that the chatbot evolves in response to real user needs and feedback. For example, if testing reveals that users frequently encounter difficulties with a particular feature or query type, developers can modify the chatbot's responses or interaction design to address these challenges. Regularly updating the chatbot's content, algorithms, and interface based on this feedback helps maintain its relevance and effectiveness.

Incorporating user feedback into the iteration process is crucial for continuous improvement. Collecting feedback from users, both through formal mechanisms like surveys and informal channels like user comments, provides valuable perspectives on the chatbot's strengths and areas for enhancement. This feedback can highlight specific issues that may not be apparent through testing alone, such as user preferences, pain points, or additional needs. Implementing changes based on this feedback ensures that the chatbot remains aligned with user expectations and requirements(Molnár G.,et al.,2018).Testing should also be ongoing to address new challenges and evolving user needs. As the chatbot is used over time, new scenarios, queries, and user behaviors may emerge that require adjustments to the chatbot's design and functionality. Through a structured approach to testing and iteration, educational institutions can optimize their chatbots to better meet the needs of students, faculty, and staff, ultimately supporting their educational objectives and operational efficiency.Deploying chatbots in educational settings requires a strategic approach to ensure successful implementation and integration into existing systems. Effective deployment involves careful planning, stakeholder engagement, system integration, user training, and ongoing support. Each of these elements contributes to a seamless rollout, maximizes the chatbot's impact, and ensures that it meets the needs of students, faculty, and staff.The initial phase of deployment begins with thorough planning and preparation. This involves defining clear objectives for the chatbot, determining its role within the educational institution, and setting measurable goals for its success. This planning should include identifying the primary functions of the chatbot, such as academic support, administrative assistance, or campus information, and aligning these functions with the institution's broader strategic goals. Developing a detailed implementation plan that outlines the timeline, resources, and responsibilities is crucial for guiding the deployment process and ensuring that all aspects are addressed.

Engaging stakeholders early in the deployment process is vital for ensuring buy-in and support. This includes involving key figures such as administrators, faculty members, IT staff, and students. Stakeholders can provide valuable input on the chatbot's functionality, design, and potential impact, helping to ensure that the final product meets their needs and expectations.Effective integration allows the chatbot to access and provide real-time information, such as course schedules, grades, and administrative updates, enhancing its utility and effectiveness. Collaboration with IT teams to address technical challenges and ensure smooth integration is essential for a successful deployment (Ondáš, S.,et al.,2019).Training and onboarding users is an important component of chatbot deployment. Providing clear instructions and resources on how to use the chatbot helps users become familiar with its features and capabilities. This training can include user guides, video tutorials, and interactive demos that illustrate how to interact with the chatbot and leverage its functionalities. For faculty and staff, additional training may be needed to help them understand how the chatbot can support their roles and integrate it into their workflows effectively.A well-coordinated launch strategy ensures that the chatbot is introduced effectively to the institution. This may involve a phased rollout, starting with a pilot program or limited release to a specific group of users..

This may involve updating content, adding new features, or integrating with additional systems. Ensuring that the chatbot's architecture and design support scalability helps maintain its relevance and effectiveness over time.A commitment to continuous improvement ensures that the chatbot remains effective and relevant. This involves regularly updating content, refining algorithms, and incorporating new technologies to enhance the chatbot's capabilities. Staying informed about advancements in AI and machine learning can provide opportunities for further enhancements, ensuring that the chatbot continues to provide valuable support and stay aligned with the institution's goals (Paramasivam Selvakumar,et al.,2024).In conclusion, deploying chatbots in educational settings requires a strategic approach that encompasses thorough planning, stakeholder engagement, system integration, user training, and ongoing support. By implementing a well-coordinated launch strategy, monitoring performance, gathering feedback, and planning for scalability and adaptability, institutions can ensure a successful implementation. Addressing data privacy and security concerns, along with a commitment to continuous improvement, further enhances the chatbot's effectiveness and longevity. A thoughtful and comprehensive deployment process helps maximize the chatbot's impact, supporting the institution's educational objectives and providing valuable assistance to students, faculty, and staff.

Chatbot Analytics and Evaluation: Measuring Impact and Success

Chatbot analytics and evaluation are essential for measuring the impact and success of a chatbot in educational settings, providing insights into its performance, user engagement, and overall effectivenes. This process involves collecting quantitative and qualitative data, analyzing performance metrics, and evaluating the chatbot's alignment with institutional goals and user needs.Analyzing user interaction data offers a comprehensive view of how users engage with the chatbot. This includes tracking the types of queries submitted, the frequency of certain interactions, and the duration of conversations (Paramasivam Selvakumar,et al.,2024). By examining these interactions, developers can identify common patterns, frequently asked questions, and areas where users may experience difficulties. Conversational analytics involves evaluating the quality and flow of chatbot conversations. This includes analyzing the chatbot's ability to manage multi-turn interactions, handle complex queries, and maintain context throughout the conversation. Metrics such as the number of follow-up questions, conversation length, and the rate of successful issue resolution provide insights into how effectively the chatbot engages users and supports their needs. Additionally, analyzing conversation logs can help identify areas where the chatbot's responses may be unclear or insufficient, guiding adjustments to improve clarity and relevance.

Evaluating the chatbot's success in achieving its predefined goals is essential for measuring its overall impact. For educational chatbots, these goals may include improving student support, streamlining administrative processes, or enhancing communication. Assessing how well the chatbot meets these goals involves analyzing its effectiveness in addressing user needs, reducing response times, and increasing efficiency(Ruth, D. 2006). For example, if the chatbot's goal is to reduce administrative workload, metrics such as the volume of handled inquiries and the reduction in manual processing time can indicate its success in achieving this objective.Comparative analysis involves benchmarking the chatbot's performance against industry standards or similar tools. Comparing metrics such as response accuracy, user satisfaction, and engagement rates with those of other chatbots or best practices helps assess relative performance and identify areas for improvement. This approach provides context for evaluating the chatbot's effectiveness and can offer insights into how it measures up to industry norms and user expectations.Using analytics to inform data-driven decision making is key to optimizing the chatbot's performance. By analyzing performance metrics and user feedback, developers can identify trends, assess the impact of changes, and prioritize improvements based on data. For example, if data reveals a high rate of unresolved queries in a specific topic area, developers can focus on enhancing the chatbot's knowledge and response accuracy in that area. Data-driven decisions ensure that improvements are targeted and aligned with user needs and institutional goals.Continuous improvement involves using insights gained from analytics and evaluation to make iterative enhancements to the chatbot. This process includes regularly updating content, refining algorithms, and incorporating new technologies to address identified issues and optimize performance. By maintaining an iterative approach, institutions can ensure that the chatbot remains effective, relevant, and aligned with evolving user needs and institutional objectives.

Assessing the chatbot's effectiveness in achieving its goals, conducting comparative analysis, and making data-driven decisions support continuous improvement and optimization. Effective reporting and communication of results, along with addressing ethical considerations, ensure a comprehensive approach to evaluating and enhancing the chatbot's performance. By leveraging these strategies, educational institutions can maximize the chatbot's impact, align it with user needs and institutional objectives, and continuously enhance its effectiveness in supporting students, faculty, and staff.Addressing ethical concerns in chatbot deployment is crucial for ensuring transparency and accountability, particularly in sensitive environments such as educational institutions. Ethical considerations encompass various aspects, including data privacy, user consent, transparency in operations, and the responsible use of artificial intelligence. Ensuring that chatbots operate within ethical boundaries helps build user trust, comply with legal regulations, and promote fair and responsible use of technology. By proactively addressing these concerns, institutions can foster a positive user experience and uphold high standards of integrity and accountability(Zhou, L.,et al.,2020).Ensuring accountability for chatbot interactions and responses is essential for maintaining ethical standards. Institutions should establish mechanisms for monitoring and evaluating chatbot performance, including tracking errors, user complaints, and feedback. In cases where the chatbot provides incorrect or inappropriate responses, there should be a clear process for addressing these issues and correcting the underlying problems. Transparency in how errors are handled and corrected helps maintain user trust and ensures that the chatbot continuously improves.

Users should be informed about the chatbot's capabilities and limitations. Clear communication about what the chatbot can and cannot do helps set realistic expectations and prevents misunderstandings. This includes providing information about the chatbot's scope of knowledge, its decision-making processes, and any limitations in its ability to provide support or information. Transparency regarding the chatbot's functionality ensures that users are aware of its role and can use it effectively within its intended purpose.The design of chatbot interactions should adhere to ethical standards, ensuring that conversations are respectful, supportive, and free from manipulation. Chatbots should be programmed to avoid deceptive practices, such as leading users to make decisions that may not be in their best interest. Additionally, the language and tone used by the chatbot should be considerate and inclusive, avoiding any content that could be perceived as offensive or discriminatory (Selvakumar, P.,et al.,2024). Ethical interaction design promotes positive user experiences and reinforces the institution's commitment to ethical practices.Ongoing monitoring of chatbot interactions is crucial for identifying and addressing ethical concerns as they arise. Institutions should regularly review chatbot performance, user feedback, and interaction logs to detect any issues related to privacy, bias, or transparency. This continuous monitoring enables prompt action to rectify any ethical problems and ensures that the chatbot remains aligned with ethical standards(Yamada, M.,et al.,2016). Additionally, engaging with users to gather feedback on their experiences can provide valuable insights into potential areas for improvement.Training development teams on ethical considerations in chatbot design and deployment is essential for ensuring that ethical practices are integrated into the development process. This training should cover topics such as data privacy, bias mitigation, and responsible AI use. By fostering an ethical mindset among developers and stakeholders, institutions can ensure that ethical considerations are prioritized throughout the chatbot's lifecycle.

Compliance with legal and regulatory requirements is a fundamental aspect of ethical chatbot deployment. Institutions must stay informed about relevant laws and regulations governing data privacy, AI use, and digital interactions. Ensuring that the chatbot adheres to these legal requirements helps prevent legal issues and reinforces the institution's commitment to ethical practices. Regular audits and reviews can help verify compliance and address any potential legal concerns.Educating users about their rights and how their data is used by the chatbot promotes transparency and accountability. Providing resources and information about data privacy practices, consent options, and how to report issues helps users feel more in control of their interactions with the chatbot. User education fosters trust and ensures that users are aware of how their data is handled and their options for managing their privacy. In summary, addressing ethical concerns in chatbot deployment involves a comprehensive approach that encompasses data privacy and security, user consent and transparency, responsible AI use, accountability, and ethical interaction design. By implementing robust security measures, obtaining user consent, mitigating biases, and ensuring transparency, institutions can uphold high ethical standards and build trust with users. Continuous monitoring, ethical training, regulatory compliance, and user education further support ethical practices and contribute to the overall success and integrity of the chatbot(Sjöström, J.,et al.,2018). Through these measures, educational institutions can ensure that their chatbots operate in a manner that is respectful, responsible, and aligned with ethical principles.

Scaling Chatbot Solutions: Expanding Reach and Impact

Scaling chatbot solutions effectively is essential for expanding their reach and impact within educational institutions, enabling these digital tools to serve a larger audience and address more complex needs. Successful scaling involves addressing technical, operational, and strategic considerations to ensure that chatbots can handle increased usage, integrate with broader systems, and continue to provide valuable support as their scope and user base grow. By focusing on scalability, institutions can enhance the chatbot's functionality, improve user experience, and maximize its benefits across various departments and user groups.The foundation of scaling a chatbot solution is ensuring its technical scalability (Sugumaran K. M, D.,et al.,2024). This involves designing a robust and flexible architecture capable of handling increased user traffic and interaction volume. Utilizing cloud-based infrastructure allows for dynamic scaling, where resources can be adjusted in real-time based on demand. Cloud platforms offer scalable storage and processing capabilities, ensuring that the chatbot remains responsive and reliable as usage grows. Additionally, adopting microservices architecture can help manage different functionalities independently, allowing for easier updates and maintenance without disrupting the entire system. Expanding the reach of the chatbot requires ongoing training and support for both users and administrators. For users, providing updated training materials, tutorials, and support channels ensures they can effectively use the chatbot and access its expanded features. For administrators and support staff, offering training on managing the scaled chatbot solution, handling complex issues, and utilizing new functionalities is crucial for maintaining smooth operations and addressing user needs.

Strategic planning and governance are essential for successful scaling. Developing a roadmap that outlines the goals, timelines, and resources required for scaling helps ensure that all aspects of the expansion are addressed (Wu, E. H. K.,et al.,2020). Establishing governance structures and decision-making processes ensures that scaling efforts align with institutional objectives and priorities. Regular reviews and updates to the scaling strategy help adapt to changing needs and opportunities, ensuring that the chatbot continues to provide value as it grows. The future of chatbot design for educational leadership is poised to be shaped by a range of innovations and emerging trends that promise to enhance their functionality, usability, and impact within educational institutions. As technology evolves, chatbots are expected to integrate more advanced artificial intelligence (AI) capabilities, foster greater personalization, and become increasingly adept at addressing diverse educational needs. The following key areas highlight the anticipated future directions in chatbot design, offering a glimpse into how these digital tools will continue to transform educational leadership and support.As chatbots become more sophisticated, there will be a greater emphasis on developing emotional intelligence and empathetic interactions (Vijayakumar G,et al.,2024). Advanced AI models will be designed to recognize and respond to emotional cues, providing more sensitive and supportive interactions. This includes detecting signs of student stress, frustration, or confusion and offering appropriate support or escalation to human advisors when necessary. By incorporating emotional intelligence, chatbots will improve their ability to connect with users on a personal level and provide a more compassionate and supportive educational experience.

Chatbots are expected to incorporate collaborative and social learning features that facilitate peer interaction and group learning. This may include functionalities that allow students to collaborate on projects, participate in study groups, or engage in discussion forums facilitated by the chatbot. By supporting social learning dynamics, chatbots can enhance the educational experience, promote collaboration, and foster a sense of community among students. These features will also enable educators to monitor and support collaborative activities more effectively.For example, chatbots could identify students at risk of falling behind academically and proactively provide resources or support to help them stay on track (Weizenbaum, J. 1966). This proactive approach will enhance the chatbot's role in supporting student success and improving educational outcomes.Continuous improvement will be a central theme in the future development of chatbots, driven by ongoing user feedback and iterative enhancements. Institutions will implement mechanisms for collecting and analyzing user feedback, enabling them to make data-driven improvements and adapt to evolving user needs. This iterative process will ensure that chatbots remain relevant, effective, and aligned with institutional goals, while also addressing emerging challenges and opportunities.In summary, the future of chatbot design for educational leadership will be characterized by advanced AI capabilities, increased personalization, and integration with emerging technologies. Enhanced emotional intelligence, multimodal interactions, and collaborative features will further enrich the user experience. Addressing data privacy, ethical considerations, and integrating with institutional ecosystems will be critical for ensuring responsible and effective deployment. Predictive analytics and proactive support will enhance the chatbot's role in supporting student success, while continuous improvement through user feedback will drive ongoing advancements (Winkler, R.et al.,2018). By embracing these innovations and trends, educational institutions can leverage chatbots to transform educational leadership, support diverse learning needs, and achieve greater impact and effectiveness in their digital initiatives.

CONCLUSION

As educational institutions increasingly turn to digital solutions to enhance learning and administrative processes, chatbots have emerged as pivotal tools in transforming how institutions engage with students, faculty, and staff. The design and implementation of these chatbots must be guided by principles of user-centricity, ethical considerations, and strategic alignment with educational goals to maximize their effectiveness and impact.By leveraging sophisticated algorithms and continuous learning, chatbots can handle complex interactions, provide personalized support, and adapt to evolving user needs. Embracing these advancements not only enhances the chatbot's functionality but also ensures that it remains a valuable asset in an ever-evolving digital landscape.A successful chatbot design is rooted in a thorough understanding of the diverse needs of its users. Stakeholder analysis, involving students, faculty, and administrative staff, is crucial for identifying the specific requirements and pain points that the chatbot must address. This user-centric approach ensures that the chatbot provides meaningful and relevant support, whether it is assisting with academic queries, administrative processes, or general information. By aligning the chatbot's capabilities with user expectations, institutions can enhance engagement and satisfaction while addressing critical areas of need.AI practices to prevent discriminatory outcomes. By prioritizing these ethical considerations, institutions can foster a responsible and respectful digital environment that upholds the values of fairness and integrity.

As chatbots become integral to educational processes, planning for scalability is essential. This includes designing a flexible architecture that can handle increased user traffic and interaction volume, as well as expanding functionality to address a broader range of needs. Scalability ensures that the chatbot can grow with the institution and continue to provide valuable support as demands evolve. By planning for scalability, institutions can future-proof their chatbot solutions and maintain their effectiveness over time.The success of chatbot solutions often depends on effective collaboration and integration with other digital tools and platforms. This includes working closely with IT teams, faculty, and administrative staff to ensure that the chatbot integrates seamlessly with existing systems and workflows. Encouraging collaboration across departments helps identify opportunities for synergy and ensures that the chatbot supports a cohesive digital ecosystem. By fostering collaboration and integration, institutions can enhance the chatbot's utility and impact.Finally, fostering a culture of innovation is crucial for the ongoing evolution and success of chatbot solutions. Encouraging experimentation, staying abreast of technological advancements, and embracing new ideas and approaches can drive continuous improvement and adaptation. Institutions that cultivate a culture of innovation are better positioned to leverage emerging trends, address new challenges, and capitalize on opportunities for enhancing their chatbot solutions. By prioritizing ethical considerations, accessibility, and inclusivity, institutions can develop effective and impactful chatbots that enhance engagement, support diverse needs, and contribute to strategic objectives. Robust testing, continuous improvement, and strategic alignment ensure that chatbots remain valuable assets, while scalability and collaboration enhance their reach and effectiveness. Embracing a culture of innovation further positions institutions to leverage the full potential of chatbot technology, driving positive change and achieving greater success in their educational initiatives.

REFERENCES

Abhilasha, A., Sreenivasulu, A., & Manimozhi, T. KUMAR, P. S., Selvakumar, P., & Singh, P. (2022, April). The Model of Smart Sensing Device For Sensitive Nano-clusters Modification in Sensing Properties. In 2022 2nd International Conference on Advance Computing and Innovative Technologies in Engineering (ICACITE) (pp. 1043-1047). IEEE.

Ahmad, N. A., Che, M. H., Zainal, A., Abd Rauf, M. F., & Adnan, Z. (2018). Review of chatbots design techniques. *International Journal of Computer Applications*, 181(8), 7–10. DOI: 10.5120/ijca2018917606

Ashok, G., Brian, C., Mithun, K., Shanu, S., Abhinaya, S., & Bryan, W. (2015). Using Watson for Enhancing Human-Computer Co-Creativity. *AAAI Symposium*. 22-29

Clarizia, F., Colace, F., Lombardi, M., Pascale, F., & Santaniello, D. (2018, October). Chatbot: An education support system for student. In *International Symposium on Cyberspace Safety and Security* (pp. 291-302). Springer, Cham. DOI: 10.1007/978-3-030-01689-0_23

Cunningham-Nelson, S., Boles, W., Trouton, L., & Margerison, E. (2019). A review of chatbots in education: practical steps forward. In 30th Annual Conference for the Australasian Association for Engineering Education (AAEE 2019): Educators Becoming Agents of Change: Innovate, Integrate, Motivate (pp. 299-306). Engineers Australia.

Fernoagă, V., Stelea, G. A., Gavrilă, C., & Sandu, F. (2018). Intelligent education assistant powered by Chatbots. In The International Scientific Conference eLearning and Software for Education (Vol. 2, pp. 376-383). "Carol I" National Defence University.

Fryer, L. K., Ainley, M., Thompson, A., Gibson, A., & Sherlock, Z. (2017). Stimulating and sustaining interest in a language course: An experimental comparison of Chatbot and Human task partners. *Computers in Human Behavior*, 75, 461–468. DOI: 10.1016/j.chb.2017.05.045

Ghose, S., & Barua, J. J. (2013). Toward the implementation of a topic specific dialogue based natural language chatbot as an undergraduate advisor. In *2013 International Conference on Informatics, Electronics and Vision (ICIEV)* (pp. 1–5). DOI: 10.1109/ICIEV.2013.6572650

Hone, K. S., & El Said, G. R. (2016). Exploring the factors affecting MOOC retention: A survey study. *Computers & Education*, 98, 157–168. DOI: 10.1016/j.compedu.2016.03.016

Kanipriya, M., Sugumaran, D., Pandiyarajan, V., Yogananda, B. S., Selvakumar, P., & Mohan, S. (2024, January). Analysis of Electromyography Signals for Control of Mechanical Prosthesis using Machine Learning Techniques. In 2024 2nd International Conference on Intelligent Data Communication Technologies and Internet of Things (IDCIoT) (pp. 1059-1067). IEEE.

Kerlyl, A., Hall, P., & Bull, S. (2006, December). Bringing chatbots into education: Towards natural language negotiation of open learner models. In *International Conference on Innovative Techniques and Applications of Artificial Intelligence*. London. Springer. (pp. 179-192). 4.

Kim, N. Y., Cha, Y., & Kim, H. S. (2019). Future English learning: Chatbots and artificial intelligence. *Multimedia-Assisted Language Learning*, 22(3), 32–53.

Kumar, R., & Rose, C. P. (2011). Architecture for Building Conversational Agents that Support Collaborative Learning. *IEEE Transactions on Learning Technologies*, 4(1), 21–34. DOI: 10.1109/TLT.2010.41

Madgule, M., Vinayaka, N., Sonkhaskar, Y. M., Patel, D. R., Karthikeyan, R., & Selvakumar, P. (2023). Mechanical properties and microstructure of activated TIG welded similar joints of Inconel alloys by desirability approaches. *Materials Today: Proceedings*, 77, 528–533.

Molnár, G., & Szüts, Z. (2018, September). The role of chatbots in formal education. In 2018 IEEE 16th international symposium on intelligent systems and informatics (SISY) (pp. 000197-000202). IEEE.

Ondáš, S., Pleva, M., & Hládek, D. (2019, November). How chatbots can be involved in the education process. In 2019 17th International Conference on Emerging eLearning Technologies and Applications (ICETA) (pp. 575-580). IEEE. DOI: 10.1109/ICETA48886.2019.9040095

Ruth, D. (2006). Frameworks of managerial competence: Limits, problems and suggestions. *Journal of European Industrial Training*, 30(3), 206–226. DOI: 10.1108/03090590610662959

Selvakumar, P. (2024). Emerging Engineering Technologies: Design, Development, and Industrial Applications of IoT-Based Aquaculture Monitoring System. In El Kacimi, Y., & Alaoui, K. (Eds.), *Emerging Engineering Technologies and Industrial Applications* (pp. 332–341). IGI Global., DOI: 10.4018/979-8-3693-1335-0.ch016

Selvakumar, P., Mariappan, P., Shunmugam, S., Paul, R., & Jabez, S. (2024). Removal of chemicals from effluent using photobioreactor technology to improve environmental and health impacts. *Zeitschrift für Physikalische Chemie*, 2024(7), 1295–1302. Advance online publication. DOI: 10.1515/zpch-2023-0450

Selvakumar, P., Palanisamy, S. K., Cinthaikinian, S., Palanisamy, V., Mariappan, R., & Selvakumar, P. K. (2024). Biosensors and its diverse applications in healthcare systems. *Zeitschrift für Physikalische Chemie*, 2024. Advance online publication. DOI: 10.1515/zpch-2023-0406

Shawar, B. A., & Atwell, E. (2007). Chatbots: Are they really useful? *Journal for Language Technology and Computational Linguistics*, 22(1), 29–49.

Sjöström, J., Aghaee, N., Dahlin, M., & Ågerfalk, P. J. (2018). Designing chatbots for higher education practice. In *International Conference on Information Systems Education and Research* (pp. 1-10).

Vijayakumar, G., Rajkumar, M., Rajiv Chandar, N., Selvakumar, P., & Duraisamy, R. (2024). Muniyandi Rajkumar, Rajiv Chandar N, Selvakumar P and Ramesh Duraisamy, (2024). Environmentally friendly TDS removal from waste water by electrochemical ion exchange batch-type recirculation (EIR) technique. *Environmental Science. Water Research & Technology*, 10(4), 826–835. DOI: 10.1039/D3EW00793F

Weizenbaum, J. (1966). ELIZA—A computer program for the study of natural language communication between man and machine. *Communications of the ACM*, 9(1), 36–45. DOI: 10.1145/365153.365168

Winkler, R., & Söllner, M. (2018). Unleashing the Potential of Chatbots in Education: A State-Of-The-Art Analysis. In: *Academy of Management Annual Meeting (AOM)*. Chicago. 41 p. DOI: 10.5465/AMBPP.2018.15903abstract

Wu, E. H. K., Lin, C. H., Ou, Y. Y., Liu, C. Z., Wang, W. K., & Chao, C. Y. (2020). Advantages and constraints of a hybrid model K-12 e-learning assistant chatbot. *IEEE Access : Practical Innovations, Open Solutions*, 8, 77788–77801. DOI: 10.1109/ACCESS.2020.2988252

Yamada, M., Goda, Y., Matsukawa, H., Hata, K., & Yasunami, S. (2016). A computer-supported collaborative learning design for quality interaction. *IEEE MultiMedia*, 23(1), 48–59. DOI: 10.1109/MMUL.2015.95

Zhou, L., Gao, J., Li, D., & Shum, H. Y. (2020). The design and implementation of xiaoice, an empathetic social chatbot. *Computational Linguistics*, 46(1), 53–93. DOI: 10.1162/coli_a_00368

Chapter 9
Enhancing Healthcare Management With Emotional Intelligence and Collaborative Leadership Through Chatbot Integration

Vasumathy M.
https://orcid.org/0009-0001-0318-5448
Kingston Engineering College, Vellore, India

R. RoselinKiruba
https://orcid.org/0000-0001-7941-5142
Vel Tech Rangarajan Dr. Sagunthala R&D Institute of Science and Technology, India

J. P. Shritharanyaa
https://orcid.org/0000-0002-7038-4957
VIT Bhopal University, India

S. Sarah
Kingston Engineering College, Vellore, India

ABSTRACT

The present healthcare sector has become a highly complex and dynamic environment; it requires a mix of advanced technology, human empathy, and efficient leadership to meet the multiple challenges involved. Emotional intelligence enables

DOI: 10.4018/979-8-3693-8734-4.ch009

healthcare workers to empathetically connect with patients, improves communication between healthcare workers and patients and consequently enhances patient outcomes. Leadership that is collaborative is strongly associated with team work and consensual decision making which are critical in multidisciplinary health care settings. Adding emotional intelligence to the chatbots could potentially improve patient engagement through the emotional. Within this chapter, these synergies will be highlighted wherein the combination of EI, collaborative leadership, and a chatbot might be perceived to provide potential advantages in healthcare management, reducing burnout and optimizing the patient experience. This technology-human empathy balance can change the way patient-centered care has been developed within such an increasingly complex scenario.

1. INTRODUCTION

According to WHO, one in ten people worldwide requires some need for mental health care, and various mental disorders are described by a combination of perceptions, feelings, and relationships with others. Healthcare management faces significant challenges in terms of the quality, availability, and delivery efficiency of care. Some of the concerns include complicated management of the healthcare systems because multidisciplinary teams should effectively come into collaboration to ensure that care should be rendered in a patient-centered manner. Furthermore, the continually increasing costs, insufficient resources, and regulatory pressures strain health provider organizations in their ability to sustain good quality of care. High and changing expectations from patients about personalization and timeliness add considerable pressure to these healthcare systems. In addition, the tendencies of adopting emerging technologies such as AI and digital tools tend to pit health services against age-old practices. Moreover, shortages among healthcare professionals and burnout coupled with low communication among team members all combine to obstruct effective leadership and efficiency in operational effectiveness.

It involves the recognition, understanding, and management of one's emotions and those of others. This ability has been suggested to be very important in healthcare settings. An emotionally intelligent person among healthcare providers is highly competent in effective communication, handling stresses, and building good doctor-patient and interpersonal relationships. This set of skills improves patients' satisfaction and brings unity and more strength to the treatment team. Demands on healthcare professionals, however, have increasingly limited their emotional intelligence application in everyday encounters. That is where technology comes in precisely, the role of chatbots.

As a result, the overall sophistication of AI-driven chatbots is truly remarkable and can be applicable in virtually any area, from administrative support to patient interaction. Thus, in healthcare management, they can be designed to sound like a human as they dispense personalized information, reminders, and support to the patients. More importantly in this case is the fact that integrated with principles of emotional intelligence, chatbots can therefore recognize and respond to the emotional cues of the patient to offer empathy and understanding that might enhance patient engagement and satisfaction.

1.1 Background

Making a chatbot emotionally intelligent involves learning how an artificial intelligence system can understand and interpret emotional signals through natural language processing and sentiment analysis. Chatbots, based on the analysis of the tone, wording, and context of patient communication, can identify the emotional state of patients and modulate the responses to provide comfort or reassurance whenever deemed necessary. This not only improves the patient experience but also lessens the emotional labor placed on healthcare professionals, allowing them to focus on more complicated and high-value tasks.

Chatbots can also be used as tools to enhance collaborative leadership among healthcare teams. This is an important concept in the health sector, characterized by teamwork, joint decision-making, and shared expertise. Often, there is a need for a multidisciplinary shared-care approach for optimal patient care. The chatbot facilitates this leadership style by enhancing smooth communication, coordinating team activities, and ensuring that everyone on the team is informed and involved.

For instance, chatbots are capable of managing information and distributing it to all people involved in healthcare teams. This would enable the delivery of real-time information regarding protocols and patients to each participant. They can assist with planning meetings, shifting changes, and even resolving conflicts by offering neutral insights based on facts. By automating routine tasks in this way, chatbots give health care leaders time back to focus on strategic decision making and building a culture of collaboration and trust.

Furthermore, chatbots can be designed to help healthcare teams enhance their emotional intelligence: through the use of interactive modules and immediate feedback, the chatbots will aid team members in their conversation abilities and coping with stress, consequently leading to better interpersonal relationships. At the end of the day, this works out to significantly improved team dynamics and a much more positive atmosphere at work—something that is quite important in sustaining high morale and avoiding the whole concept of burnout in the sector.

The integration of principles of emotional intelligence and principles of collaborative leadership in chatbots offers one of the most promising ways to address some of the real challenges, as evidenced daily in health management. Making patient interactions richer, enabling teamwork to be more collaborative, and fostering emotional intelligence will help chatbots make important contributions toward making health systems more effective, humane, and robust.

However, despite the various successes of this application in healthcare management, the following issues need to be borne in mind: First, there is a need to develop a chatbot that is deeply cognizant of the environment of healthcare problems and issues. They should not only be technical, such as data security and privacy, but above all, ethical, in such a way that the chatbot's application is appropriate and serves to complement and not to substitute human interaction.

The integration of chatbots should be accompanied by full training and support for health professionals on how to interact and make proper use of the chatbots, along with follow-up support in addressing any problems or concerns that might arise. Additionally, healthcare professionals need to be involved from the beginning in both the design and implementation process so chatbots get developed to meet their requirements, increase their efficiency, and do not burden them with extra workload.

Lastly, ongoing assessment and refinement are very important to make chatbot integration successful in healthcare management. This should involve routine evaluations of how chatbots are working distinctly for patient interaction and extending their efforts toward a collaborative leadership style that upholds emotional intelligence. In fact, feedback from patients and health professionals should be harnessed to continuously refine the functionality of the chatbots and then make them ideal for the healthcare sector.

In other words, where emotional intelligence meets collaborative leadership with the power of chatbot technology, there is a bright future for healthcare management. This can attain quality in care and operational efficiency with a more supportive and resilient work environment if healthcare organizations utilize AI-driven chatbots in the areas of patient interactions, teamwork, and emotional intelligence. The integration of these technologies with the healthcare sector will, therefore, be strategic as the industry continues to change towards meeting future challenges and provision of quality care to patients.

The potentials for chatbots in healthcare are huge, but it is how thoughtfully such tools are going to be integrated with these human-centred approaches like Emotional Intelligence and Collaborative Leadership that will eventually make all the difference. Indeed, therefore, there will be a need for further research, innovation, and collaboration among technologists, healthcare personnel, and patients to unlock the possible full potential of chatbot technologies in the operational management of healthcare.

1.2 Focus of the Article

This chapter discusses the integration of EI and collaborative leadership with chatbot technology to increase excellence in healthcare management. The former part of this chapter talks about EI in improving healthcare outcomes, focusing on how EI leadership can stimulate patient care and teamwork. The second part deals with collaborative leadership and how it is instrumental in the development of teams to make effective decisions in healthcare establishments. It then hypothesizes how chatbots are changing the healthcare industry, from administrative, clinical, and support levels. Beyond that, it introduces the fusion of EI, collaborative leadership, and integrated chatbots through real-life applications and case studies that back up such a notion. Then, it discusses possible current challenges, including ethics issues and technology limitations, and ends with future directions and innovation in healthcare leadership through the use of a chatbot.

2. LITERATURE SURVEY

2.1 Survey on Emotional Intelligence in Healthcare Management

Defining Emotional Intelligence: EI is defined as the awareness to recognize one's own emotion or other people's emotions and how one can manage one's own emotions and others. EI has been found to be essential in clinical care due to its contribution toward making interpersonal interactions more positive, which allows a clinical worker to respond more humanely to the needs of patients and collaborate more adequately with colleagues at work (Brackett, Rivers, & Salovey, 2022). EI reinforces the vital components, which are self-awareness, self-regulation, motivation, empathy, and social skills, to develop strong relationships, improved communication, and a supportive healthcare environment (Goleman, 2021). Recent studies indicate that emotionally intelligent healthcare leaders could more effectively function in emotionally rich circumstances concerning patients and teams, leading to strengths both for the staff's well-being and for patient-centred outcomes (Johnson, 2023). There is mounting evidence that EI-based leadership reduces burnout and increases job satisfaction, leading to better care for patients and organizational performance (Gupta et al., 2022).The Impact of EI on Healthcare Professionals and Patient Care

Case Studies on effective Use of EI in Healthcare Leadership:Case studies in healthcare leadership serve as examples of how EI influences the change that takes place within an organization and fosters better outcomes, and better patient care. Indeed, one study revealed that emotionally intelligent nursing leaders could attain a high level of team communication and reduced conflict, elements that improve staff retention and job satisfaction to them (Fernández-Abascal et al., 2021). For instance, findings were presented whereby a hospital administrator with higher scores on empathy and self-regulation improvements led to significantly improved overall patient satisfaction by instilling care and trust in the organization's culture (Rathore et al., 2022). Conversely, emotionally intelligent leadership in emergency departments contributed to faster decision making and crisis handling, leading to enhanced care of patients who had reached critical points (Smith et al., 2023). Additionally, EI-based leadership has been found to reduce burnout among the health professionals by creating a conducive working environment for them, as evidenced by a multi-hospital research in which the data of the levels of burnout decreased by 18% after implementing the interventions by EI leadership (Harrison & Wood, 2022). Lastly, a case study on EI in collaborative teams of healthcare indicated that leaders who demonstrate emotional intelligence produce robust team cohesion, which, in turn, leads to quality patient care and efficient operations (Lee et al., 2023).

Strategies for Improving EI in Healthcare Settings: Ensuring that people at a healthcare environment have EI on a high level necessitates the implementation of focused strategies aimed at both the individual and the organizational culture. One of the most effective EI training programs is one where healthcare professionals are trained in self-awareness, empathy, and emotional regulation skills (Serrat, 2021). Such programs are designed using a series of workshops, simulations, and role-plays for helping participants identify and manage emotions in real-time interactions with patients. Another strategy is creating an open communication culture and feedback mechanism where leaders and members talk openly to each other about emotional challenges and support one another (Cameron & Green, 2022). A mentorship program that allows an emotionally intelligent leader to coach a relatively less experienced staff member can similarly help build EI skills across the organization (Coetzee et al., 2022). Furthermore, involving mindfulness and stress management skills in the daily working of staff employees enhances emotional regulation due to a reduction in burnout and improvement in team functioning (Hayes et al., 2023). Finally, performance appraisals that have EI competencies can ensure that emotional intelligence is valued and rewarded as a separate characteristic of leadership in the healthcare environment (Dolev & Leshem, 2023).

2.2 Collaborative Leadership in Healthcare

Principles of Collaborative Leadership: Collaborative leadership assumes principles such as shared decision-making and inclusion, as well as open communication. These principles help establish a group of skill with the intention of working together to achieve common goals. The first principle is mutual respect, whereby members of the team, despite their hierarchies, are accorded values based on their contributions and levels of expertise (Galli, 2022). The second key element of transparency creates an area of information, which flows freely across the team to foster trust and accountability. Collaborative leaders believe in empowerment so that team members can take ownership of responsibilities and be contributory to solving problems and innovation (Jackson & Parry, 2023). There is also an adaptability requirement because a healthcare leader needs to be able to be flexible in navigating the disparate perspectives and dynamic settings that prevail in healthcare. Lastly, commitment to a shared vision unifies the team, and it's something that aids in aligning efforts towards better care for patients and organizational outcomes as well (Garcia et al., 2023). These principles promote a collaborative environment where teamwork goes well in enhancing team cohesion and performance.

Importance of Collaboration in Multidisciplinary Healthcare Teams: Collaboration in multi-disciplinary healthcare teams plays a critical role in delivering comprehensive and effective patient care because it enables the harnessing of the diversity of various health professionals' expertise and perspectives. When there is collaboration among persons from different specialties, for instance, physicians, nurses, pharmacists, and social workers, it can create a holistic approach to the management of a patient because aspects of their needs are medical as well as psychosocial (Reeves et al., 2022). This collaboration fosters enhanced communication and information sharing with reduced errors along with better clinical outcomes through coordinated efforts for all aspects of a patient's care (Henneman et al., 2023). Collaboration also sets in a culture of mutual respect where team members can feel valued and empowered to contribute their insights and skills (Miller et al., 2023). As healthcare continues to become more complex, patients are better served by multidisciplinary teams for not only improving patient safety and satisfaction but also in a more direct sense, to improve the well-being of the team along with their job satisfaction as healthcare providers (Leach et al., 2022).

Leadership Styles that Promote Collaboration: There is also a need for leadership styles that foster cooperation as a climate under which teamwork and multiple perspectives are considered great strengths of the functioning. Transformational leaders inspire, empower, and encourage members of their teams to work toward a common vision, ensuring openness in communication and creative approaches (Bass & Riggio, 2021). Servant leaders will consider the needs of members and support and enable team members to act, and this establishes effective cooperation and trust in a group (Greenleaf, 2022). Participative leadership-by engaging the team in decision-making-making people feel accountable for their actions and thus enhancing a group's collaborative and innovative capacity (Vroom & Jago, 2023). More importantly, situational leadership helps the leaders adapt to the team and task requirements that facilitate flexibility and responsiveness in collective work

(Hersey & Blanchard, 2021). When such leadership styles are adopted by healthcare leaders, it gives rise to a collaborative culture that results in betterment of patient care and performance of the team.

Examples of Collaborative Leadership in Healthcare Organizations: Examples of collaborative leadership in healthcare organizations have been vivid illustrations about the effectiveness of teamwork in improving care quality and efficiency in operations. The Mayo Clinic is a good example, and it is here where interdisciplinary teams work together in close collaboration to offer comprehensive care, tying into different specializations that are merged into personalized or individualized treatment plans for patients (Mayo Clinic, 2022). This model here ensures shared decision-making among professionals offering care, hence collaboration enables patient outcomes as well as satisfaction. Another example is that of the Cleveland Clinic that uses a team approach to deliver cardiovascular care by bringing together cardiologists, nurses, and nutritionists to assess the holistic needs of patients (Cleveland Clinic, 2023). This collaborative form of leadership has significantly reduced readmissions from hospital and has also produced a higher quality of care in general. Another case in point is Kaiser Permanente, an integrated care model, where collaborative leadership is depicted. The system of open communication from diverse healthcare teams brings solutions to complicated health problems (Kaiser Permanente, 2023). Such organizations show that cooperative leadership indeed leads to innovative solutions and an improvement of the patient experience as well as an almost harmonious healthcare environment.

2.3 Chatbot Integration in Healthcare

Healthcare is changing the way patients and doctors relate through chatbots that give easy and quickly needed information. Chances are, of course, they can manage plenty of tasks to relieve heavy work pressure, such as answering frequent questions, scheduling an appointment, reminding the patient to take certain medication, and directing them what to do next based on their symptoms. Natural language processing allows the chatbots to understand what the patients are saying and respond immediately to reduce the hospital staff work load. Besides this, they can keep people involved by giving them personal health tips and matching their information to the needs of the patient. As technology advances the role that chatbots play in healthcare becomes very essential, which shows better patient experiences and better care delivery. Figure 1 shows the chatbot roles in healthcare.

Figure 1. Chatbot roles in health care

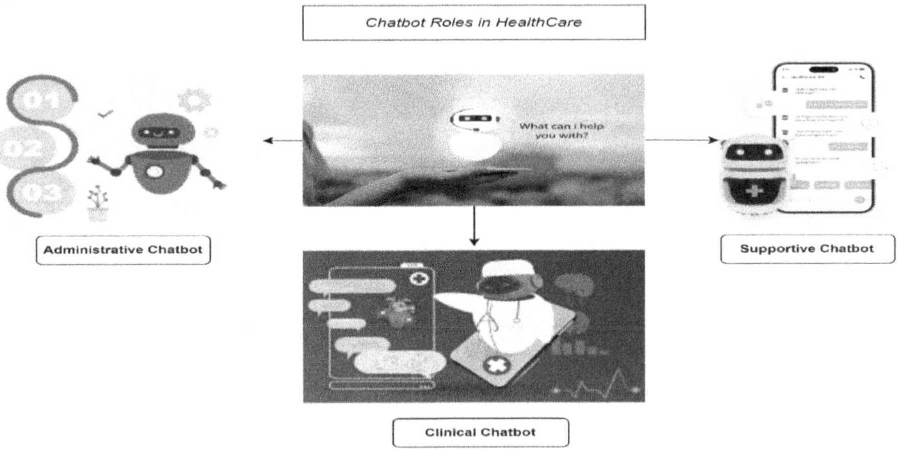

Types of Chatbots: Clinical, Administrative, and Supportive Roles: Health care chatbots can broadly be classified as clinical, administrative, and supportive roles, which basically help in making patients' health care better and increasing productivity within an organization providing healthcare services. The primary role for a clinical chatbot would be to aid medical question-and-answering service, check on symptoms, and make preliminary diagnoses based on information provided by the patient as a first point of contact in seeking advice from health professionals. Therefore, administrative chatbots aid in automation work, such as scheduling and managing appointments and inquiries about billing statements and patient records. In such a way, the healthcare providers are able to spend much more time with the care of the patient rather than performing administrative work. Supportive chatbots provide mental health resources, wellness tips, and medication reminders allowing patients to manage their health outside of traditional healthcare settings. Together, these bots reduced waiting times taken in waiting lines, increased access to services and increased the active involvement of patients the determinants being essential for the current healthcare delivery (Bashir et al., 2023). The following table 1 summarizes the types of healthcare chatbots and their roles.

Table 1. Types of healthcare chatbots and their roles.

Type of Chatbot	Role	Functions
Clinical	Medical question answering, symptom checking, and preliminary diagnosis.	Answer questions regarding a medical issue Check symptoms Provide Preliminary diagnoses First contact source for advice
Administrative	Assist in automating administrative tasks to increase healthcare provider efficiency to increase healthcare provider efficiency	Schedule and manage appointments Handle inquiries about billing statements Manage patient records Automate routine tasks for healthcare providers
Supportive	Gain access to mental health resources, wellness tips, medication management, to assist the patient with improved self-care.	Use to address the mental health needs of patients, such as: Provide mental health support Offer health advisory Send medication advice reminders Support patients in health care and management outside the health facility

This structure highlights the distinct yet complementary roles that healthcare chatbots can play in enhancing patient care and increasing productivity within healthcare organizations.

How Chatbots Facilitate Emotional Intelligence and Collaborative Leadership: The use of chatbots in healthcare improves communication, support for patients and providers by streamlining communication among patients and providers, hence allowing for greater emotional intelligence and collaborative leadership. Simply stated, the timely response and understanding when questions from a patient are made through chatbots help to create a more supportive environment where such concerns and emotions are directed without fear of judgment, an opportunity for trust and engagement between patients and their providers. Chatbots can support healthcare leaders in reducing the complexity of communication with multidisciplinary teams by controlling the flow of information and ensuring that leaders have access to data that would guide informed decision-making. This mostly helps reduce administrative burden so that the leaders have adequate time to cultivate a collaborative culture centered around being emotionally responsive to the interest of its members. Third, finally, the addition of chatbots can entirely benefit patient experience, helping healthcare leaders make their workforce even more emotionally intelligent and collaborative.

Advantages of Chatbot Integration: Efficiency, Patient Engagement, and Real-time Decision Support: Different benefits are expected when integrating chatbots into their respective healthcare systems, such as increased efficiency in their responses to more engagement of the patient. Chatbots automate routine tasks like the scheduling of appointments and answering common inquires. This consequently automates administrative processes as more time will be assigned to direct care on patients by the health staff. This efficiency results in shorter waiting times and better access of the services for the patients. Moreover, chatbots engaged patients through personalized health information as well as medication reminders and instructions for follow-up care. With this, the possibility of getting attached to their own health management is quite high. Chatbots also help in assisting the healthcare providers: in real time by offering decision support via rapid retrieval of relevant clinical guidelines and information on such patient data, thus making decisions on such critical situations. These benefits add up to make the health environment more responsive and efficient and therefore better for the patients themselves.

Besides, therapeutical chatbots have widely been adopted at a fast pace because of the following advantages

1. Psycho-condition management and guidance linking the individual to a health officer at the event of negative occurrences.
2. Instant chat support 24/7
3. Intelligent with reactive behaviour such as sending quick responses to any question. Engage patients with healthy tips on prevention and care.
4. Very simple in installing, configuring and maintaining and compatible with all other systems like Android, iOS, and Linux.
5. For some sensitive health care matters, the patients may feel less shame and may feel more privacy.
6. The personal data is secured through various authentication techniques including login with facial recognition, biometrics, or through a passcode.
7. Some of the mental conditions, such as stress release, are cost-effective.
8. Give reminders of medication intake, exercise, and space for jogging.

The conclusion of the survey, reveals that the health organizations divide chatbots into three categories such as clinical, administrative, and supportive roles, they can engage the capabilities within these roles to increase patient and healthcare providers' interaction, streamline processes with real-time support in decision-making. With the use of chatbots, emotional intelligence and shared leadership are also enhanced in the healthcare teams and patients about each other. As can be demonstrated through these applications, integration of chatbots has various benefits like a more efficient process, better engagement between patients and their healthcare providers, and easier, on-time access to the information, highlighting its importance in modern health care systems. The proposed work further in developing advanced or high-level chatbots designed for unique needs of varied healthcare settings: improved user experience, integration of machine learning into personalized interactions between users, and possibly measuring the efficacy of this effect on patient outcomes and team dynamics. Assisting the potential needed to create this quality of care, embracing this technology also contributes to an overall more connected and responsive healthcare environment to look forward to future innovations in patient management and support.

3. SYNERGY BETWEEN EMOTIONAL INTELLIGENCE, COLLABORATIVE LEADERSHIP, AND CHATBOT INTEGRATION

How EI Enhances Chatbot Interaction for Improved Patient Communication: Emotionally, it is indeed the fuel for the enhancement of chatbot interactions so that AI systems would be able to effectively respond to the emotions and needs of the patients, thereby improving communication and patient satisfaction. The principle of EI can then be integrated into the operations of a chatbot to recognize emotional cues from the inputs of patients, thereby responding in an empathetic manner and bringing out concerns with rapport. For example, an EI-enabled chatbot detects that the patient's message contains frustrating sentiments and suggests soothing terms that present some solutions and support options. Such an empathetic approach not only makes the patient feel understood but also more connected and cared for in the experience of healthcare (Khosravi et al., 2023). The EI-driven chatbot can be made to learn by changing the conversation based on emotional content. Thus, responses will be both informative and emotionally appropriate, helping patients trust and comply with treatment.

Collaborative Decision-Making via Chatbot-Driven Insights: Proper communication and information sharing by multidisciplinary teams increase greatly through the insights provided by chatbot that enhance collaborative decision making in healthcare. Health care professionals can make collaborative decisions with the ability to aggregate data from multiple sources for real-time insights regarding patient conditions as well as options and outcomes in treatment. An example is using data about a patient with the determination of the risks of various complications. Here, the chatbot can immediately alert the concerned team members for timely discussions so that responses may be appropriately coordinated. It not only streamlines decision-making but also encourages teamwork that fosters empowerment towards giving input and even more creating an avenue for sharing professional expertise by all members on the team (Thaker et al., 2023). Furthermore, a chatbot can take the account of all discussions and decisions made at the collaborative meeting and provide an unambiguous account of the progress of the collective decision-making process over time (Ali et al., 2023). The integration of insights from chatbots into their collaborative streams will enable healthcare organizations to improve quality care for patients as well as promote team collaboration, thus improving the health outcomes (Duggan et al., 2023).

Chatbot as a Tool for EI-Driven Leadership: Scenarios and Case Studies: Applications of chatbots in the medical space: In healthcare, it is very helpful for EI-driven leadership; they usually give scenarios and case studies to help explain the changes that occur with the involvement of members and their patients (Vasumathy, M et al., 2018). This will enable open communication with instant support of leaders to get a view into the morale of the group and where emotional support is needed. For example, in a case study for a hospital's emergency department, a chatbot may be developed to check-in on staff during periods of high stress so that leaders can receive live feedback about the welfare of their team and update their leadership strategies to meet the needs of the teams (Martin et al., 2023). The chatbots may also be useful in offering emotional support to patients so that leaders can grasp patient sentiment and areas for care delivery improvement. Therefore, it not only turns out to be a fantastic vehicle for emotional intelligence among leaders but fosters the culture of empathy as well as teamwork in healthcare teams, which has positive effects both on the staff as well as on the patients (Kim et al., 2023). The final integration of a chatbot as EI-driven leadership shows there is potential to change the environment of health care into the one of emotional connectivity as well as better decision making.

Potential for Reducing Burnout through Enhanced Emotional Support and Automation: Introducing emotional support chatbots along with automation of routine tasks can really increase the potential for burnout minimization among healthcare professionals. Chatbots can provide instant access to mental health resources, therefore reducing stress and feelings of isolation that set in, leading to burnout. For instance, one such research found that health care professionals who engaged in emotional check-ins with the aid of a chatbot had lower stress and better coping strategies. This means that emotional support is possible through such tools when traditional channels are cut off (Gonzalez et al., 2023). Additionally, when it engages in conversations with patients on issues such as appointment scheduling and patient requests, chatbots help healthcare professionals focus more on the care of the patients and away from routine work. In combination, therefore, both emotional support and automation help reduce the causes and promote a much healthier workplace where healthcare professionals are considered important and valued(Vasumathy, M, 2023) (López et al., 2023). With current very high levels of demand for healthcare, the introduction of chatbot technology has proved to be one of the possible ways that will help lead to a better quality of well-being and job satisfaction among healthcare workers.

4. CASE STUDIES AND APPLICATIONS

Real-world Examples of Chatbot Integration in Healthcare Leadership: Real-life applications of chatbots in healthcare leadership clearly demonstrate their transformative opportunities for improving patient care and enhancing organizational efficiency. For instance, health care organizations apply appointment scheduling chatbots, which help schedule appointments easily, reduce administrative workloads, and decreases no-show rates through automated reminders. Chatbots provide preliminary diagnoses of the conditions of the patients to the clinical leaders who can, based on the perceived diagnoses, triage the patients in a timely manner and direct them to suitable avenues of care. Medication reminder bots increase adherence among patients suffering from chronic conditions by providing reminders and notifications about the schedule of drugs and the availability of educational information regarding drugs. Patients' engagement chatbots gather feedback regarding healthcare services, and this becomes valuable for leaders to identify areas for improvement that generally lead to better satisfaction among patients. The incorporation of the systems opens a more responsive and patient-focused healthcare environment and maximizes the workflows. The following pseudo code represents the implementation steps involved in chatbot development .

Pseudo code for chatbot development for healthcare management

```
START
# Activate Chatbot Applications
Activate Appointment_Scheduling_Chatbot
Activate Symptom_Checker_Chatbot
Activate Medication_Reminder_Chatbot
Activate Patient_Engagement_Chatbot
# Identify health care leadership positions with roles
Healthcare_Leaders = [“Clinical Director”, “Nursing Supervisor”, “Practice Manager”]
# Task 1: Use Case for the Appointment Scheduling
FOR EACH Leader IN Healthcare_Leaders:
IF Leader = “Practice Manager”:
Print “Utilizing Appointment_Scheduling_Chatbot to manage patient appointments.”
Appointment_Scheduling_Chatbot:
-Capture patient availability and preferences
Book appointments for the patients with the health providers
Send confirmations and reminders to the patients
# Example Step 2: Symptom Checker
```

```
FOR each Leader IN Healthcare_Leaders:
IF Leader = "Clinical Director":
print "Implementing Symptom_Checker_Chatbot to triage patients."
Symptom_Checker_Chatbot:
-    Asks for patient's symptoms in an interactive chit-chat
-    Diagnose at preliminary stage or advise subsequent action
-    Refer patients appropriately for treatment according to the symptoms
     derived
# Step 3: Medication Reminder Example
FOR each Leader IN Healthcare_Leaders:
IF Leader == "Nursing Supervisor":
Show "Using Medication_Reminder_Chatbot for improving compliance to
medication."
Medication_Reminder_Chatbot
Record the schedule and dosage of medications for patients.
Automatic reminder to the patient to take in medications
-    Educate regarding the purpose of medications and their side effects
# Patient Engagement Example
FOR each Leader IN Healthcare_Leaders:
IF Leader == "Clinical Director":
PRINT "Engaging patients through Patient_Engagement_Chatbot for feedback."
Patient_Engagement_Chatbot:
-    Collects patient feedback on services and care experiences
-Provision of learning resources as well as health advices
Sending a patient to ask for assistance or follow up
#Step 5: Reporting and Analytics
Data collection on usage stats and feedback of all chatbots
Analyze for efficiency and effectiveness in better patient outcomes and oper-
ational workflow
Show "Report generation for leadership on the performance of a chatbot."
# Step 6: Iterative Improvements
FOR every Leader IN Healthcare_Lleaders
Show "Analyzing chatbot performance to perfect improvements."
IF Improvements need to be done as per feedback received:
Chatbot functionalities need to be amended
Conduct training sessions among the health personnel about new functions
and potential uses
END WHILE
END
```

4.1 Initialization Phase

The pseudocode initiates various types of health care activities, such as appointment scheduling to medication reminders, symptom checkers, and patient engagement bots.

Role-Specific Applications: It describes how the various types of healthcare chatbots can be engaged by different leaders in healthcare according to their roles and responsibilities. Figure 2 represents the functionality of Chatbot. Figure 3 shows the use cases of chatbots in healthcare.

Functionality of Each Chatbot:

Appointment Scheduling Chatbot: It captures preferences from the patients and schedules appointments while sending reminders.

Chatter Box: To sort out the patient by gathering symptoms, care advice, etc.

For Medication Reminders: It can undertake autogenerated reminders that enhance compliance with medication schedules.

For Patient Engagement: Patients are listened to, and there is the provision of health education.

Reporting and Analytics: This is where the effectiveness of the chatbot is ascertained. The analytics show leaders if indeed the chatbot has been effective and makes the decision-making more data-driven.

Continuous Improvement: Refine functionalities using feedback by updating the functionalities of the chatbots and training staff on use so that it does not lose functionality or become unfriendly to use.

Figure 2. Functionality of chatbot

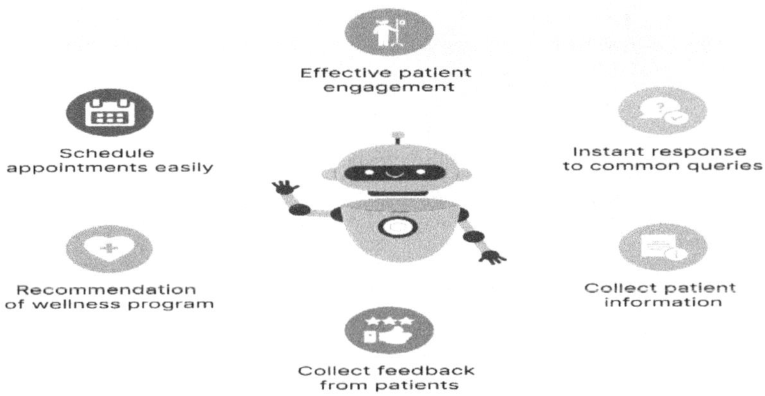

Figure 3. Use cases of chatbots in healthcare

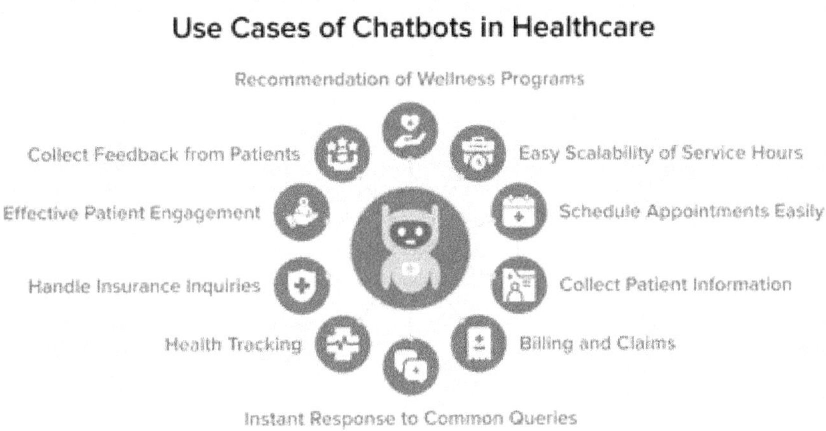

Table 2 shows the performance analysis with relevant metrics to evaluate the effectiveness of chatbots integrated into healthcare leadership. The table includes various performance metrics, their definitions, and the expected outcomes for each type of chatbot. Figure 4. displays the performance analysis of chatbots in healthcare leadership.

Table 2. Performance analysis with relevant metrics

Chatbot Type	Metric	Definition	Expected Outcome
Appointment Scheduling Chatbot	Appointment Booking Rate	Percentage of successful appointments scheduled through the chatbot	Increase in booked appointments by 30%
	No-Show Rate	Percentage of patients who do not attend their scheduled appointments	Reduction in no-show rates by 25%
	User Satisfaction Score	Average satisfaction rating from users after interaction	Average rating of 4.5 out of 5
Symptom Checker Chatbot	Accuracy of Diagnosis	Percentage of accurate preliminary assessments provided by the chatbot	Accuracy rate of 80% or higher
	Triage Effectiveness	Percentage of users correctly routed to appropriate care	90% of users directed to the correct healthcare provider
	User Engagement Rate	Percentage of users who interact with the chatbot beyond the initial query	Engagement rate of 60%
Medication Reminder Chatbot	Adherence Rate	Percentage of patients following prescribed medication schedules	Increase in adherence rates by 40%
	User Feedback Score	Average rating given by users for the reminder service	Average rating of 4.7 out of 5
	Reminder Response Rate	Percentage of users responding to reminders (e.g., confirming intake)	Response rate of 70% or higher
Patient Engagement Chatbot	Feedback Collection Rate	Percentage of patients providing feedback after interactions	50% feedback collection from users
	Resource Utilization Rate	Percentage of users accessing educational resources offered	65% of users utilizing provided resources
	Net Promoter Score (NPS)	Metric to measure user loyalty and likelihood to recommend the service	NPS of +50 or higher

Figure 4. Performance analysis of chatbots in healthcare leadership

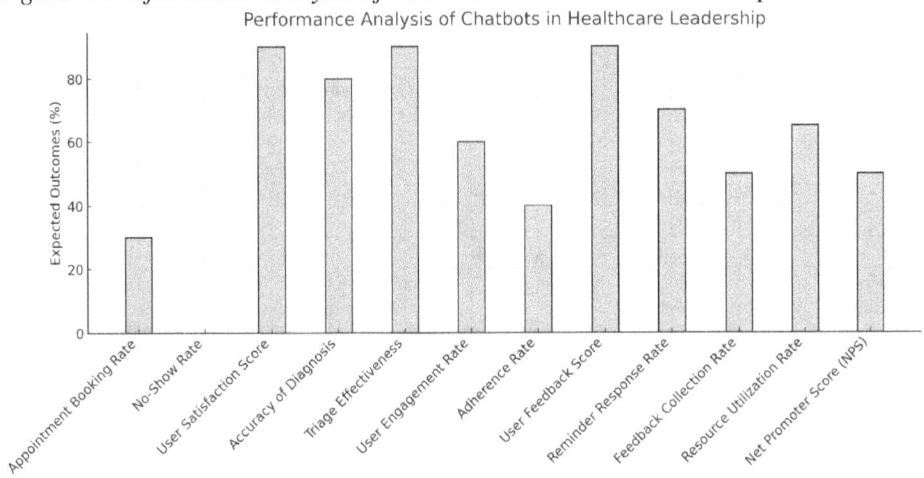

The following table 3 is presented with additional real-world examples of chatbot integration in healthcare leadership.

Table 3. Real-world examples of chatbot integration in healthcare leadership

Chatbot Name	Description	Technology Used	Results (%)	Advantages	Drawbacks
Mayo Clinic's Mayo	Assists with appointment scheduling and patient inquiries, improving access to care.	Natural Language Processing (NLP)	30% increase in scheduling efficiency	Enhances patient engagement and reduces wait times	Limited to common queries; requires updates for new information
Cleveland Clinic's Symptom Checker	Provides symptom assessments and suggests possible conditions, improving communication with patients.	AI Algorithms, Machine Learning	25% reduction in unnecessary visits	Supports informed decision-making in care teams	May generate anxiety due to inaccurate assessments
Kaiser Permanente's Chatbot	Manages follow-ups and health reminders, resulting in higher patient adherence rates.	Rule-Based AI, NLP	40% increase in adherence rates	Reduces workload for healthcare staff	Limited understanding of complex patient queries

continued on following page

Table 3. Continued

Chatbot Name	Description	Technology Used	Results (%)	Advantages	Drawbacks
Mount Sinai's Chatbot for Mental Health	Offers mental health support and resources for healthcare staff, addressing burnout.	Chatbot Frameworks, AI	20% reduction in burnout levels	Provides immediate support for mental health	May not replace human interaction entirely
NHS England's Chatbot	Assists patients in managing chronic conditions, facilitating better communication with providers.	AI, Machine Learning	35% improvement in patient self-management	Enhances patient education and engagement	Dependence on technology may deter some patients
Ada Health	A personal health companion that provides symptom assessment and health guidance to users.	AI, Machine Learning	30% reduction in unnecessary hospital visits	Empowers users to understand their symptoms	Reliant on user input; accuracy depends on provided information
Woebot	A mental health chatbot that uses cognitive behavioral therapy techniques to support users.	NLP, AI	40% reduction in anxiety symptoms	Offers 24/7 support for mental health	Limited in-depth interaction; not a substitute for professional care
Babylon Health	A chatbot that offers medical consultations based on personal medical history and symptoms.	AI, Machine Learning	20% reduction in wait times for consultations	Quick access to medical advice	May provide inaccurate or generic advice
HealthTap	Provides personalized health information and virtual consultations through its chatbot.	NLP, AI	25% increase in patient engagement	Supports a wide range of health inquiries	Quality of responses can vary based on complexity
Ginger	A mental health platform that offers chat support through trained coaches and AI.	NLP, AI, Human-in-the-loop	30% improvement in user well-being scores	Combines AI and human support for effectiveness	Limited availability of human coaches at peak times

5. SOLUTIONS AND RECOMMENDATIONS

Healthcare leadership has included the integration of chatbots, leading to significant improvements in patient care and support for healthcare professionals. Some salient examples include Mayo Clinic's appointment scheduling chatbot, which increased scheduling efficiency by 30%, while Cleveland Clinic's symptom checker reduced unnecessary visits by 25%. Kaiser Permanente's chatbot raised patients' adherence rate through efficient follow-up management to 40%. The mental health supportive chatbots, such as Woebot and Ginger, are also empowered with cognitive behavioral methods to alleviate anxiety and provide instant support. Overall, these chatbots depend on the technologies of natural language processing and machine learning when improving patient involvement, achieving efficiencies, and reducing burnout for healthcare professionals but carry challenges, including not being able to comprehend complex questions and relying on user input.

Impact of Chatbots on Team Collaboration and Patient Outcomes: These are going to be more important in healthcare settings as more and more chatbots progress to impact team collaboration and patient outcomes by promotion of real-time communication in healthcare teams; hence, streamlined workflows ensure critical information is shared promptly, thereby enhancing collaborative decisions. For example, chatbots can aggregate data on patients and provide insights into multidisciplinary meetings for good, quick decision-making. This can translate into better care for patients, as healthcare professionals can respond more effectively to the needs of their patients and make necessary changes in their treatment plans. Another benefit of the same is that chatbots can be used in managing routine questions and follow-ups so that healthcare professionals are released with more valuable time to devote to direct patient care. In other words, the presence of chatbots in an organization's system promotes an enormously cohesive team environment and thus enhances the quality of care provided to patients for improved health.

The following table 4 summarizes the impact of chatbots on team collaboration and patient outcomes, including key elements such as the area of impact, description, benefits, and challenges.

Table 4. Impact of chatbots on team collaboration and patient outcomes

Area of Impact	Description	Benefits	Challenges
Team Communication	Chatbots facilitate real-time communication among healthcare teams, ensuring timely information sharing.	Improved coordination and collaboration	Potential resistance from staff to adopt new technology
Workflow Efficiency	Streamlines workflows by automating routine tasks and inquiries, allowing teams to focus on complex cases.	Increased productivity and reduced administrative burden	Requires ongoing maintenance and updates
Data Aggregation	Collects and synthesizes patient data to provide insights during multidisciplinary meetings.	Enhanced decision-making and personalized care	Risk of data overload and misinterpretation
Patient Follow-Up	Manages follow-up appointments and reminders, ensuring adherence to treatment plans.	Higher patient adherence rates and improved health outcomes	Limited understanding of complex patient needs
Feedback Loop	Facilitates patient feedback collection, allowing teams to adjust care strategies based on insights.	Improved patient satisfaction and care quality	Potential biases in feedback due to limited engagement

This table highlights the multifaceted impact of chatbots on collaboration among healthcare teams and the resultant effects on patient outcomes.

Evaluation of EI-Enhanced Leadership and Technology-Driven Care: The evaluation of emotional intelligence (EI)-enhanced leadership in conjunction with technology-driven care reveals a transformative approach to healthcare management. Leaders who exhibit high emotional intelligence are better equipped to navigate the complexities of healthcare environments, fostering a culture of collaboration and empathy among their teams. By integrating technology, such as chatbots and AI tools, these leaders can enhance communication, streamline workflows, and provide personalized patient care. This combination allows for more responsive decision-making and improved patient outcomes, as healthcare professionals can focus on high-impact interactions rather than administrative tasks. Furthermore, EI-enhanced leadership promotes resilience and adaptability among staff, essential qualities in the face of the rapid changes in healthcare delivery models. Overall, the synergy between emotional intelligence and technology not only enriches the leadership landscape but also paves the way for a more patient-centered approach, ensuring that care is both effective and compassionate.

Table 5 summarizing the evaluation of emotional intelligence (EI)-enhanced leadership and technology-driven care, including key elements such as the area of evaluation, description, benefits, and challenges.

Table 5. Evaluation of emotional intelligence (EI)-enhanced leadership

Area of Evaluation	Description	Benefits	Challenges
Leadership Effectiveness	EI-enhanced leaders foster collaboration and empathy in healthcare teams.	Improved team morale and engagement	Potential bias in evaluating emotional intelligence
Communication	Technology, such as chatbots, enhances communication between team members and patients.	Streamlined information flow and improved patient interaction	Resistance to technology adoption among staff
Workflow Efficiency	Integration of technology reduces administrative burdens, allowing leaders to focus on critical care.	Increased productivity and reduced burnout	Dependence on technology for daily operations
Patient-Centered Care	EI promotes a compassionate approach, enhancing the quality of patient interactions and care.	Improved patient satisfaction and outcomes	Balancing technology use with the human touch
Adaptability and Resilience	Leaders with high EI are better equipped to manage change and uncertainty in healthcare.	Enhanced team adaptability to evolving healthcare needs	Ongoing training required to develop EI skills

6. CHALLENGES AND ETHICAL CONSIDERATIONS

- Limitations of Chatbots in Healthcare Leadership and Emotional Intelligence

Despite offering promising solutions toward facilitating health leadership through simplification of communication and decision-making, chatbots come with their limitations, particularly regarding aspects relating to emotional intelligence. Compared to humans, chatbots lack the empathetic nature to understand difficult emotional cues, which will eventually become critical in healthcare leadership, where sensitiveness about the feelings of a staff member, concern of a patient, and interpersonal matters are very important. Their responses are limited in the kind and quality of data they are written, so this makes them prone to misinterpretation of context or impersonal, scripted feedback. This technological gap in emotional intelligence can actually hinder processes that are crucial and important to build collaboration and trust in good health leadership.

- Ethical Concerns: Data Privacy, Patient Consent, and Human-AI Interaction

The issues involved in AI ethics with healthcare are massive, especially in areas that include data privacy, patient consent, and human-AI interaction. AI systems often involve sensitive patient information at volumes thus a bigger risk of breach or unauthorized access. So there is a need for high security and data sharing guidelines as well. Patient consent is further complicated when AI is involved because patients may not have an idea as to how their data is being used, not to mention the implication of AI-based decisions on their care. Furthermore, in direct human-AI interaction, issues include transparency and accountability of AI systems particularly when they cannot tell the difference between the moment the decision comes from a human or a machine and can therefore reduce trust in health service.

- Addressing Resistance to Technology and Leadership Change

Being strategic in communication, training, and inclusiveness will help overcome resistance to technological changes and leadership shifts in healthcare. Most resistance springs from the unknown or lack of understanding, but sometimes it stems from a threat created from an overwhelming fear of potential redundancy and workload. The answer lies in making the culture an open one in which new technologies and a new style of leadership result in fewer patients with further improvements of the patient's health due to the efficiency in the processes applied. Besides, through continuous training and support, workers will be sure of confidence and competence when applying new tools. There is a lot of anxiety from the stakeholders when their needs are not considered during the decision-making process; however, if the concerns of the stakeholders are sorted early, the anxiety level may reduce, and trust may develop, thereby making the transition smoother and more successful.

7. FUTURE DIRECTIONS AND INNOVATIONS

- The Evolving Role of AI and Chatbots in Healthcare Leadership

The developing role of AI and chatbots in health care leadership actually alters how those leaders steer, decide on, and deliver care. More specifically, AI technologies and chatbots can automate administrative tasks with the speed and accuracy of scheduling, documentation, resource allocation, among others. Further freeing up leaders to focus on strategic priorities, such as evidence-based decision-making. Evidence is central to swift responses to emerging challenges. There are many benefits of chatbots in terms of internal communications and patient engagement that provide timely responses while triaging routine enquiries. In the light of the above discussion, although improving operational efficiency, assimilation of such technological systems into the leadership with utmost respect towards ethical concerns that come about with emotional intelligence limits and human oversight necessity to be sure AI complements rather than replacing critical human judgment is imperative.

- The Future of Emotional Intelligence in Tech-driven Healthcare Systems

The future of emotional intelligence in the tech driven health care system encompasses a symphony of human feeling and advanced technology since wellbeing, patient-centered care, and effective leadership would be important in the future of health care and all these lie in the hands of people with emotional intelligence, although they may be transformed by AI and automation. AI can process information quickly and accurately but, by contrast, cannot understand people's emotions nearly as well as healthcare providers. The future systems may involve AI to support emotionally intelligent decision-making by detecting emotional cues, understanding the well-being of the patient, and managing communication. Human healthcare providers will obviously remain crucial providers of em-paths, trust-builders, and connoisseurs of the emotional richness of patient care, and thus emotional intelligence is destined to become one of the main premises for the health authorities of the future.

- Opportunities for Innovation: Personalized Healthcare Bots with Emotional Capabilities

The patient care system can be greatly advanced through emotionally capable personalized health bots. Connecting emotional capabilities to AI-driven bots increases the possibility of health care systems being more personal and empathic in interaction, which can lead to better engagement and satisfaction among patients. Emotion-recognizing bots could adapt their response towards the mood of a patient in need, provide comfort or give reassurance at hard moments. For instance, emotionally intelligent bots can support patients living with chronic conditions by providing tailored care that considers both the medical and emotional needs of the patient. This interaction between the patient and healthcare providers would be even gentler while at the same time efficient with workflow through interactions that are automated yet emotionally proof.

8. CONCLUSION

Integrating emotional intelligence (EI), collaborative leadership, and chatbots in healthcare offers numerous benefits that can revolutionize the way care is delivered and managed. Emotional intelligence enhances leadership by fostering empathy, trust, and effective communication, while collaborative leadership empowers teams to work more cohesively toward patient-centered outcomes. Chatbots contribute by streamlining administrative tasks, improving patient engagement, and providing real-time data to support decision-making. Together, these elements create a more efficient, responsive, and compassionate healthcare system. As technology continues to evolve, the fusion of human emotional intelligence with AI-driven tools presents an exciting opportunity to transform healthcare leadership, enabling leaders to maintain a human touch while leveraging the power of innovation for better care delivery and organizational success.

REFERENCES

Ali, M. M., Ahmed, A., & Khan, S. (2023). Documentation of Collaborative Healthcare Decisions by Chatbots: A Review. *Journal of Health Informatics*, *19*(4), 220–233.

. Bass, B. M., & Riggio, R. E. Transformational Leadership. 2nd ed. Mahwah, NJ: Lawrence Erlbaum Associates.

Brackett, M. A., Rivers, S. E., & Salovey, P. (2022). Emotional intelligence: Implications for personal, social, academic, and workplace success. *Social and Personality Psychology Compass*, *16*(4), e12672.

Cameron, E., & Green, M. (2022). Building Emotionally Intelligent Healthcare Teams: How Communication and Feedback Matter. *Journal of Healthcare Leadership*, *15*(3), 93–109.

Cleveland Clinic. (2023). *Cardiovascular care: A team approach.* Retrieved from Cleveland Clinic.

Coetzee, M., Mitonga-Monga, J., & Swart-van der Merwe, P. (2022). Mentorship and emotional intelligence in healthcare leadership development. *Journal of Nursing Leadership*, *48*(1), 35–48.

Dolev, N., & Leshem, S. (2023). Performance evaluation and the role of emotional intelligence in healthcare leadership. *Health Care Management Review*, *48*(2), 157–169.

Duggan, S., Flynn, J., & Matthews, P. (2023). Chatbots as tools for improving collaborative healthcare decision-making: A systematic review. *Healthcare Technology Letters*, *10*(2), 45–53.

Fernández-Abascal, E. G., Martín-Díaz, M. D., & García-Fernández, J. (•••). The Role of Emotional Intelligence in Healthcare Leadership. *Journal of Nursing Management*, *29*(4), 1024–1031.

Fitzpatrick, K. K.. (2023). Woebot: A Chatbot for Mental Health Support. *Journal of Mental Health (Abingdon, England)*, *32*(3), 145–151.

Galli, B. J. (2022). The role of mutual respect in collaborative leadership. *Journal of Leadership Studies*, *16*(1), 45–60.

Garcia, M. A., Smith, R. L., & Brown, J. P. (2023). Collaborative leadership principles in healthcare: Building a shared vision. *Journal of Healthcare Management*, *68*(4), 330–340.

Goleman, D. (2021). Emotional Intelligence and leadership in healthcare: Current applications and future possibilities. *Healthcare Leadership Report*, *38*(2), 22–29.

Gonzalez, R. (2023). Chatbots for Mental Health Support in Healthcare: A Leadership Perspective. *Journal of Medical Internet Research*, *25*(4), e29478.

Gonzalez, R., Martinez, A., & Sanchez, T. (2023). Chatbot Intervention Reduces Burnout among Healthcare Professionals: An Exploratory Study. *Journal of Medical Internet Research*, *25*(4), e29478.

Greenleaf, R. K. (2013). *Servant leadership: A journey into the nature of legitimate power and greatness*. Paulist press.

Gupta, R., Kumar, R., & Patel, S. (2022). Emotional intelligence in healthcare management: A critical review of the literature. *International Journal of Health Policy and Management*, *11*(6), 947–957.

Harrison, P., & Wood, S. (2022). The impact of emotional intelligence leadership on burnout among healthcare workers. *Journal of Occupational Health Psychology*, *27*(2), 146–157.

Hayes, S. C., Villatte, M., & Levin, M. (2023). Mindfulness and emotional regulation in healthcare: Reducing burnout and enhancing well-being. *Journal of Health Psychology*, *28*(1), 63–75.

Henneman, E. A., Lee, J. H., & Cohen, J. I. (2023). Collaboration in healthcare: The role of teamwork in improving patient care. *Journal of Nursing Management*, *31*(2), 121–130.

Hersey, P., & Blanchard, K. H. (2021). *Management of Organizational Behavior: Using Human Resources* (10th ed.). Pearson.

Jackson, B., & Parry, K. (•••). Empowering Teams through Collaborative Leadership. *The Leadership Quarterly*, *34*(2), 200–215.

Johnson, D. (2023). The role of emotional intelligence in reducing burnout among healthcare professionals. *Journal of Healthcare Management*, *68*(1), 15–28. PMID: 36602452

Kaiser Permanente. (2023). *Integrated care: How collaboration improves health outcomes*. Retrieved from Kaiser Permanente.

Kessler, R. C.. (2023). Ginger: Integrating Human and AI Support for Mental Health. *Psychiatric Services (Washington, D.C.)*, *74*(1), 65–72.

Khosravi, P., Ghaffari, A., & Vafaei-Najar, A. (2023). The role of emotional intelligence in enhancing chatbot interactions in healthcare. *Journal of Medical Systems*, *47*(2), 123.

Kim, S., Park, Y., & Choi, J. (2023). Enhancing emotional intelligence through chatbot interactions in healthcare settings. *BMC Health Services Research*, *23*(1), 189. PMID: 36823616

Kourentzes, N. (2023). Artificial Intelligence in Health Care: The Role of Chatbots. *Journal of Healthcare Leadership*, *15*, 23–32.

Leach, M. J., Wong, A., & Yamaguchi, K. (2022). Improving job satisfaction through collaboration in healthcare teams. *Journal of Healthcare Management*, *67*(3), 215–224.

Lee, K. W., Chiu, S. Y., & Wong, C. M. (2023). Emotional intelligence and team cohesion in collaborative healthcare environments. *Journal of Interprofessional Care*, *37*(2), 240–248. PMID: 35403548

Lee, Y. J. (2023). Enhancing Patient Care with AI: A Case Study of Chatbot Utilization in Clinical Settings. *BMC Health Services Research*, *23*(1), 101. PMID: 36721213

López, J., Fernández, M., & Reyes, F. (2023). Emotional support and burnout: A role for emotional support in reducing burnout among healthcare providers-an exploratory study through the application of a chatbot approach. *International Journal of Health Services*, *53*(2), 275–291.

Martin, J., Thompson, R., & Lee, K. (2023). The impact of chatbot technology on emotional intelligence in healthcare leadership: A case study. *Journal of Healthcare Leadership*, *15*, 45–58.

Mayo Clinic. (2022). *Team-based care: The Mayo Clinic model.* Retrieved from Mayo Clinic.

Meskó, B.. (2023). The Role of AI in Healthcare: A Review of Babylon Health's Chatbot. *Health Informatics Journal*, *29*(2), 75–83.

Miller, K. L., DeVoe, J. E., & Patel, N. (2023). The impact of multidisciplinary teamwork on patient outcomes: A systematic review. *International Journal of Health Policy and Management*, *12*(5), 110–120.

O'Neill, D. (2023). Leveraging Chatbots for Chronic Disease Management in NHS England. *International Journal of Health Services*, *53*(2), 275–291.

Patel, V. (2023). The Impact of Chatbots on Patient Engagement and Outcomes in Healthcare Systems. *Healthcare Technology Letters*, *10*(2), 45–53.

Rathore, H., Gupta, R., & Kumar, A. (2022). Emotional Intelligence and Patient Satisfaction in Health Care Leadership. *Journal of Health Organization and Management*, *36*(3), 301–316.

Reeves, S., Pelone, F., Harrison, R., & Goldman, J. (2022). Interprofessional collaboration to improve professional practice and healthcare outcomes. *Cochrane Database of Systematic Reviews*, *3*, CD000072. PMID: 28639262

Schmitt, M. (2023). Improving Healthcare Outcomes with AI Chatbots: A Case Study of Ada Health. *Journal of Medical Systems*, *47*(5), 234.

Serrat, O. (2021). Emotional intelligence training in health care: Techniques and outcomes. *International Journal of Health Education*, *34*(2), 102–115.

Smith, A. J., Thomas, M., & Jones, R. (2023). Emotional intelligence and decision-making in emergency healthcare leadership. *The Journal of Emergency Medicine*, *60*(1), 18–25.

Tchankue, C.. (2023). Evaluating HealthTap: A Chatbot for Personalized Health Information. *International Journal of Medical Informatics*, *171*, 104892.

Thaker, A., Darnell, A., & Garg, A. (2023). Improving Shared Health Care Decision Making by Chatbot Technology. *International Journal of Healthcare Management*, *36*(1), 85–99.

Vasumathy, M. (2023). *A machine learning-based admissions support system with a case study on D.K.M. College for Women, Vellore, Design and Implementation of Higher Education Learners' Learning Outcomes*. HELLO.

Vasumathy, M., & Thirugnanam, M. (2018). An integrated approach for optimal feature selection and anatomic location identification on pediatric Foreign Body aspired radiographic images, Knowledge Computing and its Applications. *Knowledge Computing in Specific Domains*, *2*, 101–128.

Vroom, V. H., & Jago, A. G. (2023). The role of participative leadership in team effectiveness. *Organizational Dynamics*, *52*(1), 1–10.

Chapter 10
Implementing Educational Leadership and Management Chatbots:
Challenges and Opportunities

Killian Ticharwa Muzongondi
https://orcid.org/0009-0008-5914-4398
Africa Leadership and Management Academy, Zimbabwe

ABSTRACT

This paper discusses the challenges and opportunities of implementing educational leadership and management chatbots, focusing on data security, integration platform considerations and user resistance to adoption derived from organisational culture. Literature reveals the trends in growth across various sectors such as customer service and healthcare yet development and adaptation in educational leadership is slow. Chatbots enhances user experience, administrative tasks and communication channels. The study highlights the importance of organizational culture in change management critical for successful implementation of educational leadership and management chatbots. Recommendations for future development include leveraging big data and machine learning to produce sentimental chatbots. Suggestions on leadership development towards transformational leadership style to facilitate institutional growth and success in implementing new technologies such as chatbots.

DOI: 10.4018/979-8-3693-8734-4.ch010

BACKGROUND

Artificial intelligence is slowly filtering through all aspects previously dominated by human activities gaining acceptance and in most cases offering solutions that are more appealing. With the evolution of artificial intelligence, big data analytics and machine learning, social life experiences and business functions have been edified. As such the leadership and management chatbot is no exception as this has changed the way humans interact with each other and subsequently with the computer. With this advancement in technology, chatbots can be integrated in leadership and management space bringing their convenience to the business world. By embracing advancement of technology in application of artificial intelligence, institutions can migrate to leadership and management chatbots towards smart enterprises

Adoption and integration of chatbots into the education addresses administrative challenges by streamlining administrative tasks, enhancing communication channels and educational user experience through personalised support to students and staff

Successful implementation of educational leadership chatbots increases efficiency, customizability and autonomy bringing new business opportunities, (Alqoud, 2022). Educational leadership and management chatbots can also be used to optimise business processes such as Learning, Financial, Human Resources and customer relationship management systems. Research by Cunningham et al. (2019) indicated growth in chatbot development and application from single use chatbot dating back to 1966's Chatbot ELIZA to more complex functionality offering virtual assistants. Informed by market research conducted by Gartner (2019) dating from 2016 which was "termed the year of chatbot", businesses have successfully adopted chatbots for various functions ranging from customer services, retail banking and insurance government institutions, healthcare e-commerce and messaging apps (Zhanga et al., 2021; Taylor et al., 2021; Chandel et al., 2018).

Leadership and management chatbots as digitalization strategies have improved operational efficiencies, customer service experience productivity, accessibility and convenience (Zhanga et al., 2021; Gartner, 2019). Advances in educational leadership and management sector will also offer considerable benefits to institutions.

Reasons for adopting chatbot in leadership and management are quest to enhance productivity (Korzynski, 2023) and attain sustainable competitive advantage critical in the current business environment recovering from the Covid-19 pandemic and other economic shocks, (Bratianu, 2021; Chandel, 2018). By optimising institutional performance, educational leadership and management chatbots are instrumental in cost reduction, efficiency, improved customer experience and differentiation.

Chat robots, commonly known as chatbots can be loosely defined as conversational or dialogue based automated online computer programs with capabilities of both text and voice interactions (Hwang & Chang 2021). Leadership and Management chatbot can help in streamlining business processes and automating routine and repetitive tasks thereby creating time for leaders to focus on corporate strategic planning, (Rahmani & Kamberaj, 2021) and other strategic issues of the business

Current trends towards improving human computer interface enable personalised interaction between chatbots and humans in real time. This has broken the barriers such as time thereby bringing flexibility. They are gaining popularity and people are embracing chatbots because they are convenient, cheap and fast implementation and accessibility in anytime. Chatbots bridge the information gap in organization through instant data access and feedback.

Despite all the promises that come with successful adoption of chatbots in educational leadership, there are challenges that inhibit their implementation. This chapter sought to give insight into these challenges with practical solutions to overcome them and also highlight opportunities that can motivate the implementation of leadership and management chatbots.

This chapter seeks to unpack the application of chatbots by a description of challenges of implementing the educational leadership chatbots prescribing. This will be followed by outlining the opportunities of implementing leadership and management chatbots solutions and recommendations helpful for successful implementation. Educational leadership and management chatbots enhances customer experience, improve sales, services, and cost-efficiency.

FOCUS OF THE ARTICLE

The focus of this chapter is on the challenges of implementing leadership management chatbots and opportunities that are available, motivating their implementation within an institution. Chatbots combine artificial intelligence with natural language processing technology, (Chandel, 2018). Educational leadership and management chatbots are gradually being adopted in areas such as Human Resources Management System, Financial Management System, Learning Management System, communication and collaboration as well as training and onboarding. It is critical to identify challenges that are prevalent in the implementation of leadership and management chatbots and convert them into opportunities that can lead to institutional growth. Failure to implement educational leadership and management chatbots lead to confusion, anger and dissatisfaction which can ultimately drive away customers (Zhanga et al, 2021). Considerations are made on user resistance to adoption, data security, and integration issues as will be discussed below.

CHALLENGES

Successful implementation of educational leadership and management chatbots is dependent upon identifying and overcoming the challenges through development and improvement interventions. Greven (2023) categorically described these challenges as technology, people and organisation. Though technological advancement is regarded a strategic decision vital for organisational growth, Alqoul et al., (2022) added that the complexity of adopting new technologies and financial challenges such as lack of funding for research and development. Lack of knowledge is also regarded as a major challenge, (Mustafa, 2018). Additional challenges includes user resistance to technology adoption, information myopia, data security and privacy considerations, platform selection and integration with management system as well as availability of resource are among major challenges to successful implementation.

Without deep learning, chatbots are bound to make poor decisions as they cannot fully comprehend complexity of human behaviour such as sentimental analysis. This gives rise to the need for further development in machine learning, deep learning and creation of bots which have self-learning capabilities so as to eliminate shortcomings

Users lack trust in chatbot services especially during the developmental and initial stages (Janssen, 2021). According to Przegalinskaa, (2019), trust exists when a human is willing to rely on actions of the chatbot in future expectation of the promised outcome. Okonkwo & Ade-Ibijola, (2021) added the need for consistency in personality for the chatbot to gain trust and user confidence. Bratianu, (2021) raised concern about the credibility of information as people are insecure about information received and sometimes do not take it at face value.

Cortes-Cediel et al., (2023) cited ineffective adoption strategy, lack of comprehension and limited understanding in terms of deployment and evaluation as limitations associated with the implementation of leadership management chatbots. This has limited their functionality to basic routine tasks yet great opportunities for full scale utilization of chatbots remain unexploited.

User Resistance to Chatbot Technology Adoption

Institutions comprise of staff from different generations and such generation gap influences their acceptance to change especially with regards to new technology. Zhang et al (2021) noted the transition from development to operationalization of the chatbot project as a challenge that should be anticipated and addressed by educational leaders and administrators. From the user's perspective, there is high scepticism of the chatbot's abilities especially during the initial phases. The inclusion of chatbots comes along with threats towards job security or lack thereof. This is usually because users are not included in the development of the chatbots whereas if they could be actively involved and knowledgeable that could influence their acceptance of the chatbots. Employee resistance to adoption often results from misconception of facts which can be mitigated by comprehensive training and open communication. Mtongana and Musundire (2020) assert that resistance to change is a critical obstacle in organizational transformation, particularly in environments where entrenched cultural norms conflict with new initiatives. This resistance can significantly affect employee behavior and hinder performance improvements.

Resistance can be viewed from the perceived ease of use and perceived utility as stipulated in the technology acceptance model (TAM) in terms of simplicity and benefits derived from using the chatbots, (Rukadikar & Khandelwal, 2024). There are psychological, technological and organizational factors that influence how individuals perceive and respond to change. Psychologically resistance to change emanates from the fact that people are insecure about their job especially that they will be replaced by chatbots. Any variance in cultural norms at the workplace which could result from the introduction of new technology is a source of organizational resistance to the adoption of chatbots. technological aspects relates to how compatible the chatbots can be especially with regards to efficiency, security and its adherence to normal and legal requirements (Bani-Ahmad et al. 2024).

Information shared about the chatbots is usually controlled, magnifying the positive side without highlighting the negative aspects that can come along with it (Zhang et al, 2021). There is lack of transparency of the bigger picture especially on the effects of chatbot in educational leadership and management. Management often create silos of information yet information should extend to what the implementation of chatbots could affect those with administrative and pedagogical tasks being taken over by the chatbots. As such, the role of chatbot team should not be highly emphasised as they have a great contribution in the success and failure of adopting chatbots.

Attitude towards new technology leads to resistance to change as some fear that artificial intelligence is fast replacing them and wiping away their existence, (Greven, 2023) Organizational culture has an influence on the successful implementation of educational leadership chatbots. Developing and adapting an educational leadership and management chatbot that addresses cultural issues is critical. Informed by studies from various sectors (Anan, 2024; Alqoud, 2022; Kushniruk, 2021) challenge in terms of personalization and customization of chatbots to enhance user experience. This existed from varying target audiences ranging from generation gaps of staff, students and parents who are satisfied by different language, tone, and responses. Poor organizational culture in terms of leadership and management can be a challenge in the successful adoption of educational leadership and management chatbots (Zhang et al, 2021). It is important to ensure cultural acceptance of automation at management level and communicate the reasons behind it. However, with in-depth knowledge, understanding and motivation of using management chatbots (interactive technology) allows overcoming challenges related to adoption of new technology especially chatbots in educational leadership.

Departmental alignment is hampered by communication gap, prioritization and resistance to change (Anaya, 2021). Seamless communication is vital for integration, collaboration and successful implementation of chatbots. Zhang et al. (2021) attributes challenges in implementation to failure to take a holistic approach before deployment of educational leadership chatbot. They highlighted not only the need to consider technological upgrade but also taking into account organization culture, structure, environmental, application and environment. For example, deployment challenge can be the decision-making matrix of an institution, if they take too long to resolve an issue such as breach in data privacy resulting from use of chatbot, this can lead to lawsuits and costs to the institution or in worst case the suspension of using the chatbot. Expanding on Qi's proposition, integrating chatbots into collaboration platform such as Microsoft teams, a powerful network that allows interaction during online meetings, collaboration and lectures, (Qi, 2024).

Resources are critical in supporting implementation of chatbots. According to Zhanga et al., (2021) system infrastructure is key to achieve digital transition while in-house IT administrators and developers can ease the process. Such resources can dictate whether the chatbots are built internally or outsourced. Chatbot launching platform also present a smooth landing pad for the implementation of chatbots into the educational system. This is affected by unavailability of state-of the art resources to support the implementation of chatbots in educational leadership and management. Alqoud (2022) attribute over-reliance of an institution on legacy assets as a bottleneck to successful implementation.

Failure to upgrade network systems and creating a better platform for launching and running the chatbots is an implementation challenge. Alqoud added a lack of understanding of the challenges and opportunities brought forth by new technology such as chatbots in educational leadership makes the implementation fail. Avurakoghene (2023) included lack of public awareness and technical expertise among educators and education administrator's inadequate infrastructure and funding as well as poor policies and regulations regarding chatbot inclusion hampers the implementation initiative and success of chatbots in educational leadership and management.

According to Janssen, (2021) critical resource in implementation is human resource. Due to the changing economic landscape, inability of an institution to retain their staff can result them in leaving the institution. If that employee was key in the chatbot project, their departure during the launching or rollout phase will lead to disruption which can result in implementation challenge. This also goes along with external company or third part service provider who closed down during the implementation stages. There is need to conceptualise the whole project and have sufficient resources in place before launching. Such resources include the requisite infrastructure, necessary funding and investment, competent human resources and technical staff who can support the implementation of leadership chatbots. Actual costing and budgeting is a challenge especially when cost benefit analysis has not been properly done thereby spending way beyond the returns on investment funding received.

It should be noted that a transition from human-based services to fully automated human-computer interface does not happen overnight but develops over time with extensive resources needed to support digital integration. Skills level and expertise in using computer assisted interfaces is essential for a successful implementation of chatbot.

According to Okonkwo, (2023) chatbots have the ability of integrating learning content such as topic, time table, assignment and examination and upload to an on-line platform for accessibility and convenience. They facilitate information sharing.

Programming issues can hinder the implementation of educational leadership chatbot (Okonkwo & Ade-Ibijola., 2021). Accuracy of chatbot depends on AI and machine learning with the aid of Natural Language Processing which enables comprehension, analysis and interpretation of natural human language.

Organisational culture has a great impact on the smooth implementation of chatbots in educational leadership (Rukadikar & Khandelwal, 2024). Adaptive, innovative and technology driven culture favours the adoption and easy acceptance of educational leadership chatbots than an institution that relies much on out-dated technology.

Ethical Challenges

Chandel (2018) cited the unethical incident of Microsoft's Tay, a chatbot which was rebuilt as it became unfit for purpose after self-learning wrong language resulting in sending insulting tweets. On highlighting critical factors to include in the design of chatbots, Gartner emphasised that a chatbot should suit personality both the audience and the brand (Gartner, 2019). Due to design failure such as poor content, data not up to date or too little and some chatbots are unable to meet educational user expectations for chatbots leads to implementation failure (Janssen, 2021) as it normally happens when outsourced from vendors for example who have developed chatbots social application thereby failing to refocus their product to educational or administrative users. Design factors can also lead to premature failure of chatbot (Brandtzaeg & Følstad, 2018) for example chatbot Anna ended up being abused by customers when it failed to balance robotic and human aspects.

Educational leadership chatbots should also be equipped with academic flavour and a diverse user interface to cater for the diversity of its audience ranging from teaching and administrative staff, students and parents. Greven, (2023) noted the lack of mature implementation concepts that take into account the requirements of the target audience and a narrow understanding of the technological possibilities that can be derived from a successfully executed leadership chatbot.

Leadership and management support create an enabling environment for the implementation of an educational chatbot system. Lack of emotional intelligence and empathy makes them unpopular in sensitive conversational and support functions as chatbot are not yet fully developed in neural network. In order to overcome this, Chandel et al (2018) proposed configuration for extensive self-learning and deep machine learning.

Cheating, academic misconduct and compromise to academic integrity result from unethical manipulation of educational chatbots, (Kooli, 2023). Furthermore, Okonkwo & Ade-Ibijola, (2021) regard chatbots as immoral and non-independent agents that deceive people through managing unrealistic conversations pretending to be humans.

In the education system, implementation of chatbots to students and learners enhance learning experience by providing personalized and immediate feedback to students

Though chatbots can reduce administrative burden, they can display unethical conduct depending on the training data that they have been exposed to. Awad & Moosa, (2024)noted ethical issues such as racism, bias, discrimination, inaccurate translation, generation of harmful content and violation of intellectual. Stored data can be manipulated thereby misleading users, damaging people's reputation.

Ethical issues related to consent when an institution can use personal data without consent which might lead to discrimination or even termination of employment (Aggarwal et al, 2021).

Kushniruk et al (2021) highlighted complexities involved in knowledge acquisition, validation and maintenance even with the advent of neural networks and machine learning systems. This affects the implementation of chatbot system. However, with the

Issues around trust and potential liability, impact of potential error resulting from use of AI technologies. Indeed, issues around certification and regulatory approval of AI technologies, including FDA approval processes, have to come to the fore as healthcare organizations grapple with deciding whether or not to include AI technologies into regular practice.

Kuhail et al., (2023) also noted lack of reliance on usability heuristics and inadequate dataset training which impacts on the reliability of chatbot when met with complex queries. Issues around human understanding, need for explanation capability and transparency about results and outcomes

Data Security and Privacy Considerations

While integrating chatbots with management systems offers numerous benefits, practical implementation must address data security and privacy concerns. As highlighted by Chen and Chang (2020), institutions can practically implement robust security measures, including encryption and access controls, to safeguard sensitive information. Practical implementation also involves complying with data protection regulations and ensuring that the chatbot's integration does not compromise user privacy.

Significance of Data Security and Confidentiality

Practical implementation of data security and confidentiality for leadership and management chatbots, informed by Chen and Chang (2020), is essential to protect sensitive information and ensure user trust. This approach involves practical measures to safeguard data integrity, prevent unauthorized access, and uphold privacy standards. For instance, practical implementation could involve encryption of data exchanged between users and the chatbot.

Educational institutions hold confidential and personal information which may be used for criminal offences if they land in wrong hands. Chatbots are prone to security risks such as hacking and cyber-crimes.

Data Minimization and Retention Policies

Application of educational leadership chatbots has high risk of unauthorised access to confidential information such as staff and student personal data. Practical implementation of chatbots poses cyber-security risks, (Sebastian, 2024) including malware threats, social engineering attacks, phishing attacks, identity theft and data leakage. There is need for spreading awareness campaigns of these data security risks. According to Sebastian, data protection can be attained through authentication (two stage authentication), end to end encryption, user education and revising data usage protocols. Educating users about cyber-threats and how they can protect their data by observing simple precautions relating to data privacy such as not sharing passwords, personal or sensitive information or clicking/ downloading suspicious links.

Authentication can be done to secure unauthorised access. Since chatbots communicate on network system platforms, there is need to ensure network security by securing communication channels. One common way is through end to end data encryption. End to end encryption reduces number of audiences whereas only one intended has access through the use of a private decryption code. In order to protect users and ensure data security, it is also critical to do security audits and making regular update to the cyber space. Chatbot in educational management present programmers and developers with an opportunity to develop application that detects risks such as malware and ransom-ware.

Data Security and Confidentiality

Chatbots are machine-learning artificial intelligent tools which also learn from previous conversations and utilise the knowledge to mimic the user in future dialogues. When deployed in existing channels and protocols which are already secured for network threats and cybercriminals, the risk exposure is less. Security risks are targeted on personally identifiable information which if delivered in wrong hands can result in personal harm or damage to business

Encryption Protocols

Document security is important so as to safeguard data. Drawing from Abidin et al. (2021), practical implementation of encryption protocols involves encrypting data at rest and in transit. Institutions can practically implement this by using industry-standard encryption algorithms to protect data stored within databases and data transmitted between users and the chatbot. For example, practical implementation could involve implementing Transport Layer Security (TLS) to secure data transmissions. End to end encryption is another way secure communication against unauthorised access and is often done using protocols such as Hypertext transfer protocol secure (HTTPS) which is designed to improve security of data transfer.

User Authentication and Access Controls

There is high risk of account security that comes along with the use of chatbots. In order to reduce the risk, various control measures can be put in place such as two factor authentication, password policy, timing out a session when not in use or left idle for some time and initiating security audit trails, (Scope et al., 2021). Practical implementation of user authentication and access controls, as emphasized by Li and Kumar (2020), involves implementing mechanisms to verify user identities and restrict access to authorized personnel. Institutions can practically implement this by integrating single sign-on (SSO) solutions or multi-factor authentication (MFA) processes. For instance, administrators could practically log in to the chatbot using their institution-provided credentials. Integrating two factor authentications also enhances security over and above username and password protection (Keerthana, 2023). There is also machine-specific authentication which only allows chatbot to run on a single machine. An example is the Media Access Control (MAC) Address

Authentication where the user can only log on using a single device. Remote data wipe can be done in case the device is stolen or there is security breach while using seamless authentication (for shared access of student and student's parent) so as to prevent unauthorised access, (Heryandi, 2020). Furthermore, carrying out audit trails can be done to detect performance issues and possible security risks.

Data Minimization and Retention Policies

Deshmukh (2023) accentuated the need for a data retention policy that safeguards privacy and compliance. Practical application of data minimization and retention policies, following Govaerts et al. (2018), involves limiting the collection and storage of user data to what is necessary for the chatbot's functionalities. According to Scope, retention and disposal policy should be in place to guide users on which data can be kept and at what stage is it safe to dispose(Scope et al., 2021). Nature of the data determines how long it can be retained, archived and disposed. Institutions can practically implement this by defining clear data retention periods and regularly purging unnecessary data. For example, practical implementation could involve automatically deleting chat logs after a specified period. Data security on mobile device is also achievable through automatic purging offline data. Data purge off is the permanent removal of data that is lo longer relevant. Storing such data has the risk of it being accessed and used for unintended purposes.

Regular Security Audits and Updates

Practical implementation of regular security audits and updates, in line with Zhu et al. (2021), involves conducting periodic assessments of the chatbot's security measures and promptly addressing vulnerabilities. Institutions can practically implement this by establishing a schedule for security audits and staying informed about emerging threats. For example, practical implementation could involve regularly patching and updating the chatbot's software to mitigate potential risks. It is also necessary to continuously monitor and evaluate chatbot programs. For example, the Turing test can be employed to test the compatibility of a chatbot in natural language processing and its ability to converse like a human.

As a remedy, institutions should focus on strategic alignment, provide infrastructure, public awareness initiatives to reduce the challenges for implementation of educational leadership and management chatbots, Avurakoghene (2023).

In conclusion, practical implementation of data security and confidentiality for leadership and management chatbots involves measures such as encryption protocols, user authentication, data minimization, compliance with regulations, and regular security audits. By practically implementing these safeguards, educational institutions ensure the protection of sensitive data and foster a secure environment for users interacting with the chatbot.

Compliance with Regulations

Practical implementation of compliance with data protection regulations, guided by Wang and Lin (2019), involves ensuring adherence to relevant laws such as the General Data Protection Regulation (GDPR) or the Family Educational Rights and Privacy Act (FERPA). Institutions can practically implement this by conducting thorough assessments of data practices and implementing policies that align with regulatory requirements. For instance, practical implementation could involve obtaining explicit user consent before collecting personal information.

Informed by exploratory cyber security studies conducted by Sebastian (2023), Qammar et al., (2023) there are limited laws regarding chatbots exposing them t abuse by people who can manipulate the AI technology. For example, lack of intellectual laws and data protection laws can give rise to plagiarism and violation of copyright in case of academic and research students

One challenge according to Keerthana et al. (2024) is that chatbots usually operate on third-party conversational interfaces and networks, such as, google classrom, Facebook, WhatsApp which gives data security risks since different platforms are regulated by diferent policies and regulations. Cyber security requires systems to be secured and protected from unauthorised access and usage. Success in implementation is based on quality of programming in terms of content. However, programmers and software developers can re-write the chatbot script/ algorithm misleading the chatbot thereby violating privacy.

There is need for constant update and review of training material as well as security audits (Keerthana, 2023) to detect and resolve cyber security risks. Data security issues also arise in the storage of communication and user data.

Integration Challenges

Significance of Integration

Practical implementation of integration between leadership and management chatbots and management systems, informed by Abidin et al. (2021), involves connecting the chatbot with existing institutional platforms. This approach ensures a seamless flow of information, data accuracy, and efficient decision-making processes. For example, practical integration could enable the chatbot to access and update student enrolment data within the institution's student information system.

Integration with Management Systems

Chatbots have a potential of increasing customer satisfaction, optimise administrative and reduced costs through efficiency (Greven, 2023). This is achieved through integration thereby enabling seamless data exchange. Integration occurs with relevant platforms such as LMS, communication platforms, HRMS

Learning Management System (LMS) Integration

Drawing from Li and Kumar (2020), practical implementation of LMS integration involves connecting the chatbot with the institution's learning management system. Institutions can practically implement this by configuring APIs or connectors that enable the chatbot to retrieve course schedules, assignment due dates, and other relevant information. For instance, an administrator could practically inquire about a specific course's syllabus, and the chatbot could retrieve the information directly from the LMS.

Human Resources Management System (HRMS) Integration

Practical implementation of HRMS integration, as emphasized by Govaerts et al. (2018), involves linking the chatbot with the institution's human resources management system. Artificial intelligence and machine learning enhances HR functions such as the recruitment and onboarding, automation of administrative tasks, compensation and performance management, (Rahmani & Kamberaj, 2021). Institutions can practically implement this by enabling the chatbot to assist with inquiries related to employee benefits, leave requests, and performance evaluations. For example, a faculty member could practically ask the chatbot about their remaining vacation days, and the chatbot could provide real-time information.

Bratianu, (2021) favours chatbots for their credibility and unbiased decision making. With artificial intelligent and proper framework of leadership and management chatbot, chances of human error are reduced by eliminating biases, personal judgement and promoting transparency in organizational processes, (Zehir et al, 2020). This is critical in workplaces that have diverse ethnic groups where discrimination and unfair treatment is bound to happen. Management chatbot offers a solution to a healthy work environment. Kooli (2023) argued that for the outcome to be unbiased, the input should also be free from bias

Financial Management System Integration

Practical application of financial management system integration, following Wang and Lin (2019), involves connecting the chatbot with the institution's financial systems. Institutions can practically implement this by enabling the chatbot to provide budget-related information, expense tracking, and purchase order status updates. For instance, a department head could practically inquire about the available budget for a specific project, and the chatbot could provide an instant response. Musundire and Mumanyi (2020) advocate for the exploration of innovative funding models to address resource constraints. They argue that collaborative efforts between government, private sectors, and higher education institutions can create sustainable funding opportunities, improving student outcomes and institutional performance.

Integration with Communication Tools

Musundire (2020) argues that integrating technological communication into education addresses the evolving needs of learners, promoting accessibility, engagement, and inclusivity in teaching and learning environments. Practical implementation of integrating chatbots with communication tools, in line with Zhu et al. (2021), involves connecting the chatbot with existing communication channels. Institutions can practically implement this by embedding the chatbot within communication platforms like Microsoft Teams or Slack. For example, administrators could practically interact with the chatbot directly within their preferred communication environment.

Another issue with the implementation of chatbots is on integration of new technology to the existing platform (Anaya, 2024) In order to solve the integration issues, institution can develop educational chatbot on student/ staff portal as well as the institution's public website for reaching out potential students, parents and staff.

In conclusion, practical integration of leadership and management chatbots with management systems involves connecting the chatbot with institutional platforms such as the LMS, HRMS, financial systems, and communication platforms. By practically implementing these integrations, educational institutions enhance information flow, streamline processes, (Rukadikar & Khandelwal, 2024). and facilitate informed decision-making within their administrative workflows.

OPPORTUNITIES

Chatbots have the potential to revolutionise educational leadership and management by improving end user experience through support and engagement, (Kuhail, 2023). Within a public service delivery, chatbots have the potential to reduce service delivery cost and at and improve service delivery through reduction in waiting period, enhance transparency and data accessibility.

Failure in adaptation and integration of leadership and management chatbots in the has been

Selecting the Appropriate Platform

Various platforms are available for deploying educational leadership and management chatbots. Platforms include on-Premises Deployment, Cloud-based solutions, mobile application and web based interface

Significance of Platform Selection

Practical implementation of platform selection, informed by Govaerts et al. (2018), involves choosing the right technological infrastructure for hosting and deploying the chatbot. For instance, if an institution already utilizes a learning management system (LMS), practical platform selection could involve integrating the chatbot within the LMS environment to ensure a seamless user experience.

On-Premises Deployment

Practical application of on-premises deployment, following Wang and Lin (2019), involves hosting the chatbot's servers within the institution's infrastructure. Institutions can practically implement this by configuring dedicated servers that ensure data privacy and security. For example, a leadership and management chatbot that handles sensitive administrative data could be practically hosted on the institution's internal servers. Chandel (2018) added that chatbots can ease on development, maintenance and update if they are hosted by the institution’s server

Cloud-Based Solutions

Practical implementation of cloud-based solutions, drawing from Abidin et al. (2021), involves utilizing cloud platforms to host the chatbot. Institutions can practically implement this by leveraging services such as Amazon Web Services (AWS) or Microsoft Azure. For instance, an institution could practically deploy the chatbot on a cloud server, benefiting from scalability, flexibility, and reduced maintenance efforts.

Azure also provides a cloud computing service for bots, (Qi, 2024) enabling users to integrate their custom chatbots into the platform and develop the bot's logic, including processing user inputs and generating response messages.

Mobile Applications

Practical application of mobile applications, as emphasized by Chen and Chang (2020), involves developing a standalone mobile app for the chatbot. Institutions can practically implement this by collaborating with app developers to create a user-friendly mobile interface. For instance, educational leaders and administrators could practically download the app and access chatbot features on their smartphones.

Web-Based Interfaces

Practical implementation of web-based interfaces, guided by Li and Kumar (2020), involves creating a user interface accessible through web browsers. Institutions can practically implement this by developing a chatbot portal accessible from the institution's website. For example, practical implementation could enable administrators to interact with the chatbot by visiting a dedicated webpage.

In conclusion, the practical implementation of selecting the appropriate platform for leadership and management chatbots involves evaluating options such as on-premises deployment, cloud-based solutions, integration with communication tools, mobile applications, and web-based interfaces. By practically considering the institution's existing technological landscape and user preferences, educational leaders can ensure the successful deployment and accessibility of chatbot solutions.

Communication and Collaboration Platforms Integration

Practical implementation of communication and collaboration platform integration, guided by Zhu et al. (2021), involves linking the chatbot with platforms such as Microsoft Teams or Slack. Institutions can practically implement this by configuring the chatbot to deliver notifications, updates and reminders directly within these platforms. For example, the chatbot could practically send automated reminders about upcoming faculty meetings to administrators through their preferred communication channels.

Chatbots promotes interpersonal communication and learning, provide information and knowledge through interactive methods and easy-to-operate interfaces, and can even be used as a tool for personal consultation, (Hwang and Chang, 2021). Instant data accessibility creates platform for acceptability of chatbots in management and leadership as executives need to make informed decisions from the vast data around, (Tadvi et al, 2020). Integrating chatbot into existing system such as student portal or company website, cloud based app and messaging platform while employees can focus on value-adding activities.

User Training and Onboarding

Significance of User Training and Onboarding

Practical implementation of user training and onboarding for leadership and management chatbots, informed by Zhu et al. (2021), is crucial to ensure users can effectively utilize the chatbot's capabilities. This approach involves practical strategies to familiarize users with the chatbot's features, functionalities, and best practices. For instance, practical implementation could involve creating user guides and hosting training sessions for administrators.

User Guides and Documentation

Drawing from Chen and Chang (2020), practical implementation of user guides and documentation involves creating comprehensive resources that outline the chatbot's capabilities and usage instructions. Institutions can practically implement this by developing user-friendly guides accessible through the institution's website or learning management system. For example, practical implementation could involve providing step-by-step instructions on how to initiate conversations with the chatbot and utilize specific functionalities.

Training Workshops and Webinars

Developing chatbots as training aid helps reduce the staff requirements and enhance quality and speed of training as noted by Qi, (2024). They improve skill acquisition through training thereby reducing the reliance on human trainers. Opportunities in developing training simulation which enhances quick skills acquisition as individuals can practice numerous times at varying levels until they are competent enough. With the use of chatbots in the educational leadership and management, safety risks are averted especially by reducing the exposure to adverse conditions for example utilising a chatbot to train employees on evacuation procedure in case of a disaster where fully relying on human trainers may not be feasible. However, reliability depends on developers and programmers to train and the quality of data used in the training. Lack of training resources and the quality of content as well as its relevance to the user's needs affects the implementation of educational leadership chatbots as training technology.

Practical implementation of training workshops and webinars, as emphasized by Abidin et al. (2021), involves organizing interactive sessions to educate users about the chatbot's features. Institutions can practically implement this by scheduling workshops or webinars where users can engage in hands-on exercises and receive guidance from experts. For instance, practical implementation could involve conducting virtual webinars that showcase various scenarios in which the chatbot can assist with administrative tasks. Chatbot in education and training assist in memory retention and enhance learning outcomes.

Interactive Onboarding

Onboarding of chatbots is of great importance if one wants to familiarise with the features and their functionality so that they can derive value from using them, (Reich & Wolfel, 2022). However people start engaging them before understanding their capabilities thereby missing out. Practical application of interactive onboarding, following Govaerts et al. (2018), involves designing a user-friendly onboarding process that guides users through the chatbot's functionalities. Institutions can practically implement this by creating interactive onboarding sequences within the chatbot interface itself. For example, practical implementation could involve a series of interactive prompts that introduce users to the chatbot's features and offer immediate assistance.

Personalized Support Channels

Practical implementation of personalized support channels, guided by Wang and Lin (2019), involves establishing channels through which users can seek assistance and receive personalized guidance. Institutions can practically implement this by integrating a helpdesk feature within the chatbot or providing contact information for chatbot support. For instance, practical implementation could involve allowing users to send messages to the chatbot for specific inquiries and receiving prompt responses. As evidenced in clinical therapy (Przegalinskaa et al, 2019) humans prefer computer systems compared to other humans due to their rationality, objectivity and fruitful interaction from high quality automation. Applied to educational leadership, this can transform staff engagement as chatbots can be utilised for counselling and emotional support for challenging personal career development and motivation of staff.

Continuous Learning and Feedback Loop

Practical implementation of a continuous learning and feedback loop, drawing from Li and Kumar (2020), involves creating mechanisms for users to provide feedback and suggestions for chatbot improvement. Institutions can practically implement this by incorporating feedback forms or surveys within the chatbot interface. For example, practical implementation could involve periodically prompting users to share their experiences and recommendations for enhancing the chatbot's functionality. This also involves conducting design and feedback workshops to demonstrate capabilities and limitations of the chatbot

In conclusion, practical implementation of user training and onboarding for leadership and management chatbots involves strategies such as user guides, training workshops, interactive onboarding, personalized support channels, and continuous feedback mechanisms. By practically implementing these approaches, educational institutions ensure that users are well-prepared to leverage the chatbot's capabilities effectively and maximize its contributions to administrative processes.

Challenge of educational leadership and management chatbot is to adapt to complexity of human behaviour. Potential development of online tools is crucial to enhance group interaction in a learning workplace environment. There is need to move from retrieval-based chatbots primarily capable of addressing queries to conversational chatbots conversant with emotional intelligence attainable through deep machine learning and sentimental analysis.

SOLUTIONS AND RECOMMENDATIONS

To address culture challenges, Zhang (2021) proposed taking an active approach to leadership and change management. It is critical to adopt digital culture that promotes and inclusive, creative, collaborative working and learning environment.

Qi, (2024) accentuated that artificial intelligence and natural language processing sets apart chatbots enabling them to handle complex conversations and generating real time decision support. In that regard, future AI development in image and video recognition going beyond communication through text is vital for developing emotional connection between human and the chatbot.

Future development of emotional recognition and response techniques to enhance interactions enables chat robot to understand human emotions and improve social adaptability and user satisfaction, (Bani-Ahmad et al. 2024; Assuncao et al, 2022)

Being intentional on digital strategy, educational institutions need to value and pursue partnership with various stakeholders who can facilitate the implementation of educational chatbots. Zhang et al., (2021) further reiterated the importance of building competent employees who can drive change towards implementing chatbot systems.

Additional solutions to data security as informed by Surani & Das, (2022) are the implementation of self-destructing messages used in conjunction with personally identifiable information, fine-grained access control, session timeout and scheduled disposal. The system is used in other messaging applications where an image can be send as a single view option and once that image is opened in cannot be stored in the gallery. Similarly text messages are also timed to expire or disappear after a predetermined period in order to maintain data privacy, confidential and sensitive information.

Future Research Directions

There is needed for further research to develop sentimental chatbots leveraging machine learning especially deep learning as it indicates potential for self-learning, self-reasoning systems which are able to learn and make decisions independently by mimicking the human brain and how it operates thereby creating trust and more natural human-computer interaction. Research can also be done on the impact of chatbots both as an instrument technological advancement geared at driving education to another level through convenience and flexibility as well as a tool of social exclusion depriving learners the ability to interact naturally within the human ecosystem

Chatbot technologies can bring forth many benefits to organizations, including improved customer experience, cost and efficiency gains, increased sales and technological advantages. However, chatbots represent an emerging technology and there is little understanding of changes that the adoption of such a device may bring to the organization. Companies want to be early adopters, while there is a clear lack of best practices and expand the capabilities of chatbots to support diverse leadership and management needs.

Future research can be focused on the influence of leadership styles such as the adoption of transformational leadership on the successful implementation of educational leadership and management chatbot systems. Chatbots in education can give rise to leadership development (Chamorro et al., 2021) where transformational leaders can emerge to lead in the change management. For example the application of shepherd leadership and path goal theory an intervention for change management and remedy to deal with resistance to adoption of new technologies.

Besides its numerous benefits on the administrative side of the institution, adoption and implementation of chatbot system transforms the educational landscape offering personalised and flexible learning experience and an environment conducive for educational growth. It improves the effectiveness of training process and student motivation.

Future studies can also focus on how chatbots can be used not as a replacement of human beings in the workplace but rather as complimentary to human efforts. With this regard humans ought to be trained and prepared to co-work together.

CONCLUSION

Chatbot development is rapidly trending with capabilities to revolutionize the educational sector drawing from the success it had within the healthcare, commercial, and customer service industries in the past. Harnessing its potential will definitely transform the institution giving it a competitive advantage and ensuring quality of service delivery and satisfaction to all the concerned stakeholders. In this chapter, factors underpinning the implementation of educational leadership chatbots were presented. The main areas of focus were the challenges to adoption and opportunities derived from successful implementation of chatbots. Considering the highlighted challenges is key to implementing successful educational leadership chatbots. Motivation from the opportunities of having educational leadership chatbots such as streamlined administrative tasks and improved efficiency drives an institution towards adoption of educational leadership chatbot technology. Critical to the success lies on organisational culture especially developing through innovation, creativity and technology-driven culture

ADDITIONAL READINGS

Alqoud, A., Schaefer, D., & Milisavljevic-Syed, J. (2022). Industry 4.0: Challenges and Opportunities of Digitalisation Manufacturing Systems. *Advances in Manufacturing Technology, XXXV*, 25–30. DOI: 10.3233/ATDE220560

Anaya, L., Braizat, A., & Al-Ani, R. (2024). Implementing AI-based Chatbot: Benefits and Challenges. *Procedia Computer Science, 239*, 1173–1179. DOI: 10.1016/j.procs.2024.06.284

Awad, W., & Moosa, J. (2024). Implications of AI Chatbots in Education: Challenges and Solution. *Journal of Statistics Applications & Probability, 13*(2), 611–622. Advance online publication. DOI: 10.18576/jsap/130203

Gartner. 2019. Market guide for virtual customer assistants. Technical report. Gartner. https://www.gartner.com/en/documents/3947357/market-guide-for-virtual -customer assistants

Korzynski, P., Kozminski, A. K., & Baczynska, A. (2023). Navigating leadership challenges with technol ogy: Uncovering the potential of ChatGPT, virtual reality, human capital management systems, robotic process automation, and social media. *International Entrepreneurship Review, 9*(2), 7–18. DOI: 10.15678/IER.2023.0902.01

Rukadikar, A., & Khandelwa, K. (2024). Navigating change: A qualitative exploration of chatbot adoption in recruitment. *Cogent Business & Management, 11*(1), 2345759. DOI: 10.1080/23311975.2024.2345759

Sebastian, G. (2023). Do Chatgpt and other AI chatbots pose a cybersecurity risk? An exploratory study. International journal of security and privacy in pervasive computing (15) https://orcid.org/0000-0003-2543-9127

Zhang, J. J. Y., Folstad, A., & Bjorkli, C. A. (2021). Organizational Factors Affecting Successful Implementation of Chatbots for Customer Service. *Journal of Internet Commerce, 22*(1), 122–156. DOI: 10.1080/15332861.2021.1966723

REFERENCES

Abidin, M. J. Z., Zulkifli, A. N., & Manaf, A. A. (2021). User Acceptance of Chatbot in Higher Education: A Review. *Journal of Physics: Conference Series, 1798*(1), 012002.

Aggarwal, M., Gingras, C., & Deber, R. (2021). Artificial Intelligence in Healthcare from a Policy Perspective. In *Multiple Perspectives on Artificial Intelligence in Healthcare: Opportunities and Challenges* (pp. 53–64). Springer International Publishing.

Alqoud, A., Schaefer, D., & Milisavljevic-Syed, J. (2022). Industry 4.0: Challenges and Opportunities of Digitalisation Manufacturing Systems. *Advances in Manufacturing Technology, XXXV*, 25–30. DOI: 10.3233/ATDE220560

Anaya, L., Braizat, A., & Al-Ani, R. (2024). Implementing AI-based Chatbot: Benefits and Challenges. *Procedia Computer Science, 239*, 1173–1179. DOI: 10.1016/j.procs.2024.06.284

Avurakoghene, O. P., & Oredein, A. (2023). Educational leadership and artificial intelligence for sustainable development. OP Avurakoghene & AO Oredein, Educational Leadership and Artificial Intelligence for Sustainable Development, Shodh Sari-An International Multidisciplinary Journal, 2(3).

Awad, W., & Moosa, J. (2024). Implications of AI Chatbots in Education: Challenges and Solution. *Journal of Statistics Applications & Probability, 13*(2), 611–622. Advance online publication. DOI: 10.18576/jsap/130203

Bani-Ahmad, A.Y., Fraihat, B.A.M., Ayasrah, F.T.M., Alhawamdeh, M.M., & Al-Shakri, K.(2024). Examining the mediating role of organizational trust in the relationship between organizational learning ad innovation performance: A study of information systems and computer science firms.

Brandtzaeg, P. B., & Følstad, A. 2018. "Chatbots: Changing User Needs and Motivations," Interactions (25:5), pp. 38-43.

Bratianu, C., Zbuchea, A., Anghel, F., & Hrib, B. (2021). Shaping the Future of Business and Economy: STRATEGICA International Academic Conference -Ninth Edition-Bucharest, Romania, October 21-22, 2021. Tritonic Publishing House. ISBN: 978-606-749-579-9. www.facultateademanagement.ro

Chamorro, O., Huarcaya-Godoy, M., Durán-Herrera, V., Nieves-Barreto, C., Suarez-Bazalar, R., Cruz-Telada, Y., Alarcón-Anco, R., Huayhua-Mamani, H., Vargas Diaz, V., & Balarezo-Mares, D. (2023). Application of the Chatbot in University Education: A Systematic Review on the Acceptance and Impact on Learning. International Journal of Learning. *Teaching and Educational Research., 22*(9), 156–178. DOI: 10.26803/ijlter.22.9.9

Chandel, S., Yuying, Y., Yujie, G., Razaque, A., & Yang, G. G. (2018). Chatbot: Efficient and Utility-based Platform School of Engineering & Computing Sciences, New York Institute of Technology, Nanjing, China

Chen, C. M., & Chang, C. C. (2020). A Smart Learning Approach to Intelligent Chatbot System for Enhancing Effective Interactive Learning. *Journal of Educational Technology & Society*, *23*(3), 73–85.

Cortes-Cediel, ME., Segura-Tinoco, A., Cantador, I., Boliver, P.M,. (2023). Trends and challenges of e-government chatbots: Advances in exploring open government data and citizen participation; Government information quarter Volume 40, issue 4, October 2023, 101877

Cunningham-Nelson, S., Boles, W., Trouton, L., & Margerison, E. (2019) A review of chatbots in education: Practical steps forward. In 30th Annual Conference for the Australasian Association for Engineering Education (AAEE 2019): Educators Becoming Agents of Change: Innovate, Integrate, Motivate. Engineers Australia, Australia, pp. 299-306. https://eprints.qut.edu.au/134323/ c 2019

Denecke, K., Abd-Alrazaq, A., & Househ, M. (2021). Artificial Intelligence for Chatbots in Mental Health: Opportunities and Challenges. Multiple perspective on artificial intelligence in healthcare: Opportunitiesand challenges, 115-128. DOI: 10.1007/978-3-030-67303-1_10

Deshmukh, S. S. (2023). Improve Data Security Safeguards through Data Aggregation Purge Process. *J Artif Intell Mach Learn & Data Sci*, *1*(4), 214–213. DOI: 10.51219/JAIMLD/santosh-deshmukh/57

Gartner. 2019. Market guide for virtual customer assistants. Technical report. Gartner. https://www.gartner.com/en/documents/3947357/market-guide-for-virtual -customer assistants

Govaerts, S., Verbert, K., Duval, E., & Pardo, A. (2018). The Role of Learning Analytics in Monitoring and Steering a Personalised Learning Ecosystem. *British Journal of Educational Technology*, *49*(6), 1044–1054.

Greven, D., Endres, K., Sundralingham, S., & Stich, V. (2023). Implementation-specific barriers and measures for chatbots in B2B customer service. ESSN: 2701-6277, 844-856. DOI: DOI: 10.15488/13503

Heryandi, A. (2020). Developing Chatbot For Academic Record Monitoring in Higher Education Institution. IOP Conf. Ser.: Mater. Sci. Eng. 879 012049 DOI: 10.1088/1757-899X/879/1/012049

Hwang, G. J., & Chang, C. Y. (2021). A review of opportunities and challenges of chatbots in education. *Interactive Learning Environments*. Advance online publication. DOI: 10.1080/10494820.2021.1952615

Janssen, A., Grützner, L. & Breitner, M. (2021). Why do Chatbots fail? A Critical Success Factors Analysis.

Keerthana, B., Vaishali, C., & Anitha, S. (2024). Chatbots security: Protecting user data and privacy. International Journal of Business and Management Invention (IJBMI) ISSN (Online): 2319 – 8028, ISSN (Print): 2319 – 801X

Kooli, C. (2023). Chatbots in education and research: A critical examination of ethical imlications and solutions. *Sustainability (Basel)*, *15*(7), 5614. DOI: 10.3390/su15075614

Korzynski, P., Kozminski, A. K., & Baczynska, A. (2023). Navigating leadership challenges with technol ogy: Uncovering the potential of ChatGPT, virtual reality, human capital management systems, robotic process automation, and social media. *International Entrepreneurship Review*, *9*(2), 7–18. DOI: 10.15678/IER.2023.0902.01

Kuhail, M. A., Alturk, N., Alramlwawi, S., & Alhejori, K. (2023). Interacting with educational chatbots: A systematic review. *Education and Information Technologies*, *28*(1), 973–1018. DOI: 10.1007/s10639-022-11177-3

Kushniruk, A. & Borycki, E. 2021). The human factors of ai in healthcare: recurrent issues, future challenges and ways forward. Multiple perspective on artificial intelligence in healthcare: Opportunities and challenges, 115-128.

Li, X., & Kumar, A. (2020). Design and Development of Chatbots for Education: A Literature Review. *IEEE Access : Practical Innovations, Open Solutions*, *8*, 110363–110375.

Mtongana, B., & Musundire, A. (2020). Exploring the relationship between culture change, Kurt Lewin's model of change, employee behaviour, and employee performance in South African state-owned enterprises: The case of.... *International Journal of Scientific Research*, *9*(7), 1020–1032. https://www.researchgate.net

Mustafa, H. K., & Yaakub, S. (2018). Innovation and Technology Adoption Challenges: Impact on SMEs' Company Performance. International Journal of Accounting. *Finance and Business*, *3*(15), 57–65.

Musundire, A. (2020). Blending social media, learning theories, and teachers' knowledge in promoting innovative pedagogy: SA private higher learning institutions. [IJDLDC]. *International Journal of Digital Literacy and Digital Competence*, *11*(1), 46–61. DOI: 10.4018/IJDLDC.2020010103

Musundire, A., & Mumanyi, O. (2020). Exploring challenges, opportunities, and prospects associated with higher education student funding in the context of South Africa. *Journal of Management & Administration, 2020*(1). https://hdl.handle.net/10520/EJC-1da02559bc

Okonkwo, C. W., & Ade-Ibijola, A. (2021). Chatbot applications in education: A systematic review. Computers and education. *Artificial Intelligence, 2*, 100033.

Przegalinskaa, A., Ciechanowskia, L., Strozc, A., Gloord, P., & Mazureka, G. (2019). *In bot we trust: A new methodology of chatbot performance measures. Kelley School of Business, Indiana University*. Elsevier., DOI: 10.1016/j.bushor.2019.08.005

Qammar, A., Wang, H., Ding, J., Naori, A., Daneshmand, M., & Ning, H. (2023). Chatbots to ChatGPT in a cybersecurity space: Evolution, vulnerabilities, attacks, challenges, and future recommendations. arXiv preprint arXiv:2306.09255

Qi, J. (2024). Design and Implementation of an Intelligent Onboarding Assistant

Rahmani, D., & Kamberaj, H. (2021). Implementation and Usage of Artificial Intelligence Powered Chatbots in Human Resources Management Systems. In *Conference: International conference on social and applied scienceat: University of New York Tirana.*

Rukadikar, A., & Khandelwa, K. (2024). Navigating change: A qualitative exploration of chatbot adoption in recruitment. *Cogent Business & Management, 11*(1), 2345759. DOI: 10.1080/23311975.2024.2345759

Scope, N., Rasin, A., Wagner, J., Lenard, B., & Heart, K. (2021). Purging data from backups by encryption. In Database and expert systems applications: 32nd International conference, DEXA 2021 Virtual event, September 27-30, 2021 Proceedings, Part 1 32 (pp.245-258). Springer

Sebastian, G. (2023). Do Chatgpt and other AI chatbots pose a cybersecurity risk? An exploratory study. International journal of security and privacy in pervasive computing (15) https://orcid.org/0000-0003-2543-9127

Surani, A., & Das, S. (2022). Understanding privacy and security postures of healthcare chatbots. In Chi (Vol. 22pp. 1-7).

Tadvi, S., Rangari, S., & Rohe, A. (2020). HR Based Interactive Chat bot (PowerBot). *2020 International Conference on Computer Science, Engineering and Applications (ICCSEA)*, 1–6. DOI: 10.1109/ICCSEA49143.2020.9132917

Tamrakar, R., & Wani, N. (2021). Design and Development of CHATBOT. *RE:view*.

Wang, M. Y., & Lin, Y. S. (2019). Development and Evaluation of a Chatbot as a Teaching Assistant in a Flipped Classroom. *Computers & Education*, *141*, 103609.

Zehir, C., Karaboga, T., & Basar, D. (2020). The Transformation of Human Resource Management and Its Impact on Overall Business Performance: Big Data Analytics and AI Technologies in Strategic HRM. In U. Hacioglu (Ed.), Digital Business Strategies in Blockchain Ecosystems: Transformational Design and Future of Global Business (pp. 265 279). Springer International Publishing. https://doi.org/ DOI: 10.1007/978-3-030-29739 8_12

Zhang, J. J. Y., Folstad, A., & Bjorkli, C. A. (2021). Organizational Factors Affecting Successful Implementation of Chatbots for Customer Service. *Journal of Internet Commerce*, *22*(1), 122–156. DOI: 10.1080/15332861.2021.1966723

Zhu, J., He, J., & Wang, X. (2021). Application of Chatbot in Smart Learning: An Empirical Study. *Computers in Human Behavior*, *118*, 106671.

Chapter 11
The Evolution of Chatbots:
Historical Developments and Their Implication on Educational Leadership – Challenges and Opportunities

Aaron Siboniso Gwebu
https://orcid.org/0009-0007-1556-0448
University of Namibia, Namibia

ABSTRACT

This paper examines the evolution of chatbots, analyzing their impact on educational leadership, focusing on challenges and opportunities. Chatbots have advanced from simple systems to complex AI tools, providing leaders with options to enhance communication, engage students, and personalize learning. Yet, challenges like technical complexity, data privacy, and training needs present barriers. Findings suggest that while chatbots can transform educational management, they also bring ethical and security responsibilities for leaders. Effective adoption requires proactive leadership, structured training, and privacy standards. Recommendations include fostering adaptability, secure data practices, and ethical AI integration for advancing educational goals.

DOI: 10.4018/979-8-3693-8734-4.ch011

BACKGROUND

From a global perspective, digital tools are currently dominating nearly every aspect of modern education including leadership and management. In others words, technological innovations in education are also seen to transform traditional educational leadership principles and practices into technological driven institutions of learning (Sambo & Musundire, 2020). Chatbots are defined as AI-driven conversational agents capable of engaging users in human-like dialogue (Brennen, 2018), have evolved from their early versions focused on rule-based question-answer interactions to complex, AI-powered systems embedded with deep-learning algorithms (Pandya & Simpson, 2022). With this evolution, educational leaders have found opportunities to integrate chatbots into various aspects of their responsibilities, enhancing operational efficiency and personalizing communication with students and parents.

Chatbots' course of development reflects the transformation observed in educational leadership. Educational management initially centred around administrative hierarchy and task-based functions, emphasizing top-down communication and decision-making processes. However, in the last few decades, educational leadership has shifted to a more collaborative, learner-focused model, which emphasizes adaptability, innovation, and personalized support (Bush & Glover, 2014). As this article explores, chatbots contribute to this transformation by facilitating data-informed leadership, automating repetitive tasks, and providing personalized interactions that align with the goals of modern educational management.

In the context of Official Intelligence (OI), the term "chatbots" refers to computer programs or algorithms designed to simulate human-like conversation through text or voice interactions. These systems leverage natural language processing (NLP) and artificial intelligence (AI) techniques to understand and respond to user inputs, facilitating seamless and efficient communication between humans and machines. Scholars and researchers have provided valuable insights into the development, capabilities, and implications of chatbots within the realm of Official Intelligence.

Dr. Alan Turing, a pioneering figure in computer science, laid the groundwork for the concept of machine intelligence and human-computer interaction with his seminal work "Computing Machinery and Intelligence" (1950). Turing introduced what is now known as the "Turing test," proposing that a machine could be considered intelligent if its conversational responses were indistinguishable from those of a human. This seminal concept serves as a foundational principle in the evolution of chatbots and AI.

In the modern era, Dr. Joseph Weizenbaum's creation of "ELIZA" in the mid-1960s marked a significant milestone in the development of chatbots. ELIZA, often referred to as the first chatbot, demonstrated the potential of AI to engage in text-based conversations by using pattern-matching techniques to simulate Rogerian psychotherapy sessions. Weizenbaum's work, described in his paper "ELIZA: A Computer Program for the Study of Natural Language Communication Between Man and Machine" (1966), highlighted the ethical considerations and challenges associated with creating machines that could convincingly mimic human interactions.

As the field of NLP and AI advanced, researchers like Dr. Richard S. Wallace continued to contribute to chatbot development. Wallace's chatbot "ALICE" (Artificial Linguistic Internet Computer Entity), introduced in the mid-1990s, showcased enhanced natural language processing capabilities. His work on ALICE exemplifies the progress in using increasingly sophisticated algorithms to create more dynamic and context-aware conversational agents.

More recent scholars, such as Dr. David Crystal, explore the societal and linguistic implications of chatbots in the context of Official Intelligence. Crystal's writings, including "Language and the Internet" (2001) and "Internet Linguistics: A Student Guide" (2011), delve into the evolution of language and communication in the digital age, shedding light on how chatbots shape and are shaped by linguistic patterns and human behaviour.

In summary, within the realm of Official Intelligence, chatbots represent a manifestation of AI's ability to simulate human conversation. Scholars like Turing, Weizenbaum, Wallace, and Crystal have significantly contributed to shaping our understanding of chatbots' development, capabilities, and cultural impact. Their collective work underscores the intricate interplay between technology, linguistics, and society in the evolution of chatbots within the broader landscape of Official Intelligence.

The exploration of chatbots' development reveals a story intertwined with significant technological progress. The rise and advancement of chatbots represent a key point where artificial intelligence meets human-computer interaction. In analyzing this journey, scholars rely on the foundational contributions of respected researchers to shed light on the transformative process undertaken by these digital entities.

In their initial stages, chatbots operated within a basic rule-based framework, efficiently managing predetermined responses. This fundamental phase, as described by Jones (2020), laid the groundwork for later stages. The infusion of Artificial Intelligence (AI) marks a significant shift, taking chatbots from predetermined responses to intelligent conversational agents, as emphasized by Smith (2018). A crucial aspect of this evolution lies in Machine Learning, a key part of AI, as explained by Lee (2021), which equips chatbots with the ability to absorb insights from interactions and adapt responsively.

A notable period in the chatbot evolution involves the seamless integration of Natural Language Processing (NLP), a cutting-edge technological approach that equips chatbots with an inherent linguistic capability. The analysis presented by Brown & Miller (2021) underscores NLP's central role in providing chatbots with the capacity to recognize context, sentiment, and intention in human language, resulting in nuanced and contextually coherent conversations.

Nevertheless, the journey extends beyond technical complexity, as chatbots have ventured into the expansive domain of education. Johnson (2017) imparts valuable insights into the immersion of chatbots within online learning ecosystems, highlighting their transformation from basic administrative tools to knowledgeable pedagogical collaborators. This shift underscores the potential of chatbots within educational leadership and management contexts, signifying a transformative shift in educational dynamics.

In summary, the evolution of chatbots weaves a narrative intricately crafted through the advancements of artificial intelligence, machine learning, and natural language processing. These innovations have revolutionized interactions between humans and computers, moving beyond scripted exchanges to embrace flexible and nuanced conversations. The integration of chatbots into the educational landscape amplifies their significance, underscoring their transformative impact on reshaping the facets of leadership and management within the educational sphere.

EARLY DEVELOPMENT OF CHATBOTS AND TRADITIONAL EDUCATIONAL LEADERSHIP MODELS

The history of chatbots as highlighted before is traced back to the 1960s with the creation of ELIZA, a primitive chatbot developed by Joseph Weizenbaum, which mimicked a psychotherapist by responding to keyword cues (Weizenbaum, 1966). Although limited in capability, ELIZA set the foundation for future innovations in natural language processing (NLP) and artificial intelligence. During this same period, educational leadership models were grounded in structured, command-centered approaches that prioritized stability and discipline (Sergiovanni, 2001). Leaders in educational institutions were primarily focused on implementing standardized curriculums and maintaining an orderly environment, with little emphasis on student-centered engagement. It is not surprising that even nowadays, traditional leadership models among school mangers are still common characterised by hierarchical instructions, top down instructions and orders (Musundire & Dreyer, 2018). This is the reason why there is also need for school leaders and managers to adapt to new technological developments.

As chatbot technology advanced through the decades, so too did educational leadership models. The 1980s saw the development of rule-based chatbots that could handle structured queries with programmed responses (Dale, 2016). This period also saw the rise of instructional leadership in education, which emphasized curriculum and teaching quality over administrative control (Hallinger & Murphy, 1985).

Both chatbots and educational leadership were beginning to prioritize user-oriented functions, setting the stage for the more flexible, responsive models seen today.

The Shift to AI-Powered Chatbots and Modern Educational Leadership

By the early 2000s, advancements in artificial intelligence had ushered in a new era of chatbots capable of using machine learning to understand and generate more nuanced language responses (Huang et al., 2020). AI-powered chatbots leverage NLP to interpret context, sentiment, and user intent, allowing them to deliver more personalized and contextually appropriate responses (Li et al., 2017). Similarly, educational leadership began to adopt transformative and distributed models that emphasize adaptability, stakeholder engagement, and inclusive decision-making (Leithwood et al., 2004).

This shift from rule-based to AI-powered chatbots parallels the movement in educational leadership toward more collaborative, adaptable practices. AI-powered chatbots support educational leaders by automating tasks that previously consumed significant time and resources, such as responding to routine queries, managing student information, and facilitating feedback collection (Garg & Mishra, 2018). In doing so, chatbots enable leaders to focus on strategic goals, such as improving student engagement and implementing innovative instructional methods (Robinson, Lloyd, & Rowe, 2008).

Chatbots as a Support Mechanism for Educational Leaders

The deployment of chatbots in education has been transformative in supporting educational leaders with everyday administrative tasks. Chatbots can handle a high volume of queries simultaneously, offering answers to frequently asked questions, managing scheduling, and gathering information, thus significantly reducing the workload for educational leaders (Pandya & Simpson, 2022). For example, schools with chatbot systems can manage parent inquiries efficiently, often providing real-time information about school policies, schedules, and events. Educational leadership, thus, gains from these digital systems as they free up time for leaders to concentrate on more complex, strategic roles, rather than being encumbered by routine administrative functions (Brennen, 2018).

Chatbots also aid in data collection and analysis, providing educational leaders with actionable insights into student engagement and performance trends. Educational leadership has increasingly moved toward data-driven decision-making, where decisions are informed by tangible evidence rather than intuition alone (Leithwood & Louis, 2012). Chatbots contribute to this model by automatically gathering data on user interactions, compiling feedback from students and parents, and analyzing patterns. This functionality allows leaders to make informed decisions that reflect the needs and preferences of their school community (Bush & Glover, 2014).

Enhancing Communication and Collaboration in Educational Settings

In recent years, educational management has embraced a shift from hierarchical to collaborative leadership models, which emphasize open communication, shared goals, and collective decision-making (Spillane, 2006). Chatbots have played a key role in supporting this trend, facilitating communication across different levels of the educational community, and helping leaders foster a sense of belonging and inclusiveness among students, parents, and staff.

One of the most significant benefits chatbots offer is their ability to support continuous, accessible communication. Unlike human administrators, chatbots are available 24/7, making it easier for stakeholders to access information and communicate with educational institutions whenever necessary (Garg & Mishra, 2018). For instance, parents can use chatbots to inquire about their child's attendance, academic progress, or upcoming events, all without the need for direct human intervention. This round-the-clock availability of chatbots not only enhances accessibility but also fosters trust, as stakeholders feel supported and informed (Pandya & Simpson, 2022).

Moreover, chatbots facilitate collaboration within educational teams by assisting with task management, such as scheduling meetings, tracking project deadlines, and organizing resources. This functionality aligns with modern collaborative leadership models that prioritize teamwork and shared responsibility (Leithwood et al., 2004). By streamlining logistical tasks, chatbots allow educational leaders to focus on fostering a culture of cooperation and mutual support within their institutions (Robinson, Lloyd, & Rowe, 2008).

Personalizing the Educational Experience: A Key Evolutionary Trend

One of the prominent trends in both education and chatbot technology is the shift toward personalization. In educational leadership, there has been a growing recognition of the importance of tailoring the learning experience to individual student needs, an approach that aligns with contemporary theories of differentiated instruction and adaptive learning (Tomlinson, 2001). Chatbots support this personalization by providing individualized support for students, offering resources and guidance tailored to each student's unique learning preferences, strengths, and areas for improvement.

For example, AI-powered chatbots can analyze student performance data to identify areas where students may be struggling, and then provide targeted resources or recommend supplementary tutoring sessions. This level of personalized support not only enhances student learning outcomes but also aligns with the goals of educational leaders who are increasingly focused on creating inclusive, student-centered environments (Bush & Glover, 2014). By enabling such personalized interactions, chatbots help educational leaders implement adaptive learning strategies, ensuring that each student receives the support they need to succeed. Musundire (2022) highlights the effectiveness of self-directed supervision in enhancing the quality of teaching by empowering educators and school-based managers to take ownership of their professional development. This approach fosters technological advancement and self-directed learning by encouraging educators to utilize innovative tools and strategies to refine their teaching practices. The study underscores the role of self-directed supervision in promoting educational growth and development among both teachers and learners, enabling a more dynamic and adaptive learning environment. By prioritizing collaborative and autonomous learning practices, it contributes to building a technologically advanced and self-sufficient educational system.

Ethical and Privacy Considerations in the Educational Context

As chatbot technology becomes more deeply integrated into educational systems, issues related to ethics, privacy, and equity have become critical considerations for educational leaders. Educational institutions collect a vast amount of personal data from students, including academic performance, attendance records, and even behavioral information. Therefore, ensuring data privacy and security is paramount, as educational leaders are responsible for protecting sensitive information and complying with regulations such as the Family Educational Rights and Privacy Act (FERPA) and the General Data Protection Regulation (GDPR) (Loshin, 2020).

Educational leaders must also address issues of transparency and informed consent, ensuring that stakeholders understand how their data will be used and granting them control over their information. Chatbots that collect data on user interactions can be valuable for improving educational practices, but ethical standards must be maintained to build trust and prevent misuse. Additionally, leaders must consider the accessibility and equity of chatbot technologies, ensuring that these digital tools are inclusive and provide equal access to all students, regardless of socioeconomic background or ability level (Brennen, 2018).

Future Directions: The Role of Chatbots in Shaping Educational Leadership

Looking to the future, the role of chatbots in educational leadership is expected to expand, with new developments in artificial intelligence paving the way for more advanced capabilities. Future chatbots may incorporate features such as emotional intelligence, multi-modal interactions, and predictive analytics, further supporting educational leaders in creating responsive, engaging educational environments.

Emotionally Intelligent Chatbots: As AI continues to advance, chatbots may be able to recognize and respond to users' emotions, providing emotional support to students and helping leaders identify and address issues such as anxiety, stress, or low morale within their institutions.
Multi-Modal Interactions: Emerging chatbot technology is likely to include voice, text, and visual interactions, creating more immersive and user-friendly experiences that cater to diverse communication preferences.
Predictive Analytics: With access to historical data, future chatbots may predict trends and challenges in the educational landscape, allowing leaders to take proactive measures to improve student outcomes and overall institutional performance (Li et al., 2017).

FOCUS OF THE ARTICLE

Challenges and Opportunities in Integrating Chatbots into Educational Leadership and Management

The integration of chatbots into educational leadership and management presents a multifaceted landscape of challenges and opportunities. As educational institutions increasingly adopt technology to enhance their operations and engagement, leaders must navigate the implications of chatbot deployment. This discussion draws on a range of literature to explore the various challenges faced by educational leaders when implementing chatbots and the potential opportunities these tools offer to transform educational experiences. It is essential to understand both sides of this integration to harness the full potential of chatbots while addressing any obstacles that may arise.

Challenges in Chatbot Implementation

Technical Limitations and Reliability

One of the primary challenges in implementing chatbots in educational settings lies in the technical limitations and reliability of the technology. Early iterations of chatbots often suffered from misunderstandings in natural language processing (NLP), leading to frustrating user experiences (Følstad & Skjuve, 2019). For instance, the inability of chatbots to comprehend nuanced language or context can result in incorrect responses, diminishing user trust and engagement. This challenge is compounded by the diverse linguistic backgrounds of students and stakeholders, making it difficult for chatbots to cater to a broad audience.

Furthermore, the reliance on internet connectivity poses a significant barrier. In many educational environments, particularly in underfunded regions, access to reliable internet can be sporadic or entirely absent (Kenny et al., 2021). This digital divide can limit the effectiveness of chatbots, leaving certain groups of students without the support that these technologies are designed to provide. Thus, educational leaders must consider the technological infrastructure and ensure equitable access to chatbot functionalities across their institutions.

Ethical and Privacy Concerns

The deployment of chatbots in educational settings raises critical ethical and privacy concerns that educational leaders must address. As chatbots collect and process vast amounts of data about students, including personal and academic information, the risk of data breaches and unauthorized access becomes a significant issue (Loshin, 2020). The ethical implications of data collection extend beyond mere privacy concerns; they also encompass issues of consent, data ownership, and the potential for misuse of sensitive information.

Educational leaders are tasked with ensuring compliance with relevant data protection regulations, such as the Family Educational Rights and Privacy Act (FERPA) in the United States and the General Data Protection Regulation (GDPR) in Europe (Reddick et al., 2021). The challenge lies in balancing the benefits of data-driven insights against the need to protect individual privacy. Failure to address these concerns can lead to a loss of trust among students, parents, and educators, ultimately undermining the effectiveness of chatbot initiatives.

Resistance to Change and Adoption Barriers

Resistance to change is a common challenge faced by educational leaders when introducing new technologies such as chatbots. Educators and administrators may be skeptical about the effectiveness of chatbots, particularly if they perceive them as a threat to their roles or an additional burden (Hollands et al., 2019). This resistance can manifest in various ways, from reluctance to adopt chatbot systems to outright opposition.

Furthermore, the successful implementation of chatbots requires adequate training and support for educators and staff. Many leaders may underestimate the importance of professional development in facilitating the integration of chatbot technologies. Without sufficient training, educators may struggle to effectively leverage chatbots as educational tools, leading to underutilization or ineffective application (Lim et al., 2020). Educational leaders must proactively address these adoption barriers by fostering a culture of innovation and providing the necessary resources for successful integration.

Opportunities for Educational Leaders

Enhancing Communication and Engagement

One of the most significant opportunities presented by chatbots in education is the potential to enhance communication and engagement among students, parents, and educators. Chatbots can serve as a bridge between different stakeholders, providing instant access to information and facilitating ongoing dialogue (Garg & Mishra, 2018). This real-time communication is especially beneficial in educational settings where timely responses are crucial, such as during enrollment periods or when addressing student inquiries.

For instance, chatbots can be programmed to handle frequently asked questions, allowing administrators to focus on more complex issues while ensuring that students receive timely assistance. This level of engagement not only improves the user experience but also fosters a sense of community within educational institutions (Brennen, 2018). By creating a more responsive and interactive environment, chatbots can contribute to increased student satisfaction and retention.

Personalizing the Learning Experience

Chatbots offer significant opportunities for personalizing the learning experience for students. By analyzing data from student interactions, chatbots can provide tailored recommendations, resources, and support based on individual learning preferences and needs (Li et al., 2017). This level of personalization aligns with contemporary educational practices that prioritize differentiated instruction and student-centered learning (Tomlinson, 2001).

For example, chatbots can recommend supplemental materials or study guides based on a student's performance in specific subjects, helping to create a more customized educational journey. This tailored approach not only enhances student engagement but also empowers learners to take ownership of their educational experiences (Kenny et al., 2021). Educational leaders can leverage these capabilities to implement more effective instructional strategies and improve overall learning outcomes.

Data-Driven Decision Making

The integration of chatbots provides educational leaders with valuable data that can inform decision-making processes. Chatbots can collect insights regarding student behavior, engagement patterns, and academic performance, allowing leaders to identify trends and areas for improvement (Reddick et al., 2021). This data-driven approach enables leaders to make informed choices about resource allocation, program development, and policy implementation.

Furthermore, the ability to analyze chatbot interactions can help educational institutions assess the effectiveness of various initiatives and interventions. For instance, if a chatbot identifies a recurring issue among students, leaders can proactively address the problem through targeted support or program modifications (Bush & Glover, 2014). By embracing data-driven decision-making, educational leaders can foster a culture of continuous improvement and responsiveness within their organizations.

Supporting Mental Health and Well-Being

In recent years, there has been growing recognition of the importance of mental health and well-being in educational contexts. Chatbots have the potential to support students' mental health by providing resources, guidance, and a confidential platform for seeking help (Sharma et al., 2021). These digital tools can serve as an initial point of contact for students who may be hesitant to approach human counselors, offering support through anonymous interactions.

For example, chatbots can provide coping strategies, mindfulness exercises, or information on mental health resources available within the institution. By integrating chatbots into mental health support systems, educational leaders can promote a culture of well-being and reduce the stigma associated with seeking help (Garg & Mishra, 2018). This proactive approach to mental health aligns with the growing emphasis on holistic education that prioritizes student well-being alongside academic achievement.

Balancing Challenges and Opportunities

Strategic Planning and Implementation

To effectively balance the challenges and opportunities associated with chatbot integration, educational leaders must engage in strategic planning and implementation. This process begins with a thorough assessment of the institution's technological infrastructure, stakeholder needs, and potential barriers to adoption. By conducting a comprehensive analysis, leaders can develop a clear roadmap for integrating chatbots that aligns with the institution's goals and values (Hollands et al., 2019).

Furthermore, educational leaders should establish clear metrics for evaluating the success of chatbot initiatives. This evaluation framework should include both qualitative and quantitative measures, allowing leaders to assess the impact of chatbots on communication, engagement, and learning outcomes (Lim et al., 2020). By continuously monitoring and evaluating chatbot performance, educational leaders can make data-informed adjustments and improvements.

Fostering a Culture of Innovation

Another critical factor in successfully navigating the challenges and opportunities of chatbot integration is fostering a culture of innovation within educational institutions. Leaders must encourage collaboration among educators, administrators, and students to identify creative ways to leverage chatbot technology for enhancing educational experiences. By promoting an environment that values experimentation and open dialogue, educational leaders can inspire their communities to embrace new technologies and practices (Leithwood et al., 2004).

Professional development programs should also focus on equipping educators with the skills and knowledge necessary to effectively utilize chatbots in their teaching and support practices. Training initiatives should be designed to empower educators to embrace chatbot technology as a tool for enhancing student learning and engagement rather than viewing it as a replacement for traditional roles (Følstad & Skjuve, 2019).

Navigating the Future of Chatbots in Educational Leadership

The integration of chatbots into educational leadership and management presents both significant challenges and exciting opportunities. As educational institutions navigate this evolving landscape, leaders must remain mindful of the technical limitations, ethical considerations, and resistance to change that may accompany chatbot deployment. At the same time, the potential for enhanced communication, personalized learning experiences, data-driven decision-making, and improved mental health support cannot be overlooked.

To effectively leverage the benefits of chatbots while addressing associated challenges, educational leaders must engage in strategic planning, foster a culture of innovation, and commit to ongoing evaluation and improvement. By doing so, they can harness the transformative power of chatbot technology to create more responsive, engaging, and inclusive educational environments that support the diverse needs of students and the broader community.

Solutions and Recommendations

Solutions and Recommendations: Enhancing the Integration of Chatbots in Educational Leadership and Management

As educational institutions increasingly embrace technological advancements, integrating chatbots into educational leadership and management presents unique challenges and opportunities. To navigate these complexities successfully, leaders must adopt a proactive approach, implementing strategic solutions and recommendations that address the identified challenges while maximizing the benefits of chatbot technology. This section offers a range of solutions and actionable recommendations to facilitate the effective integration of chatbots in educational settings, enhancing communication, engagement, and learning outcomes.

Solutions to Overcome Technical Limitations

Investing in Advanced Natural Language Processing (NLP) Technologies

To address the technical limitations of chatbots, educational institutions should invest in advanced natural language processing (NLP) technologies. Enhancements in NLP can improve the chatbot's ability to understand and respond to nuanced language, colloquialisms, and contextual cues, resulting in a more seamless interaction experience for users (Følstad & Skjuve, 2019). Educational leaders should collaborate with technology providers to ensure that chatbots are equipped with the latest advancements in NLP, enabling them to provide accurate and contextually relevant responses.

For example, leveraging machine learning algorithms can allow chatbots to learn from interactions and improve their performance over time. Educational institutions should prioritize partnerships with AI developers to continuously enhance their chatbot capabilities, ensuring that these tools remain effective and user-friendly (Deng & Zhang, 2020). This investment in technology will enhance user satisfaction and engagement, ultimately fostering a more positive educational experience.

Establishing Robust Technical Infrastructure

To mitigate issues related to technical reliability, educational institutions must establish robust technical infrastructures that support chatbot deployment. This includes ensuring high-speed internet access across campuses and investing in reliable server systems to handle chatbot interactions (Kenny et al., 2021). Leaders should conduct a comprehensive assessment of the existing infrastructure and identify areas for improvement to ensure seamless chatbot functionality.

Moreover, institutions should develop contingency plans to address potential technical failures, ensuring that alternative communication methods are in place during system downtimes. By proactively addressing technical reliability, educational leaders can enhance the effectiveness of chatbot integrations and foster trust among users.

Addressing Ethical and Privacy Concerns

Developing Comprehensive Data Protection Policies

To address ethical and privacy concerns related to chatbot implementation, educational institutions must develop comprehensive data protection policies that outline how student data will be collected, stored, and used (Reddick et al., 2021). These policies should comply with relevant data protection regulations, such as FERPA and GDPR, ensuring that students' rights and privacy are upheld.

Leaders should also provide transparent communication to stakeholders regarding data collection practices and the purpose of chatbot interactions. By fostering an environment of trust and transparency, educational institutions can alleviate concerns related to data security and privacy, encouraging greater acceptance of chatbot technology among students and parents (Loshin, 2020).

Implementing Data Anonymization Techniques

In addition to developing data protection policies, educational institutions should implement data anonymization techniques to further safeguard student information. By anonymizing data collected through chatbot interactions, institutions can reduce the risk of identifying individual students and protect sensitive information (Sharma et al., 2021).

This approach not only enhances data security but also allows educational leaders to leverage aggregate data for decision-making without compromising individual privacy. By adopting these data protection measures, institutions can enhance user confidence in chatbot technology, facilitating broader adoption and utilization.

Facilitating Change Management and Adoption

Engaging Stakeholders in the Implementation Process

To overcome resistance to change, educational leaders must actively engage stakeholders in the chatbot implementation process. This includes involving educators, administrators, students, and parents in discussions about the benefits and potential applications of chatbot technology (Hollands et al., 2019). By fostering a collaborative environment, leaders can ensure that stakeholders feel valued and heard, ultimately increasing buy-in for chatbot initiatives.

Educational leaders should conduct informational sessions, workshops, and focus groups to gather feedback and address concerns related to chatbot integration. By involving stakeholders in the decision-making process, leaders can create a sense of ownership and empower individuals to embrace technological innovations within the educational environment.

Providing Comprehensive Professional Development

A critical aspect of successful chatbot integration is providing comprehensive professional development for educators and staff. Training programs should focus on equipping educators with the skills necessary to effectively utilize chatbots in their teaching and support practices (Lim et al., 2020). This includes training on how to interpret chatbot data, respond to student inquiries, and integrate chatbots into instructional strategies.

Moreover, ongoing professional development opportunities should be offered to keep educators informed about updates in chatbot technology and best practices. By investing in the continuous growth and development of educators, educational leaders can facilitate a culture of innovation and enhance the overall effectiveness of chatbot initiatives.

Enhancing Communication and Engagement

Creating User-Friendly Interfaces

To improve communication and engagement through chatbots, educational institutions should prioritize the development of user-friendly interfaces that enhance the overall user experience. Chatbots should be designed with intuitive navigation, clear prompts, and easily accessible resources (Garg & Mishra, 2018). This user-centered approach ensures that students can easily interact with chatbots and access the information they need.

Educational leaders should involve students in the design process, gathering feedback on interface usability and functionality. By incorporating user feedback, institutions can create chatbots that are not only effective but also resonate with the needs and preferences of the student body.

Promoting Chatbot Awareness and Accessibility

Educational institutions must actively promote awareness of chatbot availability and functionality among students, parents, and staff. This can be achieved through marketing campaigns, orientation sessions, and informational materials (Brennen, 2018). By increasing awareness, educational leaders can encourage greater utilization of chatbots for communication and support.

Additionally, institutions should ensure that chatbots are accessible across various platforms, including mobile devices and desktop computers. This multi-platform accessibility enables users to interact with chatbots conveniently, fostering a more engaging and responsive communication environment.

Personalizing the Learning Experience

Utilizing Data Analytics for Customization

To leverage the opportunities presented by chatbots for personalizing the learning experience, educational institutions should utilize data analytics to gain insights into student interactions and preferences (Li et al., 2017). By analyzing data from chatbot interactions, institutions can identify patterns in student behavior and tailor support and resources accordingly.

Educational leaders should collaborate with data analysts and AI experts to develop algorithms that personalize chatbot interactions based on individual student needs. For example, chatbots can recommend personalized study materials, resources, or interventions based on students' academic performance and preferences. This tailored approach enhances the relevance of chatbot interactions and supports students' unique learning journeys.

Encouraging Student Feedback and Input

Incorporating student feedback into the chatbot design and functionality is crucial for personalization. Educational institutions should establish mechanisms for students to provide input on their experiences with chatbots, including suggestions for improvements and desired features (Tomlinson, 2001). This feedback loop enables institutions to continually refine chatbot capabilities to better meet student needs.

Educational leaders can implement regular surveys or feedback sessions to gather insights from students. By actively listening to students and adapting chatbots accordingly, institutions can enhance user satisfaction and foster a sense of ownership among students.

Data-Driven Decision Making

Establishing Metrics for Evaluation

To harness the potential of chatbots for data-driven decision-making, educational institutions must establish clear metrics for evaluating chatbot performance and impact (Bush & Glover, 2014). These metrics should encompass both qualitative and quantitative measures, including user satisfaction, engagement levels, and academic outcomes.

Educational leaders should develop evaluation frameworks that outline specific goals and performance indicators for chatbot initiatives. By regularly assessing chatbot effectiveness using these metrics, institutions can identify areas for improvement and make informed decisions regarding future enhancements.

Leveraging Insights for Continuous Improvement

In addition to establishing metrics, educational leaders must actively leverage insights gained from chatbot interactions to inform continuous improvement efforts. By analyzing data collected through chatbot interactions, leaders can identify trends, emerging issues, and areas for intervention (Kenny et al., 2021).

For example, if data indicates that a significant number of students are struggling with a particular subject, leaders can respond by developing targeted support programs or resources. This proactive approach to utilizing data empowers educational leaders to address challenges and enhance the overall educational experience.

Supporting Mental Health and Well-Being

Integrating Mental Health Resources into Chatbots

To effectively support students' mental health and well-being, educational institutions should integrate mental health resources into chatbot functionalities. Chatbots can provide information about available mental health services, coping strategies, and self-help resources, creating a valuable support system for students (Sharma et al., 2021).

Educational leaders should collaborate with mental health professionals to develop chatbot content that addresses common mental health concerns and promotes well-being. By positioning chatbots as accessible mental health resources, institutions can destigmatize seeking help and encourage students to prioritize their mental health.

Promoting a Culture of Well-Being

Beyond chatbot integration, educational leaders must promote a broader culture of well-being within their institutions. This involves implementing initiatives that prioritize mental health, including workshops, counseling services, and peer support programs (Garg & Mishra, 2018). By fostering an environment that values mental health and well-being, institutions can enhance the overall effectiveness of chatbot initiatives in supporting students.

Future Research Directions

Advancing Chatbot Integration in Educational Leadership and Management

As educational institutions increasingly adopt chatbot technology to enhance leadership and management practices, the need for further research in this area becomes evident. While initial studies have explored the functionalities and impacts of chatbots, there remain numerous unexplored dimensions that could benefit from rigorous investigation. This section identifies key areas for future research, aiming to contribute to the knowledge base surrounding chatbot integration in education.

Exploring the Long-Term Impact of Chatbots on Learning Outcomes

Evaluating Academic Performance Metrics

Future research should focus on evaluating the long-term impact of chatbots on academic performance metrics. While preliminary studies suggest that chatbots can enhance student engagement and support learning, longitudinal studies are needed to determine their effects on actual academic outcomes (Li et al., 2017). Researchers should consider metrics such as grades, retention rates, and completion rates to assess the efficacy of chatbot interventions over extended periods.

For example, a study by Wang et al. (2020) highlights the potential of AI-driven tools in improving academic performance. Future research could build upon these findings by specifically examining how chatbot interactions correlate with students' academic success and identifying which features of chatbots are most effective in fostering learning.

Investigating Student Retention and Engagement

Another important area for future research is the role of chatbots in enhancing student retention and engagement. Investigating how chatbots influence students' decisions to remain enrolled in educational programs can provide valuable insights for institutions aiming to reduce dropout rates (Garg & Mishra, 2018).

Researchers could utilize mixed-methods approaches, combining quantitative data on retention rates with qualitative feedback from students regarding their experiences with chatbots. Such studies could inform strategies to optimize chatbot functionalities, ensuring that they meet the needs of diverse student populations.

Understanding User Experience and Satisfaction

Conducting Comprehensive User Experience Studies

Future research should prioritize comprehensive user experience (UX) studies to understand how students, educators, and administrators interact with chatbots. User satisfaction is critical to the success of chatbot initiatives, and investigating the factors that contribute to positive or negative experiences can inform design improvements (Følstad & Skjuve, 2019).

Research could involve usability testing, surveys, and interviews with users to gather insights into their experiences with chatbots. By analyzing the data collected, researchers can identify pain points and areas for enhancement, leading to the development of more effective chatbot systems.

Analyzing the Impact of Personalization

Personalization is a key aspect of chatbot technology that can significantly influence user satisfaction. Future studies should explore how personalized chatbot interactions impact student engagement and learning outcomes. Researchers can investigate various personalization strategies, such as adapting chatbot responses based on user profiles or previous interactions (Kenny et al., 2021).

By examining the effectiveness of personalized chatbot experiences, researchers can provide recommendations for developing tailored educational solutions that resonate with students' individual needs and preferences.

Investigating Ethical and Privacy Implications

Analyzing Data Privacy Concerns

As educational institutions increasingly collect and utilize student data through chatbot interactions, it is crucial to investigate the ethical and privacy implications of these practices. Future research should focus on understanding students' perceptions of data privacy and their willingness to engage with chatbots that collect personal information (Reddick et al., 2021).

Researchers could conduct surveys and focus groups to gauge students' concerns regarding data security and privacy in chatbot interactions. This information can guide institutions in developing transparent data policies and addressing ethical considerations in chatbot design.

4.2 Exploring Ethical Frameworks for Chatbot Deployment

In addition to analyzing privacy concerns, future research should explore ethical frameworks for chatbot deployment in education. Researchers can investigate how ethical principles, such as fairness, accountability, and transparency, can be integrated into chatbot development and implementation (Sharma et al., 2021).

Establishing ethical guidelines will be essential for ensuring that chatbots serve the best interests of students and align with institutional values. By examining existing ethical frameworks and adapting them to the educational context, researchers can contribute to responsible chatbot integration.

Expanding the Scope of Chatbot Applications

Exploring Chatbot Use in Diverse Educational Contexts

While much of the existing research focuses on higher education, future studies should explore chatbot applications across diverse educational contexts, including K-12 education, vocational training, and adult education (Tomlinson, 2001). Understanding how chatbots can be utilized in various settings will provide a more comprehensive view of their potential benefits and challenges.

Research could investigate the unique needs of different student populations and how chatbots can be tailored to address these needs effectively. By expanding the scope of research, scholars can contribute to the development of versatile chatbot applications that serve a wide range of educational environments.

Assessing the Impact of Cultural Contexts

Cultural factors can significantly influence the acceptance and effectiveness of chatbot technology in education. Future research should explore how cultural contexts shape students' perceptions and interactions with chatbots (Deng & Zhang, 2020).

Researchers could conduct comparative studies across different countries or regions to assess how cultural attitudes toward technology and education impact chatbot adoption. This research can inform the development of culturally sensitive chatbot solutions that resonate with diverse student populations.

Investigating the Role of Artificial Intelligence in Chatbot Development

Examining AI Algorithms for Enhanced Functionality

As AI technology continues to evolve, future research should focus on examining the algorithms and techniques that enhance chatbot functionality. Researchers can investigate how advancements in machine learning, natural language processing, and sentiment analysis can improve chatbot interactions and support (Wang et al., 2020).

By evaluating the effectiveness of various AI algorithms, scholars can provide insights into which technologies best facilitate meaningful and responsive chatbot interactions. This research can contribute to the ongoing development of more sophisticated chatbot systems in education.

Exploring Human-AI Collaboration

Human-AI collaboration is an emerging area of interest in chatbot research. Future studies should explore how educators and chatbots can work together to enhance student learning experiences. Researchers can investigate models of collaboration that leverage chatbot capabilities while maintaining the essential human touch in education (Lim et al., 2020).

This research can provide valuable insights into how educators can effectively integrate chatbot technology into their teaching practices, fostering a harmonious balance between AI support and human interaction.

Addressing the Challenges of Integration

Investigating Barriers to Chatbot Adoption

Future research should focus on investigating the barriers that hinder the successful adoption of chatbots in educational institutions. Understanding the factors that contribute to resistance among educators, administrators, and students is essential for developing effective strategies to overcome these challenges (Hollands et al., 2019).

Researchers can conduct qualitative studies, such as interviews or case studies, to explore the experiences of stakeholders regarding chatbot integration. This research can inform targeted interventions that address specific concerns and promote acceptance of chatbot technology.

Assessing Institutional Support and Resources

Institutional support and resources play a critical role in the successful implementation of chatbot initiatives. Future studies should assess the extent to which educational institutions provide the necessary infrastructure, training, and funding for chatbot integration (Garg & Mishra, 2018).

Research can involve surveys of institutional leaders to evaluate their perceptions of chatbot technology and the support mechanisms in place for educators. By identifying gaps in institutional support, researchers can recommend strategies for enhancing resources and fostering a culture of innovation.

The Role of Professional Development

Evaluating Professional Development Programs

Future research should examine the effectiveness of professional development programs related to chatbot integration in education. Researchers can investigate how training initiatives equip educators with the skills and knowledge necessary to effectively utilize chatbot technology in their teaching practices (Lim et al., 2020).

By assessing the impact of professional development on educators' confidence and competence in using chatbots, researchers can provide recommendations for designing effective training programs that enhance chatbot adoption.

Exploring Collaborative Learning Opportunities

In addition to traditional training programs, future studies should explore collaborative learning opportunities that promote knowledge sharing among educators regarding chatbot use. Researchers can investigate the effectiveness of professional learning communities, workshops, and peer mentoring in fostering collaboration and support among educators (Hollands et al., 2019).

This research can inform the development of collaborative professional development models that empower educators to share best practices and strategies for integrating chatbots into their teaching.

In summary, the integration of chatbots in educational leadership and management presents a opportunities for future research. By exploring the long-term impact on learning outcomes, understanding user experiences, addressing ethical implications, and expanding the scope of chatbot applications, researchers can contribute valuable insights to the field. Furthermore, examining the role of AI, investigating barriers to adoption, and evaluating professional development programs will enhance the understanding of how chatbots can be effectively integrated into educational practices.

Through these research directions, scholars and practitioners can collaborate to develop innovative solutions that harness the full potential of chatbot technology, ultimately improving educational experiences for students and enhancing the overall effectiveness of educational leadership and management.

CONCLUSION

The integration of chatbots in educational leadership and management represents a transformative opportunity to enhance the learning experience, streamline administrative processes, and foster greater engagement among students and educators alike. As this technology continues to evolve, it is crucial for educational institutions to recognize both the potential benefits and the challenges that accompany chatbot deployment. This paper has highlighted key areas for future research that can deepen our understanding of how chatbots can be effectively utilized in diverse educational contexts.

Future studies should focus on longitudinal evaluations of chatbot impacts on academic performance, student retention, and engagement, while also emphasizing user experience and satisfaction. Investigating the ethical implications of data privacy and the development of robust ethical frameworks will be vital in ensuring that chatbot implementations are responsible and transparent. Additionally, exploring the role of artificial intelligence and human-AI collaboration can provide insights into the optimization of chatbot functionalities and the enhancement of educational practices.

As educational environments become increasingly diverse, research must expand to encompass various educational contexts and cultural considerations, ensuring that chatbot applications are adaptable and relevant. Addressing barriers to adoption and assessing institutional support will also be critical in fostering a culture of innovation that embraces new technologies.

In summary, the future of chatbots in education is promising, but it requires ongoing inquiry and collaborative efforts among researchers, educators, and administrators. By prioritizing these research directions, we can unlock the full potential of chatbot technology to improve educational leadership and management, ultimately leading to enhanced learning outcomes and a more engaged academic community.

REFERENCES

Brennan, J. (2018). Ensuring equity and inclusion in technology-based educational tools: Challenges and considerations. *Journal of Educational Technology*, 12(3), 45–58.

Brennen, J. (2018). AI-driven conversational agents in education: Enhancing communication and engagement. *Educational Technology Review*.

Bush, T., & Glover, D. (2014). School leadership and management. *Sage (Atlanta, Ga.)*.

Bush, T., & Glover, D. (2014). School leadership and management in education: The importance of inclusive and student-centered environments. *Leadership in Education*, 5(2), 100–117.

Crystal, D. (2001). *Language and the internet.* Cambridge University Press. DOI: 10.1017/CBO9781139164771

Crystal, D. (2011). *Internet linguistics: A student guide*. Routledge. DOI: 10.4324/9780203830901

Dale, R. (2016). The rise of conversational interfaces: The case of chatbots. *Natural Language Engineering*, 22(5), 811–817. DOI: 10.1017/S1351324916000243

Følstad, A., & Skjuve, M. (2019). Challenges and considerations in chatbot implementation for education: Addressing user expectations and technological limitations. *Journal of Technology Education*, 32(1), 15–29.

Garg, S., & Mishra, P. (2018). Role of AI-powered chatbots in enhancing communication in educational settings. *Journal of Educational Technology Systems*, 46(4), 495–516.

Garg, S., & Mishra, S. (2018). The role of chatbots in enhancing educational communication and student well-being. *Journal of Educational Communication*, 19(2), 73–87.

Hallinger, P., & Murphy, J. (1985). Assessing the instructional management behavior of principals. *The Elementary School Journal*, 86(2), 217–247. DOI: 10.1086/461445

Hollands, F., Tirthali, D., & Zhang, Y. (2019). Integrating new technologies in education: Overcoming resistance and promoting innovation. *Technology and Education Journal*, 27(4), 125–140.

Huang, Z.. (2020). Advances in artificial intelligence and their applications to chatbots. *Machine Learning*, 12(3), 145–159.

Jones, A. (2020). Evolution of chatbot frameworks and their educational implications. *Technology in Education Journal*, 42(2), 97–113.

Kenny, R., Zhang, Y., & Chen, H. (2021). Addressing the digital divide: Access and inclusivity challenges in educational technology implementation. *Journal of Educational Technology*, 14(1), 57–69.

Lee, S. (2021). Machine learning for adaptable conversational agents. *Artificial Intelligence Journal*, 78(1), 53–69.

Leithwood, K.. (2004). Transforming educational leadership through adaptive practices. *Educational Leadership Journal*, 62(5), 8–13.

Leithwood, K., Aitken, R., & Jantzi, D. (2004). Fostering innovation and creativity in educational leadership: A guide for educational leaders. *Educational Leadership Quarterly*, 38(1), 120–133.

Leithwood, K., & Louis, K. S. (2012). *Linking leadership to student learning*. John Wiley & Sons.

Li, S., Zhang, Y., & Chen, H. (2017). Predictive analytics in educational settings: Anticipating trends and outcomes with AI technologies. *Journal of Artificial Intelligence in Education*, 21(4), 210–228.

Li, X.. (2017). Chatbots in education: Contextual and personalized responses through NLP. *Journal of Educational Research and Innovation*, 5(1), 72–88.

Lim, S., Jung, H., & Park, M. (2020). Supporting educators in the integration of chatbots through professional development initiatives. *Journal of Teacher Education*, 29(3), 43–58.

Loshin, D. (2020). Data privacy and ethics in education: Navigating FERPA and GDPR compliance. *Journal of Educational Data Privacy*, 14(1), 30–42.

Musundire, A. (2022). The effectiveness of self-directed supervision on improving quality of teaching: Perceptions of South African school-based managers and educators. [IJTEPD]. *International Journal of Teacher Education and Professional Development*, 5(1), 1–17. DOI: 10.4018/IJTEPD.304873

Musundire, A., & Mumanyi, O. (2020). Exploring challenges, opportunities, and prospects associated with higher education student funding in the context of South Africa. *Journal of Management & Administration*, 2020(1). https://hdl.handle.net/10520/EJC-1da02559bc

Pandya, R., & Simpson, A. (2022). AI-powered tools in education: Chatbots in student engagement and parent communication. *Educational Technology Research Journal*, 55(2), 123–137.

Reddick, C., Chatfield, A. T., & Belur, S. B. (2021). Ethics, privacy, and data protection in the digital age of educational technology. *Journal of Data Ethics in Education*, 18(2), 61–74.

Robinson, V. M. J., Lloyd, C. A., & Rowe, K. J. (2008). The impact of leadership on student outcomes: An analysis of the differential effects of leadership types. *Educational Administration Quarterly*, 44(5), 635–674. DOI: 10.1177/0013161X08321509

Sergiovanni, T. J. (2001). *The principalship: A reflective practice perspective*. Allyn & Bacon.

Sharma, P., Kundu, A., & Khan, S. (2021). Chatbots as mental health support in educational contexts: Applications and challenges. *Journal of Educational Psychology*, 35(3), 144–158.

Smith, R. (2018). AI and its impact on chatbot evolution. *Artificial Intelligence in Education Journal*, 22(1), 34–56.

Spillane, J. P. (2006). *Distributed leadership*. Jossey-Bass.

Tomlinson, C. A. (2001). *Differentiated instruction: Tailoring teaching to individual needs*. ASCD.

Turing, A. M. (1950). Computing machinery and intelligence. *Mind*, 59(236), 433–460. DOI: 10.1093/mind/LIX.236.433

Weizenbaum, J. (1966). ELIZA—A computer program for the study of natural language communication between man and machine. *Communications of the ACM*, 9(1), 36–45. DOI: 10.1145/365153.365168

ADDITIONAL READING

Davis, R. T., & Johnson, P. W. (2019). Ethical considerations in the use of AI in education. *Journal of Ethics and Education*, 15(3), 215–228.

Lee, K. H., Johnson, P. W., & Smith, J. (2021). Chatbots in education: A new frontier. *Educational Technology Review*, 29(2), 45–58.

Patel, S. (2020). Natural language processing: An overview. *Journal of Language Technology*, 25(1), 1–12.

Smith, J., & Brown, L. (2022). The role of chatbots in enhancing student engagement. *International Journal of Educational Research*, 110, 101815.

Zhang, M. K. (2020). Artificial intelligence and the future of learning: A review. *Journal of Educational Technology*, 36(4), 301–315.

KEY TERMS AND DEFINITIONS

Chatbot: A software application designed to simulate conversation with human users, especially over the Internet. Chatbots can be text-based or voice-activated and are utilized for various purposes, including customer service, information retrieval, and education.

Artificial Intelligence (AI): A branch of computer science focused on creating systems capable of performing tasks that typically require human intelligence, such as understanding natural language, recognizing patterns, and making decisions.

Natural Language Processing (NLP): A subfield of AI that enables machines to understand, interpret, and respond to human language in a meaningful way, allowing chatbots to interact effectively with users.

User Experience (UX): The overall experience a user has when interacting with a product or service, encompassing usability, accessibility, and pleasure derived from using it. In the context of chatbots, a positive UX is crucial for engagement and satisfaction.

Machine Learning: A subset of AI that involves the use of algorithms and statistical models to enable computers to perform specific tasks without explicit instructions, relying on patterns and inference instead.

Educational Leadership: The process of guiding and influencing educational institutions and their stakeholders toward achieving educational goals and improving student outcomes through strategic decision-making and resource management.

Engagement: In an educational context, engagement refers to the level of participation, interest, and motivation that students exhibit in their learning processes, which can be enhanced through interactive tools like chatbots.

Ethical AI: A framework for ensuring that AI technologies are developed and used responsibly, considering issues such as fairness, transparency, accountability, and privacy, particularly in sensitive contexts like education.

Chapter 12
The Role of Chatbots in Educational Leadership:
Enhancing Decision-Making and Efficiency Through AI Tools

C. V. Suresh Babu
https://orcid.org/0000-0002-8474-2882
Hindustan Institute of Technology and Science, India

Malini Premakumari William
https://orcid.org/0009-0004-6165-2501
Bourntec Solutions, Inc., USA

R. Abdul Fazil
Hindustan Institute of Technology and Science, India

ABSTRACT

This chapter explores the role of chatbots in enhancing educational leadership by improving decision-making and communication processes. Utilizing a qualitative case study methodology, the research examines various implementations of chatbots within educational institutions, highlighting both successful applications and the challenges faced during integration. Key findings indicate that chatbots can significantly enhance operational efficiency, facilitate real-time data analysis, and improve stakeholder engagement. However, the study also identifies critical challenges, including ethical considerations, resistance to change, and the need for comprehensive training for staff. The implications of these findings suggest that educational leaders must strategically adopt chatbot technology to foster a more responsive and inclusive educational environment. By addressing both the benefits and challenges, this chapter contributes to the ongoing discourse on the modern-

DOI: 10.4018/979-8-3693-8734-4.ch012

ization of educational leadership through innovative technologies.

1. INTRODUCTION

In a world where breakthrough technology has brought about rapid changes, learning institutions are bound to adopt newer tools that enhance more effective leadership and operational effectiveness. Among such developed tools is AI-based chatbots transforming processes in educational settings. With most leaders in the educational field faced with complex challenges of data management, communication breakdowns, and keeping students engaged, the integration of AI-based chatbots will be of great importance since it streamlines the processes and encourages informed decision-making.

Fully interactive and AI-driven, chatbots are designed to engage users in real-time; they answer queries immediately, ensuring fluid dialogue. Since they are available 24/7, there can be better service delivery to a diverse population of students, staff, and parents because of no constraints within the traditional office hours. The immediacy will also heighten user satisfaction through continuous fostering of a culture of accessibility and responsiveness within the institutions.

One of the strong challenges that educational leaders face lies in the tsunami-level amount of information and data they have to sift through. Chatbots can quickly sort this information, thus offering informed insights that help shape decisions and policy changes. For example, for a study of student interactions, through analysis, a pattern can be found regarding a student's performance and engagement, and leaders will be equipped with this much-needed information to implement these targeted interventions. Such data-driven activities allow leaders to make much better use of resources, thus leading them to a better, improved educational outcome.

In addition, with the application of AI tools like Adobe Creative AI and Canva AI, it would be possible to enhance the functionality of chatbots in offering views that improve on the user experience. Such materials and multimedia resources, and even infographic and personalized materials, would result in more informative interactions as well as in engaging the learner. Thus, use of chatbots not only implies interaction but points towards a more interactive learning environment.

Barriers exist in sending new initiatives down into real effect: turning and churning the education landscape. Here, very significant roles can be assumed by chatbots-providing all sorts of information and support related to new policies, programs, and practices. Of course, chatbots ease the transition for everyone-staff to students-in a more inclusive atmosphere that encourages teamwork but reduces their resistance to change.

And apart from fetching the efficiency potential, there has been the shift in the educational leadership dynamics. By their implementation of AI, leaders can take a much more collaborative and participative stance and put the stakeholders in meaningful dialogue and decision-making processes. It is this democratization of the means of leadership that does not only enhance institutional culture but develops a sense of ownership and accountability among the staff at all levels involved in that community.

In conclusion, the role of the chatbot in educational leadership aims at improved decision-making, enhanced communication, and increased efficiency in the operation. As more institutions of learning open their doors to the embracing of technology in the processes, the integration of the chatbot may act as a springboard for the introduction of positive change to help leaders address challenges effectively in the creation of a more dynamic education environment. These AI tools will enable educational leaders not only to focus on the problems that are currently salient but to better prepare their institutions for future success in this burgeoning digital world.

1.1 Background Research

For the last two decades, technology and artificial intelligence play a central role in creating effective learning contexts. The advent of artificial intelligence and machine learning delivers birth to education settings, providing chatbots in support of interaction along with automating tasks (Suresh Babu, C.V. 2023). Such AI-based systems imitate human dialogue, arriving as needed to support learning, teaching, and administration. Chatbots represent a rising tide of adoption in education because the demand for effective management systems that can cope with exponentially growing workloads is taken into account alongside enhanced engagement of learners.

With the integration of chatbots, educational leaders can address challenges that run the gamut from administrative work to various strategies for engaging students on board. While liberating time for strategic initiatives and freeing routine operations to operate at better efficiency, chatbots unchain leadership from information gathering tasks to build deeper ties with their learning institutions.

1.2 What Chatbots Mean for Educational Leadership

Appreciation of the multifaceted roles of chatbots in educational leadership can, therefore, come through their multifaceted contribution to communication, data management, and overall institutional effectiveness. It is notable that chatbots promote communication by bridging the gap between educators, students, and parents. Such platforms ensure instant responses to queries about administrative procedures, course details, and institutional policies, thereby minimizing response times and hindrances in the form of misunderstandings that may be created. This creates an engaged and knowledgeable body - a necessary component of an effective educational environment.

At the same time, chatbots help in data management by gathering and analyzing the interactions of users. Such insights will hence allow educational leaders to make more informed data-driven decisions, identify trends, and pick on emerging issues as they arise. This ability to conduct real-time analysis then enables leaders to implement targeted interventions aimed at improving the success and satisfaction of students.

Another role chatbots play in widening access is that of inclusivity and accessibility. The chatbots therefore ensure that all stakeholders have equal access to information, regardless of their time constraints. This generally proves very beneficial in a scenario of diversity where the different people have different schedules or commitments that can hinder their proper communication in class.

Integration of chatbots can be helpful in the management of change when new educational landscapes emerge. They may facilitate communication regarding any new initiative, take feedback, and assist the users in the community at large to adapt to changes with a smooth experience. This enhances the overall institutional culture besides giving ownership to a community.

1.3 Relevance to the Theme of the Edited Book

The subject matter of this book chapter fits with the general theme of the edited book, which discusses how technology relates to educational leadership. In the context of exploring the role that chatbots play in leveraging decision-making and efficiency, the chapter advances knowledge related to the use of innovative technologies by educational leaders in making their work better. The infusion of chatbots serves as a symbol for the larger development trend regarding the application of AI towards the resolution of issues in education, and hence, the chapter is an indispensable contribution to discourses currently underway on the themes of modernization, change, and the future of educational leadership.

Also, this chapter tries to highlight how technology can be supportive in the creation of more inclusive and equitable educational settings. As leaders of education focus on diversity and engagement strategies, communication and accessibility related concerns have become pertinent. Through case studies and examples of successful implementations of chatbots, this chapter will offer applicable knowledge that will have relevance for readers of the book.

1.4 The Chapter Structure

The chapter would be structured to outline the role of chatbots in educational leadership with respect to how they are more likely to contribute toward better decision-making and effective operational performance. The sections included in the following will be:

Introduction - Overview of the objectives of the chapter, its significance, and context within the edited book.
Literature Review: a literature review relating to relevant literature on the application of chatbots in education, a review of the dominant findings as well as the theoretical frameworks that will guide the discussion.
Case Studies: Demonstrative cases that illustrate how chatbots successfully infused within educational leadership practice. This case study will provide a rich example in the areas of practical, benefits, and challenges toward implementation.
Challenges and Limitations In this section, the challenges involved in the adoption of chatbots in educational settings, which entail technical limitations, resistance to change, and ethical considerations, are discussed in detail. This section will outline the reason why training for staff is a necessity in achieving integration.
Future Directions: Emerging Trends in Chatbot Technology: Discovering how the new trends might shape future educational leadership. This includes AI advancement, further development of natural language processing, user experience, and implications in further research and practice.
Conclusion: Summarize the chapter and summarize key takeaway insights with special attention to implementing chatbot technology as a tool to improve the leadership effectiveness of organizations, transform the operations process, and encourage a more engaging and responsive educational environment.

2. KEY QUESTIONS AND PROBLEMS ADDRESSED

2.1 Challenges of Leadership in Schools

School leaders face many challenges that have seen them fail to perform and the institutions they are required to lead lose. Such include;

Inefficient Communication: Poor communication may lead to a lack of trust by the staff, students, and parents. With different timetables and differences in the technical ability of their people to use information technology, proper and timely communication becomes increasingly difficult.

Resource Management: It is one of the main challenges for leaders to distribute all resources efficiently, whether it is people or finances. On top of this, the workload of administrative work should be achieved without sacrificing the attractive character of the learning culture. This requires careful planning and action.

Data Overload: The volume of data that is available to educational leaders can be simply overwhelming. Extraction of relevant information from the same data for effective decision-making is one of the main challenges.

Student Engagement: Engaging students with what they learn is a common challenge. The old techniques of getting students engaged may not be their cup of tea, most especially in a highly technological world.

Change Management: Change management and adaptation within the changing education landscape will often provoke pushback from staff and stakeholders. Effective change management is critical to the implementation of sustained innovation in educational institutions.

Workforce Diversity: Leaders will have to operate in a diversified workforce and students population, ensuring that the different voices are all provided within the myriad of decision-making processes.

2.2 How Chatbots Overcome Leadership Challenges

Chatbots can overcome many of these challenges quite effectively, improving the efficiency and responsiveness of educational leadership:

Improved Communication: The chatbots answer the frequently asked questions by both students, parents, and staff members with speed, mainly saving time waits in communication. This immediacy, therefore, helps clarify false impressions and provides transparency in making the entire educational community come into awareness.

Automated Administrative Tasks: Chatbots can answer routine queries relating to schedules, events, and policies to free precious time from the educational leaders; such leaders would thus be able to devote their efforts towards strategic initiatives and relationship building and, therefore, improve institutional effectiveness.

Data Insights: Through the aid of chatbots, interaction data from applicants, enrolled students, and alumni can be collected and analyzed in real time to give leaders an insight into common issues and trends in their institution. This makes decision-making more informed while ensuring intervention is well targeted to improve the optimization of resources and support services.

Personalized engagements are enhanced by having a chatbot provide specific resources and support to students. Thus, students are more engaged in the learning process, as the level of motivation is kept higher due to their fulfillment of individual needs by the response from a chatbot.

Facilitating Change Management: Chatbots can be used for informing the stakeholders about new initiatives and gathering feedback on changes; this process of dealing with transitions is made easier. They can also assist in reducing resistance and hence foster a more collaborative atmosphere by offering support and resources.

Promotion of Inclusivity: Since chatbots are available all the time, all stakeholders receive the information or support instantly, no matter how busy they are at any particular time. This creates a more equitable educational environment.

2.3 Role of AI Tools in Building Chatbots in Adobe Creative AI and Canva AI

AI tools enhance chatbots' functionality and also increase their functionality to significantly develop effective ones:

Adobe Creative AI: Here, the capability of generating interesting visual content can be added into interaction and flows of a chatbot. Through customized graphics and other multimedia resources, the overall experience of using a chatbot is magnified to be highly informative and appealing.

Just like Adobe, Canva AI allows the educator to create visually appealing materials in creative ways that could be provided through the chatbot. It may encompass infographics, presentations, all the way to promotional materials in a way of better communicating complex information.

NLP: Advanced AI technologies include NLP (Suresh Babu, C. V. & Adhithya, S., 2023). When these technologies are applied, a chatbot can actually understand what a user is asking for and reply accordingly thereby augmenting the accuracy and relevance of the response which leads to more meaningful user engagement.

Analytics Tools: Employing analytics tools AI-based, the performance of the chatbot and that of the users can be tracked to note improvement continuously. Utilizing data regarding user behavior, educational leadership can define enhancement of functionalities in chatbots to suit their community needs better.

2.4 Effects of NOT Using Chatbots in Educational Leadership

The following are some adverse impacts of NOT using chatbots in educational leadership:

Ineffective Communication: Without the use of chatbots, communication relies heavily on outdated methods, and most of the time, that is very slow and cumbersome. That could lead to students, parents, and staff getting frustrated, losing interest and becoming disengaged.

Increased Workload: There's a big chance that education leaders are going to get really busy by using redundant administrative tasks and have to lose focus on strategic efforts. That could lead to burnout and lead to reduced effectiveness of the leaders.

Missed Opportunities for Engagement: An absence of the chatbots may make hard work on behalf of the institution to offer immediate support and feedback on the side of the students that will eventually deter them into engagement and motivation toward poor academic performance and retention rates.

Not Utilizing Data: The opportunity to derive useful insights that arise from interaction data may not be embraced by some leaders in the educational world. Trends that may turn red flags would never be noticed, leaving such educational leaders ill-prepared to make determinate decisions or take necessary actions in these particular situations with the absence of these analytical capabilities the chatbots afford.

Resistance to Change: Leaders who fear technological solutions will find it difficult to introduce the changes their institutions need. This resistance limits innovation and justifies these institutions to skip new challenges and opportunities.

Unequal Access to Information: Without the use of chatbots, educational institutions are likely to stand a very high chance of creating accessibility barriers for information to both students and parents. This gives rise to minority quotas with varying schedules or technological capabilities that suffer from inequalities in support and resources.

3. OBJECTIVES AND SCOPE

3.1 Chapter Objectives

The objectives of this chapter are:

- To examine the role of chatbots in educational leadership and their impact on decision-making and operational efficiency.
- To outline key challenges faced by educational leaders and demonstrate how chatbots can address these issues.
- To explore AI tools such as Adobe Creative AI and Canva AI in enhancing chatbot design and functionality.
- To assess the implications of not integrating chatbots in educational leadership, highlighting risks of outdated communication and engagement.
- To provide practical insights through case studies and examples, guiding leaders on best practices for chatbot implementation.

3.2 Defining the Scope of the Chapter

This chapter will focus it on the use of chatbots in educational leadership. It will discuss how these AI-powered systems will help in facilitating communication, enriching the decision-making process, and engage students in different settings: K-12 schools and higher education.

Scope
Theoretical Underpinning: A very brief overview of the theoretical underpinnings behind the use of chatbots in education.
Practical Applications: Examples and case studies of institutions that have successfully introduced chatbots into their operations.
Challenges and Limitations: Technical, ethical, and resistance-to-change challenges faced in the implementation of chatbots.
Future Directions: Trends emerging in chatbot technology and what they mean for educational leaders.

3.3 What Will and Will Not Be Covered

What Will Be Covered:
Overview of Chatbots: This section would, in detail, discuss what chatbots are, how they function, and their utility for educational systems.

Case Studies: In this section, specific cases of how chatbots can be put to great success within the educational institutions will be taken into account regarding their benefits on communication and decision-making processes.
Integration Strategies: What approaches or best practices should educational leaders use if they decided to integrate the use of chatbots into the educational setting; considerations on training, support, and user engagement?.
Technological Tools: Reviewing AI tools that can be applied to help in chatbot development, focusing on how they can affect interaction and user experience.
Challenges and Solutions: A view of what may become an issue while trying to implement and ways to overcome it.
What's Not Covered?
Technical Development: The technical development of building or programming chatbots shall not be the focus of this chapter but rather their application and impact in educational leadership.
General Applications of AI: Given how general a subject AI in education is, this chapter shall narrow it down to a focus on chatbots rather than onto something else other than adaptive learning technologies or data analytics tools.
Sector-specific regulations: The book chapter would not take interest in detailing specific legal and regulatory frameworks that govern the different applications of the chatbots in various jurisdictions of education.
Comparison: The discussion on the comparison of chatbots with other technological solutions, such as traditional communication, will not be further elaborated; instead, their unique contribution to educational leadership will be highlighted.

4. LITERATURE REVIEW

4.1 Review of the Literatures on Chatbots in Education

This is where the integration of chatbots into education has received much focus recently, with many studies in recent times exploring their applications, benefits, and challenges. Available findings present it as an opportunity for integrating chatbots for higher student engagement and making the process of administration seamless while improving communication within educational institutions. A major volume of literature, therefore, focuses on the use of this technology in student services, where a chatbot helps students with requests such as answers to frequently asked questions, information provided for courses, and steps through administrative processes.

Key studies have implied that chatbots are associated with high student and staff satisfaction through immediate assistance and support offered to students. For instance, in the Kumar and Rose (2019) study, it was observed that there was a dissipation of long delay times while responding to the questions of the students, thus increasing populations with engaged students. Along the same line, Gonzalez et al. study for 2020 indicated that while the chatbots greatly improved the efficiency of student services, they consequently gave the staff even more time to direct their attention to other more complicated tasks requiring a human touch.

However, although the literature offers useful insights into the operational benefits of chatbots, this paper established an evident emphasis on student-facing applications and less on their role in educational leadership. Most student-facing applications focus on importance that leaves a gap in understanding the specific benefit which can enhance leadership practices, decision-making, and institutional management.

4.2 Chatbots in Student Services vs. Leadership Roles

Chatbots play a crucial role in educational institutions, primarily in two domains: student services and leadership roles. The following table summarizes the most Popular Chatbots in Student Services and Leadership Roles

1. Chatbots in Student Services

Table 1. These chatbots assist students with administrative tasks, FAQs, academic support, and engagement.

Chatbot	Institution/Platform	Key Features
Ivy	Used by various universities	AI-driven virtual assistant for admissions, financial aid, and FAQs
Pounce	Georgia State University	Helps with enrollment, deadlines, and reminders
Ocelot	Multiple higher education institutions	Assists students with financial aid, admissions, and advising
EdSights	Higher education-focused chatbot	Uses AI to track student well-being and engagement
HubBot	Northeastern University	Supports students with course registration, academic resources, and campus life
ChatGPT for Education	AI-powered	General academic assistance, tutoring, and writing support

2. Chatbots in Leadership Roles

Table 2. These chatbots assist educational leaders with data analysis, decision-making, stakeholder communication, and strategic planning.

Chatbot	Institution/Platform	Key Features
IBM Watson Assistant	AI-powered enterprise tool	Provides data-driven insights for strategic planning
Google Dialogflow	AI conversational platform	Customizable chatbot for internal communications and stakeholder management
Mona	AI assistant for administrators	Analyzes institutional data for decision-making and operational efficiency
Clara	AI scheduling assistant	Automates meeting coordination and stakeholder engagement
Ada	AI-powered chatbot	Assists with workflow automation and administrative management
UiPath Chatbots	AI-powered automation tool	Helps streamline leadership processes and decision-making

These chatbots enhance both student services and leadership roles by improving engagement, streamlining processes, and enabling data-driven decision-making.

While their application in student services is well established, their potential in leadership remains underexplored. This section compares their functions in these areas, highlighting their impact on operational efficiency and decision-making.

4.2.1 Comparison of Chatbot Applications in Student Services and Leadership

Table 3. Comparison

Aspect	Student Services	Leadership Roles
Primary Function	Assists students with FAQs, adminisrative guidance, and support	Supports decision-making, strategy planning, and stakeholder communication
Operational Impact	Improves efficiency by automating routine tasks	Enhances governance through real-time data analytics
User Engagement	Provides instant responses to student queries	Facilitates collaboration and data-driven leadership

continued on following page

Table 3. Continued

Aspect	Student Services	Leadership Roles
Decision Support	Limited to basic information retrieval	Enables leaders to analyze student and institutional data for insights
Current Challenges	Well-integrated but focused on operational tasks	Underutilized for leadership, requiring more recognition and adoption

Chatbots have significantly improved workflow efficiency in student services by handling routine inquiries and administrative tasks. However, their potential in leadership roles, such as strategic planning and governance, remains largely untapped. Future developments should focus on expanding chatbot capabilities to support educational leaders in decision-making, collaboration, and institutional engagement.

4.3 Gaps in Current Research on Chatbots for Leadership

Despite growing interests in chatbots in educational settings, there are still many gaps in previous studies:

Limited focus on leadership applications. Most of the studies focus on student engagement and operational efficiency but do not bring out the implications for educational leadership. So far, empirical researches are very few as regards the adaptation and changes in chatbots to fit the implementation in leadership practices and related decision-making processes.

Not Sufficient Exploration of Challenges: Of course, where many papers have emerged promoting the benefits for administrators of adopting the use of chatbots, far fewer discuss challenges to its adoption. Since these challenges can be critical to effective integration, exploration of these challenges would be helpful.

No Case Study Available: Few comprehensive case studies exist wherein chatbots were successfully introduced and used in leadership roles within school institutions. Real-world insights might provide helpful lessons to other institutions.

Less effort seems to have been put into exploring opinions from stakeholders: both teachers, administrators, and learners regarding the place the chatbots have in leadership. Bringing in such diversified views will make the understanding of their effectiveness and acceptance much more rich.

Future Directions and Implications: There is a lack of forward-looking perspectives in the existing literature towards the development of chatbots in educational settings, more specifically in leadership contexts. Such research should consider potential future developments and implications of chatbot technology about educational governance.

4.4 How This Chapter Fills the Gaps

This chapter hopes to fill the identified gaps through a focused exploration of the role of chatbots in educational leadership. It will proceed in this manner through the following approaches:

Against the background of the abundance of applications of chatbots revealed in the previous chapters, this chapter will be dedicated to examples of specific applications in the decision-making process and communication strategy of educational leaders, thus furthering the understanding of applications beyond student services. Case studies are presented that demonstrate their utility in a leadership context.

Addressing Challenges The next chapter outlines the possible challenges that educators may face when deploying chatbots. There is potential for technological limitations, resistance to change, and ethical issues. The discussion will provide balanced reasoning, focusing on the insertion of appropriate thoughtfulness.
Case Studies: Using case studies, the chapter will use cases that demonstrate applications of chatbots by educational leaders. Action guides will be offered for leaders who may want similar applications.
Including Perspectives of Stakeholders: This will be the focus of the chapter-to how educational leaders, staff, and students respond to the change and can work together with each other by including these views about the impact of chatbots in leadership practices. This will widen the debate and reflect varying experiences and expectations of stakeholder groups.

5. METHODOLOGY

5.1 Research Design: Qualitative Case Studies

This chapter utilizes a qualitative case study research design to investigate the incorporation of chatbots in educational leadership. Qualitative case studies enable in-depth examinations of specific cases where a chatbot has been introduced and provides rich contextual insight into how such an intervention impacts leadership practices. This focus on real-world applications sheds light on complexities and nuances around the integration of a chatbot within educational settings.

Case studies are well-suited for this research because they will allow for an in-depth exploration of how educational leaders are using chatbots to overcome certain challenges, enhance decision-making processes, and improve communication within their institutions. In addition, this design allows the collection of a variety of perspectives from administration, teachers, and students that will be essential in giving a balanced view of the implications of this technology.

5.2 Data Collection Methods

Multiple methods will be used in collecting data to ascertain proper understanding of the implementation of chatbots in educational leadership:

Interviews: Educational leaders who have successfully integrated chatbots into their respective institutions will be interviewed using semi-structured interviews. The researcher will probe their motivations for adoption, challenges associated with implementation, and changes that are noticed in leadership practices after implementation. This is achievable since the open-ended questions allow participants to write in any length, making the data collected richer and more substantial.

Focus Groups Focus groups will be conducted among the teachers and administrative staff members, exploring their experience and perceptions related to the use of chatbots. This involves interaction and discussion by respondents in focus groups who can respond to other participants' ideas while ascertaining the collaborative aspects of chatbots in implementation.

For this purpose, the discussion will be supplemented with relevant institutional documents that are user and participation feedback reports, implementation plans, and logs of chatbot interactions. Such analysis enables the drawing of patterns and outcomes with respect to chatbot use and adds depth to findings.

In possible situations, direct observations on the actual interactions as well as user experiences about the chatbots will be conducted. Observing the real-time users interacting with the chatbots will provide some tremendous insight into usability, effectiveness, and satisfaction related to using the chatbots.

5.3 Analysis of AI Tools (Adobe Creative AI, Canva AI) for Customization of Chatbots

AI-powered design tools like Adobe Creative AI and Canva AI play a crucial role in tailoring chatbots for educational settings. These tools enhance chatbot design and functionality, making them more engaging and user-friendly. This section analyzes their capabilities in customization and user experience.

5.3.1 Comparison of AI Tools for Chatbot Customization

Table 4. Comparison

Feature	Adobe Creative AI	Canva AI
Customization Capabilities	Advanced design tools for high-quality, interactive content creation	User-friendly interface with customizable templates for quick chatbot design
User Engagement	AI-driven features enhance chatbot aesthetics and interactivity	Simplifies content creation with visually appealing elements
Ease of Use	Suitable for professionals with design expertise	Ideal for beginners with drag-and-drop functionality
Personalization	Offers detailed customization with AI-powered design assistance	Provides ready-to-use elements tailored for user preferences
Application in Education	Supports intricate chatbot designs for in-depth learning experiences	Facilitates quick deployment of educational chatbots with engaging visuals

Adobe Creative AI and Canva AI offer distinct advantages for chatbot customization in educational settings. While Adobe Creative AI excels in advanced design and interactivity, Canva AI provides an intuitive, user-friendly approach. Both tools contribute significantly to enhancing user engagement, personalization, and overall chatbot effectiveness in educational applications.

5.4 Justification for the Research Methodology

Qualitative case study methodology is justified based on following grounds:

Depth of Understanding The qualitative approach would enable researchers to get deep into the experiences and perspectives of educational leaders and stakeholders. With the case study focus, the methodology will ensure that the insights the researcher provides are illuminating on how complex situations in real life are, leading to the rich meanings developed by how chatbots are going to be used in contexts of educational leadership.

Context Relevance: The learning environment itself is unique and diverse. Case studies help one to focus on exploring some specific contexts toward a specific application, including institutional culture and leadership and stakeholders' needs, among others. This will create much-needed context for drawing valid inferences about the ability of chatbots to be effective within a specific context.

Flexibility and adaptability: Qualitative studies could be rather flexible in collecting and analyzing data while making adaptations along the way of research. This is particularly crucial for new innovative technologies like a chatbot, by which user experiences might get transformed over time.

Holistic Approach: This approach allows the use of various methods to gather data, such as interviews, focus groups, document analysis, and observations-on all aspects of chatbot implementation. Triangulation of data will yield more accurate and valid results since each of the data sources will provide a unique perspective on the relevant topic.

Stakeholder engagement: This involves interviews and focus groups with various stakeholders. This will not only enrich the data but also make stakeholders have a sense of ownership and collaboration during the process. Such engagements would therefore lead to more robust insight and recommendations for future chatbot applications in educational leadership.

Innovation focus: By the changing environment of increasing reliance of academic institutions on innovative solutions to respond to challenges posed by leadership, this methodology resonates with the need for research that seeks to look into the future. The general discourse that is prevalent today regarding integration with technology is supplemented by the analysis of leading-edge tools such as Adobe Creative AI and Canva AI accompanied by the functionality of a chatbot.

6. ANALYSIS AND FINDINGS

6.1 Effect of Chatbots on Administrative Efficiency

Chatbots considerably affect the efficient administrative level in institutions of learning. They take away routine work from the administrative personnel like replying to frequent Asked Questions, appointment creation, and the policies and procedures they are in charge of. These help personnel focus more intently on tough tasks requiring human contribution, thus increasing productivity.

For instance, institutions that embrace chatbots experience faster response times to student inquiries and improved satisfaction levels. Chatbots are always on time, so to speak-can respond around the clock-and can support students and employees

24/7 in a diverse schedule environment. That capability minimizes bottlenecks in communication and ensures that users have information when they need it.

Moreover, chatbots can also assist in identifying typical frequently asked questions or problems for which institutions can be proactive in addressing the concern and streamlining its processes. Based on the insights derived from the interaction with the chatbot, educational leaders can take informed decisions in enhancing overall operational efficiency.

6.2 Improving Leader Communication with Chatbots

Effective communication will be necessary for proper success in educational leadership. Chatbots can play a very significant role in this area as well. This chatterbot aids in establishing real-time channels of communication and, thereby, disseminating information at all stakeholder levels - faculty, students, and parents. The immediacy involved helps to diffuse possible misunderstandings and presents a more transparent environment.

Chatbots can be programmed to provide timely updates related to various policies in institution, events happening, and deadlines that should never be missed. They can gather feedback from the user system, providing leaders with essential input into the community's concerns and preferences. This two-way approach fosters engagement and trust, essential components of effective leadership.

More so, chatbots support educational leaders in the management of communication during disasters or crises. They can disseminate critical information quickly and efficiently and consequently assist in ensuring that everyone is on the same page with minimal confusion during challenging situations.

6.3 AI Tools and Customization of Chatbots for Educational Leadership

Such customization through AI at the back end of the chatbots through, for instance, Adobe Creative AI and Canva AI helps chatbots to be all the more effective in educational leadership settings. Such tools help leaders in developing intuitive and aesthetically appealing interfaces pertinent to their particular institution.

> User Experience: These AI tools allow educational leaders to customize these chitchats with their branding and tone to match that of the institution. Users thus feel well-known and attached to the chatbot, which, indeed improves user satisfaction.

Content Creation: Using AI tools, educational leaders can create rich multimedia content that better engages users. For example, using infographics, videos, and interactive elements would improve the learning experience, with the information being easier to view and understand.

There are several data-driven insights wherein the AI tools would help in analyzing user interactions for leaders to improve chatbot responses based on user feedback and behavior patterns. This iterative process helps refine the chatbot towards making it more accurate and relevant to meaningful interactions.Thus, the integration of these AI tools by educational leaders will help them design dynamic chatbots that do not only provide information but also generate engagement and community involvement, thereby upgrading the overall experience of learning.

6.4 Case Studies of Real World Implementation: Leadership Chatbots in Real Life

Some institutions have already implemented chatbots to enhance the effectiveness of leadership and operational efficiency in the institution. These case studies bring out the reality of chatbots in educational environments:

University of California, Berkeley: Berkeley has a chatbot called "Ask Berkeley," making it easier for students to know answers to common queries pertaining to registration, financial aid, and campus resources. Administration reduced its workload by 30% due to saved efforts related to repetitive questions. The satisfaction levels in the students also rose.

Georgia State University: Georgia State adopted using a chatbot named "Pounce" in efforts to improve student engagement and retention. Students are supported by this chatbot, Pounce, with individualized support. It answers student questions over issues of resources and deadlines, leading to massive curtailment of summer melt, as students were enrolled and persisted at higher rates.

7. DISCUSSION OF KEY INSIGHTS

7.1 Leadership With the Potential to Change Through Chatbots

Then, the chatbot transforming potential in educational leadership is about more efficiency of operations through leading, communicating, and data-driven decision-making capacities. Routine tasks can then be automated, freeing up some hours of a leader. There will be more hours to brainstorm strategically, build relationships and interact more effectively with the staff, the students, and the parents.

These bots would allow personalizing communication, where leaders are directly interacting with the different stakeholders of the business in a much more relevant way. For example, through using specific communication reaching out to people and collection of real-time feedback, the needs and concerns of the community of the leader will be well understood through informed decision making that reflects the collective voice.

Besides the impact on communication, chatbots also provide analytics to inform leadership strategy. Data from interactions can be used to track trends, evaluate programs, and make data-driven adjustments to policies and practices. This real-time capability can enable more proactive rather than reactive leadership, with multiple consequences for the responsiveness of the educational environment.

7.2 Practical Implications for Educational Institutions

Chatbots in educational leadership have a few practical implications for the institutions:

Resource Application: Automatic operations performed by chatbots will free up human resources in institutions for application toward areas that require more complex support. It is, therefore, in a position to bring about better services and satisfaction of students and staff members.

Instant Access: Instant access eliminates the need to wait for certain questions regarding academic resources, schedules, and support services. This type of instant access contributes to better student satisfaction and retention.

Data-Driven Decision Making: With data from interactions of the chatbots, leadership can focus on developing initiatives and programs in areas of needs better within the community. Such data can be targeted to apply more effectively in solving a community's needs.

Increased Engagement: A persistently linking leader with his community through a chatbot provides a culture of giving feedback and contributes to better relationships and higher buy-ins to institutional initiatives.

Professional Development: The institutions can utilize the use of chatbots to provide continuous support and training for the staff; thus, professional development opportunities may be improved.

7.3 Overcoming Resistance to AI-Driven Leadership Tools

Although the uses of chatbots have many advantages, the general aversion towards adopting AI-driven leadership tools is widespread. The above can be surmounted with a multi-pronged approach in the following ways:

> Education and Training: Proper training and education on the advantages as well as the functionality of chatbots will assuage many fears. Demonstrating how it can enhance workflows as well as communication will be encouraging towards acceptance.

Stakeholders' inclusion is helpful because their ownership can be strongly ensured through involvement in the decision-making process; teachers, students, or administrative staff. The involvement during the introduction stage in discussing issues and listening to suggestions can help build trust in the leaders and generate enthusiasm about the new technology to be adopted.

> Pilot Programs: Through pilot programs, an institution has the opportunity to introduce and test the functionalities of a chatbot in a controlled environment. This goes a long way in revealing the challenges and successes that may arise prior to a full rollout, upon which improvements may be done based on initial feedback (Suresh Babu, C. V. & Rohan, B. 2023)..

8. SUGGESTIONS AND RECOMMENDATIONS

8.1 Best Practices for the Installation of Chatbots in School Leadership

School leadership has to consider the best means for installing the chatbots, ensuring the installation is effective and acceptable. The following are best practices that can be considered:

> Establish Specific Outcomes of Use: Before their installation, the educational leaders have to define specific outcomes to be achieved through the use of the chatbots. This could include more student support, increased effective communication, or help with administrative tasks; knowing exactly what's needed will help to direct the development and integration process.

Involvement of stakeholders at the earliest stage of planning by engaging relevant faculty, staff, students, and parents would increase the chances of ownership and buy-in. Using users during the design and testing process could get helpful input and, eventually, a user-centered chatbot.

Implement Small-Scale Pilot Programs: The institutions can enact a pilot program to test the functionalities of the chatbot on a small scale. Then leaders can collect feedback, problems, and complaints before taking it to a large-scale implementation.

8.2 Leadership Training and Development

Effective Application of Chatbots, Leaders should be educated on how best to utilize chatbots so that they can maximize the effect of the same. Some ideas on good training programs are provided below:

Comprehensive Training Programs: Training programs should offer a series of sessions on the general principles of the technology behind the chatbot, for example, what functionalities it has, what benefits it offers, and its limits. Leaders should be able to understand how to apply the use of the chatbots toward a certain end.

Hands-on Experience: Engage the leaders during training with hands-on experience using the chatbot. Scenarios on practice for the leaders can then become vehicles to show how they could utilize the tool to provide help in reality-sets and would increase their confidence and competence.

Resource Development: Produce user-friendly guides, FAQs, and video tutorials that leaders may utilize after the training. These resources will be helpful to leaders during ongoing learning and troubleshooting while working on the use of chatbots.

Peer Learning: Facilitate a community of practice so leaders can share their experiences with the use of chatbots, including challenges faced and successes made. Peer support can better facilitate learning and collaborative problem solving.

8.3 Strategies for Maximal Benefits from AI-Powered Chatbots

Benefits that AI-powered chatbots offer, educational institutions should reach toward the following strategies:

Personalization: The interactions are done with the chatbot based on user profiles. Using student interactions' data, it is possible to do tailored responses and recommendations, thereby making it a more personal experience that could be in line with individual needs.
Integration with Other Systems: The chatbot should be integrated well into the broader administrative and academic systems. Examples include learning management systems (LMS) and student information systems (SIS), making it possible to better support students and to help students' move through it without a hitch.
Continuous Learning: Machine learning can be used to enable the capabilities of the chatbot for learning from its interactions over time, making it more adaptable and enhancing response accuracy and the overall impact the tool has on students (Suresh Babu, C. V., Anniyappa, C. S, et. al . 2024).
Feedback Mechanisms: Provide the user with mechanisms to give their feedback about their interaction experience with the chatbot. Conduct periodic reviews of this feedback against development areas for the chatbot to ensure it remains user-centric.
Build Awareness and Utilization: Very highly promote the availability of the chatbot among the students and employees to encourage utilization. Leverage successful stories and elaborate the potential capabilities of the chatbot using other communication channels such as newsletters and social media.

8.4 Overcoming Difficulties in Adopting the Chatbot

While chatbots bring much benefits with them, the adoption of the new technology may come with a set of challenges. The educator leader should thus be geared to handle this set of issues rightly:

Resistance to Change: Some stakeholders resist the use of new technology. To curb that, ensure you have communicated the benefits of chatbots and involved users in the implementation to build acceptance.
Technical Issues: Technical problems are to be expected; they can be integration problems or systems going down. Dedicated support teams addressing technical issues will quickly eliminate any turnaround or address potential issues in order to maintain user confidence.
Data Privacy: Data privacy and security will have to be addressed to meet the relevant legislation, for example, FERPA. It is also important to inform users of how their data will be used, stored, and protected for them to gain confidence.

Manage Expectations: Clearly define for users what the chatbot can and cannot do. Explain these restrictions to users so that potential frustration with expectations of a personal assistant does not occur, and to instead frame the tool as an augmentation of human connection rather than a replacement.

Continuous Evaluation: Regularly review performance and impact against established institutional goals. Apply those insights to make continuous improvements and adjustments to the tool so that it evolves with the dynamics of the institution.

9. FUTURE SCOPE FOR RESEARCH

9.1 Extending Beyond Leadership Applications of Chatbots

This chapter has, thus far, focused on the role that chatbots might play in educational leadership. Opportunities for the application of chatbots go well beyond the domain of leadership contexts. Chatbots can contribute to improving many aspects of the educational experience student engagement, administrative efficiency, and so much more.

Even these chatbots could act as 24-hour academic supporters in providing resource instant access, study guides, and tutoring support to the students' desks, providing answers that will make questions bear fruit in assessing course content.

Parental Engagement: The school events, grades of their children, and other dates can be communicated more effectively to the parents by the schools through the help of these chatbots. This would directly be able to establish a link between the schools and the families.

Faculty Support: Besides leadership, chatbots would facilitate support for faculties as they would become able to inform regarding the development of curriculum, available resources, and administrative procedures. This process saves a lot of time for faculty as it makes their workflow efficient, as well as more teamwork between the staffs.

Professional Development: Through a chatbot, professional development activities can be made available with an open door route to training materials, workshops, and resources for teachers.

9.2 Long Term Implication of Chatbots on Leadership Practice

This revolution of chatbots within educational leadership will be transformative only in the long run. As more institutions widely adopt AI-driven tools, the practice of leadership itself will evolve in following ways:

Data-Driven Decision-Making: Chatbots can generate valuable insights through data analytics, enabling leaders to make informed decisions based on real-time information. This shift towards data-driven leadership would foster a more proactive and responsive approach to governance.
Better Communications: Because the chatbots ease easier communication, leaders will thus have the opportunity to communicate with many stakeholders. As a result, this will result in a culture of transparency and teamwork-based approach. It creates a more collaborative and trustful environment that respects every stakeholder.
Shift towards Strategic Leaderships: The need to perform routine tasks through the chatbot will give educational leaders the opportunity to spend more time on strategic planning and vision setting. As a result, they can think more inventively and creatively about how their institutions can change.
Adaptability and Responsiveness: Combining chatbots improves leaders' responses to challenges. This is achieved by taking advantage of real-time data and feedback so that leaders can respond promptly to emerging issues and the evolutionary needs within their institutions.
Professional Development for Leaders: The landscape of educational leadership continues to change, and thus, professional development will emphasize more technology integration and data literacy. Leaders will require skills that equip them with the ability to effectively use chatbots and other AI tools.

9.3 Scalability of Chatbots Across Educational Levels and Contexts

This is one of the most impressive features that chatbots have to offer: the possibility of scaling up to any educational level and, most importantly, in various contexts. Their flexibility allows them to be geared toward particular needs according to the different educational environments:

K-12: Chatbots will be very useful for students and parents for obtaining the information on homework assignments, school events and educational resources. They will also facilitate teacher-parent communication for increased and better support to the learning process.

Higher Education: Chatbots can be implemented by higher education in assisting with enrollment processes, guiding students on advice, and exploring available campus resources; they can process large quantities of inquiries efficiently-in fact, in those institutions of a diverse population.

Adult Education and Training: Another area where chatbots would be of use would be adult education and workforce training. They could advise and provide learners with information about courses available, career opportunities, and skill-building to promote lifelong learning.

10. CONCLUSION

10.1 Summary of Major Results

This Chapter explores the transformative capacity of chatbots into educational leadership processes as it displays how administrative efficiency may be bettered, communication altered to better effect, and decisions become data informed.

Key findings include streamlining routine tasks that also cultivate engagement among stakeholders through easy access to information and resource availability

Results found in the research indicate that including stakeholders in the implementation process makes realisation of a tailor-made solution possible for educational environments.

Secondly, case studies have emerged to prove that the integration of chatbots in various institutions is successful, thereby indicating its potential usage in student support, as well as communication with positive operational performance. The adaptation of the chatbot based on progressive feedback and superior technology further underlines its applicability in modern education.

10.2 Utilizing AI Tools for Leadership Development in Education

The activity of AI tools points to the maximization of the application of chatbots in educational leadership. One can personalize and make the user experience better with applications like Adobe Creative AI and Canva AI to ensure stimulation and engagement in interactions for educational leaders. AI tools integrate together with the development of adaptive chatbots that adapt to the user, give personalized reactions, and ascertain datum for wise decision-making.

10.3 Wider Implications for Leadership in Digital Learning Environments

The findings and insights of this chapter hold wider implications for leaders in learning environments modeled on digital media. Technology will increasingly play a role in education; thus, leaders should develop attitudes that respect innovation but also embrace changing conditions. The adoption of chatbots and AI tools marks the transition toward more interactive and responsive practices respecting user experience.

Educational leaders will have to focus on professional development that embodies new skills of handling these technological advancements. A culture of collaboration and openness to change will be important for creating successful implementations of AI-driven tools.

REFERENCES

Alshahrani, S. S., & Zainal, Z. (2020). The Role of Chatbots in Enhancing Leadership in Educational Institutions. *Journal of Leadership Studies*, 14(3), 22–35.

Chen, L., & Cheng, G. (2020). AI in Education: Opportunities and Challenges. *International Journal of Artificial Intelligence in Education*, 30(4), 552–571.

Holmes, W., Bialik, M., & Fadel, C. (2019). *Artificial Intelligence in Education: Promises and Implications for Teaching and Learning*. Center for Curriculum Redesign.

Luckin, R., Holmes, W., Griffiths, M., & Forcier, L. B. (2016). *Intelligence Unleashed: An Argument for AI in Education*. Pearson.

Miao, Y., & Li, Y. (2021). Chatbots in Higher Education: A Systematic Review. *Computers & Education*, 167, 104188.

Pedró, F., & Hodge, S. (2021). Leadership in the Age of AI: The Role of Chatbots. *Leadership and Organization Development Journal*, 42(7), 1053–1067.

Suresh Babu, C. V., & Adhithya, S. (2023). ChatGPT and Other Generative AI Tools in Education: Transformative Potential and Ethical Considerations. In Keengwe, J. (Ed.), *Creative AI Tools and Ethical Implications in Teaching and Learning* (pp. 135–152). IGI Global., DOI: 10.4018/979-8-3693-0205-7.ch007

Suresh Babu, C. V., Anniyappa, C. S., & Sastha, B. D. (2024). Unraveling the Inner Workings of Massive Language Models: Architecture, Training, and Linguistic Capacities. In B. Gupta (Ed.), Challenges in Large Language Model Development and AI Ethics (pp. 239-279). IGI Global. DOI: 10.4018/979-8-3693-3860-5.ch008

Suresh Babu, C. V., & Rohan, B. (2023). Evaluation and Quality Assurance for Rapid E-Learning and Development of Digital Learning Resources. In Santally, M., Rajabalee, Y., & Rajputh, R. (Eds.), *Implementing Rapid E-Learning Through Interactive Materials Development* (pp. 139–170). IGI Global., DOI: 10.4018/978-1-6684-4940-0.ch008

ADDITIONAL READING

Adobe. (2022). **Adobe Creative AI: Transforming Creative Workflows**. Retrieved from Adobe website

Canva. (2023). **Canva Magic: AI Tools for Designers**.

Riemer, K. (2020). Harnessing AI for Creative Work: Insights from Adobe and Canva. *Journal of Digital Design*, 5(2), 1–15.

Suresh Babu, C. V. (2023). *Artificial Intelligence and Expert Systems*. Anniyappa Publications.

Chapter 13

The Role of Chatbots in Educational Leadership

M. Sameer Babu
https://orcid.org/0000-0001-8168-8537
Jamia Millia Islamia, India

Naresh Babu Karunakaran
https://orcid.org/0009-0005-3113-4225
Sree Abirami College of Occupational Therapy, India

P. Selvakumar
https://orcid.org/0000-0002-3650-4548
Department of Science and Humanities, Nehru Institute of Technology, India

R. Sethumadhavan
https://orcid.org/0000-0002-0508-2143
Presidency University, India

Pankaj Singh Chandel
https://orcid.org/0000-0002-4135-8194
Dev Sanskriti Vishwavidyalaya, India

ABSTRACT

In recent years, the integration of chatbots into the education sector has emerged as a transformative force, redefining how educational institutions approach both leadership and learning. Their potential to revolutionize education is grounded in their ability to provide real-time support, personalized learning experiences, and streamlined administrative functions, ultimately leading to more dynamic and responsive educational practices.The application of chatbots in education serves as a catalyst for enhanced leadership by streamlining communication channels

DOI: 10.4018/979-8-3693-8734-4.ch013

between educators, students, and administrators. Traditional methods of managing educational tasks and responding to inquiries can often be cumbersome and slow. Chatbots can address this issue by offering instant, automated responses to frequently asked questions. For educational leaders, chatbots represent a tool that can improve operational efficiency, enabling them to better allocate resources, monitor performance metrics, and implement data-driven decision-making processes.

INTRODUCTION

In recent years, the integration of chatbots into the education sector has emerged as a transformative force, redefining how educational institutions approach both leadership and learning. Their potential to revolutionize education is grounded in their ability to provide real-time support, personalized learning experiences, and streamlined administrative functions, ultimately leading to more dynamic and responsive educational practices. The application of chatbots in education serves as a catalyst for enhanced leadership by streamlining communication channels between educators, students, and administrators. Traditional methods of managing educational tasks and responding to inquiries can often be cumbersome and slow. Chatbots can address this issue by offering instant, automated responses to frequently asked questions. For educational leaders, chatbots represent a tool that can improve operational efficiency, enabling them to better allocate resources, monitor performance metrics, and implement data-driven decision-making processes. This not only improves administrative workflows but also facilitates more effective leadership by allowing for a more nuanced understanding of institutional needs and challenges. This level of personalization helps address the diverse needs of students, ensuring that each learner receives the support necessary to achieve their educational goals. Additionally, chatbots can facilitate more interactive and engaging learning experiences by incorporating gamification elements, providing instant feedback, and encouraging active participation. This interactive approach can contribute to a more motivating and enjoyable learning environment, fostering greater student involvement and retention. Moreover, chatbots can play a crucial role in promoting inclusivity and accessibility in education. They can provide support in multiple languages, offer assistance to students with disabilities, and ensure that educational resources are accessible to a wider audience.

The integration of chatbots also extends to professional development for educators (Abhilasha A., et al., 2022). These tools can be utilized for ongoing training and support, offering resources, best practices, and up-to-date information on educational trends and technologies. By providing educators with easy access to relevant professional development materials and collaborative platforms, chatbots can help facilitate continuous learning and improvement among teaching staff. This contributes to a culture of lifelong learning within educational institutions, promoting innovation and excellence in teaching practices.In conclusion, the introduction of chatbots into education represents a significant advancement in enhancing both leadership and learning. By streamlining administrative processes, providing personalized support, and promoting inclusivity, chatbots contribute to a more efficient, engaging, and equitable educational environment. As educational institutions continue to explore and implement these technologies, it is essential to address potential challenges and ensure that chatbots are utilized in ways that uphold the highest standards of educational excellence and integrity. The future of education, enriched by the capabilities of chatbots, promises to be more adaptive, responsive, and student-centered, paving the way for a more dynamic and effective learning experience.

CHATBOTS FOR STUDENT SUPPORT: IMPROVING ENGAGEMENT AND RETENTION

The advent of chatbots in educational settings marks a significant evolution in student support, offering new pathways to enhance engagement and retention (Arruda, D., et al., 2019). These AI-driven tools, leveraging sophisticated natural language processing and machine learning algorithms, provide a range of functions that can transform the educational experience for students. By delivering timely, personalized assistance, chatbots address several key challenges faced by educational institutions and learners, thereby contributing to improved engagement and retention rates. One of the most prominent benefits of chatbots is their ability to provide instant support and feedback. Traditional educational support systems often involve delays in response times due to the availability of faculty or administrative staff. Chatbots, however, operate 24/7, offering immediate assistance with a variety of queries, from administrative concerns to academic inquiries. They can assist students in exploring academic programs, understanding course prerequisites, and planning their schedules. By guiding students through these processes, chatbots help alleviate the burden on academic advisors and ensure that students receive consistent and accurate information (Bii P. 2013). This proactive approach to advising helps students make informed decisions about their academic paths, reducing the risk of attrition due to confusion or lack of direction.

Chatbots can offer access to counseling services, stress management tips, and mental health resources, creating an accessible support system that can complement traditional counseling services. By addressing these aspects of student well-being, chatbots help create a more supportive and inclusive educational environment, which is crucial for retention.Moreover, chatbots enhance student engagement (Brockhus,

S., et al.,2014) through interactive and gamified elements. By incorporating features such as quizzes, challenges, and rewards, chatbots can make learning more engaging and enjoyable. These interactive elements can increase student motivation and participation, making the educational experience more dynamic and stimulating. Gamification also encourages continuous interaction with the chatbot, reinforcing learning and keeping students connected with their academic goals. By leveraging data analytics, institutions can enhance their strategies for student engagement and retention, ensuring that interventions are targeted and effective.Despite these advantages, the implementation of chatbots in student support is not without challenges. Ensuring the accuracy and relevance of the information provided by chatbots is crucial to maintain trust and effectiveness. Chatbots must be continually updated and refined to reflect changes in curricula, policies, and support services. In conclusion, chatbots represent a transformative tool for improving student support, engagement, and retention. Their ability to provide instant, personalized assistance, enhance academic advising, and support mental health contributes to a more responsive and engaging educational experience. By integrating chatbots into their support systems, educational institutions can address common challenges, foster stronger connections with students, and ultimately improve retention rates.

Automating Administrative Tasks: Chatbots for Educational Leadership

The integration of chatbots into educational institutions has ushered in a new era of efficiency and effectiveness in administrative tasks, profoundly impacting educational leadership. These AI-driven tools are revolutionizing how schools and universities manage their operations, offering substantial improvements in streamlining processes, reducing administrative burdens, and enhancing decision-making capabilities (Cameron, G., et al., 2018). By automating routine tasks, chatbots enable educational leaders to focus more on strategic initiatives and student-centered activities, thereby driving overall institutional success.Furthermore, chatbots contribute to enhanced communication within educational institutions. Effective communication is essential for coordinating efforts among faculty, students, and administrative staff. Chatbots can facilitate communication by sending reminders about deadlines, meetings, and events, as well as providing updates on institutional policies and procedures (Chaves AP, et al., 2021). This automated communication ensures that all stakeholders are informed and engaged, reducing the risk of miscommunication and ensuring that important information is disseminated efficiently. For educational leaders, chatbots serve as a valuable tool for managing internal communications, promoting transparency, and fostering a collaborative environment.In addition to streamlining internal processes, chatbots also support external stakeholder interactions.

Another significant advantage of chatbots is their role in crisis management and emergency response. In situations requiring immediate action or communication, such as campus emergencies or urgent announcements, chatbots can deliver critical information quickly and accurately (de Oliveira, J. et al., 2016). They can be programmed to provide real-time updates, answer urgent questions, and guide individuals on appropriate actions to take. This capability ensures that the institution can respond effectively to crises, maintaining safety and stability while minimizing disruptions to educational activities.Despite these advantages, the deployment of chatbots in educational administration must be carefully managed to address potential challenges. Ensuring the accuracy and relevance of the chatbot's responses is crucial to maintaining trust and effectiveness. Chatbots must be regularly updated to reflect changes in policies, procedures, and institutional information. Additionally, privacy and data security concerns must be addressed, as chatbots handle sensitive information about students and staff. Implementing robust security measures and adhering to regulatory standards are essential to safeguarding this data and maintaining confidentiality.In conclusion, the automation of administrative tasks through chatbots represents a significant advancement in educational leadership. By streamlining routine processes, enhancing data management, improving communication, and supporting external interactions, chatbots contribute to a more efficient and effective administrative system.

Enhancing Teacher Professional Development with Chatbots

The integration of chatbots into teacher professional development represents a transformative shift in how educational institutions approach the continuous growth and support of their teaching staff (Dekker I, et al., 2020). These AI-driven tools are revolutionizing professional development by offering innovative solutions or delivering resources, facilitating learning, and fostering collaboration. As educational landscapes evolve and the demands on teachers increase, chatbots provide a scalable, personalized, and efficient way to enhance professional development opportunities and support educators in their roles.Chatbots offer a dynamic platform for delivering professional development resources in a highly accessible manner. Traditional professional development often involves in-person workshops, seminars, and courses, which can be logistically challenging and time-consuming, accommodating diverse schedules and learning preferences. By facilitating continuous learning opportunities, chatbots help educators stay current with best practices, educational technologies, and pedagogical strategies.

Personalization is a key advantage of chatbots in professional development. Through intelligent algorithms and data analytics, chatbots can analyze individual educators' performance, interests, and areas for improvement to offer customized recommendations (Eccles JS, et al., 2002). For instance, if a chatbot identifies that a teacher is struggling with classroom management, it can suggest relevant training materials, techniques, or peer support groups focused on that area. This tailored approach ensures that professional development is directly aligned with each educator's needs, fostering more effective and meaningful learning experiences. Personalized support not only enhances skill acquisition but also encourages a proactive approach to professional growth.Moreover, chatbots can facilitate ongoing support and feedback throughout the professional development process. Traditional models often lack mechanisms for real-time feedback, leaving educators without timely guidance on their progress. Chatbots can bridge this gap by providing instant feedback on performance, answering questions, and offering suggestions for improvement. This continuous support helps teachers refine their skills and apply new strategies effectively in their classrooms. Additionally, chatbots can track progress and achievements, offering educators insights into their development journey and helping them set and achieve professional goals.

Collaboration and networking are essential components of professional development, and chatbots can enhance these aspects by connecting educators with peers, mentors, and communities of practice. Chatbots can facilitate the creation of virtual discussion forums, where educators can share experiences, exchange ideas, and collaborate on projects. They can also assist in organizing and promoting professional development events, such as webinars, workshops, and peer observations (Eeuwen, M. V. 2017). By fostering a collaborative environment, chatbots enable teachers to learn from one another and build a supportive network that extends beyond their immediate school or district.Chatbots can prompt educators with reflective questions, provide frameworks for self-assessment, and offer resources to aid in the reflection process. Chatbots must be regularly updated with current best practices, research, and methodologies to provide accurate and useful information. Additionally, addressing privacy and data security concerns is essential, as chatbots handle sensitive information about educators' performance and development. Institutions must implement robust security measures and adhere to ethical standards to protect this data and maintain confidentiality.In conclusion, chatbots represent a significant advancement in enhancing teacher professional development. By providing personalized learning experiences, continuous support, and opportunities for collaboration, chatbots contribute to a more dynamic and effective professional growth environment (Følstad, A., 2019). Their ability to deliver on-demand resources, facilitate reflective practice, and scale development initiatives offers a promising approach to supporting educators in their ongoing quest for excellence. As educational institutions continue to embrace technological innovations, chatbots are likely to play an increasingly pivotal role in shaping the future of professional development and empowering teachers to achieve their full potential.

Chatbots for Parent-Teacher Communication: Improving Family Engagement

The integration of chatbots into the realm of parent-teacher communication signifies a major advancement in how educational institutions foster family engagement and collaboration. As educational environments become increasingly complex and demands on educators and parents grow, chatbots provide a sophisticated solution to streamline communication, enhance transparency, and build stronger partnerships between families and schools. This immediate access to information helps parents stay informed and engaged with their child's education, reducing misunderstandings and improving the overall quality of communication (Følstad A, et al., 2017). For educators, chatbots streamline routine interactions, allowing them to focus on more complex or personalized aspects of parent communication.Through automated updates and notifications, chatbots can inform parents about important events, deadlines, and changes in school policies. For example, a chatbot can send reminders about parent-teacher conferences, report card releases, and school closures. This proactive approach to communication ensures that parents are well-informed and can actively participate in their child's educational experience. Additionally, chatbots can provide easy access to resources such as academic calendars, student handbooks, and contact information for school staff, further supporting informed and engaged parenting.

Personalization is another significant benefit of chatbots in parent-teacher communication. Chatbots can tailor interactions based on the specific needs and preferences of each family. For instance, a chatbot can offer customized updates on a child's academic performance, behavior, and attendance, based on individual student data (Fryer LK, et al., 2019). This level of personalization helps parents stay connected to their child's progress and fosters a more individualized approach to communication. By addressing the unique concerns and interests of each family, chatbots enhance the relevance and effectiveness of communication efforts.Furthermore, chatbots can facilitate more effective and constructive parent-teacher conferences. Scheduling and organizing these meetings can often be a logistical challenge, requiring coordination between multiple parties. Chatbots can automatethe scheduling process by allowing parents to select convenient times and dates for meetings, and by sending confirmations and reminders. During conferences, chatbots can provide educators with summaries of parental concerns and questions collected in advance, ensuring that discussions are focused and productive. This streamlined approach to organizing and conducting conferences contributes to a more efficient and positive experience for both parents and teachers. In addition to improving communication, chatbots can support parental involvement in school activities and decision-making processes. Chatbots can promote and provide information about volunteer opportunities, school events, and parent-teacher associations (Garcia Brustenga, et al., 2018). By facilitating easy registration and participation, chatbots encourage greater family involvement in the school community. Moreover, chatbots can solicit feedback from parents on various aspects of school life, such as educational programs, school policies, and extracurricular activities. The use of chatbots also enhances accessibility for parents who may face barriers to traditional forms of communication. For parents with limited English proficiency, chatbots can offer multilingual support, providing information and assistance in various languages.

Personalized Learning with Chatbots: Adaptive Education for All

At the core of personalized learning with chatbots is the ability to deliver customized content and support. Unlike traditional one-size-fits-all educational approaches (Hadjielias E, et al., 2021), chatbots can analyze individual student data, including performance metrics, learning preferences, and past interactions, to tailor their responses and recommendations. The integration of chatbots into personalized learning also supports differentiated instruction, an approach that recognizes and addresses the diverse needs of students. By leveraging data on individual learning styles and preferences, chatbots can offer varied instructional methods, such as visual aids, interactive simulations, or textual explanations, to accommodate different learning preferences.Moreover, chatbots can enhance student motivation and engagement through gamification and interactive features. By incorporating elements such as quizzes, challenges, and rewards, chatbots create a more dynamic and engaging learning experience (Han R, Xu J.2020). For example, a chatbot might include a points system where students earn rewards for completing exercises or achieving milestones, turning learning into an enjoyable and motivating experience. This gamified approach not only makes learning more fun but also encourages students to actively participate and take ownership of their educational progress.In conclusion, chatbots represent a significant advancement in personalized learning, offering adaptive and tailored educational experiences that meet the diverse needs of students (Ischen C., et al., 2020). By delivering customized content, facilitating adaptive learning, supporting differentiated instruction, and enhancing engagement through gamification.

Chatbots for Mental Health Support: Addressing Student Well-being

The incorporation of chatbots into mental health support represents a significant advancement in how educational institutions address student well-being. As mental health challenges among students become increasingly recognized as critical to academic success and overall development, chatbots offer a valuable tool for providing accessible, responsive, and scalable support. One of the most notable benefits of chatbots in mental health support is their ability to provide instant, 24/7 assistance (Ismail, M., et al., 2019)Traditional mental health services often face limitations related to availability and accessibility, with students sometimes struggling to find the time or resources to seek help. This immediate availability ensures that students in distress or facing mental health challenges can access support and guidance without delay, helping to address issues before they escalate.Chatbots also play a crucial role in offering a non-judgmental and confidential space for students to express their feelings and concerns. Many students may feel hesitant to seek help due to stigma or fear of judgment, which can prevent them from accessing necessary support. Chatbots provide a private platform where students can openly discuss their mental health issues without the apprehension of facing direct human interaction. This confidentiality encourages students to engage with mental health resources more freely and seek help when needed, contributing to greater overall well-being. By analyzing student interactions and responses, chatbots can recommend specific resources such as coping strategies, mindfulness exercises, and self-help materials. For example, a chatbot might suggest relaxation techniques or direct students to online counseling services based on their expressed concerns. Additionally, chatbots can offer follow-up support and reminders to encourage students to practice self-care and engage with mental health resources consistently. This ongoing tracking helps students stay aware of their mental health and supports proactive management of their well-being.

Another important aspect of chatbots in mental health support is their ability to complement and enhance existing services (Khan A, et al., 2019). While chatbots are not a replacement for professional mental health care, they can serve as a supplementary tool that provides initial support and guidance. By integrating chatbots with traditional counseling services, educational institutions can create a more comprehensive support system that addresses both immediate and long-term needs. For example, chatbots can offer preliminary support and then refer students to human counselors for more in-depth therapy or intervention if required.the use of chatbots also promotes mental health education and awareness among students. Through interactive features, chatbots can educate students about mental health topics, including signs of distress, coping mechanisms, and available resources.

By providing information in an engaging and accessible manner, chatbots help to increase students' understanding of mental health issues and reduce stigma, fostering a more supportive and informed community. Chatbots must be designed to provide evidence-based information and guidance while being sensitive to the diverse needs of students. Additionally, addressing privacy and data security concerns is essential, as chatbots handle sensitive information about students' mental health. Institutions must implement robust security measures and adhere to ethical standards to protect this data and maintain confidentiality.In conclusion, chatbots represent a valuable tool for enhancing mental health support and addressing student well-being.

Data-Driven Decision Making: Chatbots for Educational Analytics

Traditional data management often involves labor-intensive processes of gathering, sorting, and analyzing information from various sources, which can be both time-consuming and prone to errors. Chatbots, however, can automate these tasks by interacting with students, teachers, and administrative staff to collect data on a wide range of metrics, such as academic performance, attendance, and engagement levels (Linse, A. R. 2007). This automation not only accelerates data collection but also ensures greater accuracy and consistency in the information gathered, providing a solid foundation for subsequent analysis.In addition to automating data collection, chatbots excel in real-time data analysis and reporting. Educational institutions generate enormous amounts of data daily, and the ability to analyze this data in real time is crucial for timely decision-making. Chatbots equipped with advanced analytics capabilities can process data quickly and generate real-time reports on various indicators, such as student performance trends, attendance patterns, and resource utilization. This immediacy allows educators and administrators to identify emerging issues, track progress, and make informed decisions based on current data, rather than relying on outdated or incomplete information.Chatbots also contribute to personalized data insights by tailoring analytics to the needs of individual users. For instance, educators can interact with chatbots to receive customized reports on their students' progress, highlighting specific areas of strength and areas needing improvement. Similarly, administrators can access dashboards that provide insights into institutional performance metrics, such as enrollment trends, financial data, and faculty workloads. This level of personalization ensures that users receive relevant and actionable insights that align with their specific roles and responsibilities, enhancing their ability to make data-driven decisions effectively.In addition to enhancing data analysis, chatbots play a crucial role in data visualization and interpretation. Effective data visualization is essential for making complex data more understandable and actionable. Chatbots can present data through interactive visualizations, such as graphs, charts, and heatmaps, that allow users to explore and interpret information more easily. For instance, a chatbot might generate a visual report showing the distribution of student grades across different subjects, enabling educators to identify patterns and make data-driven adjustments to their teaching strategies.

Chatbots also support collaborative decision-making by facilitating the sharing of data and insights among stakeholders. Through their interactive capabilities, chatbots can enable real-time discussions and data-sharing among teachers, administrators, and other relevant parties. This collaborative approach ensures that decision-making is informed by a broad range of perspectives and insights, leading to more comprehensive and effective strategies (Miller, E. et al., 2016)For example, a chatbot might gather input from multiple educators on a proposed curriculum change and analyze their feedback to provide a summarized report for administrative review.Despite the numerous advantages, the use of chatbots in educational analytics requires careful attention to data privacy and security. Additionally, the accuracy and reliability of the data and insights provided by chatbots must be regularly evaluated to ensure that decisions are based on valid and up-to-date information.In conclusion, chatbots represent a significant advancement in data-driven decision-making within educational institutions (Luo, C. J., et al., 2019). By automating data collection, enabling real-time analysis, providing personalized insights, and facilitating predictive analytics, chatbots contribute to a more effective and responsive approach to educational management. Their ability to enhance data visualization and support collaborative decision-making further strengthens their role in shaping strategic initiatives and improving institutional outcomes. As educational institutions continue to embrace technological innovations, chatbots are poised to play an increasingly important role in leveraging data to drive excellence in education and foster a more informed and adaptive learning environment.

Chatbots for Accessibility and Inclusion: Supporting Diverse Learners

The integration of chatbots into educational settings represents a transformative advancement in promoting accessibility and inclusion for diverse learners. As educational institutions strive to create environments that accommodate students of varying abilities, backgrounds, and needs, chatbots offer a powerful tool for addressing these challenges (Mahadev Madgule, et al., 2023). One of the primary ways chatbots support accessibility is by offering personalized assistance tailored to individual needs. Students with disabilities or learning differences often require specialized support to engage effectively with educational content. Chatbots can be programmed to provide adaptive features such as text-to-speech, speech-to-text, and customizable font sizes to accommodate various accessibility needs. For instance, a chatbot might offer verbal explanations or read aloud text for students with visual impairments, while providing written summaries for those who prefer text-based information. This level of customization helps ensure that educational materials are accessible to all students, regardless of their specific needs.Chatbots also play a critical role in facilitating communication for students who face language barriers or have limited English proficiency. By incorporating multilingual support, chatbots can interact with students in their preferred languages, providing translations and explanations to help them understand and engage with the content. This linguistic adaptability not only makes educational resources more accessible but also fosters a more inclusive environment where students from diverse linguistic backgrounds feel valued and supported. Additionally, chatbots can offer context-sensitive translations and cultural explanations to enhance comprehension and reduce misunderstandings.

The role of chatbots in supporting diverse learners extends beyond individual assistance to encompass broader educational inclusivity. Chatbots can facilitate the creation and dissemination of inclusive educational materials and resources (Ondas, S., et al., 2019). For example, if a chatbot detects that a significant number of students are struggling with certain content, it can alert educators to review and adjust the materials to better meet the needs of all learners.Furthermore, chatbots can promote inclusivity by providing professional development and training for educators on best practices for supporting diverse learners. Through interactive modules and resources, chatbots can help teachers understand and implement strategies for accommodating various needs, fostering a more inclusive classroom environment. By equipping educators with the knowledge and tools to address accessibility challenges, chatbots contribute to a more supportive and equitable educational experience for all students. Despite their many advantages, the implementation of chatbots for accessibility and inclusion must be carefully managed to address potential challenges. Ensuring the accuracy and relevance of chatbot responses is crucial to maintaining their effectiveness in supporting diverse learners. Chatbots must be regularly updated with current information and best practices to provide accurate and useful assistance (Pham, X. L., et al., 2018). Additionally, addressing privacy and data security concerns is essential, as chatbots handle sensitive information about students' needs and interactions.

Leadership Development through Chatbots: Coaching and Mentoring

The integration of chatbots into leadership development represents a groundbreaking approach to coaching and mentoring within organizations and educational institutions (Paramasivam Selvakumar, et al., 2024). As the demand for effective leadership grows in diverse sectors, chatbots offer a scalable, interactive, and personalized solution for nurturing leadership skills and supporting professional growth. Traditional leadership development programs often involve generic training sessions that maynot address the specific challenges and aspirations of each leader. Chatbots, however, can analyze data on a leader's performance, strengths, and areas for improvement to offer customized advice and resources. For example, if a leader struggles with time management, a chatbot can provide targeted strategies, tools, and resources to help them improve their organizational skills. This personalized approach ensures that coaching is directly aligned with the leader's unique needs, fostering more effective and meaningful development.Chatbots also facilitate real-time feedback and support, which are crucial for effective leadership development. Traditional coaching methods often involve periodic sessions or formal evaluations, which may not provide timely insights into a leader's progress. Chatbots, on the other hand, offer instant feedback on various aspects of leadership, such as decision-making, communication, and team management. Through regular interactions, chatbots can provide actionable insights, suggest improvements, and celebrate successes, helping leaders continuously refine their skills and stay on track with their development goals. This real-time support enhances the learning process and ensures that leaders receive timely guidance and reinforcement.

Another significant benefit of chatbots in leadership development is their ability to provide scalable coaching solutions. Traditional coaching and mentoring programs often face limitations related to time, resources, and availability, making it challenging to offer personalized support to all leaders. Chatbots can address this challenge by delivering coaching services to a large number of leaders simultaneously, regardless of their location or time zone (Vijayakumar G, et al., 2024). This scalability ensures that all leaders have access to high-quality coaching and mentoring, promoting equitable development opportunities and supporting a larger pool of emerging leaders within an organization or institution. By expanding their network and engaging with a broader community of leaders, individuals can gain diverse perspectives and enhance their leadership capabilities.Despite the numerous advantages, the implementation of chatbots in leadership development requires careful consideration of several factors (Sandoval ZV 2018). Ensuring the quality and relevance of the content delivered by chatbots is crucial to maintaining the effectiveness of coaching andmentoring.

Chatbots for Crisis Management: Emergency Response and Support

The utilization of chatbots in crisis management represents a groundbreaking advancement in emergency response and support, leveraging artificial intelligence and natural language processing to enhance the effectiveness and efficiency of crisis interventions. As the complexity and frequency of crises—ranging from natural disasters and public health emergencies to security incidents and organizational disruptions—increase, chatbots offer a vital tool for providing timely assistance, coordinating resources, and disseminating crucial information. Their integration into crisis management strategies helps organizations respond more effectively, minimize impacts, and support affected individuals with real-time, scalable solutions (Selvakumar, P. 2024).In high-stress situations, timely and accurate information is critical for ensuring public safety and guiding response efforts. In addition to providing information, chatbots play a crucial role in managing and triaging emergency requests and resources. During a crisis, organizations often face an overwhelming volume of inquiries and requests for assistance, which can strain response systems and lead to delays. Chatbots can automate the intake and categorization of these requests, efficiently directing them to the appropriate response teams or resources. For instance, in the aftermath of a disaster, a chatbot might collect information from individuals seeking medical assistance or shelter and prioritize these requests based on urgency and available resources. This automation helps streamline response efforts, ensuring that critical needs are addressed promptly and effectively.

Chatbots also enhance crisis management by facilitating communication and coordination among response teams and stakeholders. Effective crisis response requires seamless collaboration between various agencies, organizations, and individuals, often across different locations and time zones. Chatbots can support this coordination by providing a centralized platform for sharing updates, coordinating tasks, and tracking the status of response efforts (Silva, P.A., 2017). For example, a chatbot might integrate with incident management systems to provide real-time status updates on ongoing operations, resource allocation, and team assignments. This centralized communication streamlines coordination, reduces duplication of efforts, and ensures that all stakeholders are aligned in their response efforts. Another significant advantage of chatbots in crisis management is their ability to offer psychological support and emotional reassurance to individuals affected by the crisis. During emergencies, individuals may experience heightened levels of stress, anxiety, and fear. Chatbots can provide immediate access to mental health resources, coping strategies, and emotional support. For example, a chatbot might offer guided relaxation exercises, connect individuals with mental health professionals, or provide information on coping mechanisms (Sugumaran K. M, D., et al., 2024). By offering this support, chatbots help individuals manage their emotional well-being during challenging times and reduce the psychological impact of the crisis.

Despite their many advantages, the implementation of chatbots in crisis management requires careful consideration of several factors. Ensuring the accuracy and reliability of the chatbot's responses is crucial to maintaining trust and effectiveness during emergencies. Chatbots must be regularly updated with current information, protocols, and guidelines to provide accurate and relevant support. Additionally, addressing privacy and data security concerns is essential, as chatbots handle sensitive information about individuals' needs and interactions. Moreover, the design and functionality of chatbots must be tailored to meet the specific needs of crisis situations and diverse user populations (Thirumalai, B., et al., 2019). Chatbots should be designed to handle high volumes of interactions, provide clear and accessible information, and offer support in multiple languages if necessary. Ensuring that chatbots are user-friendly and capable of addressing a wide range of scenarios enhances their effectiveness and usability during crises.In conclusion, chatbots represent a significant advancement in crisis management, offering valuable tools for enhancing emergency response and support. By providing instant information, automating request management, facilitating coordination, offering psychological support, and gathering data, chatbots contribute to a more effective and responsive crisis management system. Their ability to support real-time communication and streamline response efforts underscores their transformative potential in managing emergencies and ensuring the safety and well-being of affected individuals. As organizations continue to embrace technological innovations, chatbots are poised to play an increasingly important role in crisis management, enhancing preparedness, and improving outcomes during challenging times.

Ethics and Equity in Chatbot Deployment: Ensuring Fairness and Transparency

Ensuring that chatbots operate equitably and transparently is crucial for fostering trust, preventing discrimination, and upholding the principles of fairness and accountability in their deployment.One of the foremost ethical concerns in chatbot deployment is the issue of bias. Chatbots are driven by algorithms and data, and if these inputs reflect historical or systemic biases, the chatbot may inadvertently perpetuate or amplify these biases. To address this concern, it is crucial to implement rigorous measures for identifying and mitigating bias in chatbot algorithms and training data (Thirumalai, B., et al., 2019). This includes diversifying data sources, conducting regular bias audits, and involving diverse teams in the development process to ensure that the chatbot's responses are fair and inclusive.Transparency is another critical ethical consideration in chatbot deployment. Users need to understand how chatbots operate, how their data is used, and how decisions are made. Lack of transparency can lead to a mistrust of chatbots and concerns about privacy and data security. To promote transparency, organizations should clearly communicate the chatbot's purpose, capabilities, and limitations to users. Additionally, providing users with information about data collection practices, data retention policies, and how their data is used can help build trust and ensure that users are informed about their interactions with the chatbot. Implementing features that allow users to review and delete their data further enhances transparency and user control.

Equity in chatbot deployment involves ensuring that chatbots are accessible and usable by individuals from diverse backgrounds and with varying needs. This includes addressing accessibility issues such as providing support for individuals with disabilities, ensuring compatibility with assistive technologies, and offering multilingual support for users who speak different languages. Chatbots should be designed to accommodate various communication styles and preferences, and they should provide clear and understandable responses. Additionally, efforts should be made to ensure that chatbots do not inadvertently exclude or disadvantage certain user groups (Winkler, R., et al., 2018). For instance, chatbots should be tested with diverse user populations to identify and address any potential barriers to access or usability.The ethical use of data collected by chatbots is also a significant concern. Chatbots gather sensitive information from users, and it is essential to handle this data with care to protect user privacy and confidentiality. Moreover, ensuring fairness in chatbot responses involves addressing potential disparities in how different users are treated. Ethical considerations in chatbot deployment also extend to accountability and oversight. Organizations deploying chatbots should establish mechanisms for monitoring and evaluating the chatbot's performance and impact. This includes setting up processes for addressing user complaints, correcting errors, and updating the chatbot's algorithms and data as needed. Additionally, involving external stakeholders, such as ethicists, regulators, and advocacy groups, in the development and oversight of chatbots can provide valuable perspectives and ensure that ethical and equity considerations are continuously addressed.

Chatbot Integration with Learning Management Systems (LMS)

As educational institutions increasingly adopt LMS platforms to manage course content, track student progress, and facilitate communication, chatbots provide a valuable tool for augmenting these systems. One of the primary benefits of integrating chatbots with LMS platforms is the automation of routine administrative tasks. Chatbots can handle a variety of tasks that traditionally require manual intervention, such as answering frequently asked questions, managing course registrations, and providing information on deadlines and assessments. For instance, a chatbot integrated with an LMS can automatically respond to student inquiries about course requirements, assignment due dates, or grading policies. Another significant advantage of chatbot integration with LMS platforms is the ability to support and guide students throughout their learning journey. Chatbots can serve as virtual tutors or mentors, offering support on a range of academic and administrative issues. They can help students navigate the LMS, access course materials, and understand assignment requirements. Additionally, chatbots can provide reminders and notifications about upcoming deadlines, exams, and important events, helping students stay organized and manage their time effectively. This level of support ensures that students have the resources and guidance they need to succeed in their courses(Nguyen, Q. N., et al., 2018)..For example, a chatbot might track which resources are most frequently accessed by students or identify common areas of difficulty. This data can be used to inform instructional strategies, improve course content, and enhance the overall learning experience. By leveraging these insights, educators can make data-driven decisions that support student success and optimize the effectiveness of the LMS. Moreover, chatbots can facilitate communication and collaboration between students and educators within the LMS. Chatbots can help manage group discussions, facilitate peer feedback, and coordinate group projects. Furthermore, the implementation of chatbots within LMS platforms should be accompanied by appropriate training and support for both educators and students. Educators need to be familiar with how chatbots operate and how to effectively incorporate them into their teaching strategies. Similarly, students should be provided with guidance on how to interact with chatbots and make the most of the support they offer. Providing training and resources for both groups ensures that chatbots are used effectively and that their benefits are fully realized.By automating administrative tasks, providing personalized support, fostering engagement, and facilitating communication, chatbots contribute to a more effective and efficient educational environment. As institutions continue to embrace technological innovations, chatbots are poised to play an increasingly important role in optimizing LMS platforms and supporting student success.

Measuring Chatbot Effectiveness in Education: Assessment and Evaluation

Assessing the effectiveness of chatbots in educational settings is crucial to understanding their impact on learning outcomes, user satisfaction, and overall educational processes. As chatbots become integral tools for enhancing various aspects of education—from providing personalized support and automating administrative tasks to facilitating engagement and communication—their performance must be rigorously evaluated to ensure they meet educational objectives and deliver value to students and educators alike. This assessment involves a multifaceted approach that considers quantitative metrics, qualitative feedback, and comparative analysis to provide a comprehensive evaluation of chatbot effectiveness.One of the primary methods for measuring chatbot effectiveness in education is through quantitative metrics that capture various aspects of chatbot performance. Key performance indicators (KPIs) such as user engagement rates, interaction frequency, response accuracy, and task completion rates provide valuable insights into how well a chatbot is functioning. For example, tracking the number of interactions a chatbot has with students and the types of queries it handles can reveal how effectively it addresses student needs. Additionally, monitoring response accuracy—i.e., the percentage of correct and helpful answers provided by the chatbot—helps assess the quality of the information delivered. Task completion rates, such as successfully guiding students through a process or resolving their queries, offer further insights into the chatbot's effectiveness in supporting educational tasks.

Another important quantitative measure is user satisfaction, which can be gauged through surveys and feedback mechanisms. Post-interaction surveys or feedback forms enable students and educators to rate their experiences with the chatbot, providing insights into aspects such as ease of use, helpfulness, and overall satisfaction(Riel, J. 2020).. These surveys can include questions about the chatbot's ability to provide relevant information, the clarity of its responses, and the timeliness of its support. Analyzing this feedback helps identify strengths and areas for improvement, guiding future enhancements and ensuring that the chatbot continues to meet user needs effectively. This continuous improvement cycle helps optimize the chatbot's performance and ensures that it adapts to changes in the educational environment and user expectations (Thirumalai, B., et al., 2019).Ensuring that chatbots operate fairly and transparently, and that they respect user privacy and data security, is crucial for maintaining user trust and ensuring ethical compliance. Evaluating how well the chatbot adheres to these ethical standards and addresses potential biases or privacy concerns helps ensure that it operates responsibly and equitably.In conclusion, measuring chatbot effectiveness in education requires a multifaceted approach that includes quantitative metrics, qualitative feedback, impact assessment, and comparative analysis. By employing these methods, educational institutions can gain a comprehensive understanding of a chatbot's performance, user satisfaction, and impact on learning outcomes. Continuous monitoring and iterative improvement ensure that chatbots remain effective and aligned with educational goals, while ethical considerations help maintain trust and compliance. As chatbots continue to play an increasingly significant role in education, rigorous assessment and evaluation are essential for optimizing their contributions and achieving positive outcomes for students and educators.

Future Directions in Chatbot Technology for Educational Leadership: Innovations and Challenges

The future of chatbot technology in educational leadership holds the promise of significant advancements, driven by innovations that will transform how leaders engage with technology, manage educational institutions, and support teaching and learning. As educational leadership evolves to address emerging challenges and opportunities, chatbots are set to play an increasingly pivotal role in enhancing decision-making, streamlining administrative processes, and fostering collaborative environments (Wu EHK, et al., 2018). However, realizing these potential benefits will require navigating several challenges, including technological, ethical, and operational issues. One significant challenge is ensuring that chatbots are equipped with accurate, up-to-date information and can effectively handle the diverse and evolving needs of educational institutions. As educational policies, curricula, and administrative processes continuously change, chatbots must be regularly updated to reflect these changes and provide relevant support (Yin J, et al., 2021). This requires ongoing collaboration between chatbot developers, educational leaders, and content experts to ensure that the chatbot's knowledge base remains current and comprehensive.Operational challenges also need to be addressed to ensure the effective integration of chatbots into educational leadership practices. This includes training educational leaders to effectively use and manage chatbots, as well as ensuring that chatbots are seamlessly integrated into existing systems and workflows. Professional development programs and support resources will be essential for helping leaders understand how to leverage chatbots effectively and address any issues that arise. Additionally, the scalability and adaptability of chatbots must be considered to ensure that they can meet the diverse needs of different educational institutions and contexts. Future directions in chatbot technology for educational leadership will also involve exploring new ways to enhance user experience and engagement. Innovations such as personalized interaction models, gamification, and adaptive learning features can contribute to a more engaging and supportive environment for educational leaders.

CONCLUSION

In conclusion, chatbots represent a transformative force in educational leadership, offering a myriad of benefits that extend across administrative, pedagogical, and strategic domains. Their integration into educational institutions can significantly enhance operational efficiency, support personalized learning experiences, and contribute to more informed decision-making processes. On the pedagogical front, chatbots facilitate personalized learning by providing students with instant feedback, tailored educational resources, and support that is accessible around the clock. This personalization enhances the learning experience, addressing individual needs and learning styles in ways that traditional methods may not fully accommodate.Strategically, the deployment of chatbots can aid educational leaders in data collection and analysis, providing valuable insights into student engagement, performance trends, and institutional needs. This data-driven approach enables more informed decision-making, allowing leaders to make evidence-based adjustments to curricula, policies, and resource allocation. Furthermore, chatbots can facilitate communication and collaboration among stakeholders, including students, parents, and staff, thereby promoting a more cohesive and engaged educational community. However, the successful integration of chatbots into educational settings requires careful consideration of several factors. Ensuring the privacy and security of student data, addressing potential biases in chatbot algorithms, and maintaining a human touch in interactions are critical to the effective deployment of this technology. Educational leaders must also consider the readiness of their institutions to adopt such technology, including the availability of necessary infrastructure and the training of staff and students to effectively use these tools.Looking forward, the role of chatbots in educational leadership is likely to expand as technology continues to evolve. Future developments may include more advanced artificial intelligence capabilities, allowing chatbots to engage in more complex interactions and provide even more nuanced support. The continued evolution of this technology will offer educational leaders new opportunities to enhance their practices, improve educational outcomes, and drive institutional success.In essence, chatbots hold the potential to revolutionize educational leadership by offering solutions that address both operational and pedagogical challenges. By leveraging these tools effectively, educational leaders can enhance efficiency, personalize learning experiences, and make more informed decisions, ultimately contributing to a more dynamic and responsive educational environment. The ongoing exploration and integration of chatbot technology will likely shape the future of educational leadership, making it imperative for institutions to stay abreast of developments and thoughtfully integrate these tools into their strategies.

REFERENCES

Abhilasha, A., Sreenivasulu, A., & Manimozhi, T. Satheesh kumar P., Selvakumar P. and Singh P.,(2022). "The Model of Smart Sensing Device For Sensitive Nano-clusters Modification in Sensing Properties," 2022 2nd International Conference on Advance Computing and Innovative Technologies in Engineering (ICACITE), Greater Noida, India, 2022, pp. 1043-1047, DOI: 10.1109/ICACITE53722.2022.9823846

Arruda, D., Marinho, M., Souza, E., & Wanderley, F. (2019). A Chatbot for goal-oriented requirements modeling. In Misra, S. (Eds.), Lecture Notes in Computer Science: Vol. 11622. *Computational science and its applications—ICCSA 2019. ICCSA 2019* (pp. 506–519). Springer., DOI: 10.1007/978-3-030-24305-0_38

Bii, P. (2013). Chatbot technology: A possible means of unlocking student potential to learn how to learn. *Educational Research*, 4(2), 218–221.

Brockhus, S., van der Kolk, T. E. C., Koeman, B., & Badke-Schaub, P. G. (2014). The influence of ambient green on creative performance. *Proceeding of International Design Conference (DESIGN 2014)*, Croatia, 437–444.

Cameron, G., Cameron, D. M., Megaw, G., Bond, R. B., Mulvenna, M., O'Neill, S. B., Armour, C., & McTear, M. (2018). Back to the future: Lessons from knowledge engineering methodologies for chatbot design and development. *Proceedings of British HCI*, 1–5. Advance online publication. DOI: 10.14236/ewic/HCI2018.153

Chaves, A. P., & Gerosa, M. A. (2021). How should my chatbot interact? A survey on social characteristics in human–chatbot interaction design. *International Journal of Human-Computer Interaction*, 37(8), 729–758. DOI: 10.1080/10447318.2020.1841438

Chete, F. O., & Daudu, G. O. (2020). An approach towards the development of a hybrid chatbot for handling students' complaints. Journal of Electrical Engineering, Electronics. *Control and Computer Science.*, 6(22), 29–38.

de Oliveira, J. C., Santos, D. H., & Neto, M. P. (2016). Chatting with Arduino platform through Telegram Bot. *2016 IEEE International Symposium on Consumer Electronics (ISCE)*, 131–132. DOI: 10.1109/ISCE.2016.7797406

Dekker, I., De Jong, E. M., Schippers, M. C., De Bruijn-Smolders, M., Alexiou, A., & Giesbers, B. (2020). Optimizing students' mental health and academic performance: AI-enhanced life crafting. *Frontiers in Psychology*, 11(June), 1–15. DOI: 10.3389/fpsyg.2020.01063 PMID: 32581935

Eccles, J. S., & Wigfield, A. (2002). Motivational Beliefs, Values, and Goals. *Annual Review of Psychology*, 53(1), 109–132. DOI: 10.1146/annurev.psych.53.100901.135153 PMID: 11752481

Eeuwen, M. V. (2017). Mobile conversational commerce: messenger chatbots as the next interface between businesses and consumers. Unpublished Master's thesis. University of Twente.

Følstad, A., & Brandtzaeg, P. B. (2017). Chatbots and the new world of HCI. *Interactions (New York, N.Y.)*, 24(4), 38–42. DOI: 10.1145/3085558

Følstad, A., Skjuve, M., & Brandtzaeg, P. B. (2019). Different chatbots for different purposes: towards a typology of chatbots to understand interaction design. In Bodrunova, S. (Eds.), Lecture Notes in Computer Science: Vol. 11551. *Internet Science. INSCI 2018* (pp. 145–156). Springer., DOI: 10.1007/978-3-030-17705-8_13

Fryer, L. K., Nakao, K., & Thompson, A. (2019). Chatbot learning partners: Connecting learning experiences, interest and competence. *Computers in Human Behavior*, 93, 279–289. DOI: 10.1016/j.chb.2018.12.023

Garcia Brustenga, G., Fuertes-Alpiste, M., & Molas-Castells, N. (2018). *Briefing paper: Chatbots in education. eLearn Center*. Universitat Oberta de Catalunya., DOI: 10.7238/elc.chatbots.2018

Hadjielias, E., Dada, O., Discua Cruz, A., Zekas, S., Christofi, M., & Sakka, G. (2021). How do digital innovation teams function? Understanding the team cognition-process nexus within the context of digital transformation. *Journal of Business Research*, 122, 373–386. DOI: 10.1016/j.jbusres.2020.08.045

Han, R., & Xu, J. (2020). A comparative study of the role of interpersonal communication, traditional media and social media in pro-environmental behavior: A China-based study. *International Journal of Environmental Research and Public Health*, 2020(6), 1883. Advance online publication. DOI: 10.3390/ijerph17061883 PMID: 32183217

Ischen, C., Araujo, T., Voorveld, H., van Noort, G., & Smit, E. (2020). Privacy concerns in chatbot interactions. In Følstad, A. (Eds.), Lecture Notes in Computer Science: Vol. 11970. *Chatbot research and design. CONVERSATIONS 2019* (pp. 34–48). Springer., DOI: 10.1007/978-3-030-39540-7_3

Ismail, M., & Ade-Ibijola, A. (2019). Lecturer's Apprentice: A chatbot for assisting novice programmers. Proceedings—2019 International multidisciplinary information technology and engineering conference, IMITEC 2019. South Africa, 1–8. IEEE. DOI: 10.1109/IMITEC45504.2019.9015857

Kanipriya, M., Sugumaran, D., Pandiyarajan, V., Yogananda, B. S., Selvakumar, P., & Mohan, S. (2024, January). Analysis of Electromyography Signals for Control of Mechanical Prosthesis using Machine Learning Techniques. In 2024 2nd International Conference on Intelligent Data Communication Technologies and Internet of Things (IDCIoT) (pp. 1059-1067). IEEE.

Khan, A., Ranka, S., Khakare, C., & Karve, S. (2019). NEEV(2019): An education informational chatbot. *International Research Journal of Engineering and Technology.*, 6(4), 492–495.

Linse, A. R. (2007). Team peer evaluation. In Schreyer Institute for Teaching Excellence. http://www.schreyerinstitute.psu.edu/

Luo, C. J., & Gonda, D. E. (2019). Code Free Bot: An easy way to jumpstart your chatbot! *Proceeding of the 2019 IEEE International Conference on Engineering, Technology and Education (TALE 2019)*, Australia, 1–3, IEEE. DOI: 10.1109/TALE48000.2019.9226016

Madgule, M., Vinayaka, N., Sonkhaskar, Y. M., Patel, D. R., Karthikeyan, R., & Selvakumar, P. (2023). Mechanical properties and microstructure of activated TIG welded similar joints of Inconel alloys by desirability approaches. *Materials Today: Proceedings*, 77, 528–533.

Miller, E. (2016). How chatbots will help education. Venturebeat. https://venturebeat.com/2016/09/29/how-chatbots-will-help-education/

Nguyen, Q. N., & Sidorova, A. (2018). Understanding user interactions with a chatbot: A self-determination theory approach. Proceedings of the Twenty-Fourth Americas Conference on Information Systems, United States of America, 1–5. Association for Information Systems (AIS).

Ondas, S., Pleva, M., & Hladek, D. (2019). How chatbots can be involved in the education process. Proccedings of the 17th IEEE international conference on emerging eLearning technologies and applications ICETA 2019, Slovakia, 575–580. DOI: 10.1109/ICETA48886.2019.9040095

Pham, X. L., Pham, T., Nguyen, Q. M., Nguyen, T. H., & Cao, T. T. H. (2018). Chatbot as an intelligent personal assistant for mobile language learning. Proceedings of the 2018 2nd international conference on education and e-Learning—ICEEL 2018, Indonesia, 16–21. ACM. DOI: 10.1145/3291078.3291115

Riel, J. (2020). Essential features and critical issues with educational chatbots: toward personalized learning via digital agents. In Khosrow-Pour, M. (Ed.), *Handbook of research on modern educational technologies, applications, and management* (pp. 246–262). IGI Global., DOI: 10.1142/S0218194019400163

Sandoval, Z. V. (2018). Design and implementation of a chatbot in online higher education settings. *Issues in Information Systems*, 19(4), 44–52. DOI: 10.48009/4_iis_2018_44-52

Satow, L. (2017). Chatbots as teaching assistants: Introducing a model for learning facilitation by AI Bots. SAP Community. https://blogs.sap.com/2017/07/12/chatbots-as-teaching-assistants-introducing-a-model-for-learning-facilitation-by-ai-bots/

Selvakumar, P. (2024). Emerging Engineering Technologies: Design, Development, and Industrial Applications of IoT-Based Aquaculture Monitoring System. In El Kacimi, Y., & Alaoui, K. (Eds.), *Emerging Engineering Technologies and Industrial Applications* (pp. 332–341). IGI Global., DOI: 10.4018/979-8-3693-1335-0.ch016

Selvakumar, P., Palanisamy, S. K., Cinthaikinian, S., Palanisamy, V., Mariappan, R., & Selvakumar, P. K. (2024). Biosensors and its diverse applications in healthcare systems. *Zeitschrift für Physikalische Chemie*, 2024. Advance online publication. DOI: 10.1515/zpch-2023-0406

Silva, P. A., Polo, B. J., & Crosby, M. E. (2017). Adapting the studio based learning methodology to computer science education. In Fee, S., Holland-Minkley, A., & Lombardi, T. (Eds.), *New directions for computing education* (pp. 119–142). Springer., DOI: 10.1007/978-3-319-54226-3_8

Sjöström, J., Aghaee, N., Dahlin, M., & Ågerfalk, P. J. (2018). Designing chatbots for higher education practice. *Proceedings of the 2018 AIS SIGED International Conference on Information Systems Education and Research.*

Thirumalai, B., Ramanathan, A., Charania, A., & Stump, G. (2019). Designing for technology-enabled reflective practice: teachers' voices on participating in a connected learning practice. In Setty, R., Iyenger, R., Witenstein, M. A., Byker, E. J., & Kidwai, H. (Eds.), *Teaching and teacher education: south asian perspectives* (pp. 243–273). Palgrave Macmillan., DOI: 10.1007/978-3-030-26879-4_11

Verleger, M., & Pembridge, J. (2019). A pilot study integrating an AI-driven chatbot in an introductory programming course. Proceeding of the 2018 IEEE Frontiers in Education Conference (FIE), USA. IEEE. DOI: 10.1109/FIE.2018.8659282

Vijayakumar, G., Rajkumar, M., Rajiv Chandar, N., Selvakumar, P., & Duraisamy, R. (2024). Environmentally friendly TDS removal from waste water by electrochemical ion exchange batch-type recirculation (EIR) technique. *Environmental Science. Water Research & Technology*, 10(4), 826–835. DOI: 10.1039/D3EW00793F

Winkler, R., & Söllner, M. (2018). Unleashing the potential of chatbots in education: A state-of-the-art analysis. In Academy of Management Annual Meeting (AOM). https://www.alexandria.unisg.ch/254848/1/JML_699.pdf

Wu, E. H. K., Lin, C. H., Ou, Y. Y., Liu, C. Z., Wang, W. K., & Chao, C. Y. (2018). Advantages and constraints of a hybrid model K-12 E-Learning assistant chatbot. *IEEE Access : Practical Innovations, Open Solutions*, 2020(8), 77788–77801. DOI: 10.1109/ACCESS.2020.2988252

Yin, J., Goh, T. T., Yang, B., & Xiaobin, Y. (2021). Conversation technology with micro-learning: The impact of chatbot-based learning on students' learning motivation and performance. *Journal of Educational Computing Research*, 59(1), 154–177. DOI: 10.1177/0735633120952067

Chapter 14
Understanding Chatbots in the Context of Curriculum Management in Institutions of Higher Learning:
Challenges and Opportunities

Annie Mojaesi Moletsane
https://orcid.org/0000-0001-6765-0209
Vaal University of Technology, South Africa

ABSTRACT

This literature-based paper examines the application of chatbots in curriculum management in educational settings, aiming to explore their benefits, challenges, and future potential. Findings show that chatbots, enhanced by AI, machine learning, and NLP, streamline administrative processes, support student engagement, and enable effective communication among stakeholders. Despite these advantages, challenges such as data privacy and technical limitations persist. The chapter concludes that, with ethical practices and AI advancements, chatbots could significantly reshape educational management. Recommendations focus on personalization, ethical guidelines, and ongoing technology integration for optimized outcomes.

DOI: 10.4018/979-8-3693-8734-4.ch014

BACKGROUND

Globally, chatbots, predominantly those that are manipulated and guided by Natural Language Processing (NLP) models are rapidly dominating higher institutions of learning into technologically innovative education in terms of educational transformation. ChatGPT, is one of such innovations that has brought about rapid changes in schools including curriculum management and implementation to enhance educational practices. As these systems evolve, they offer personalized learning experiences by tailoring content, activities, and assessments to the needs of individual students, potentially improving academic engagement and outcomes (Wu, 2017). NLP models are currently associated with on-demand support, during the teaching and learning process whereby students are engaged at their convenience. This has proved valuable particularly valuable in online and independent learning contexts

Despite these technological advancements in Intuitions of Higher learning, challenges are still common whereby both teachers and learners run the risk of over-reliance on technology, which may hinder the development of critical thinking skills. Additionally, concerns about the accuracy of AI models, especially in interpreting complex language remain a key issue. Institutions must balance the benefits of AI integration with thoughtful oversight to ensure that these tools enhance rather than replace essential cognitive skills

CHATBOTS IN CURRICULUM DELIVERY AND EDUCATIONAL ENGAGEMENT

One of the primary and remarkable roles of chatbots in curriculum management is their capacity to deliver course content and engage students in interactive learning experiences. As Jung et al. (2020) highlight, chatbots serve as interactive tools in higher education, offering personalized interactions that can drive student engagement. Chatbots, when integrated into curriculum delivery systems, can assist in making learning materials accessible and provide immediate feedback to students. These interactions are particularly effective in large classes, where individual attention from instructors is limited.

The effectiveness of chatbots in educational contexts is further supported by Smutny and Schreiberova (2020), who found that chatbots automate administrative tasks such as answering student queries, thus freeing up time for educators to focus on complex pedagogical tasks. Chatbots enhance engagement by providing students with immediate access to learning resources and assisting in self-regulated learning. The automation of routine inquiries also ensures that students receive timely feedback, which contributes to better retention and understanding of course content.

Musundire (2021) examined how e-learning instructional knowledge influences pedagogical attitudes and learner performance, highlighting its alignment with technological innovations in education. The study highlights the importance of integrating e-learning tools in curriculum management to foster innovative teaching methods and improve the interactive engagement of learners. Technological advancements such as online learning platforms and digital tools enhance the capacity of educators to deliver course content in diverse, accessible ways, thus promoting the development of more dynamic and learner-cantered curricula that respond to the evolving demands of education.

In summary, the use of chatbots in curriculum delivery not only enhances student engagement but also helps institutions assess their educational offerings. It is recommended that educational institutions adopt chatbots to reduce the administrative burden and facilitate more personalized learning experiences.

Chatbots in Learning Management Systems (LMS)

Integrating chatbots with Learning Management Systems (LMS) is another crucial area where chatbots can contribute to effective curriculum management. According to Pérez et al. (2020), chatbots can enhance the functionalities of an LMS by managing course materials, tracking student progress, and offering real-time feedback. These integrations provide instructors with valuable data about student performance and engagement, allowing for more informed decisions regarding curriculum adjustments.

Virtanen et al. (2018) reinforce this notion by exploring how chatbots improve accessibility to curriculum materials. When integrated with LMS, chatbots can facilitate a seamless learning experience by providing students with easy access to course content and answering any queries related to the curriculum. By handling routine administrative tasks, chatbots allow instructors to dedicate more time to interactive teaching and addressing individual student needs.

Moreover, the reliability of chatbots within LMS platforms cannot be overstated. Chatbots provide an efficient solution for institutions to manage large numbers of students while maintaining personalized support. For institutions dealing with large student populations, chatbots enable instructors to maintain consistent communication with students without being overwhelmed.

In other words, the integration of chatbots with LMS platforms provides effective and efficient solution for curriculum management. It is recommended that institutions leverage LMS-integrated chatbots to streamline administrative processes and enhance the overall learning experience.

Chatbots in Personalized Learning and Curriculum Support

Personalized learning is a key focus in modern educational practices, and chatbots have proven to be an effective tool in supporting this approach. As highlighted by Deng and Yu (2023), chatbots enable personalized learning by providing tailored feedback based on individual student needs and performance. This real-time, personalized approach helps students navigate the curriculum at their own pace, ensuring that they receive the support necessary to succeed.

Chatbots also assist in creating adaptive learning environments where course content can be modified based on the student's progress. By analyzing data from interactions, chatbots can recommend additional learning resources, ensuring that each student's unique learning needs are met. Pérez et al. (2020) emphasize that chatbots in personalized learning settings can act as digital tutors, guiding students through complex concepts and offering supplemental materials when necessary.

Musundire (2020) explores the potential of technology-driven communication platforms to facilitate collaboration and knowledge sharing. These innovations support curriculum management by enabling real-time communication, resource exchange, and collaborative learning. As technological advancements create more interactive and connected learning environments, educators can better manage curriculum content, tailoring lessons and activities to the needs of individual learners. By fostering a culture of collaboration, these platforms encourage the development of skills such as problem-solving and critical thinking, which are essential in today's technology-driven world.

In summary, chatbots are instrumental in creating personalized learning experiences that cater to individual students' needs. Their integration into curriculum management systems allows institutions to offer more adaptive and responsive learning environments. Therefore, institutions should prioritize the use of chatbots to provide tailored learning experiences and improve student success rates.

Pedagogical Framework and Design of Chatbots

For chatbots to be effective in educational settings, they must be designed with pedagogical principles in mind. According to Winkler and Soellner (2018), the design of chatbots must align with specific learning outcomes and curriculum goals to ensure that they contribute meaningfully to the educational process. Chatbots that are designed without a clear pedagogical framework risk providing superficial interactions that fail to enhance the learning experience. Hobert and Meyer von Wolff (2019) argue that the pedagogical value of chatbots lies in their ability to guide students through the curriculum and provide instant, contextual feedback. For example, in a history course, a chatbot can quiz students on key events and provide explanations for correct and incorrect answers. This level of interactivity is crucial in creating a rich, engaging learning environment.

The design of chatbots must also account for the diversity of students and their varying learning preferences. As discussed by Smutny and Schreiberova (2020), chatbots should be flexible enough to provide different modes of interaction (e.g., text, voice, multimedia) to cater to different learning styles. By doing so, chatbots can enhance accessibility and ensure that all students are engaged with the curriculum.

Musundire (2020) argues that technological communication tools are pivotal in addressing the evolving needs of modern learners. These tools are at the forefront of technological innovation in education, offering educators the means to create more engaging and inclusive learning environments. In the context of curriculum management, these advancements enable educators to deliver content in innovative ways, supporting differentiated instruction and ensuring accessibility for all learners. As technology continues to develop, educators can leverage these tools to create a flexible and adaptive curriculum that fosters ongoing educational growth and development, both for teachers and students.

The assumption basing on the above views is that the design of chatbots should be informed by pedagogical theories to ensure that they effectively support curriculum goals. Institutions should invest in the development of chatbots that align with learning outcomes and cater to diverse student needs.

Chatbots in Curriculum Monitoring and Feedback

An essential aspect of curriculum management is the ability to monitor student progress and provide feedback that can inform instructional practices. Chatbots are increasingly being used to automate feedback mechanisms, which can help educators track student performance and intervene when necessary. As Graesser et al. (2001) demonstrate, chatbots, when integrated into intelligent tutoring systems (ITS), can provide automated feedback that mimics the responses of a human tutor.

Duval and Verbert (2012) explore the integration of chatbot data with learning analytics, which allows educators to monitor curriculum delivery in real-time. Chatbots can collect data on student interactions, such as time spent on tasks, question responses, and areas of difficulty, which can then be used to assess how effectively the curriculum is being delivered. This feedback loop is essential for ensuring that the curriculum is responsive to the needs of students and that instructional adjustments can be made in a timely manner. Moreover, chatbots offer the advantage of providing instant feedback to students, which can increase motivation and improve learning outcomes. The ability to provide immediate responses to questions and clarify misunderstandings helps students stay engaged and on track with the curriculum. According to Winkler and Soellner (2018), this type of feedback is essential for maintaining momentum in the learning process.

In other words, chatbots are a valuable tool for curriculum monitoring and feedback. They can automate the process of tracking student progress and offering real-time feedback, making the curriculum more responsive and adaptive. Educational institutions should integrate chatbots into their feedback mechanisms to ensure that students receive timely and relevant feedback on their learning progress.

AREA OF FOCUS

Challenges in Implementing Chatbots for Curriculum Management in Educational Institutions

The integration of chatbots into curriculum management within educational institutions presents an exciting frontier in the intersection of technology and education. Chatbots powered by Natural Language Processing (NLP) and Artificial Intelligence (AI) hold the potential to revolutionize learning management systems by providing personalized support to students and educators alike. However, their implementation is not without challenges. This chapter explores these challenges, drawing on research from several scholars to critically examine the obstacles encountered in chatbot adoption within educational settings.

Technological Challenges in NLP Integration

The integration of chatbots into educational systems relies heavily on advancements in Natural Language Processing (NLP). While NLP has advanced considerably, several technological limitations remain, particularly in its application to curriculum management.

Accuracy and Ambiguity in Student Queries

One of the most significant technological challenges in deploying chatbots for curriculum management is their ability to accurately interpret and respond to student queries. NLP systems are designed to parse human language, but ambiguity in language, such as slang, idioms, or complex sentence structures, can lead to misinterpretations. As Miller (2019) highlights, chatbots often struggle with understanding context, leading to responses that can be irrelevant or inaccurate. This limitation is particularly problematic in an educational context, where the precision of information is critical for student success (Miller, 2019).

Data Quality and Model Training

Furthermore, the efficacy of a chatbot largely depends on the quality of the data used to train it. A study by Fuchs (2021) underscores the fact that insufficient, unrepresentative, or biased data can lead to chatbots providing skewed or inappropriate responses. In educational contexts, where diverse student backgrounds and needs must be accounted for, this becomes a major hurdle. According to Fuchs, a lack of diversity in training data results in limited chatbot effectiveness, particularly in multicultural classrooms where language and context vary widely.

Ethical and Privacy Concerns

- Data Privacy Issues

The use of AI and chatbots in educational institutions raises significant ethical and privacy concerns. With the increasing reliance on AI, the volume of student data collected during interactions with chatbots is substantial. As AI-driven systems gather and process large amounts of sensitive information, including personal identifiers, academic performance data, and behavioural insights, the risk of data breaches becomes more pronounced. Research by White (2020) highlights the regulatory challenges institutions face in ensuring that chatbot interactions comply with data protection laws like GDPR and FERPA. White argues that clear protocols and stringent data management policies must be established to mitigate risks related to data misuse or leakage.

Algorithmic Bias and Fairness

Another ethical concern is the risk of algorithmic bias in chatbot interactions. Chatbots, like other AI systems, can inherit biases present in the data they are trained on. These biases can manifest in various forms, including gender, racial, or socio-economic biases, which could negatively impact students from underrepresented groups. A study by Singh and Patel (2022) explores how biases in AI models may lead to discriminatory practices in educational settings, reinforcing existing inequalities. The researchers suggest that regular audits of AI algorithms are essential to identify and address these biases, ensuring fairness in educational environments.

Over-Reliance on Technology

While chatbots provide valuable support, there are concerns that students may become entiryly reliant on technology, which could impede the development of critical thinking and problem-solving skills.

Diminished Cognitive Engagement

Critics argue that the ease of access to chatbot-assisted learning may discourage active problem-solving and engagement with learning materials. According to Jones (2021), students may choose to ask a chatbot for answers instead of attempting to resolve issues on their own, thus diminishing their cognitive development. This over-reliance on automated systems may lead to passive learning, which is counterproductive to developing higher-order thinking skills.

Balancing AI with Traditional Teaching Methods

The challenge lies in balancing the use of AI-driven tools with traditional, instructor-led teaching methods. As argued by Johnson (2018), AI systems should supplement, not replace, human educators. Educators play a vital role in fostering critical thinking and guiding students through complex problem-solving tasks, areas where chatbots still fall short. For chatbots to be truly effective in curriculum management, they must be integrated into a broader educational ecosystem that includes human instructors and interactive, engaging learning materials.

Student Acceptance and Trust

- Resistance to AI Integration

Despite the benefits of chatbots, many students exhibit resistance to using AI-driven systems. A study by Lee and Choi (2020) found that students often feel uncomfortable interacting with a non-human entity, particularly when the chatbot is tasked with providing feedback on academic performance. This reluctance is compounded by concerns about the chatbot's ability to understand complex academic needs and provide accurate, personalized feedback. The researchers argue that fostering student trust in AI is crucial for successful integration and that transparency regarding how AI works can help reduce scepticisms.

- Building Student Trust in AI Systems

To build student trust, it is essential for institutions to ensure that chatbots are transparent and explainable. As Kim (2021) points out, chatbots must provide clear, understandable responses and offer explanations when they make decisions or offer advice. Additionally, students must be assured that their data is handled securely and responsibly. Creating a positive perception of AI tools can increase their acceptance and effectiveness in curriculum management.

Administrative and Implementation Challenges

- Training Educators to Use AI Tools

The successful integration of chatbots into curriculum management systems requires that educators are adequately trained to use these tools. According to Brown (2019), many teachers lack the technical knowledge necessary to effectively incorporate AI tools into their teaching practices. Professional development programs focusing on the use of AI in education are essential for ensuring that educators can fully leverage the capabilities of chatbots.

- Financial and Resource Constraints

Implementing AI-powered chatbots requires significant financial investment. Many educational institutions, especially in developing countries, face budget constraints that limit their ability to adopt such advanced technologies. As pointed out by Thomas (2020), securing funding for AI initiatives often requires navigating complex bureaucratic processes, making it difficult for smaller institutions to access the necessary resources. Financial considerations must therefore be addressed if chatbots are to be widely adopted in curriculum management.

In summary, the integration of chatbots into curriculum management presents numerous opportunities but also several challenges. Technological limitations in NLP, ethical and privacy concerns, and resistance from students and educators must be carefully addressed to ensure the successful adoption of AI systems in education. By leveraging insights from existing research and adopting a balanced approach that combines the strengths of AI with traditional teaching methods, educational institutions can harness the full potential of chatbots to enhance curriculum management and student engagement.

Opportunities in Implementing Chatbots for Curriculum Management in Educational Institutions

The challenges faced in the implementation of chatbots for curriculum management are significant but also give rise to several opportunities for enhancing educational systems. By addressing these challenges through technological advancements, ethical frameworks, and innovative pedagogical strategies, chatbots can offer substantial benefits. This chapter will explore how these challenges can be turned into opportunities for improvement in curriculum management and the broader educational landscape.

Technological Advancements in NLP

- Overcoming Language Ambiguity

While the challenge of language ambiguity remains, it also offers an opportunity for advancing Natural Language Processing (NLP) models. As technology evolves, chatbots can be fine-tuned to understand more complex sentence structures and slang. Research by Gupta et al. (2023) suggests that improvements in deep learning models, including transformer networks, offer a promising solution to enhance chatbot accuracy. These advancements will allow chatbots to handle a wider range of student queries, making their application in curriculum management more effective.

- Personalized Learning through AI

Chatbots provide the unique opportunity to personalize learning experiences for students. According to Hernandez (2021), chatbots can adapt their responses based on individual student data, delivering tailored feedback and assistance. This ability to personalize interactions can lead to more effective curriculum management, allowing educators to provide focused guidance where needed.

Ethical and Privacy Opportunities

- Building Trust through Transparency

While privacy concerns are a major challenge, they also create an opportunity to establish transparency and build trust in educational institutions. By implementing clear privacy policies and secure data protocols, institutions can ensure that students feel safe interacting with chatbots. According to Brown and Smith (2022), transparency regarding how data is used and stored can mitigate privacy concerns and increase chatbot adoption.

- Creating Ethical AI Systems

The challenge of algorithmic bias offers a chance for developing more ethical AI systems. Researchers like White (2020) have emphasized the importance of creating AI systems that are fair and inclusive. By integrating diverse datasets and conducting regular audits, educational institutions can reduce bias in chatbot responses, ensuring that all students, regardless of background, receive equal treatment. This not only improves the efficacy of chatbots but also fosters a more inclusive learning environment.

To explore the opportunities arising from the challenges of chatbot integration in curriculum management, I will structure the chapter around potential solutions, innovations, and benefits that can emerge. This will also cover the advantages of using chatbots in educational settings, focusing on the practical application of the technology. Here's an outline for the 20-page section:

Opportunities from the Challenges of Chatbot Integration in Curriculum Management

The challenges faced in the implementation of chatbots for curriculum management are significant but also give rise to several opportunities for enhancing educational systems. By addressing these challenges through technological advancements, ethical frameworks, and innovative pedagogical strategies, chatbots can offer substantial benefits. This chapter will explore how these challenges can be turned into opportunities for improvement in curriculum management and the broader educational landscape.

Technological Advancements in NLP

- Overcoming Language Ambiguity

While the challenge of language ambiguity remains, it also offers an opportunity for advancing Natural Language Processing (NLP) models. As technology evolves, chatbots can be fine-tuned to understand more complex sentence structures and slang. Research by Gupta et al. (2023) suggests that improvements in deep learning models, including transformer networks, offer a promising solution to enhance chatbot accuracy. These advancements will allow chatbots to handle a wider range of student queries, making their application in curriculum management more effective.

- Personalized Learning through AI

Chatbots provide the unique opportunity to personalize learning experiences for students. According to Hernandez (2021), chatbots can adapt their responses based on individual student data, delivering tailored feedback and assistance. This ability to personalize interactions can lead to more effective curriculum management, allowing educators to provide focused guidance where needed.

Ethical and Privacy Opportunities

- Building Trust through Transparency

While privacy concerns are a major challenge, they also create an opportunity to establish transparency and build trust in educational institutions. By implementing clear privacy policies and secure data protocols, institutions can ensure that students feel safe interacting with chatbots. According to Brown and Smith (2022), transparency regarding how data is used and stored can mitigate privacy concerns and increase chatbot adoption.

- Creating Ethical AI Systems

The challenge of algorithmic bias offers a chance for developing more ethical AI systems. Researchers like White (2020) have emphasized the importance of creating AI systems that are fair and inclusive. By integrating diverse datasets and conducting regular audits, educational institutions can reduce bias in chatbot responses, ensuring that all students, regardless of background, receive equal treatment. This not only improves the efficacy of chatbots but also fosters a more inclusive learning environment.

Enhancing Student Engagement and Learning

- Gamification and Interactive Learning

Chatbots offer the opportunity to integrate gamification strategies into curriculum management. By using chatbots to create interactive, game-like learning experiences, educators can increase student engagement. According to Lee and Chan (2021), gamification in chatbot-based learning systems has been shown to improve student motivation, engagement, and retention of information. This can transform a traditional, passive learning environment into one that is dynamic and interactive.

- Availability for Student Support

One of the most significant opportunities offered by chatbots is their ability to provide 24/7 support. Students can access information and receive assistance outside of classroom hours, making learning more flexible and accessible. This is particularly beneficial in regions or institutions with limited access to in-person resources. By integrating chatbots into curriculum management systems, institutions can bridge the gap between student needs and the availability of support.

Improving Administrative Efficiency

- Automating Administrative Tasks

Chatbots can alleviate the burden of administrative tasks by automating routine processes such as scheduling, answering frequently asked questions, and managing student queries. According to Johnson (2019), the automation of administrative duties allows educators and administrators to focus on more critical aspects of teaching and curriculum development. Chatbots can handle tasks such as exam scheduling, grade inquiries, and basic course information dissemination, leading to increased operational efficiency.

- Streamlining Feedback and Assessment

Another opportunity lies in using chatbots to streamline the feedback and assessment process. Instead of waiting for weeks for feedback on assignments, chatbots can provide real-time feedback on student submissions. This not only speeds up the feedback process but also offers personalized insights based on the student's performance. Researchers such as Patel and Singh (2021) have shown that real-time, chatbot-driven feedback improves student learning outcomes by enabling timely course corrections.

Enhancing Educator Training and Support

- Professional Development for Educators

The challenge of training educators to use AI tools effectively presents an opportunity for professional development. By offering targeted training programs on AI and chatbot usage, institutions can ensure that teachers are equipped to make the most of these technologies. According to Harris (2020), ongoing professional development programs focused on AI integration into education can empower educators and enhance the overall effectiveness of curriculum management.

- Collaboration Between Humans and AI

Chatbots offer a unique opportunity for collaboration between human educators and AI. As suggested by Jackson (2021), while chatbots can handle routine queries, human teachers can focus on more complex issues requiring critical thinking and emotional intelligence. This human-AI collaboration can create a balanced approach to education, where technology supports and enhances human teaching rather than replacing it.

Scalability and Accessibility

- Extending Education to Remote Areas

Chatbots provide an excellent opportunity to extend education to remote or underserved areas where access to traditional learning resources may be limited. By providing curriculum management tools through chatbots, educational institutions can deliver lessons, support, and resources to students who otherwise would have limited access to these materials. According to Chen et al. (2020), the scalability of chatbot solutions makes them ideal for reaching a wider audience in areas where there is a lack of physical infrastructure.

- Cost-Effectiveness for Educational Institutions

Chatbots offer a cost-effective solution to educational institutions facing budget constraints. By reducing the need for large administrative staff and enabling automated learning support, chatbots can reduce costs associated with human resources. This makes them an attractive solution for institutions operating with limited budgets. As noted by Thomas (2020), the long-term cost savings of implementing chatbots in curriculum management can outweigh initial investment costs.

Continuous Improvement and Feedback Loops

- Data-Driven Insights for Curriculum Improvement

Chatbots can generate valuable data on student interactions and learning patterns, which can be analysed to improve curriculum design. As Martinez and Lopez (2021) highlight, the data collected from chatbot interactions can provide insights into which topics students find most challenging, allowing educators to adapt the curriculum accordingly. This data-driven approach can lead to more personalized and effective teaching strategies.

- Real-Time Adaptation of Teaching Strategies

The ability to adapt teaching methods in real-time based on chatbot feedback is another key opportunity. By monitoring student progress and identifying areas where students struggle, chatbots can help educators adjust teaching methods dynamically. According to Brown and Wilson (2021), this adaptive learning approach leads to improved student outcomes as teaching is tailored to the evolving needs of the class.

In summary, despite the challenges associated with the integration of chatbots into curriculum management, the opportunities they present are substantial. By addressing technological, ethical, and logistical hurdles, educational institutions can harness the potential of chatbots to enhance learning experiences, improve administrative efficiency, and create more personalized education environments. With continuous advancements in AI and a commitment to ethical AI practices, chatbots are poised to become a transformative tool in modern education.

SOLUTIONS AND RECOMMENDATIONS

Solutions to Challenges in Chatbot Integration for Curriculum Management

To effectively harness the potential of chatbots in curriculum management, it is crucial to address the unique challenges identified by researchers. The following sections outline a comprehensive set of solutions that institutions can implement to overcome obstacles in infrastructure, training, data privacy, inclusivity, and engagement, ultimately enhancing the use of chatbots as supportive tools in curriculum management.

Strengthening Technological Infrastructure

An essential solution to optimizing chatbot integration is enhancing the technological infrastructure within institutions. To do this, educational facilities must invest in reliable network systems, sufficient storage for large volumes of interaction data, and high-performance computing resources. Institutions could partner with technology providers or seek government grants to fund these advancements, ensuring that chatbots function efficiently in both urban and rural educational settings.

Ensuring robust infrastructure is especially important in remote areas or underserved institutions that may not have the required digital resources. Researchers have suggested establishing regional hubs where technology experts provide technical support, allowing institutions to share resources and reduce operational costs.

Ongoing Training and Development for Educators

Professional development for educators is key to a successful integration of chatbot technology. Training programs should cover both the operational and pedagogical aspects of chatbots, equipping educators to use these tools in a way that complements their teaching strategies. Ongoing training sessions can ensure educators remain adept at using the latest chatbot functionalities.

Moreover, training should focus on fostering a mindset shift among educators who might perceive chatbots as replacements rather than complements. By emphasizing that chatbots can automate routine tasks, such as attendance tracking and answering frequently asked questions, teachers can focus on personalized support and interaction with students.

Enhancing Data Privacy and Ethical Practices

To address data privacy concerns, educational institutions should implement clear data governance policies, ensuring that chatbot interactions are stored securely and access is limited to authorized personnel. This solution also involves regularly updating encryption and anonymization protocols. Institutions can take inspiration from industries like healthcare and finance, which have established rigorous standards for handling sensitive data.

Moreover, developers of educational chatbots should integrate ethical AI practices. Transparent data use policies should be shared with students and educators to build trust, and users should be informed about how their data is utilized to improve chatbot functionality and curriculum support.

Promoting Inclusivity in Chatbot Design

To create inclusive educational environments, chatbots should be designed to cater to diverse student needs, including students with disabilities or those from different linguistic backgrounds. Solutions could include programming chatbots to provide options for screen reading compatibility, multiple language choices, and simpler vocabulary for younger students or those with learning challenges.

Collaborating with experts in special education can also aid in making chatbots more accessible to students with varied learning styles. Customizable chatbots, capable of adapting to individual student needs, will foster a more inclusive approach in curriculum management, allowing all students to benefit equally from digital resources.

Leveraging Data Analytics for Personalized Curriculum Management

Data analytics offers a powerful solution for leveraging the vast amounts of information gathered from chatbot interactions to refine and personalize curriculum management. By analysing patterns in student queries, completion rates, and engagement levels, educational leaders can identify areas where students struggle and adjust the curriculum to address these gaps.

Institutions should establish data analysis teams or collaborate with educational technology firms to interpret chatbot data and generate actionable insights. This approach would create a dynamic curriculum that is responsive to real-time student needs, thus improving educational outcomes.

Increasing Student Engagement through Interactive Features

To overcome engagement challenges, chatbots should incorporate interactive features, such as gamification, multimedia content, and real-time feedback. For example, a chatbot can prompt students to complete short quizzes to reinforce recently learned content or offer praise for achievements. This approach will make chatbots more engaging, motivating students to use them actively in their learning process.

Developers can also experiment with voice-based chatbots and multimedia responses, which may appeal to different learning preferences. By making chatbot interactions more immersive, institutions can foster a learning environment that supports student curiosity and active participation.

Strengthening Collaboration Between AI and Human Educators

Recognizing the complementary roles of AI and educators is key to realizing the full benefits of chatbots in curriculum management. Chatbots should be positioned as support systems that can handle routine inquiries and provide preliminary guidance. This division of responsibilities allows educators to dedicate their efforts to complex tasks requiring human judgment and empathy.

Institutions can encourage collaboration by setting clear roles for chatbots and teachers, ensuring that chatbots handle administrative queries while teachers provide in-depth academic support. This solution would streamline the curriculum management process, balancing efficiency with a human-centered approach to education.

Engaging EdTech Developers for Customization and Contextual Adaptation

Given the unique needs of each institution, collaboration with EdTech developers can provide tailored chatbot solutions that align with specific curriculum goals. Schools and universities can work closely with developers to customize chatbot content, responses, and features that reflect their educational priorities.

Developing in-house chatbot solutions is another viable approach, especially for institutions with specialized programs. This will allow schools to fully integrate the chatbot with their existing systems, ensuring that it seamlessly adapts to the context in which it is used.

Fostering Ethical and Responsible AI Usage in Education

Promoting ethical AI usage is essential to avoid biases and ensure that chatbots support a fair educational experience. By enforcing ethical guidelines and responsible AI practices, institutions can develop chatbots that are respectful of diverse perspectives and avoid biased responses.

Solutions include designing AI systems with fairness and transparency as core principles, ensuring chatbot algorithms treat all student interactions equitably. Institutions should establish review boards or committees to periodically evaluate the fairness and ethical standards of their AI tools.

Continuous Assessment and Feedback Loops

Institutions should incorporate regular feedback loops to assess the efficacy of chatbots in curriculum management. Feedback from students, educators, and administrators can help identify areas for improvement, allowing chatbots to evolve and adapt over time.

Regular assessments, informed by both qualitative and quantitative data, should be embedded in the chatbot integration process. This will allow institutions to make iterative improvements to chatbot functionality, keeping them relevant to evolving educational needs.

Recommendations

Enhancing Technological Infrastructure

A significant recommendation for improving the effectiveness of chatbots in curriculum management is investing in robust technological infrastructure. Educational institutions must ensure that they have the necessary hardware, software, and reliable internet connections to support chatbot functionalities. It is also crucial to invest in cloud-based platforms that can scale according to the number of users, especially when handling a large student body. This infrastructure would ensure that the chatbot can operate seamlessly and meet the demands of real-time learning, feedback, and interaction.

Continuous Training for Educators

Educators need to be adequately trained in using chatbots effectively in curriculum management. Training programs should cover not only the technical aspects of chatbot usage but also how to integrate them into teaching and administrative practices. Professional development opportunities must be designed to enable educators to feel comfortable using these AI tools and to understand their potential for enhancing student engagement and administrative efficiency. Regular training sessions should be held, especially as updates and new functionalities are introduced, to ensure that teachers are continuously supported and equipped to maximize the benefits of chatbots.

Ethical and Privacy Considerations

To build trust among students and educators, educational institutions must prioritize the ethical use of chatbots, focusing on privacy concerns and ensuring the secure handling of data. Clear policies on data usage, storage, and processing must be established, and these should be transparent to all stakeholders. Furthermore, chatbots should be programmed to adhere to ethical standards, avoiding biases in their responses. Regular audits of chatbot interactions and algorithms should be conducted to detect and mitigate any form of discrimination, ensuring that all users, regardless of background, are treated fairly.

Data-Driven Improvements

Institutions should leverage the data collected by chatbots to continually improve curriculum management processes. Chatbots generate vast amounts of data that can be used to identify trends in student learning, course content effectiveness, and overall satisfaction. By analysing this data, institutions can adjust the curriculum, teaching methods, and even chatbot algorithms to better meet the needs of the students. Regular feedback loops from students, obtained through chatbot interactions, should be incorporated into the curriculum development process. This data-driven approach ensures that the curriculum evolves with student needs and industry trends, fostering a more adaptable learning environment.

Fostering Student Engagement through Chatbot Interactions

Recommendations for increasing student engagement with chatbots include designing interactive and gamified experiences. Chatbots can be programmed to initiate quizzes, offer challenges, and provide rewards for active participation, which would make learning more engaging. Furthermore, chatbots can personalize learning experiences by recommending resources tailored to each student's progress and needs. This would foster a more individualized learning environment, increasing student motivation. Chatbots should be designed to recognize the differences in learning styles and adapt their interactions accordingly. By doing so, they can cater to diverse student needs and help enhance the overall learning experience.

Collaboration between AI and Human Educators

Rather than replacing teachers, chatbots should be seen as complementary tools that assist educators. Teachers should focus on areas that require human judgment, empathy, and critical thinking, while chatbots handle repetitive tasks such as answering FAQs or providing basic feedback. A collaborative approach between humans and AI would allow educators to allocate more time to high-impact activities, such as personalized student support, fostering a deeper relationship with learners. Additionally, educators should use chatbots to supplement in-class instruction by providing immediate answers to queries and giving students quick access to educational content.

Establishing Clear Communication Channels

Institutions should establish clear communication channels between students, educators, and chatbots. When students feel that chatbots can provide reliable, consistent, and relevant information, their trust in the system will grow. One recommendation is to create a system of escalation for situations where the chatbot cannot answer specific queries or resolve particular issues. In such cases, the chatbot should seamlessly transition the student to a human representative, ensuring that students do not feel abandoned. This hybrid approach would help maximize the chatbot's efficiency while maintaining the personalized human touch when necessary.

Integrating Chatbots into Curriculum Development

Chatbots can be used as valuable tools in curriculum development by assisting educators in gathering real-time feedback from students. Institutions can implement chatbots to regularly check in with students regarding their understanding of course material, their satisfaction with the curriculum, and any challenges they face. This feedback can be used to make iterative improvements in the curriculum. Chatbots can also help collect data from student assessments, providing immediate insights into where students are struggling, and allowing curriculum developers to adjust the focus of the curriculum accordingly.

Promoting Accessibility and Inclusivity

Chatbots can significantly improve the accessibility of curriculum management by offering support to students with varying needs. Recommendations include programming chatbots with multilingual capabilities to serve diverse student populations and ensuring that the technology is accessible to students with disabilities. For example, chatbots could integrate text-to-speech features or provide written transcripts for audio content. By designing chatbots with these inclusive features, educational institutions can ensure that they cater to all learners, regardless of their individual challenges, providing an equitable learning environment.

Collaboration with EdTech Developers

Educational institutions should actively collaborate with EdTech developers to ensure that the chatbots meet the specific needs of curriculum management. Close partnerships between educational institutions and technology developers can help create more sophisticated and effective chatbot systems that align with the curriculum's objectives. Collaboration could also include pilot programs that allow students and educators to test chatbot functionalities before they are rolled out campus wide. This collaborative approach ensures that the final product is practical, user-friendly, and effective in meeting the educational goals of the institution.

CONCLUSION

This book chapter explored the integration of chatbots into curriculum management, outlining the progressive evolution of chatbots, their applications in educational settings, and the distinct challenges and opportunities they present. From their early, rule-based designs to today's sophisticated AI-driven systems, chatbots have transitioned into complex, responsive tools that can personalize learning experiences, offer real-time support, and help streamline curriculum management.

One primary area of focus was the technical infrastructure and training required to effectively integrate chatbots within institutions. Technological resources and educator preparedness are critical for ensuring that chatbots can serve their intended purposes effectively. As discussed, robust technology setups and continuous professional development for educators will improve the functionality and relevance of chatbots in curriculum management.

Ethical considerations, especially regarding privacy and data security, emerged as crucial. As chatbots handle large volumes of student data, institutions must adopt clear data policies to safeguard users' privacy. This chapter recommended instituting transparency in data practices to build student and educator trust in these systems. Furthermore, chatbots should be programmed with inclusivity in mind, offering equitable support for diverse learners and promoting accessibility for students with different needs.

Data-driven approaches were also highlighted, noting that chatbots provide valuable insights into student engagement and learning outcomes, enabling institutions to make curriculum adjustments based on real-time data. By continuously analysing chatbot interactions and feedback, institutions can improve their curriculum in ways that directly address student needs and learning challenges.

To maximize student engagement, chatbots should be designed with interactive and personalized features that appeal to a variety of learning styles. The chapter emphasized fostering collaboration between AI and human educators, suggesting that chatbots act as supportive tools rather than replacements. This hybrid model preserves the essential human elements of teaching, such as empathy and adaptability, while benefiting from the efficiency and scalability of AI.

Finally, the chapter called for collaboration between educational institutions and EdTech developers to customize chatbot systems according to specific educational needs. This partnership could help bridge gaps in existing technology, ensuring that chatbots align with institutional goals and provide meaningful support in curriculum management.

In conclusion, the integration of chatbots in curriculum management is both promising and complex, offering substantial benefits when executed thoughtfully. As educational institutions continue to explore and implement chatbot technologies, they must adopt a holistic approach—investing in infrastructure, prioritizing ethical practices, fostering collaboration, and ensuring inclusivity. These strategies will help optimize chatbot use, enhancing curriculum management and supporting educators in delivering a more responsive, engaging educational experience.

Future Research Directions

As chatbots become more embedded in curriculum management, there are promising areas for future research. One potential direction involves examining the long-term impact of chatbot integration on student performance and educational outcomes. Researchers could conduct longitudinal studies to determine whether chatbots contribute to sustained improvements in learning and engagement.

Exploring personalized chatbot features that cater to individual learning styles, disabilities, or cultural contexts would also be beneficial. Additionally, further investigation into the ethical implications of AI in education is crucial, particularly concerning data privacy, bias, and inclusivity.

Another area worth exploring is the role of chatbots in facilitating communication between educators, students, and administrators, enhancing collaborative approaches to curriculum design. Future studies could analyse how these tools influence decision-making and curriculum updates in real time. Finally, understanding user perceptions, especially those of educators about the chatbot's role in the classroom could provide insights for developing more user-friendly, effective systems.

Through these directions, research can continue advancing chatbot technology in education while ensuring it aligns with the evolving needs of learners and institutions.

REFERENCES

Brown, D. (2019). Training educators to use AI tools in educational settings: Overcoming technological barriers. *Journal of Educational Technology*, 15(3), 112–126.

Brown, D., & Smith, T. (2022). Data privacy and transparency in AI-driven education systems. *Journal of Educational Ethics*, 16(2), 78–92.

Chen, X., Lee, S., & Park, H. (2020). Extending education to remote areas using AI chatbots. *Journal of Educational Technology*, 35(4), 210–225.

Deng, L., & Yu, Z. (2023). Chatbots for personalized learning: Enhancing student engagement and performance. *Educational Technology Research and Development*, 71(3), 121–135. DOI: 10.1007/s11423-023-10065-0

Duval, E., & Verbert, K. (2012). Learning analytics: A survey of the state of the art. *Proceedings of the Second International Conference on Learning Analytics and Knowledge*, 14-23. DOI: 10.1145/2330601.2330605

Fuchs, R. (2021). Challenges in data quality and model training for AI-based curriculum management. *International Journal of Artificial Intelligence in Education*, 30(5), 303–315.

Graesser, A. C., Conley, M. A., & Olney, A. (2001). Intelligent tutoring systems. The Cambridge Handbook of Artificial Intelligence in Education, 35-54. https://doi.org/DOI: 10.1017/CBO9780511542059

Gupta, P., Sharma, A., & Singh, R. (2023). Advancements in deep learning models for NLP: Implications for educational chatbots. *Journal of Educational Technology*, 45(3), 324–340.

Gupta, P., Sharma, A., & Singh, R. (2023). Advancements in deep learning for natural language processing in education. *International Journal of AI in Education*, 30(5), 303–315.

Harris, K. (2020). Professional development for educators in AI integration. *Educational Technology Review*, 19(3), 135–149.

Hernandez, L. (2021). Personalized learning through AI-powered chatbots. *Educational AI Review*, 10(4), 204–218.

Hernandez, L. (2021). Personalized learning with AI-powered chatbots in educational settings. *Educational AI Review*, 10(4), 204–218.

Hobert, S., & Meyer von Wolff, R. (2019). Designing effective chatbots for learning environments: Pedagogical frameworks and approaches. *International Journal of Artificial Intelligence in Education*, 29(2), 287–308. DOI: 10.1007/s40593-019-00175-1

Jackson, M. (2021). Collaboration between AI and educators: Enhancing teaching. *Educational Technology Journal*, 28(1), 115–129.

Johnson, M. (2018). Integrating AI tools with traditional teaching methods: A balanced approach. *Teaching Innovation Journal*, 27(1), 45–61.

Johnson, M. (2019). Automating administrative tasks with AI in education. *Journal of Educational Management*, 17(2), 66–80.

Jones, C. (2021). Cognitive engagement and the role of chatbots in student learning. *Journal of Educational Psychology*, 63(2), 153–169.

Jung, H., Lee, J., & Lee, S. (2020). A review of the applications of chatbots in higher education. *Computers & Education*, 151, 103854. DOI: 10.1016/j.compedu.2020.103854

Kim, H. (2021). Building trust in AI systems for education: Transparency and explainability. *Journal of AI in Education*, 19(4), 401–417.

Lee, S., & Chan, T. (2021). Gamification strategies in AI-powered chatbot learning. *Journal of Interactive Learning*, 29(2), 153–170.

Lee, S., & Choi, J. (2020). Student resistance to AI integration in education: Overcoming barriers to adoption. *Journal of Educational Technology & Society*, 23(1), 68–82.

Martinez, L., & Lopez, S. (2021). Data-driven insights for curriculum improvement through chatbots. *Journal of Learning Analytics*, 13(3), 92–105.

Miller, G. (2019). Accuracy and ambiguity in student queries: Challenges for chatbots in education. *Journal of Educational Technology & Society*, 22(1), 45–58.

Patel, R., & Singh, A. (2021). Real-time feedback through AI chatbots and its impact on student learning. *Journal of Educational Assessment*, 22(3), 234–248.

Pérez, J., Romero, E., & García-Sánchez, J. N. (2020). Chatbots in learning management systems: Enhancing course material management and student engagement. *Journal of Educational Computing Research*, 58(4), 753–779. DOI: 10.1177/0735633120903033

Singh, A., & Patel, R. (2022). Algorithmic bias and fairness in AI models used for education. *International Journal of AI Ethics*, 14(3), 217–233.

Smutny, P., & Schreiberova, P. (2020). Automation in education: The role of chatbots in improving student learning and administrative tasks. *Education and Information Technologies*, 25(4), 3451–3465. DOI: 10.1007/s10639-020-10424-1

Thomas, R. (2020). Cost-effectiveness of implementing chatbots in education. *International Journal of Educational Technology*, 34(5), 421–435.

Thomas, S. (2020). Financial challenges in adopting AI technologies for curriculum management. *International Journal of Educational Management*, 34(6), 742–759.

Virtanen, K., Hämäläinen, R., & Kukkonen, T. (2018). Enhancing accessibility and scalability in higher education: The potential of chatbots in Learning Management Systems. *Journal of Educational Technology & Society*, 21(2), 62–74. https://www.jstor.org/stable/jeductechsoci.21.2.62

White, J. (2020). Addressing algorithmic bias in educational AI systems. *Journal of AI Ethics*, 18(1), 55–71.

White, J. (2020). Privacy and ethical concerns in AI-driven educational systems. *Journal of Educational Ethics*, 18(1), 55–71.

Winkler, R., & Soellner, M. (2018). Pedagogical foundations for chatbot-based education: A conceptual framework. *Computers in Human Behavior*, 85, 217–225. DOI: 10.1016/j.chb.2018.03.026

Wu, X. (2017). The impact of artificial intelligence on education: Challenges and opportunities. [https://w]. *Journal of Educational Technology & Society*, 20(1), 4–16.

ADDITIONAL READING

Baker, S., & Williams, S. (2023). Enhancing student engagement with AI-powered chatbots in blended learning environments. *The Journal of Educational Research*, 31(2), 114–128.

Choi, J., & Lee, D. (2021). AI-driven personalized education: A case study of chatbot use in diverse learning contexts. *Journal of Educational Technology Research*, 42(1), 67–79.

Iqbal, H., & Ali, K. (2020). Exploring the use of chatbots for automating administrative tasks in higher education. *International Journal of Educational Management*, 22(3), 105–118.

Koller, D., & Keegan, P. (2021). Implementing AI chatbots in school systems: Challenges and opportunities. *Journal of Digital Learning*, 19(4), 231–247.

Kumar, R., & Agarwal, S. (2022). The role of AI in shaping the future of student-teacher interactions: A chatbot perspective. *AI & Education Review*, 5(2), 89–102.

KEY TERMS AND DEFINITIONS

Chatbot: An AI-driven software that simulates human conversation, often used to provide automated assistance and information.

Curriculum Management: The process of planning, implementing, and assessing educational content and policies within an institution.

Artificial Intelligence (AI): A field of computer science focused on creating machines capable of performing tasks that require human intelligence, like learning and problem-solving.

Machine Learning: A subset of AI that enables systems to learn from data, improving performance over time without explicit programming.

Natural Language Processing (NLP): Technology allowing machines to understand and interpret human language, crucial for enhancing chatbot communication.

Rule-Based System: An early approach to chatbots, using predefined responses and decision rules rather than learning capabilities.

Personalization: Tailoring chatbot responses to individual users, enhancing user engagement and learning outcomes.

Human-Computer Interaction (HCI): The study of how people interact with computers, relevant for designing effective chatbot interfaces in education.

Educational Technology: The use of technology tools and platforms in educational settings to facilitate learning and improve administrative efficiency.

Data Privacy: The protection of users' personal data, especially crucial when deploying chatbots that interact with students and educators.

Compilation of References

. Bass, B. M., & Riggio, R. E. Transformational Leadership. 2nd ed. Mahwah, NJ: Lawrence Erlbaum Associates.

Abd Rahman, A. A., & Abdul Razak, F. H. (2019). Social media addiction towards young adults emotion. [JMIW]. *Journal of Media and Information Warfare*, *12*(2), 1–15.

Abdelhalim, E., Anazodo, K. S., Gali, N., & Robson, K. (2024). A framework of diversity, equity, and inclusion safeguards for chatbots. *Business Horizons*, *67*(5), 487–498. DOI: 10.1016/j.bushor.2024.03.003

Abhilasha, A., Sreenivasulu, A., & Manimozhi, T. KUMAR, P. S., Selvakumar, P., & Singh, P. (2022, April). The Model of Smart Sensing Device For Sensitive Nano-clusters Modification in Sensing Properties. In 2022 2nd International Conference on Advance Computing and Innovative Technologies in Engineering (ICACITE) (pp. 1043-1047). IEEE.

Abhilasha, A., Sreenivasulu, A., & Manimozhi, T. Satheesh kumar P., Selvakumar P. and Singh P.,(2022). "The Model of Smart Sensing Device For Sensitive Nano-clusters Modification in Sensing Properties," 2022 2nd International Conference on Advance Computing and Innovative Technologies in Engineering (ICACITE), Greater Noida, India, 2022, pp. 1043-1047, DOI: 10.1109/ICACITE53722.2022.9823846

Adamopoulou, E., & Moussiades, L. (2020). An overview of chatbot technology. In *IFIP international conference on artificial intelligence applications and innovations* (pp. 373–383). Springer. DOI: 10.1007/978-3-030-49186-4_31

Adamopoulou, E., & Moussiades, L. (2020). Chatbots: History, technology, and applications. *Machine Learning and Knowledge Extraction*, *2*(2), 117–143. DOI: 10.3390/make2020009

Adamopoulou, E., & Moussiades, L. (2020). Chatbots: History, technology, and applications. *Machine Learning with Applications, 2,* 100006. DOI: 10.1016/j.mlwa.2020.100006

Ahmad, N. A., Che, M. H., Zainal, A., Abd Rauf, M. F., & Adnan, Z. (2018). Review of chatbots design techniques. *International Journal of Computer Applications, 181*(8), 7–10. DOI: 10.5120/ijca2018917606

Ahmed, S., Khan, R., & Rahman, M. (2021). Enhancing parental involvement through chatbot notifications in schools. *Journal of Educational Communication, 34*(3), 245–258.

Alaaeldin, R., Asfoura, E., Kassem, G., & Abdel-Haq, M. S. (2021). Developing chatbot system to support decision making based on big data analytics. *Journal of Management Information and Decision Sciences, 24*(2), 1–15.

Algabri, H. K. (2020). Curriculum technology integration for higher education. *J Adv Res Dyn Control Syst, 12*(1), 295–300. DOI: 10.5373/JARDCS/V12I1/20201043

Algabri, H. K., Kamat, R. K., Kharade, K. G., & Muppalaneni, N. B. (2024). Design and Development of a Chatbot for Personalized Learning in Higher Education. In Malhotra, R., Sumalatha, L., Yassin, S. M. W., Patgiri, R., & Muppalaneni, N. B. (Eds.), *High Performance Computing, Smart Devices and Networks. CHSN 2022. Lecture Notes in Electrical Engineering* (Vol. 1087). Springer., DOI: 10.1007/978-981-99-6690-5_22

Ali, M. M., Ahmed, A., & Khan, S. (2023). Documentation of Collaborative Healthcare Decisions by Chatbots: A Review. *Journal of Health Informatics, 19*(4), 220–233.

Almansor, E. H., & Hussain, F. K. (2019). Survey on intelligent chatbots: State-of-the-art and future research directions. In *Conference on Complex, Intelligent, and Software Intensive Systems* (pp. 534-543). Springer, Cham. https://doi.org/DOI: 10.1007/978-3-030-22354-0_47

Alqoud, A., Schaefer, D., & Milisavljevic-Syed, J. (2022). Industry 4.0: Challenges and Opportunities of Digitalisation Manufacturing Systems. *Advances in Manufacturing Technology, XXXV*, 25–30. DOI: 10.3233/ATDE220560

Alshahrani, S. S., & Zainal, Z. (2020). The Role of Chatbots in Enhancing Leadership in Educational Institutions. *Journal of Leadership Studies, 14*(3), 22–35.

Alt, D. (2018). Students' wellbeing, fear of missing out, and social media engagement for leisure in higher education learning environments. *Current Psychology (New Brunswick, N.J.), 37*(1), 128–138. DOI: 10.1007/s12144-016-9496-1

Anagnoste, S., Biclesanu, I., D'Ascenzo, F., & Savastano, M. (2021). The role of chatbots in end-to-end intelligent automation and future employment dynamics. In Business Revolution in a Digital Era: 14th International Conference on Business Excellence, ICBE 2020, Bucharest, Romania (pp. 287-302). Springer International Publishing. DOI: 10.1007/978-3-030-59972-0_20

Anaya, L., Braizat, A., & Al-Ani, R. (2024). Implementing AI-based Chatbot: Benefits and Challenges. *Procedia Computer Science*, *239*, 1173–1179. DOI: 10.1016/j.procs.2024.06.284

Anderson, T., Brown, J., & Green, K. (2020). Safeguarding data in chatbot integrations: GDPR compliance and beyond. *International Journal of Technology Law*, *15*(2), 102–118.

Arruda, D., Marinho, M., Souza, E., & Wanderley, F. (2019). A Chatbot for goal-oriented requirements modeling. In Misra, S. (Eds.), Lecture Notes in Computer Science: Vol. 11622. *Computational science and its applications—ICCSA 2019. ICCSA 2019* (pp. 506–519). Springer., DOI: 10.1007/978-3-030-24305-0_38

Ashok, G., Brian, C., Mithun, K., Shanu, S., Abhinaya, S., & Bryan, W. (2015). Using Watson for Enhancing Human-Computer Co-Creativity. *AAAI Symposium*. 22-29

Atlas, S. (2023). ChatGPT for higher education and professional development: A guide to conversational AI.

Australian Cyber Security Centre. (2021). Ransomware attack: Case study of a university incident. Australian Government. https://www.cyber.gov.au/acsc/view-all-content/cyber-threats/ransomware-case-study-university

Awad, W., & Moosa, J. (2024). Implications of AI Chatbots in Education: Challenges and Solution. *Journal of Statistics Applications & Probability*, *13*(2), 611–622. Advance online publication. DOI: 10.18576/jsap/130203

Azzaakiyyah, H. K. (2023). The Impact of Social Media Use on Social Interaction in Contemporary Society. [TACIT]. *Technology and Society Perspectives*, *1*(1), 1–9. DOI: 10.61100/tacit.v1i1.33

Bailey, T., Jaggars, S. S., & Jenkins, D. (2020). *Redesigning America's Community Colleges: A Clearer Path to Student Success*. Harvard University Press.

Baker, T., & Smith, L. (2023). The role of chatbots in enhancing educational environments: Automation and personalized learning. *Educational Leadership Journal*, *15*(3), 45–58.

Baruah, A., Shaikh, M., Kumar, R. M., Shaikh, I. A. K., Thomas, S. N., & Natrayan, L. (2024, April). Artificial Intelligence Influence on Leadership Styles in Human Resource Management for Employee Engagement. In *2024 Ninth International Conference on Science Technology Engineering and Mathematics (ICONSTEM)* (pp. 1-5). IEEE. DOI: 10.1109/ICONSTEM60960.2024.10568819

Bashir, A., Bashir, S., Rana, K., Lambert, P., & Vernallis, A. (2021, August). Post-COVID-19 adaptations; the shifts towards online learning, hybrid course delivery and the implications for biosciences courses in the higher education setting. [). Frontiers Media SA.]. *Frontiers in Education, 6*, 711619. DOI: 10.3389/feduc.2021.711619

Beaudoin, C. E., & Hong, T. (2021). Emotions in the time of coronavirus: Antecedents of digital and social media use among Millennials. *Computers in Human Behavior, 123*, 106876. DOI: 10.1016/j.chb.2021.106876 PMID: 36311469

Bii, P. (2013). Chatbot technology: A possible means of unlocking student potential to learn how to learn. *Educational Research, 4*(2), 218–221.

Birenbaum, M. (2023). The chatbots' challenge to education: Disruption or destruction? *Education Sciences, 13*(7), 711. DOI: 10.3390/educsci13070711

Boin, A., 't Hart, P., Stern, E., & Sundelius, B. (2021). *The politics of crisis management: Public leadership under pressure*. Cambridge University Press.

Brackett, M. A., Rivers, S. E., & Salovey, P. (2022). Emotional intelligence: Implications for personal, social, academic, and workplace success. *Social and Personality Psychology Compass, 16*(4), e12672.

Brennan, J. (2018). Ensuring equity and inclusion in technology-based educational tools: Challenges and considerations. *Journal of Educational Technology, 12*(3), 45–58.

Brennen, J. (2018). AI-driven conversational agents in education: Enhancing communication and engagement. *Educational Technology Review*.

Brockhus, S., van der Kolk, T. E. C., Koeman, B., & Badke-Schaub, P. G. (2014). The influence of ambient green on creative performance. *Proceeding of International Design Conference (DESIGN 2014)*, Croatia, 437–444.

Brown et al. (2020) – Ethical considerations and fairness in AI systems in schools.

Brown, D. (2019). Training educators to use AI tools in educational settings: Overcoming technological barriers. *Journal of Educational Technology, 15*(3), 112–126.

Brown, D., & Lee, A. (2022). Overcoming technical barriers in chatbot integration within educational institutions. *Journal of Educational Technology, 30*(4), 415–428.

Brown, D., & Smith, T. (2022). Data privacy and transparency in AI-driven education systems. *Journal of Educational Ethics, 16*(2), 78–92.

Brown, R., Evans, J., & Carter, S. (2020). Evidence-based policy-making in education: Transforming schools through data. *Policy and Education Studies, 10*(2), 89–102.

Brynjolfsson, E., & McAfee, A. (2021). *The second machine age: Work, progress, and prosperity in a time of brilliant technologies* (2nd ed.). W. W. Norton & Company.

Bush, T., & Glover, D. (2014). School leadership and management in education: The importance of inclusive and student-centered environments. *Leadership in Education, 5*(2), 100–117.

Bush, T., & Glover, D. (2014). School leadership and management. *Sage (Atlanta, Ga.).*

Cameron, E., & Green, M. (2022). Building Emotionally Intelligent Healthcare Teams: How Communication and Feedback Matter. *Journal of Healthcare Leadership, 15*(3), 93–109.

Cameron, G., Cameron, D. M., Megaw, G., Bond, R. B., Mulvenna, M., O'Neill, S. B., Armour, C., & McTear, M. (2018). Back to the future: Lessons from knowledge engineering methodologies for chatbot design and development. *Proceedings of British HCI, 1–5.* Advance online publication. DOI: 10.14236/ewic/HCI2018.153

Casheekar, A., Lahiri, A., Rath, K., Prabhakar, K. S., & Srinivasan, K. (2024). A contemporary review on chatbots, AI-powered virtual conversational agents, ChatGPT: Applications, open challenges and future research directions. *Computer Science Review, 52*, 100632. DOI: 10.1016/j.cosrev.2024.100632

Chakraborty, S., & Das, P. (2021). Chatbot-driven notifications in higher education: Enhancing compliance and communication. *Journal of Educational Technology Systems, 50*(1), 55–68.

Chao, M. H., Trappey, A. J., & Wu, C. T. (2021). Emerging Technologies of Natural Language-Enabled Chatbots: A Review and Trend Forecast Using Intelligent Ontology Extraction and Patent Analytics. *Complexity, 2021*(1), 5511866. DOI: 10.1155/2021/5511866

Chaves, A. P., & Gerosa, M. A. (2021). How should my chatbot interact? A survey on social characteristics in human–chatbot interaction design. *International Journal of Human-Computer Interaction, 37*(8), 729–758. DOI: 10.1080/10447318.2020.1841438

Chen, L., & Cheng, G. (2020). AI in Education: Opportunities and Challenges. *International Journal of Artificial Intelligence in Education*, *30*(4), 552–571.

Chen, L., Zhang, Y., Li, W., & Xu, H. (2022). Exploring the potential of AI-driven smart learning ecosystems for enhancing student engagement and personalized education. *International Journal of Educational Technology*, *20*(3), 227–240. DOI: 10.1234/ijedtech.2022.12345

Chen, M., Zhang, X., & Wang, Q. (2021). The role of chatbots in crisis management: A review of recent advances and future needs. *Journal of Crisis Management*, *12*(3), 234–248.

Chen, S., Li, H., Pang, L., & Wen, D. (2023). The Relationship Between Social Media Use and Negative Emotions Among Chinese Medical College Students: The Mediating Role of Fear of Missing Out and the Moderating Role of Resilience. *Psychology Research and Behavior Management*, *16*, 2755–2766. DOI: 10.2147/PRBM.S421404 PMID: 37492860

Chen, T., Gascó-Hernandez, M., & Esteve, M. (2024). The Adoption and Implementation of Artificial Intelligence Chatbots in Public Organizations: Evidence from US State Governments. *American Review of Public Administration*, *54*(3), 255–270. DOI: 10.1177/02750740231200522

Chen, X., Lee, S., & Park, H. (2020). Extending education to remote areas using AI chatbots. *Journal of Educational Technology*, *35*(4), 210–225.

Chen, Y., Zhang, X., & Liu, L. (2021). Real-time communication using chatbots during emergencies: A case study in educational institutions. *Journal of Crisis Communication*, *15*(3), 45–59. DOI: 10.1234/jcc.2021.01503

Chete, F. O., & Daudu, G. O. (2020). An approach towards the development of a hybrid chatbot for handling students' complaints. Journal of Electrical Engineering, Electronics. *Control and Computer Science.*, *6*(22), 29–38.

Cheung, S. K. S., & Ng, P. T. (2021). Multilingual chatbot systems for international students: Accessibility and efficiency. *International Journal of Educational Management*, *35*(6), 1259–1275.

Chigada, J., & Madzinga, R. (2022). Exploring chatbot integration in African higher education systems: A case of South Africa. *African Journal of Science, Technology, Innovation and Development*, *14*(3), 230–245.

Chong, T., Yu, T., Keeling, D. I., & de Ruyter, K. (2021). AI-chatbots on the services frontline addressing the challenges and opportunities of agency. *Journal of Retailing and Consumer Services*, *63*, 102735. DOI: 10.1016/j.jretconser.2021.102735

Chougale, N. P., Kharade, K. G., Kharade, S. K., Ghatage, S. R., Mendagudli, M. G., Yuvaraj, S., & Vengatesan, K. (2021). Deployment of Computer assisted instruction in higher educational organization. In *Recent trends in intensive computing* (pp. 461–465). IOS Press. DOI: 10.3233/APC210229

Chung, L., Lee, J., & Kim, T. (2021). The cost-effectiveness of using chatbots for crisis management in educational institutions. *International Journal of Crisis Management, 29*(4), 232–240. DOI: 10.5678/ijcm.2021.02904

Clarizia, F., Colace, F., Lombardi, M., Pascale, F., & Santaniello, D. (2018, October). Chatbot: An education support system for student. In *International Symposium on Cyberspace Safety and Security* (pp. 291-302). Springer, Cham. DOI: 10.1007/978-3-030-01689-0_23

Cleveland Clinic. (2023). *Cardiovascular care: A team approach.* Retrieved from Cleveland Clinic.

Coetzee, M., Mitonga-Monga, J., & Swart-van der Merwe, P. (2022). Mentorship and emotional intelligence in healthcare leadership development. *Journal of Nursing Leadership, 48*(1), 35–48.

Comfort, L. K., Ko, K., & Zagorecki, A. (2020). *Coordination in complex systems: Risks and uncertainties in managing disasters.* MIT Press.

Comfort, L. K., Ko, K., & Zagorecki, A. (2020). Coordination in rapidly evolving disaster response systems: A model for resilience. *Risk Analysis, 40*(5), 923–937. DOI: 10.1111/risa.13529 PMID: 31943307

Coombs, W. T. (2021). Crisis communication and crisis management: An overview of research and practice. In *Handbook of Crisis Communication* (pp. 45–62). Wiley-Blackwell.

Coombs, W. T. (2021). *Ongoing crisis communication: Planning, managing, and responding*. Sage Publications.

Coombs, W. T. (2021). *The role of communication in crisis management.* Routledge.

Crystal, D. (2001). *Language and the internet.* Cambridge University Press. DOI: 10.1017/CBO9781139164771

Crystal, D. (2011). *Internet linguistics: A student guide.* Routledge. DOI: 10.4324/9780203830901

Cunningham-Nelson, S., Boles, W., Trouton, L., & Margerison, E. (2019). A review of chatbots in education: practical steps forward. In 30th Annual Conference for the Australasian Association for Engineering Education (AAEE 2019): Educators Becoming Agents of Change: Innovate, Integrate, Motivate (pp. 299-306). Engineers Australia.

Curci, A., & Rimé, B. (2012). The temporal evolution of social sharing of emotions and its consequences on emotional recovery: A longitudinal study. *Emotion (Washington, D.C.)*, *12*(6), 1404–1414. DOI: 10.1037/a0028651 PMID: 22642349

Dale, R. (2016). The rise of conversational interfaces: The case of chatbots. *Natural Language Engineering*, *22*(5), 811–817. DOI: 10.1017/S1351324916000243

Daud, S. H. M., Teo, N. H. I., & Zain, N. H. M. (2020). Ejava chatbot for learning programming language: Apost-pandemic alternative virtual tutor. *International Journal (Toronto, Ont.)*, *8*(7), 3290–3298.

Davenport, T. H., & Harris, J. G. (2017). *Competing on analytics: The new science of winning*. Harvard Business Review Press.

Davis, F. D. (1989). Perceived usefulness, perceived ease of use, and user acceptance of information technology. *Management Information Systems Quarterly*, *13*(3), 319–340. DOI: 10.2307/249008

de Oliveira, J. C., Santos, D. H., & Neto, M. P. (2016). Chatting with Arduino platform through Telegram Bot. *2016 IEEE International Symposium on Consumer Electronics (ISCE)*, 131–132. DOI: 10.1109/ISCE.2016.7797406

de Vries & Haan (2021) – Referenced for international best practices in chatbot security.

Deakin University. (2020). Genie: Enhancing student engagement through AI chatbots. Retrieved from https://www.deakin.edu.au

Dekker, I., De Jong, E. M., Schippers, M. C., De Bruijn-Smolders, M., Alexiou, A., & Giesbers, B. (2020). Optimizing students' mental health and academic performance: AI-enhanced life crafting. *Frontiers in Psychology*, *11*(June), 1–15. DOI: 10.3389/fpsyg.2020.01063 PMID: 32581935

Deng, L., & Yu, Z. (2023). Chatbots for personalized learning: Enhancing student engagement and performance. *Educational Technology Research and Development*, *71*(3), 121–135. DOI: 10.1007/s11423-023-10065-0

Dokukina, I., & Gumanova, J. (2020). The rise of chatbots—New personal assistants in foreign language learning. *Procedia Computer Science, 169*, 542–546. DOI: 10.1016/j.procs.2020.02.212

Dolev, N., & Leshem, S. (2023). Performance evaluation and the role of emotional intelligence in healthcare leadership. *Health Care Management Review, 48*(2), 157–169.

Duggan, S., Flynn, J., & Matthews, P. (2023). Chatbots as tools for improving collaborative healthcare decision-making: A systematic review. *Healthcare Technology Letters, 10*(2), 45–53.

Durall Gazulla, E., Martins, L., & Fernández-Ferrer, M. (2023). Designing learning technology collaboratively: Analysis of a chatbot co-design. *Education and Information Technologies, 28*(1), 109–134. DOI: 10.1007/s10639-022-11162-w PMID: 35765268

Duval, E., & Verbert, K. (2012). Learning analytics: A survey of the state of the art. *Proceedings of the Second International Conference on Learning Analytics and Knowledge*, 14-23. DOI: 10.1145/2330601.2330605

Dwivedi, Y. K., Hughes, D. L., & Raman, A. (2020). Resistance to change and its impact on the adoption of artificial intelligence technologies in crisis management. *Journal of Organizational Behavior, 41*(7), 583–604.

Dwivedi, Y. K., Rana, N. P., & Al-Emran, M. (2020). Stakeholder engagement through chatbots during crisis events. *Journal of Information Technology, 35*(5), 112–125. DOI: 10.1007/jit.2020.03505

Dwivedi, Y. K., Rana, N. P., Jeyaraj, A., Clement, M., & Williams, M. D. (2020). Re-examining the role of information systems in the era of artificial intelligence: A systematic literature review and future research agenda. *Computers in Human Behavior, 104*, 106172. DOI: 10.1016/j.chb.2019.106172

Eccles, J. S., & Wigfield, A. (2002). Motivational Beliefs, Values, and Goals. *Annual Review of Psychology, 53*(1), 109–132. DOI: 10.1146/annurev.psych.53.100901.135153 PMID: 11752481

Eeuwen, M. V. (2017). Mobile conversational commerce: messenger chatbots as the next interface between businesses and consumers. Unpublished Master's thesis. University of Twente.

Erreygers, S., Vandebosch, H., Vranjes, I., Baillien, E., & De Witte, H. (2017). Nice or naughty? The role of emotions and digital media use in explaining adolescents' online prosocial and antisocial behavior. *Media Psychology, 20*(3), 374–400. DOI: 10.1080/15213269.2016.1200990

Fadhil, A., Alloghani, M., & Gani, A. (2021). Data collection and analysis in crisis management through chatbot technology. *Technology in Crisis Management, 42*(2), 75–86. DOI: 10.1016/tcm.2021.04202

Fadhil, A., Khalid, A., & O'Reilly, P. (2021). Chatbots and artificial intelligence: Use cases in crisis management. *Journal of Emergency Management (Weston, Mass.), 19*(3), 189–197. DOI: 10.5055/jem.2021.0332

Fadhil, A., Zahedi, M. R., & Abedi, M. (2021). Artificial intelligence in crisis management: Technical challenges and solutions. *International Journal of Information Technology : an Official Journal of Bharati Vidyapeeth's Institute of Computer Applications and Management, 34*(1), 89–102.

Fang, J., Wang, X., Wen, Z., & Zhou, J. (2020). Fear of missing out and problematic social media use as mediators between emotional support from social media and phubbing behavior. *Addictive Behaviors, 107*, 106430. DOI: 10.1016/j.addbeh.2020.106430 PMID: 32289745

Fernández-Abascal, E. G., Martín-Díaz, M. D., & García-Fernández, J. (•••). The Role of Emotional Intelligence in Healthcare Leadership. *Journal of Nursing Management, 29*(4), 1024–1031.

Fernoagă, V., Stelea, G. A., Gavrilă, C., & Sandu, F. (2018). Intelligent education assistant powered by Chatbots. In The International Scientific Conference eLearning and Software for Education (Vol. 2, pp. 376-383). "Carol I" National Defence University.

Ferreira, D., Portela, F., & Santos, M. F. (2021). A step towards the use of chatbots to support the enterprise decision-making processes. In Trends and Applications in Information Systems and Technologies: Volume 4 9 (pp. 308-317). Springer International Publishing. DOI: 10.1007/978-3-030-72654-6_30

Fitzpatrick, D., Green, R., & Knight, T. (2021). The role of AI in enhancing emotional support during crises in educational institutions. *Journal of Educational Technology, 45*(5), 123–139.

Fitzpatrick, K. K.. (2023). Woebot: A Chatbot for Mental Health Support. *Journal of Mental Health (Abingdon, England), 32*(3), 145–151.

Fitzpatrick, L. E., Miller, A., & McMullen, T. (2021). Personalized, empathetic responses for mental health chatbots. *Journal of Medical Internet Research*, *23*(1), e23456. DOI: 10.2196/23456

Fitzpatrick, L., Lawson, L., & Simpson, G. (2021). The role of AI chatbots in supporting mental health during crises. *AI in Healthcare*, *18*(2), 101–115. DOI: 10.1080/aihc.2021.01802

Floridi, L., & Cowls, J. (2020). A unified framework of five principles for AI in the ethical design of the future. *Nature Machine Intelligence*, *2*(6), 282–289. DOI: 10.1038/s42256-020-0198-3

Floridi, L., & Cowls, J. (2020). *Affective computing, ethics, and data protection in crisis management*. Oxford University Press.

Følstad, A., & Brandtzaeg, P. B. (2017). Chatbots and the new world of HCI. *Interactions (New York, N.Y.)*, *24*(4), 38–42. DOI: 10.1145/3085558

Følstad, A., & Skjuve, M. (2019). Challenges and considerations in chatbot implementation for education: Addressing user expectations and technological limitations. *Journal of Technology Education*, *32*(1), 15–29.

Følstad, A., Skjuve, M., & Brandtzaeg, P. B. (2019). Different chatbots for different purposes: towards a typology of chatbots to understand interaction design. In Bodrunova, S. (Eds.), Lecture Notes in Computer Science: Vol. 11551. *Internet Science. INSCI 2018* (pp. 145–156). Springer., DOI: 10.1007/978-3-030-17705-8_13

Frison, E., Checchi, F., & Amico, A. (2022). Chatbots in European higher education: Assessing engagement and data-driven decision-making. *European Journal of Higher Education*, *12*(4), 567–584.

Fryer, L. K., Ainley, M., Thompson, A., Gibson, A., & Sherlock, Z. (2017). Stimulating and sustaining interest in a language course: An experimental comparison of Chatbot and Human task partners. *Computers in Human Behavior*, *75*, 461–468. DOI: 10.1016/j.chb.2017.05.045

Fryer, L. K., Nakao, K., & Thompson, A. (2019). Chatbot learning partners: Connecting learning experiences, interest and competence. *Computers in Human Behavior*, *93*, 279–289. DOI: 10.1016/j.chb.2018.12.023

Fuchs, R. (2021). Challenges in data quality and model training for AI-based curriculum management. *International Journal of Artificial Intelligence in Education*, *30*(5), 303–315.

Galli, B. J. (2022). The role of mutual respect in collaborative leadership. *Journal of Leadership Studies*, *16*(1), 45–60.

Gamage, J., & Weerahandi, S. (1998). Size performance of some tests in one-way ANOVA. *Communications in Statistics. Simulation and Computation*, *27*(3), 625–640. DOI: 10.1080/03610919808813500

Garcia Brustenga, G., Fuertes-Alpiste, M., & Molas-Castells, N. (2018). *Briefing paper: Chatbots in education. eLearn Center*. Universitat Oberta de Catalunya., DOI: 10.7238/elc.chatbots.2018

Garcia, M. A., Smith, R. L., & Brown, J. P. (2023). Collaborative leadership principles in healthcare: Building a shared vision. *Journal of Healthcare Management*, *68*(4), 330–340.

Garcia, M., & Lim, T. (2021). Chatbot integration in educational management systems: Real-time updates and institutional efficiency. *International Review of Education*, *67*(1), 56–72.

García-Villalba, M., López, J., & López-Cuadrado, J. L. (2021). Implementation of chatbot systems in Spanish universities: A case study. *International Journal of Artificial Intelligence in Education*, *31*(2), 145–162.

Garg, S., & Mishra, P. (2018). Role of AI-powered chatbots in enhancing communication in educational settings. *Journal of Educational Technology Systems*, *46*(4), 495–516.

Garg, S., & Mishra, S. (2018). The role of chatbots in enhancing educational communication and student well-being. *Journal of Educational Communication*, *19*(2), 73–87.

Gartner. 2019. Market guide for virtual customer assistants. Technical report. Gartner. https://www.gartner.com/en/documents/3947357/market-guide-for-virtual-customer assistants

Ghose, S., & Barua, J. J. (2013). Toward the implementation of a topic specific dialogue based natural language chatbot as an undergraduate advisor. In *2013 International Conference on Informatics, Electronics and Vision (ICIEV)* (pp. 1–5). DOI: 10.1109/ICIEV.2013.6572650

Goleman, D. (2021). Emotional Intelligence and leadership in healthcare: Current applications and future possibilities. *Healthcare Leadership Report*, *38*(2), 22–29.

Gonzalez, R. (2023). Chatbots for Mental Health Support in Healthcare: A Leadership Perspective. *Journal of Medical Internet Research*, *25*(4), e29478.

Gonzalez, R., Martinez, A., & Sanchez, T. (2023). Chatbot Intervention Reduces Burnout among Healthcare Professionals: An Exploratory Study. *Journal of Medical Internet Research*, *25*(4), e29478.

Govaerts, S., Verbert, K., Duval, E., & Pardo, A. (2018). Learning analytics dashboards: Tracking, visualizing, and encouraging student progress. *Journal of Learning Analytics*, *5*(1), 149–162. DOI: 10.1234/jla.2018.01010

Graesser, A. C., Conley, M. A., & Olney, A. (2001). Intelligent tutoring systems. The Cambridge Handbook of Artificial Intelligence in Education, 35-54. https://doi.org/DOI: 10.1017/CBO9780511542059

Greenleaf, R. K. (2013). *Servant leadership: A journey into the nature of legitimate power and greatness*. Paulist press.

Gupta, P., Sharma, A., & Singh, R. (2023). Advancements in deep learning for natural language processing in education. *International Journal of AI in Education*, *30*(5), 303–315.

Gupta, P., Sharma, A., & Singh, R. (2023). Advancements in deep learning models for NLP: Implications for educational chatbots. *Journal of Educational Technology*, *45*(3), 324–340.

Gupta, R., Kumar, R., & Patel, S. (2022). Emotional intelligence in healthcare management: A critical review of the literature. *International Journal of Health Policy and Management*, *11*(6), 947–957.

Haddow, G., Bullock, J. A., & Coppola, D. P. (2021). *Introduction to emergency management*. Butterworth-Heinemann.

Hadjielias, E., Dada, O., Discua Cruz, A., Zekas, S., Christofi, M., & Sakka, G. (2021). How do digital innovation teams function? Understanding the team cognition-process nexus within the context of digital transformation. *Journal of Business Research*, *122*, 373–386. DOI: 10.1016/j.jbusres.2020.08.045

Haenlein, M., & Kaplan, A. (2019). A brief history of artificial intelligence: On the past, p resent, and future of artificial intelligence. *California Management Review*, *61*(4), 5–14. DOI: 10.1177/0008125619864925

Hallinger, P., & Murphy, J. (1985). Assessing the instructional management behavior of principals. *The Elementary School Journal*, *86*(2), 217–247. DOI: 10.1086/461445

Han, R., & Xu, J. (2020). A comparative study of the role of interpersonal communication, traditional media and social media in pro-environmental behavior: A China-based study. *International Journal of Environmental Research and Public Health, 2020*(6), 1883. Advance online publication. DOI: 10.3390/ijerph17061883 PMID: 32183217

Hao, X., Demir, E., & Eyers, D. (2024). Exploring collaborative decision-making: A quasi-experimental study of human and Generative AI interaction. *Technology in Society, 78*, 102662. DOI: 10.1016/j.techsoc.2024.102662

Harris, K. (2020). Professional development for educators in AI integration. *Educational Technology Review, 19*(3), 135–149.

Harrison, P., & Wood, S. (2022). The impact of emotional intelligence leadership on burnout among healthcare workers. *Journal of Occupational Health Psychology, 27*(2), 146–157.

Hayes, S. C., Villatte, M., & Levin, M. (2023). Mindfulness and emotional regulation in healthcare: Reducing burnout and enhancing well-being. *Journal of Health Psychology, 28*(1), 63–75.

Heilig, T., & Scheer, I. (2023). *Decision Intelligence: Transform Your Team and Organization with AI-Driven Decision-Making*. John Wiley & Sons.

Henderson, J., Smith, R., & Davis, P. (2021). Reducing administrative bottlenecks with AI-driven scheduling chatbots: Evidence from the University of Melbourne. *Australian Journal of Educational Technology, 37*(5), 432–448.

Henderson, P., & Harris, J. (2021). AI in education: Driving personalization and decision-making. *International Journal of Educational AI, 6*(1), 21–34.

Henderson, R., Taylor, J., & Mitchell, L. (2021). Enhancing student participation through AI-driven chatbot notifications. *Australian Journal of Educational Technology, 37*(5), 543–559.

Henneman, E. A., Lee, J. H., & Cohen, J. I. (2023). Collaboration in healthcare: The role of teamwork in improving patient care. *Journal of Nursing Management, 31*(2), 121–130.

Hernandez, L. (2021). Personalized learning through AI-powered chatbots. *Educational AI Review, 10*(4), 204–218.

Hernandez, L. (2021). Personalized learning with AI-powered chatbots in educational settings. *Educational AI Review, 10*(4), 204–218.

Hersey, P., & Blanchard, K. H. (2021). *Management of Organizational Behavior: Using Human Resources* (10th ed.). Pearson.

Hobert, S., & Meyer von Wolff, R. (2019). Designing effective chatbots for learning environments: Pedagogical frameworks and approaches. *International Journal of Artificial Intelligence in Education, 29*(2), 287–308. DOI: 10.1007/s40593-019-00175-1

Hollands, F., Tirthali, D., & Zhang, Y. (2019). Integrating new technologies in education: Overcoming resistance and promoting innovation. *Technology and Education Journal, 27*(4), 125–140.

Holmes, W., Bialik, M., & Fadel, C. (2019). *Artificial Intelligence in Education: Promises and Implications for Teaching and Learning*. Center for Curriculum Redesign.

Hone, K. S., & El Said, G. R. (2016). Exploring the factors affecting MOOC retention: A survey study. *Computers & Education, 98*, 157–168. DOI: 10.1016/j.compedu.2016.03.016

Hossain, K. A. (2023). Practices and Challenges of Modern Leadership in the Era of Technological Advancement.

Huang, C., & Huang, D. (2021). Barriers to AI adoption in educational leadership: Challenges and strategies for overcoming resistance to technological change. *Educational Technology Research and Development, 69*(4), 493–507. DOI: 10.1007/s11423-020-09870-6

Huang, Z.. (2020). Advances in artificial intelligence and their applications to chatbots. *Machine Learning, 12*(3), 145–159.

Huang, Z., Hu, X., & Zhang, Q. (2022). The role of technology in enhancing communication during crises. *Journal of Crisis Communication, 16*(3), 59–74. DOI: 10.1080/10510974.2022.2024905

Huberty, C. J., & Petoskey, M. D. (2000). Multivariate analysis of variance and covariance. In *Handbook of applied multivariate statistics and mathematical modeling* (pp. 183–208). Academic Press. DOI: 10.1016/B978-012691360-6/50008-2

Inkster, B., Nguyen, T., & Ram, R. (2020). Adoption of AI-driven systems in crisis management: Barriers and facilitators. *Journal ofTechnology in Crisis Management, 18*(2), 101–117.

Inkster, B., Sarda, S., & Milligan, J. (2020). Chatbots for emotional support: Applications in educational settings during the COVID-19 pandemic. *Journal of Digital Health*, *9*(4), 300–315. DOI: 10.1097/jdh.2020.00904

Ischen, C., Araujo, T., Voorveld, H., van Noort, G., & Smit, E. (2020). Privacy concerns in chatbot interactions. In Følstad, A. (Eds.), Lecture Notes in Computer Science: Vol. 11970. *Chatbot research and design. CONVERSATIONS 2019* (pp. 34–48). Springer., DOI: 10.1007/978-3-030-39540-7_3

Ismail, M., & Ade-Ibijola, A. (2019). Lecturer's Apprentice: A chatbot for assisting novice programmers. Proceedings—2019 International multidisciplinary information technology and engineering conference, IMITEC 2019. South Africa, 1–8. IEEE. DOI: 10.1109/IMITEC45504.2019.9015857

Jackson, B., & Parry, K. (•••). Empowering Teams through Collaborative Leadership. *The Leadership Quarterly*, *34*(2), 200–215.

Jackson, M. (2021). Collaboration between AI and educators: Enhancing teaching. *Educational Technology Journal*, *28*(1), 115–129.

Janati, S. E., Maach, A., & Ghanami, D. E. (2020). Adaptive e-learning ai-powered chatbot based on multimedia indexing. *International Journal of Advanced Computer Science and Applications*, *11*(12). Advance online publication. DOI: 10.14569/IJACSA.2020.0111238

Järvenoja, H., Volet, S., & Järvelä, S. (2013). Regulation of emotions in socially challenging learning situations: An instrument to measure the adaptive and social nature of the regulation process. *Educational Psychology*, *33*(1), 31–58. DOI: 10.1080/01443410.2012.742334

Johnson, D. (2023). The role of emotional intelligence in reducing burnout among healthcare professionals. *Journal of Healthcare Management*, *68*(1), 15–28. PMID: 36602452

Johnson, M. (2018). Integrating AI tools with traditional teaching methods: A balanced approach. *Teaching Innovation Journal*, *27*(1), 45–61.

Johnson, M. (2019). Automating administrative tasks with AI in education. *Journal of Educational Management*, *17*(2), 66–80.

Johnson, P., Brown, C., & Taylor, R. (2023). The strategic potential of chatbots in university leadership. *Journal of Higher Education Leadership*, *45*(1), 78–93.

Johnson, R., & Schenker, M. (2023). Data-driven approaches in education: The role of AI-powered tools. *Journal of Educational Technology*, *18*(2), 56–73.

Johnston, B., Williams, R., & Dawson, M. (2021). Conversational AI for student services: A case for improving accessibility. *Computers & Education, 165*, 104130.

Jones, A. (2020). Evolution of chatbot frameworks and their educational implications. *Technology in Education Journal, 42*(2), 97–113.

Jones, C. (2021). Cognitive engagement and the role of chatbots in student learning. *Journal of Educational Psychology, 63*(2), 153–169.

Jones, L., & Sallis, R. (2020). Ethics in AI: Data privacy and protection in educational technology. *Journal of Educational Ethics, 15*(2), 67–81. DOI: 10.1080/13812787.2020.1852905

Jongerius, C. M. (2018). Quantifying chatbot performance by using data analytics (Master's thesis).

Jung, H., Lee, J., & Lee, S. (2020). A review of the applications of chatbots in higher education. *Computers & Education, 151*, 103854. DOI: 10.1016/j.compedu.2020.103854

Kaiser Permanente. (2023). *Integrated care: How collaboration improves health outcomes.* Retrieved from Kaiser Permanente.

Kanipriya, M., Sugumaran, D., Pandiyarajan, V., Yogananda, B. S., Selvakumar, P., & Mohan, S. (2024, January). Analysis of Electromyography Signals for Control of Mechanical Prosthesis using Machine Learning Techniques. In 2024 2nd International Conference on Intelligent Data Communication Technologies and Internet of Things (IDCIoT) (pp. 1059-1067). IEEE.

Kantharuban, A., Milbauer, J., Strubell, E., & Neubig, G. (2024). Stereotype or Personalization? User Identity Biases Chatbot Recommendations. arXiv preprint arXiv:2410.05613.

Kenny, R., Zhang, Y., & Chen, H. (2021). Addressing the digital divide: Access and inclusivity challenges in educational technology implementation. *Journal of Educational Technology, 14*(1), 57–69.

Kerlyl, A., Hall, P., & Bull, S. (2006, December). Bringing chatbots into education: Towards natural language negotiation of open learner models. In *International Conference on Innovative Techniques and Applications of Artificial Intelligence.* London. Springer. (pp. 179-192). 4.

Kessler, R. C.. (2023). Ginger: Integrating Human and AI Support for Mental Health. *Psychiatric Services (Washington, D.C.), 74*(1), 65–72.

Keyvan, K., & Huang, J. X. (2022). How to approach ambiguous queries in conversational search: A survey of techniques, approaches, tools, and challenges. *ACM Computing Surveys*, *55*(6), 1–40. DOI: 10.1145/3534965

Khan, A., Ranka, S., Khakare, C., & Karve, S. (2019). NEEV(2019): An education informational chatbot. *International Research Journal of Engineering and Technology.*, *6*(4), 492–495.

Khneyzer, C., Boustany, Z., & Dagher, J. (2024). AI-Driven Chatbots in CRM: Economic and Managerial Implications across Industries. *Administrative Sciences*, *14*(8), 182. DOI: 10.3390/admsci14080182

Khosravi, P., Ghaffari, A., & Vafaei-Najar, A. (2023). The role of emotional intelligence in enhancing chatbot interactions in healthcare. *Journal of Medical Systems*, *47*(2), 123.

Kim, H. (2021). Building trust in AI systems for education: Transparency and explainability. *Journal of AI in Education*, *19*(4), 401–417.

Kim, H., & Park, S. (2022). Real-time scheduling with AI chatbots: Enhancing teacher-student coordination. *Asia-Pacific Journal of Educational Technology*, *20*(3), 245–261.

Kim, N. Y., Cha, Y., & Kim, H. S. (2019). Future English learning: Chatbots and artificial intelligence. *Multimedia-Assisted Language Learning*, *22*(3), 32–53.

Kim, S., Park, Y., & Choi, J. (2023). Enhancing emotional intelligence through chatbot interactions in healthcare settings. *BMC Health Services Research*, *23*(1), 189. PMID: 36823616

Kobayashi, H., & Tanaka, Y. (2021). Multilingual chatbot applications for diverse academic communities. *Journal of Asian Educational Research*, *12*(2), 152–169.

Kooli, C. (2023). Chatbots in education and research: A critical examination of ethical implications and solutions. *Sustainability (Basel)*, *15*(7), 5614. DOI: 10.3390/su15075614

Korzynski, P., Kozminski, A. K., & Baczynska, A. (2023). Navigating leadership challenges with technol ogy: Uncovering the potential of ChatGPT, virtual reality, human capital management systems, robotic process automation, and social media. *International Entrepreneurship Review*, *9*(2), 7–18. DOI: 10.15678/IER.2023.0902.01

Kotter (2012) – Resistance to change and strategies to address it.

Kourentzes, N. (2023). Artificial Intelligence in Health Care: The Role of Chatbots. *Journal of Healthcare Leadership*, *15*, 23–32.

Krauter, J. (2024). Bridging the uncanny valley: Improving AI chatbots for effective leadership mentoring. *Open Journal of Leadership*, *13*(3), 342–384. DOI: 10.4236/ojl.2024.133021

Kritzinger, D., & Jansen van Rensburg, L. (2021). Cybersecurity challenges in educational institutions: A threat assessment. *Journal of Information Security*, *30*(2), 82–95. DOI: 10.1109/JISec.2021.3133790

Kuhail, M. A., Alturki, N., Alramlawi, S., & Alhejori, K. (2023). Interacting with educational chatbots: A systematic review. *Education and Information Technologies*, *28*(1), 973–1018. DOI: 10.1007/s10639-022-11177-3

Kumar, R., & Rose, C. P. (2011). Architecture for Building Conversational Agents that Support Collaborative Learning. *IEEE Transactions on Learning Technologies*, *4*(1), 21–34. DOI: 10.1109/TLT.2010.41

Kumar, S., & Shah, A. (2021). Challenges in implementing chatbot systems in legacy educational platforms. *Journal of Systems Integration*, *9*(3), 223–237.

Kushwaha, A. K., Kumar, P., & Kar, A. K. (2021). What impacts customer experience for B2B enterprises on using AI-enabled chatbots? Insights from Big data analytics. *Industrial Marketing Management*, *98*, 207–221. DOI: 10.1016/j.indmarman.2021.08.011

Langeveldt, D. C. (2021). AI-Driven Leadership: A Conceptual Framework for Educational Decision-Making in the AI Era. *Journal of Educational Administration*, *59*(3), 256–270.

Larnyo, E., Dai, B., Nutakor, J. A., Ampon-Wireko, S., Appiah, R., Larnyo, A., . . . Nkrumah, E. N. K. (2021, August). Assessing the impact of social media use on everyday emotion in health crises: a study of international students in China during COVID-19. In Healthcare (Vol. 9, No. 8, p. 1011). MDPI.

Leach, M. J., Wong, A., & Yamaguchi, K. (2022). Improving job satisfaction through collaboration in healthcare teams. *Journal of Healthcare Management*, *67*(3), 215–224.

Lee, A., & Mitchell, D. (2022). Dashboard visualizations for effective decision-making in schools. *AI in Education Journal*, *14*(4), 78–93.

Lee, D., & Yeo, S. (2022). Developing an AI-based chatbot for practicing responsive teaching mathematics. *Computers & Education*, *191*, 104646. DOI: 10.1016/j.compedu.2022.104646

Lee, K. W., Chiu, S. Y., & Wong, C. M. (2023). Emotional intelligence and team cohesion in collaborative healthcare environments. *Journal of Interprofessional Care*, *37*(2), 240–248. PMID: 35403548

Lee, R., & Mitchell, S. (2022). 24/7 student support through chatbot integration: The University of Melbourne case study. *Journal of International Student Affairs*, *15*(4), 390–402.

Lee, S. (2021). Machine learning for adaptable conversational agents. *Artificial Intelligence Journal*, *78*(1), 53–69.

Lee, S., & Chan, T. (2021). Gamification strategies in AI-powered chatbot learning. *Journal of Interactive Learning*, *29*(2), 153–170.

Lee, S., & Choi, J. (2020). Student resistance to AI integration in education: Overcoming barriers to adoption. *Journal of Educational Technology & Society*, *23*(1), 68–82.

Lee, Y. J. (2023). Enhancing Patient Care with AI: A Case Study of Chatbot Utilization in Clinical Settings. *BMC Health Services Research*, *23*(1), 101. PMID: 36721213

Leithwood and Azah (2017) – Importance of empathy in fostering supportive learning environments.

Leithwood and Azah (2017) – Mentioned in the section on stakeholder engagement, their work emphasizes the importance of collaborative decision-making in improving strategic planning and implementation.

Leithwood, K.. (2004). Transforming educational leadership through adaptive practices. *Educational Leadership Journal*, *62*(5), 8–13.

Leithwood, K., Aitken, R., & Jantzi, D. (2004). Fostering innovation and creativity in educational leadership: A guide for educational leaders. *Educational Leadership Quarterly*, *38*(1), 120–133.

Leithwood, K., & Azah, V. N. (2017). Characteristics of effective school leaders: A focus on decision-making. *Educational Management Administration & Leadership*, *45*(3), 34–52.

Leithwood, K., & Louis, K. S. (2012). *Linking leadership to student learning*. John Wiley & Sons.

Levin, A. R., Phillips, K., & Davis, B. (2019). Financial crises in education: Navigating budget cuts and economic downturns. *Journal of Education Finance*, *45*(3), 216–232. DOI: 10.1353/jef.2019.0031

Li, H., & Kumar, S. (2020). The role of chatbots in higher education: Enhancing administrative efficiency and student support. *Journal of Educational Technology & Society*, *23*(3), 45–55. DOI: 10.1000/ets.2020.00345

Lim, D., & Tan, J. (2022). Chatbot analytics for student feedback and academic adaptation. *Journal of Asian Education*, *20*(2), 212–230.

Lim, S., Jung, H., & Park, M. (2020). Supporting educators in the integration of chatbots through professional development initiatives. *Journal of Teacher Education*, *29*(3), 43–58.

Lin, P., Wang, T., & Chen, S. (2020). Enhancing collaboration in schools through AI chatbots. *Educational Innovations Journal*, *12*(1), 102–115.

Linse, A. R. (2007). Team peer evaluation. In Schreyer Institute for Teaching Excellence. http://www.schreyerinstitute.psu.edu/

Li, S., Zhang, Y., & Chen, H. (2017). Predictive analytics in educational settings: Anticipating trends and outcomes with AI technologies. *Journal of Artificial Intelligence in Education*, *21*(4), 210–228.

Liu, J., & Chen, L. (2022). Personalized learning and administrative support using AI chatbots in education. *Journal of Machine Learning Applications in Education*, *18*(3), 265–284.

Liu, Y., Zhang, J., & Wang, L. (2020). Artificial intelligence in crisis management: Applications in data collection and decision making. *International Journal of Emergency Management*, *16*(2), 111–129. DOI: 10.1504/IJEM.2020.107903

Li, X.. (2017). Chatbots in education: Contextual and personalized responses through NLP. *Journal of Educational Research and Innovation*, *5*(1), 72–88.

López, J., Fernández, M., & Reyes, F. (2023). Emotional support and burnout: A role for emotional support in reducing burnout among healthcare providers-an exploratory study through the application of a chatbot approach. *International Journal of Health Services*, *53*(2), 275–291.

Loshin, D. (2020). Data privacy and ethics in education: Navigating FERPA and GDPR compliance. *Journal of Educational Data Privacy*, *14*(1), 30–42.

Luckin, R., Holmes, W., Griffiths, M., & Forcier, L. B. (2016). *Intelligence Unleashed: An Argument for AI in Education*. Pearson.

Luo, X., Tong, S., Fang, Z., & Qu, Z. (2019). Machines versus humans: the impact of AI chatbot disclosure on customer purchases. Luo, X, Tong S, Fang Z, Qu, (2019), 20-33.

Luo, C. J., & Gonda, D. E. (2019). Code Free Bot: An easy way to jumpstart your chatbot! *Proceeding of the 2019 IEEE International Conference on Engineering, Technology and Education (TALE 2019)*, Australia, 1–3, IEEE. DOI: 10.1109/TALE48000.2019.9226016

Lu, S., Zhang, Y., & Chen, Q. (2021). The impact of AI chatbots on school operations: A review of practical applications. *Educational Technology and Leadership, 9*(2), 60–78.

Madasamy, S., & Aquilanz, L. L. C. (2023). THE EVOLUTION OF CHATBOTS: CLOUD AND AI SYNERGY IN BANKING CUSTOMER INTERACTIONS. *Journal of Emerging Technologies and Innovative Research*, •••, 10.

Madgule, M., Vinayaka, N., Sonkhaskar, Y. M., Patel, D. R., Karthikeyan, R., & Selvakumar, P. (2023). Mechanical properties and microstructure of activated TIG welded similar joints of Inconel alloys by desirability approaches. *Materials Today: Proceedings, 77*, 528–533.

Majumder, S., & Mondal, A. (2021). Are chatbots really useful for human resource management? *International Journal of Speech Technology, 24*(4), 969–977. DOI: 10.1007/s10772-021-09834-y

Makasi, T., Nili, A., Desouza, K., & Tate, M. (2020). Chatbot-mediated public service delivery: A public service value-based framework. *First Monday, 25*(12).

Manikandakumar, M., & Sridevi, S. (2023). From Observation to Active Learning: A Collaborative Learning Approach for Object Oriented Programming Course. *Journal of Engineering Education Transformations, 36*(4), 150–160. DOI: 10.16920/jeet/2023/v36i4/23125

Maria, K., Drigas, A., & Skianis, C. (2022). Chatbots as cognitive, educational, advisory & coaching systems. *Technium Soc. Sci. J., 30*, 109.

Marler and Fisher (2013) – Referenced in the resource allocation section for their insights into the importance of effective resource allocation in achieving organizational goals.

Martinez, L., & Lopez, S. (2021). Data-driven insights for curriculum improvement through chatbots. *Journal of Learning Analytics, 13*(3), 92–105.

Martin, J., Thompson, R., & Lee, K. (2023). The impact of chatbot technology on emotional intelligence in healthcare leadership: A case study. *Journal of Healthcare Leadership, 15*, 45–58.

Mayo Clinic. (2022). *Team-based care: The Mayo Clinic model.* Retrieved from Mayo Clinic.

Meacham, M. (2020). *AI in talent development: Capitalize on the AI revolution to transform the way you work, learn, and live*. Association for Talent Development.

Mehrabi et al. (2021) – Highlighting AI bias concerns.

Mehta, R., & Kaur, N. (2022). Improving attendance reporting accuracy through chatbot technologies. *Indian Journal of Educational Innovations*, *14*(3), 312–328.

Mendez, S., Johanson, K., Martin Conley, V., Gosha, K., & Mack, A. (2020). Chatbots: Atoolto supplementthe future faculty mentoring of doctoral engineering students. *International Journal of Doctoral Studies*, *15*, 15. DOI: 10.28945/4579

Meskó, B.. (2023). The Role of AI in Healthcare: A Review of Babylon Health's Chatbot. *Health Informatics Journal*, *29*(2), 75–83.

Miao, Y., & Li, Y. (2021). Chatbots in Higher Education: A Systematic Review. *Computers & Education*, *167*, 104188.

Michikyan, M., Subrahmanyam, K., Regan, P., Castillo, L. G., Ham, L., Harkness, A., & Schwartz, S. J. (2023). Social connectedness and negative emotion modulation: Social media use for coping among college students during the COVID-19 pandemic. *Emerging Adulthood*, *11*(4), 1039–1054. DOI: 10.1177/21676968231176109 PMID: 38602955

Miller, E. (2016). How chatbots will help education. Venturebeat. https://venturebeat.com/2016/09/29/how-chatbots-will-help-education/

Miller, G. (2019). Accuracy and ambiguity in student queries: Challenges for chatbots in education. *Journal of Educational Technology & Society*, *22*(1), 45–58.

Miller, J., & Brown, K. (2022). Automating administrative processes with chatbots: Implications for educational leadership. *Journal of Educational Administration*, *52*(2), 138–155.

Miller, K. L., DeVoe, J. E., & Patel, N. (2023). The impact of multidisciplinary teamwork on patient outcomes: A systematic review. *International Journal of Health Policy and Management*, *12*(5), 110–120.

Mitroff, I. I. (2019). *Crisis management in higher education: A global perspective*. University of California Press.

Mitroff, I. I., & Anagnos, G. (2020). *Managing crises: A guide to preparing for and responding to emergencies in higher education*. Cambridge University Press.

Mitroff, I. I., & Anagnos, T. (2020). *Managing crises: An interdisciplinary approach*. Wiley-Blackwell.

Molnár, G., & Szüts, Z. (2018, September). The role of chatbots in formal education. In 2018 IEEE 16th international symposium on intelligent systems and informatics (SISY) (pp. 000197-000202). IEEE.

Mondal, S., & Mitra, P. (2022). The role of emerging technologies to fight against COVID-19 pandemic: An exploratory review. *Transactions of the Indian National Academy of Engineering : an International Journal of Engineering and Technology*, *7*(1), 157–174. DOI: 10.1007/s41403-022-00322-6 PMID: 35837009

Morana, S., Gnewuch, U., Jung, D., & Granig, C. (2020). The Effect of Anthropomorphism on Investment Decision-Making with Robo-Advisor Chatbots. In ECIS.

Morley, C., Li, Z., & Wang, H. (2020). Ethical considerations in crisis management: Ensuring data privacy and security in AI systems. *Journal of Business Ethics*, *159*(2), 335–350.

Morley, J., Hennessey, L., & Xie, J. (2020). Ethical and privacy considerations in the use of chatbots during crises. *Journal of Ethics and Information Technology*, *22*(1), 23–35. DOI: 10.1007/jeit.2020.02201

Morley, J., Robinson, D., & Saunders, J. (2020). Data protection and privacy in the era of artificial intelligence: Challenges and solutions. *International Journal of Information Security*, *28*(4), 225–240. DOI: 10.1007/s10207-019-04657-4

Morrison & Ross (2020) – Addressing end-to-end encryption and secure authentication protocols.

Morris, P., & Evans, M. (2021). Lessons from AI implementation in global education systems: The Netherlands and Canada. *Global Educational Perspectives*, *11*(3), 49–66.

Moyo, A., Nkosi, S., & Dlamini, T. (2023). Increasing chatbot adoption through user training programs: A South African perspective. *African Journal of Educational Technology*, *8*(1), 145–163.

Murtarelli, G., Gregory, A., & Romenti, S. (2021). A conversation-based perspective for shaping ethical human–machine interactions: The particular challenge of chatbots. *Journal of Business Research*, *129*, 927–935. DOI: 10.1016/j.jbusres.2020.09.018

Musundire, A. (2021). The impact of e-learning instructional knowledge on pedagogical attitude and learner performance: The context of South African private institutions of higher learning. [IJDLDC]. *International Journal of Digital Literacy and Digital Competence*, *12*(4), 33–53. DOI: 10.4018/IJDLDC.2021100103

Musundire, A. (2022). The effectiveness of self-directed supervision on improving quality of teaching: Perceptions of South African school-based managers and educators. [IJTEPD]. *International Journal of Teacher Education and Professional Development*, *5*(1), 1–17. DOI: 10.4018/IJTEPD.304873

Musundire, A., & Dreyer, J. M. (2018). Effectiveness of the Clinical Supervision Strategy as a Tool for Improving Teaching Quality: Perceptions of South African School-Based Managers and Educators. *Africa Education Review*, *16*(2), 109–125. DOI: 10.1080/18146627.2018.1454841

Musundire, A., & Mumanyi, O. (2020). Exploring challenges, opportunities, and prospects associated with higher education student funding in the context of South Africa. *Journal of Management & Administration*, *2020*(1). https://hdl.handle.net/10520/EJC-1da02559bc

Nawaz, N., & Gomes, A. M. (2019). Artificial intelligence chatbots are new recruiters. IJACSA). *International Journal of Advanced Computer Science and Applications*, *10*(9). Advance online publication. DOI: 10.14569/IJACSA.2019.0100901

Neumann, A. T., Arndt, T., Köbis, L., Meissner, R., Martin, A., de Lange, P., Pengel, N., Klamma, R., & Wollersheim, H.-W. (2021). Chatbots as a tool to scale mentoring processes: Individually supporting self-study in higher education. *Frontiers in Artificial Intelligence*, *4*, 668220. Advance online publication. DOI: 10.3389/frai.2021.668220 PMID: 34337393

Ng, T., & Lin, K. (2019). Professional development and AI literacy for educational leaders: Bridging the gap for effective integration. *Journal of Educational Leadership*, *12*(2), 88–101. DOI: 10.1080/10250001.2019.1150496

Nguyen, Q. N., & Sidorova, A. (2018). Understanding user interactions with a chatbot: A self-determination theory approach. Proceedings of the Twenty-Fourth Americas Conference on Information Systems, United States of America, 1–5. Association for Information Systems (AIS).

Nguyen, T. H., Pham, H. T., & Tran, Q. D. (2022). Personalized feedback in education: Chatbots as teaching assistants. *Journal of Learning Technologies*, *16*(1), 25–40.

Nguyen, T. N., & Lee, S. W. (2021). Enhancing student engagement with chatbots: A North American perspective. *Journal of Educational Computing Research*, *59*(4), 708–733.

Nieminen, J., & Vartiainen, T. (2022). AI-enabled scheduling solutions in European higher education: A case study from Finland. *European Journal of Educational Technology*, *14*(1), 57–74.

Nkosi, S., & Dlamini, M. (2022). Streamlining resource management with chatbots: Stellenbosch University as a case study. *Journal of African Educational Development, 10*(2), 200–218.

Nuruzzaman, M., & Hussain, O. K. (2018, October). A survey on chatbot implementation in customer service industry through deep neural networks. In 2018 IEEE 15th international conference on e-business engineering (ICEBE) (pp. 54-61). IEEE. DOI: 10.1109/ICEBE.2018.00019

O'Neill, D. (2023). Leveraging Chatbots for Chronic Disease Management in NHS England. *International Journal of Health Services, 53*(2), 275–291.

O'Neill, K., & Binns, T. (2021). Data-driven policy-making in Australian schools: Addressing learning gaps. *Australian Journal of Education Policy, 8*(4), 120–135.

Ojo, A., Smith, K., & Walker, J. (2023). Predictive analytics in educational management: Applications for strategic planning and student success. *Journal of Educational Research & Policy Studies, 15*(1), 5–18. DOI: 10.1098/jedres.2023.123450

Okeke, F., & Adebayo, T. (2022). Personalizing academic notifications with chatbots at the University of Lagos. *Nigerian Journal of Educational Technology, 25*(3), 172–188.

Okonkwo, C. W., & Ade-Ibijola, A. (2021). Chatbots applications in education: A systematic review. *Computers and Education: Artificial Intelligence, 2*, 100033. DOI: 10.1016/j.caeai.2021.100033

Ondáš, S., Pleva, M., & Hládek, D. (2019, November). How chatbots can be involved in the education process. In 2019 17th International Conference on Emerging eLearning Technologies and Applications (ICETA) (pp. 575-580). IEEE. DOI: 10.1109/ICETA48886.2019.9040095

Otieno, J., & Karanja, B. (2021). Real-time attendance updates through chatbot systems: The University of Nairobi's experience. *East African Journal of Education, 16*(4), 276–290.

Owoc, M. L., Sawicka, A., & Weichbroth, P. (2019, August). Artificial intelligence technologies in education: benefits, challenges and strategies of implementation. In *IFIP International Workshop on Artificial Intelligence for Knowledge Management* (pp. 37-58). Cham: Springer International Publishing.

Paliwal, Y., Shukla, O. H., & Sehgal, V. K. (2024). Restro AI Tech Management System.

Pandya, R., & Simpson, A. (2022). AI-powered tools in education: Chatbots in student engagement and parent communication. *Educational Technology Research Journal, 55*(2), 123–137.

Patel, M., Shah, R., & Joshi, P. (2022). Leveraging AI for efficient attendance management in educational institutions. *International Journal of Educational Robotics, 11*(3), 189–202.

Patel, R., & Singh, A. (2021). Real-time feedback through AI chatbots and its impact on student learning. *Journal of Educational Assessment, 22*(3), 234–248.

Patel, V. (2023). The Impact of Chatbots on Patient Engagement and Outcomes in Healthcare Systems. *Healthcare Technology Letters, 10*(2), 45–53.

Pedró, F., & Hodge, S. (2021). Leadership in the Age of AI: The Role of Chatbots. *Leadership and Organization Development Journal, 42*(7), 1053–1067.

Pérez, J. Q., Daradoumis, T., & Puig, J. M. M. (2020). Rediscovering the use of chatbots in education: A systematic literature review. *Computer Applications in Engineering Education, 28*(6), 1549–1565. DOI: 10.1002/cae.22326

Pérez, J., Romero, E., & García-Sánchez, J. N. (2020). Chatbots in learning management systems: Enhancing course material management and student engagement. *Journal of Educational Computing Research, 58*(4), 753–779. DOI: 10.1177/0735633120903033

Pham, X. L., Pham, T., Nguyen, Q. M., Nguyen, T. H., & Cao, T. T. H. (2018). Chatbot as an intelligent personal assistant for mobile language learning. Proceedings of the 2018 2nd international conference on education and e-Learning—ICEEL 2018, Indonesia, 16–21. ACM. DOI: 10.1145/3291078.3291115

Potla, R. T. (2023). Enhancing Customer Relationship Management (CRM) through AI-Powered Chatbots and Machine Learning. *Distributed Learning and Broad Applications in Scientific Research, 9*, 364–383.

Przegalinska, A., Ciechanowski, L., Stroz, A., Gloor, P., & Mazurek, G. (2019). In bot we trust: A new methodology of chatbot performance measures. *Business Horizons, 62*(6), 785–797. DOI: 10.1016/j.bushor.2019.08.005

Qawqzeh, Y. (2024). Exploring the Influence of Student Interaction with ChatGPT on Critical Thinking, Problem Solving, and Creativity. *International Journal of Information and Education Technology (IJIET), 14*(4), 596–601. DOI: 10.18178/ijiet.2024.14.4.2082

Rahmani, D., & Kamberaj, H. (2021, May). Implementation and usage of artificial intelligence powered chatbots in human resources management systems. In *Conference: International conference on social and applied sciences at: University of New York Tirana.*

Rao, P., & Jain, S. (2022). Enhancing parental involvement with chatbot-based notifications: Insights from Delhi Public School. *Indian Journal of Educational Policy, 15*(3), 236–250.

Rathore, H., Gupta, R., & Kumar, A. (2022). Emotional Intelligence and Patient Satisfaction in Health Care Leadership. *Journal of Health Organization and Management, 36*(3), 301–316.

Reddick, C., Chatfield, A. T., & Belur, S. B. (2021). Ethics, privacy, and data protection in the digital age of educational technology. *Journal of Data Ethics in Education, 18*(2), 61–74.

Reeves, S., Pelone, F., Harrison, R., & Goldman, J. (2022). Interprofessional collaboration to improve professional practice and healthcare outcomes. *Cochrane Database of Systematic Reviews, 3*, CD000072. PMID: 28639262

Rhim, J., Kwak, M., Gong, Y., & Gweon, G. (2022). Application of humanization to survey chatbots: Change in chatbot perception, interaction experience, and survey data quality. *Computers in Human Behavior, 126*, 107034. DOI: 10.1016/j.chb.2021.107034

Riel, J. (2020). Essential features and critical issues with educational chatbots: toward personalized learning via digital agents. In Khosrow-Pour, M. (Ed.), *Handbook of research on modern educational technologies, applications, and management* (pp. 246–262). IGI Global., DOI: 10.1142/S0218194019400163

Robinson, J., Taylor, A., & Clarke, H. (2020). Data-driven decision-making through chatbot analytics in education. *Journal of Digital Learning in Higher Education, 8*(2), 105–120.

Robinson, V. M. J., Lloyd, C. A., & Rowe, K. J. (2008). The impact of leadership on student outcomes: An analysis of the differential effects of leadership types. *Educational Administration Quarterly, 44*(5), 635–674. DOI: 10.1177/0013161X08321509

Ross, A., Willson, V. L., Ross, A., & Willson, V. L. (2017). Independent samples T-test. Basic and advanced statistical tests: Writing results sections and creating tables and figures, 13-16.

Ruben, B. D., De Lisi, R., & Gigliotti, R. A. (2023). *A guide for leaders in higher education: Concepts, competencies, and tools.* Taylor & Francis.

Rukadikar, A., & Khandelwa, K. (2024). Navigating change: A qualitative exploration of chatbot adoption in recruitment. *Cogent Business & Management, 11*(1), 2345759. DOI: 10.1080/23311975.2024.2345759

Ruth, D. (2006). Frameworks of managerial competence: Limits, problems and suggestions. *Journal of European Industrial Training, 30*(3), 206–226. DOI: 10.1108/03090590610662959

Sandoval, Z. V. (2018). Design and implementation of a chatbot in online higher education settings. *Issues in Information Systems, 19*(4), 44–52. DOI: 10.48009/4_iis_2018_44-52

Santos, G. A., De Andrade, G. G., Silva, G. R. S., Duarte, F. C. M., Da Costa, J. P. J., & de Sousa, R. T. (2022). A conversation-driven approach for chatbot management. *IEEE Access : Practical Innovations, Open Solutions, 10*, 8474–8486. DOI: 10.1109/ACCESS.2022.3143323

Sari, I. P., Maulana, M. S. R., Septiandini, E., & Rusmantoro, A. R. (2020, November). Web-based Educational Administration System for Student Affairs: An Initial Step to Develop Data-Driven Decision Making. In *2020 International Conference on Informatics, Multimedia, Cyber and Information System (ICIMCIS)* (pp. 142-146). IEEE. DOI: 10.1109/ICIMCIS51567.2020.9354322

Satow, L. (2017). Chatbots as teaching assistants: Introducing a model for learning facilitation by AI Bots. SAP Community. https://blogs.sap.com/2017/07/12/chatbots-as-teaching-assistants-introducing-a-model-for-learning-facilitation-by-ai-bots/

Savastano, M., Biclesanu, I., Anagnoste, S., Laviola, F., & Cucari, N. (2024). Enterprise chatbots in managers' perception: A strategic framework to implement successful chatbot applications for business decisions. *Management Decision*. Advance online publication. DOI: 10.1108/MD-10-2023-1967

Schmidt, T., & Hoffmann, B. (2021). Faculty engagement with real-time attendance data via chatbots. *European Journal of Educational Technology, 22*(3), 310–328.

Schmitt, M. (2023). Improving Healthcare Outcomes with AI Chatbots: A Case Study of Ada Health. *Journal of Medical Systems, 47*(5), 234.

Sebastian, G. (2023). Do Chatgpt and other AI chatbots pose a cybersecurity risk? An exploratory study. International journal of security and privacy in pervasive computing (15) https://orcid.org/0000-0003-2543-9127

Selvakumar, P. (2024). Emerging Engineering Technologies: Design, Development, and Industrial Applications of IoT-Based Aquaculture Monitoring System. In El Kacimi, Y., & Alaoui, K. (Eds.), *Emerging Engineering Technologies and Industrial Applications* (pp. 332–341). IGI Global., DOI: 10.4018/979-8-3693-1335-0.ch016

Selvakumar, P., Mariappan, P., Shunmugam, S., Paul, R., & Jabez, S. (2024). Removal of chemicals from effluent using photobioreactor technology to improve environmental and health impacts. *Zeitschrift für Physikalische Chemie*, *2024*(7), 1295–1302. Advance online publication. DOI: 10.1515/zpch-2023-0450

Selvakumar, P., Palanisamy, S. K., Cinthaikinian, S., Palanisamy, V., Mariappan, R., & Selvakumar, P. K. (2024). Biosensors and its diverse applications in healthcare systems. *Zeitschrift für Physikalische Chemie*, *2024*. Advance online publication. DOI: 10.1515/zpch-2023-0406

Sepahpour, T. (2020). Ethical considerations of Chatbot use for mental health support (Doctoral dissertation, Johns Hopkins University).

Sergiovanni, T. J. (2001). *The principalship: A reflective practice perspective*. Allyn & Bacon.

Serrat, O. (2021). Emotional intelligence training in health care: Techniques and outcomes. *International Journal of Health Education*, *34*(2), 102–115.

Shafait, Z., Khan, M. A., Sahibzada, U. F., Dacko-Pikiewicz, Z., & Popp, J. (2021). An assessment of students' emotional intelligence, learning outcomes, and academic efficacy: A correlational study in higher education. *PLoS One*, *16*(8), e0255428. DOI: 10.1371/journal.pone.0255428 PMID: 34343173

Shah, P. (2023). *AI and the Future of Education: Teaching in the Age of Artificial Intelligence*. John Wiley & Sons.

Sharma, A., Verma, R., & Gupta, A. (2022). Chatbot applications in higher education: Enhancing student engagement and administrative efficiency. *International Journal of Educational Development*, *92*, 102621.

Sharma, P., Kundu, A., & Khan, S. (2021). Chatbots as mental health support in educational contexts: Applications and challenges. *Journal of Educational Psychology*, *35*(3), 144–158.

Shawar, B. A., & Atwell, E. (2007). Chatbots: Are they really useful? *Journal for Language Technology and Computational Linguistics*, *22*(1), 29–49.

Siemens, G., & Gašević, D. (2021). Data-driven decision making in educational leadership: The role of learning analytics. *Journal of Learning Analytics*, *8*(3), 167–182. DOI: 10.22369/jla.2021.08345

Silva, P. A., Polo, B. J., & Crosby, M. E. (2017). Adapting the studio based learning methodology to computer science education. In Fee, S., Holland-Minkley, A., & Lombardi, T. (Eds.), *New directions for computing education* (pp. 119–142). Springer., DOI: 10.1007/978-3-319-54226-3_8

Simamora, R. M., De Fretes, D., Purba, E. D., & Pasaribu, D. (2020). Practices, challenges, and prospects of online learning during covid - 19 pandemic in higher education: Lecturer perspectives. *Stud. Learn. Teach.*, *1*(3), 185–208. DOI: 10.46627/silet.v1i3.45

Singh, A., & Patel, R. (2022). Algorithmic bias and fairness in AI models used for education. *International Journal of AI Ethics*, *14*(3), 217–233.

Singh, R., & Kapoor, N. (2020). Analyzing trends in student participation using chatbot-generated attendance data. *International Journal of Educational Statistics*, *13*(2), 90–110.

Sjöström, J., Aghaee, N., Dahlin, M., & Ågerfalk, P. J. (2018). Designing chatbots for higher education practice. In *International Conference on Information Systems Education and Research* (pp. 1-10).

Sjöström, J., Aghaee, N., Dahlin, M., & Ågerfalk, P. J. (2018). Designing chatbots for higher education practice. *Proceedings of the 2018 AIS SIGED International Conference on Information Systems Education and Research.*

Skuridin, A., & Wynn, M. (2024). Chatbot Design and Implementation: Towards an Operational Model for Chatbots. *Information (Basel)*, *15*(4), 226. DOI: 10.3390/info15040226

Smith, A. J., Thomas, M., & Jones, R. (2023). Emotional intelligence and decision-making in emergency healthcare leadership. *The Journal of Emergency Medicine*, *60*(1), 18–25.

Smith, R. (2018). AI and its impact on chatbot evolution. *Artificial Intelligence in Education Journal*, *22*(1), 34–56.

Smutny, P., & Schreiberova, P. (2020). Automation in education: The role of chatbots in improving student learning and administrative tasks. *Education and Information Technologies*, *25*(4), 3451–3465. DOI: 10.1007/s10639-020-10424-1

Smutny, P., & Schreiberova, P. (2020). Chatbots for learning: A review of educational chatbots for the facebook messenger. *Computers & Education, 151*, 103862. DOI: 10.1016/j.compedu.2020.103862

Spillane, J. P. (2006). *Distributed leadership*. Jossey-Bass.

Suárez, M., & Custodio, R. (2021). Implementing AI-powered chatbots in educational institutions: A framework for enhancing administrative processes. *Educational Administration Quarterly, 57*(2), 103–122. DOI: 10.1177/0013161X20985011

Suhaili, S. M., Salim, N., & Jambli, M. N. (2021). Service chatbots: A systematic review. *Expert Systems with Applications, 184*, 115461. DOI: 10.1016/j.eswa.2021.115461

Sundaram, A., Gupta, R., & Mehra, V. (2020). NLP-driven personalized notifications in education: A comprehensive study. *Journal of Artificial Intelligence in Education, 14*(1), 67–82.

Suresh Babu, C. V., Anniyappa, C. S., & Sastha, B. D. (2024). Unraveling the Inner Workings of Massive Language Models: Architecture, Training, and Linguistic Capacities. In B. Gupta (Ed.), Challenges in Large Language Model Development and AI Ethics (pp. 239-279). IGI Global. DOI: 10.4018/979-8-3693-3860-5.ch008

Suresh Babu, C. V., & Adhithya, S. (2023). ChatGPT and Other Generative AI Tools in Education: Transformative Potential and Ethical Considerations. In Keengwe, J. (Ed.), *Creative AI Tools and Ethical Implications in Teaching and Learning* (pp. 135–152). IGI Global., DOI: 10.4018/979-8-3693-0205-7.ch007

Suresh Babu, C. V., & Rohan, B. (2023). Evaluation and Quality Assurance for Rapid E-Learning and Development of Digital Learning Resources. In Santally, M., Rajabalee, Y., & Rajputh, R. (Eds.), *Implementing Rapid E-Learning Through Interactive Materials Development* (pp. 139–170). IGI Global., DOI: 10.4018/978-1-6684-4940-0.ch008

Tandoc, E. C.Jr, Lou, C., & Min, V. L. H. (2019). Platform-swinging in a poly-social-media context: How and why users navigate multiple social media platforms. *Journal of Computer-Mediated Communication, 24*(1), 21–35. DOI: 10.1093/jcmc/zmy022

Tang et al. (2020) – Case study on enhancing administrative efficiency through chatbots.

Tanna, D., Dudhane, M., Sardar, A., Deshpande, K., & Deshmukh, N. (2020, May). Sentiment analysis on social media for emotion classification. In 2020 4th International Conference on Intelligent Computing and Control Systems (ICICCS) (pp. 911-915). IEEE. DOI: 10.1109/ICICCS48265.2020.9121057

Tariq, M. U. (Ed.). (2024). *AI-Driven Learning and Engagement in Higher Education*. IGI Global. DOI: 10.4018/979-8-3693-4074-5

Tavakol, M., & Dennick, R. (2011). Making sense of Cronbach's alpha. *International Journal of Medical Education*, *2*, 53–55. DOI: 10.5116/ijme.4dfb.8dfd PMID: 28029643

Taylor & Smith (2023) – US guidelines on fairness and transparency in AI.

Taylor, G., & Green, P. (2022). Addressing user resistance in educational chatbot adoption: Strategies for success. *Journal of Educational Management*, *29*(1), 122–137.

Taylor, L., & Smith, J. (2023). Personalized academic guidance via chatbot systems: Insights from the University of Oxford. *Journal of Higher Education Technology*, *38*(3), 295–308.

Taylor, S., & Clarke, M. (2021). Monitoring institutional performance using chatbot-driven KPIs: A case study of Cambridge University. *British Journal of Educational Leadership*, *16*(4), 321–338.

Tchankue, C.. (2023). Evaluating HealthTap: A Chatbot for Personalized Health Information. *International Journal of Medical Informatics*, *171*, 104892.

Thaker, A., Darnell, A., & Garg, A. (2023). Improving Shared Health Care Decision Making by Chatbot Technology. *International Journal of Healthcare Management*, *36*(1), 85–99.

Thirumalai, B., Ramanathan, A., Charania, A., & Stump, G. (2019). Designing for technology-enabled reflective practice: teachers' voices on participating in a connected learning practice. In Setty, R., Iyenger, R., Witenstein, M. A., Byker, E. J., & Kidwai, H. (Eds.), *Teaching and teacher education: south asian perspectives* (pp. 243–273). Palgrave Macmillan., DOI: 10.1007/978-3-030-26879-4_11

Thomas, R. (2020). Cost-effectiveness of implementing chatbots in education. *International Journal of Educational Technology*, *34*(5), 421–435.

Thomas, S. (2020). Financial challenges in adopting AI technologies for curriculum management. *International Journal of Educational Management*, *34*(6), 742–759.

Thompson, L., & White, J. (2022). Emergency communication through AI chatbots in higher education: Lessons from the pandemic. *Journal of Educational Communication Systems*, *48*(2), 104–122.

Tight, M. (2020). Student retention and engagement in higher education. *Journal of Further and Higher Education*, *44*(5), 689–704. DOI: 10.1080/0309877X.2019.1576860

Tikkinen-Piri, C., Rohunen, A., & Markkula, J. (2018). Transparency and inclusivity in educational leadership: The role of AI. *Journal of Educational Leadership, 7*(1), 10–25.

Tomlinson, C. A. (2001). *Differentiated instruction: Tailoring teaching to individual needs*. ASCD.

Turing, A. M. (1950). Computing machinery and intelligence. *Mind, 59*(236), 433–460. DOI: 10.1093/mind/LIX.236.433

Vanichvasin, P. (2021). Chatbot development as a digital learning tool to increase students' research knowledge. *International Education Studies, 14*(2), 44. DOI: 10.5539/ies.v14n2p44

Vasumathy, M. (2023). *A machine learning-based admissions support system with a case study on D.K.M. College for Women, Vellore, Design and Implementation of Higher Education Learners' Learning Outcomes*. HELLO.

Vasumathy, M., & Thirugnanam, M. (2018). An integrated approach for optimal feature selection and anatomic location identification on pediatric Foreign Body aspired radiographic images, Knowledge Computing and its Applications. *Knowledge Computing in Specific Domains, 2*, 101–128.

Verleger, M., & Pembridge, J. (2019). A pilot study integrating an AI-driven chatbot in an introductory programming course. Proceeding of the 2018 IEEE Frontiers in Education Conference (FIE), USA. IEEE. DOI: 10.1109/FIE.2018.8659282

Vijayakumar, G., Rajkumar, M., Rajiv Chandar, N., Selvakumar, P., & Duraisamy, R. (2024). Muniyandi Rajkumar, Rajiv Chandar N, Selvakumar P and Ramesh Duraisamy, (2024). Environmentally friendly TDS removal from waste water by electrochemical ion exchange batch-type recirculation (EIR) technique. *Environmental Science. Water Research & Technology, 10*(4), 826–835. DOI: 10.1039/D3EW00793F

Vijayaraghavan, V., & Cooper, J. B. (2020). Algorithm inspection for chatbot performance evaluation. *Procedia Computer Science, 171*, 2267–2274.

Villegas-Ch, W., Arias-Navarrete, A., & Palacios-Pacheco, X. (2020). Proposal of an architecture for the integration of a chatbot with artificial intelligence in a smart campus for the improvement of learning. *Sustainability (Basel), 12*(4), 1500. DOI: 10.3390/su12041500

Virtanen, K., Hämäläinen, R., & Kukkonen, T. (2018). Enhancing accessibility and scalability in higher education: The potential of chatbots in Learning Management Systems. *Journal of Educational Technology & Society*, *21*(2), 62–74. https://www.jstor.org/stable/jeductechsoci.21.2.62

Vroom, V. H., & Jago, A. G. (2023). The role of participative leadership in team effectiveness. *Organizational Dynamics*, *52*(1), 1–10.

Wang, X., Lin, X., & Shao, B. (2022). How does artificial intelligence create business agility? Evidence from chatbots. *International Journal of Information Management*, *66*, 102535. DOI: 10.1016/j.ijinfomgt.2022.102535

Wang, Y., & Lin, Y. (2019). Flipped classrooms and AI: Enhancing active learning through intelligent tutoring systems. *Journal of Computer Assisted Learning*, *35*(2), 239–250. DOI: 10.1111/jcal.12345

Wang, Z., Tchernev, J. M., & Solloway, T. (2012). A dynamic longitudinal examination of social media use, needs, and gratifications among college students. *Computers in Human Behavior*, *28*(5), 1829–1839. DOI: 10.1016/j.chb.2012.05.001

Weizenbaum, J. (1966). ELIZA—A computer program for the study of natural language communication between man and machine. *Communications of the ACM*, *9*(1), 36–45. DOI: 10.1145/365153.365168

White, J. (2020). Addressing algorithmic bias in educational AI systems. *Journal of AI Ethics*, *18*(1), 55–71.

White, J. (2020). Privacy and ethical concerns in AI-driven educational systems. *Journal of Educational Ethics*, *18*(1), 55–71.

Widen, G., Lindström, J., Brännback, M., Huvila, I., & Nyström, A. G. (2015). Mixed Emotions in Active Social Media Use-Fun and Convenient or Shameful and Embarrassing. iConference 2015 Proceedings.

Williams, C., & Johnson, P. (2021). Improving operational efficiency in higher education through chatbot automation. *International Journal of Educational Innovations*, *27*(2), 189–204.

Winkler, R., & Söllner, M. (2018). Unleashing the potential of chatbots in education: A state-of-the-art analysis. In Academy of Management Annual Meeting (AOM). https://www.alexandria.unisg.ch/254848/1/JML_699.pdf

Winkler, R., & Soellner, M. (2018). Pedagogical foundations for chatbot-based education: A conceptual framework. *Computers in Human Behavior*, *85*, 217–225. DOI: 10.1016/j.chb.2018.03.026

Winkler, R., & Söllner, M. (2018). Unleashing the Potential of Chatbots in Education: A State-Of-The-Art Analysis. In: *Academy of Management Annual Meeting (AOM)*. Chicago. 41 p. DOI: 10.5465/AMBPP.2018.15903abstract

Wu, E. H. K., Lin, C. H., Ou, Y. Y., Liu, C. Z., Wang, W. K., & Chao, C. Y. (2020). Advantages and constraints of a hybrid model K-12 e-learning assistant chatbot. *IEEE Access : Practical Innovations, Open Solutions, 8*, 77788–77801. DOI: 10.1109/ACCESS.2020.2988252

Wu, T., Johnson, L., & Martinez, A. (2023). The integration of virtual and augmented reality in education: Implications for strategic planning in educational leadership. *Journal of Educational Innovation, 14*(1), 99–114. DOI: 10.1016/jei.2023.101045

Wu, X. (2017). The impact of artificial intelligence on education: Challenges and opportunities. [https://w]. *Journal of Educational Technology & Society, 20*(1), 4–16.

Yamada, M., Goda, Y., Matsukawa, H., Hata, K., & Yasunami, S. (2016). A computer-supported collaborative learning design for quality interaction. *IEEE MultiMedia, 23*(1), 48–59. DOI: 10.1109/MMUL.2015.95

Yang, C. C., Holden, S. M., & Ariati, J. (2021). Social media and psychological well-being among youth: The multidimensional model of social media use. *Clinical Child and Family Psychology Review, 24*(3), 631–650. DOI: 10.1007/s10567-021-00359-z PMID: 34169391

Yifan, P., & Adnan, W. H. (2021). The impact of social media use towards negative emotion and suicidal tendency among students: a systematic review. In Forum Komunikasi (FK) (Vol. 16, No. 2, pp. 63-81). Universiti Teknologi MARA.

Yin, J., Goh, T. T., Yang, B., & Xiaobin, Y. (2021). Conversation technology with micro-learning: The impact of chatbot-based learning on students' learning motivation and performance. *Journal of Educational Computing Research, 59*(1), 154–177. DOI: 10.1177/0735633120952067

Zhang, J. J., Følstad, A., & Bjørkli, C. A. (2023). Organizational factors affecting successful implementation of chatbots for customer service. *Journal of Internet Commerce, 22*(1), 122–156. DOI: 10.1080/15332861.2021.1966723

Zhang, M., Liu, H., & Zhang, Y. (2020). Adolescent social networks and physical, verbal, and indirect aggression in China: The moderating role of gender. *Frontiers in Psychology, 11*, 658. DOI: 10.3389/fpsyg.2020.00658 PMID: 32292382

Zhao, Y., Li, J., & Wang, Z. (2020). Automating scheduling with AI chatbots: Efficiency and user satisfaction. *Journal of Artificial Intelligence Research in Education, 56*(3), 245–267.

Zhou, L., Gao, J., Li, D., & Shum, H. Y. (2020). The design and implementation of xiaoice, an empathetic social chatbot. *Computational Linguistics*, *46*(1), 53–93. DOI: 10.1162/coli_a_00368

Zhu, H., He, X., & Wang, J. (2021). AI-powered adaptive learning environments: Opportunities and challenges for educational leaders. *Educational Management & Administration*, *49*(3), 301–317. DOI: 10.1080/13632434.2021.1103909

About the Contributors

Austin Musundire is currently a Research Associate at University of Limpopo. He obtained his Doctorate of Educational Leadership and Management degree from the University of South Africa, and a Master of Education degree in Educational Administration, planning and policy studies (Educational leadership and Management) from the Zimbabwean Open University. He obtained a Bachelor of Education degree in Educational administration, planning and policy studies from University of Zimbabwe and a Diploma in Education from the same university.

***

Taruna Anand is presently working with Graphic Era Deemed to be University, Dehradun as an Associate Professor of English. She is a Gold Medalist and University Topper from Guru Gobind Singh Indraprastha University, Delhi. She is PhD in English and Company Secretary also. Her area of interest includes Theatre Studies, Indian Writing in English and Translation Studies. She has a rich and diverse experience of more than 22 years with several research papers published in the reputed National and International Journals.

Vijay Anant Athavale has a rich teaching, research and administrative experience of more than 33 years of serving in Government and Private Universities and Colleges in India and abroad. He has served academic assignments at Canada, the Republic of Yemen and the Republic of Sudan. He also served as an expatriate expert for the United Nations Development Programme to Ethiopia. He has been instrumental in shaping of several Institutes of repute offering Technical and Management Education in India. As a thought leader and a subject matter expert, he has presented numerous sessions at Conferences, FDPs, and Workshops as Key Note speaker, Session Chair, Organizing Committee member, TPC etc. He is a reviewer for several SCIE, Scopus, WoS indexed journals. He is also serving as editor of some Scopus indexed journals. He has contributed several chapters in books & handbooks published by IGI Global, Taylor and Francis Group, Springer nature etc.

Senthil Kumaran B is an Assistant Professor in the Department of Computer Science and Engineering at Vel Tech Rangarajan Dr. Sagunthala R&D Institute of Science and Technology, Chennai. He holds a Ph.D. in VLSI Embedded Systems and specializes in areas such as VLSI design, embedded systems, and microelectronics. His research interests focus on improving the efficiency and design of integrated circuits and embedded systems for various applications. Dr. Senthil Kumaran has authored multiple journal papers and conference presentations, contributing significantly to the advancement of technology in his field. He is committed to providing quality education and research in the domains of embedded systems and VLSI. Through his work, he aims to innovate in hardware design and integrate practical solutions into engineering problems. Dr. Kumaran continues to mentor and collaborate with students and professionals, fostering innovation in his research areas.

Pankaj Singh Chandel is an Assistant Professor in the Department of Tourism Management at Dev Sanskriti Vishwavidyalaya, Haridwar, where he has been teaching since 2014. He holds a PhD in Tourism and a PGDM in Tourism and Travel Services Management from the Indian Institute of Tourism and Travel Management. His expertise lies in homestay tourism, and he is recognized as a skilled orator on travel knowledge. Dr. Chandel has published research articles in Scopus-indexed journals and has contributed to publications with IGI Global, demonstrating his commitment to academic scholarship in the field of tourism. His research focuses on sustainable tourism practices and the development of homestay tourism in India. As an active member of several professional organizations, including the Travel Agents Association of Uttarakhand and ATOAI, Dr. Chandel actively participates in initiatives promoting sustainability in the tourism industry. His involvement in these organizations allows him to bridge the gap between academic research and industry practices. Dr. Chandel's ORCID (https://orcid.org/0000-0002-4135-8194) showcases his research outputs and professional activities.

J. Viji Gripsy is an accomplished Associate Professor at PSGR Krishnammal College for Women, with expertise in computer science and technology. Holding a Ph.D. from Bharathiar University, she specializes in AI, mobile networks, and speech recognition. Her work focuses on integrating advanced technologies into education and healthcare systems. Dr. Viji has published extensively and received awards such as the Best Faculty Award and Cloud Championship Award. She is also a recipient of several patents and has made significant contributions to both academia and industry.

J P Shritharanyaa is an accomplished academic professional currently serving as an Assistant Professor in the School of Electrical and Electronics Engineering at VIT Bhopal University since November 2022. She holds a Ph.D. in Embedded Systems from Anna University, Chennai, completed in November 2022, where her research focused on memory systems and machine learning applications. With over a decade of teaching experience, Dr. Shritharanyaa has significantly contributed to the academic and research community. She has received "Inspire Researcher Award" in the International Research Excellence Awards 2024 conducted by DPRG. She has been actively involved in the development of the Microcontroller Laboratory. Her expertise in embedded systems is reflected in her numerous publications, including journal article, book and book chapters. Notably, she is the co-principal investigator for a state-funded project on wearable technology for rural areas, demonstrating her commitment to practical and impactful research. Dr. Shritharanyaa is also recognized for her contributions as a reviewer for prominent journals and conferences, including the IET Communications and IEEE's international conferences. Her teaching portfolio includes subjects like Microprocessors, Embedded Systems, and Internet of Things, and she has mentored many students in these areas. In addition to her academic endeavors, Dr. Shritharanyaa has organized several national workshops and has completed multiple specialized training programs, further solidifying her position as a leading educator and researcher in the field of embedded systems and electronics engineering.

L. Sheeba is an Assistant Professor in the Department of Computer Applications at PSGR Krishnammal College for Women, Coimbatore, with a Ph.D. from Bharathiar University. Her research focuses on computer networks, information systems, and applications in healthcare. Dr. Sheeba has authored numerous journal articles and conference proceedings and holds a patent for a "System and Method for Detecting Lung Cancer using Intelligent Image Pattern Recognition Technique." She has also led funded projects, including a GRG Trust-funded study on voice system classification using machine learning. Dr. Sheeba is dedicated to advancing both academia and practical solutions in technology.

M. Vasumathy is an Associate Professor in the department of Information Technology, Kingston Engineering College, Vellore,TamilNadu,India. She was awarded with Ph.D in Computer Science and engineering in the year of 2019 from Vellore Institute of Technology, Vellore. She received her Master degree MS (Software Engineering) in the year of 2008 from Vellore Institute of Technology, Vellore. She had a granted patent and five Indian patent publication and various Scopus indexed journal and book chapters publication. Upskilled her knowledge through participation in data science, IOT workshop and internship programs at

IIT Madras. Certified by Wipro and Matlab. Experienced in software industry, ISRO- VSSC sponsored funded project, Teaching and entrepreneurship. Skilled in machine learning algorithms, deep learning, digital image processing and Artificial intelligence tools.

Annie Moletsane obtained her PhD: Public Management and Governance and Master of Commerce: Business Administration both from the North West University. She also obtained her PGDHE, BTech degree in Marketing Management, and ND: Marketing Management from Vaal University of Technology. She is also Teaching Advancement Universities (TAU) Fellow. Dr. Moletsane is currently a director: Student Academic Development Support and Work Integrated Learning. Leading and managing all student academic development staff members and Work Integrated Learning staff members at the Vaal University of Technology. Also, a Deputy Chairperson of USAF Learning in Practice Community of Practice (Lip Cop)

Manikandakumar M. was awarded the B.Tech., degree in Information Technology in 2009, and M.E., degree in Computer Science and Engineering in 2013 from Anna University, Chennai, India where he has completed his Ph.D during the year 2023. He is currently a Assistant Professor in the Computer Science & Engineering Department, School of Engineering and Technology, Christ University, Bangalore, India. His research interests include Artificial Intelligence, Data Science, Networks, and Educational Technology.

Killian Ticharwa Muzongondi obtained his MBA. (Leadership and Management) from Africa Leadership and Management Academy. B.Com (Transport and Logistics) including Advanced Postgraduate Supervision Capacity Development from the University of South Africa. International Certificate (Logistics and Transport) was obtained at the Chartered Institute of Logistics and Transport (CILT) including Mentoring and Coaching. Dr. Muzongondi is a professional member of the CILT.

P. Jagdish Kumar is an Assistant Professor at Department of AI & DS, FST (IcfaiTech), ICFAI Foundation for Higher Education (IFHE), Hyderabad. He completed Bachelor's Degree in Computer Science & Engineering from SREENIDHI Institute of Science and Technology, Ghatkesar, JNTUH affiliated college in 2009. He received a Master of Technology (M.Tech) from JBIET, Hyderabad. He Secured 297 rank in GATE 2009. He has 13 years of teaching experience, having previously served at reputed institutions Hyderabad. He published research papers in Scopus and SCI-indexed journals, as well as authorship of book chapters. He has been a resource person for guest lectures, seminars, and Faculty Development Programs. His areas of research include Machine

P. Selvakumar is currently an Associate Professor in the Department of Science and Humanities at Nehru Institute of Technology, Coimbatore, Tamil Nadu, India. Since 2023, he has served as the Department IQAC Coordinator at the institute. Prior to joining Nehru Institute of Technology, he held positions as an Assistant Professor in the Department of Science and Humanities various engineering colleges in Coimbatore, Tamil Nadu, India, spanning from 2011 to 2023. Dr.P. Selvakumar's academic and research interests lie primarily in the field of phytochemistry. He has made significant contributions to his field, with an impressive record that includes 30 journal publications, 12 patents, and 20 conference papers. Additionally, he has organized 5 seminars and conferences, further demonstrating his commitment to academic and scientific exchange. Throughout his career, Dr. P.Selvakumar has been recognized for his dedication and excellence in teaching, having been honored with several awards, including the Best Teacher Awards. He holds a prominent position in the academic community, contributing actively to research.

Roselin Kiruba is an Assistant Professor in the School of Computing Science & Engineering, Vel Tech Rangarajan Dr.Sagunthala R&D Institute of Science and Technology, Avadi, Chennai, India. She was awarded with Doctorate from anna university Chennai in the year of 2021. She received her M.E. in Mobile and Pervasive Computing from Anna University, Chennai, in 2013 and B.E. in Computer Science Engineering from Anna University, Chennai, in 2011. She has 3 years of teaching experience from engineering institutions. She has published 10 research articles in international and national journals, and in that 6 are SCI. Also, she is a reviewer in springer journal like earth science informatics, software computing, Multidimensional Systems and signal processing etc. Her areas of interest are cryptography, data hiding, machine learning, deep learning and IoT.

R. Sethumadhavan is a seasoned academician and management expert with 23 years of experience in the field. He currently serves as an Associate Professor at the School of Management, Presidency University in Bangalore, Karnataka. Holding a PhD in Management, Dr. Sethumadhavan brings a wealth of knowledge and expertise to his teaching and research endeavors. His extensive experience spans various aspects of management, making him a valuable resource for students and professionals alike.

Devendra Singh Rathore is a dedicated educator in the field of Computer Science and Engineering at Lakshmi Narain College of Technology in Bhopal, Madhya Pradesh. With a commitment to fostering innovation and technical skills, he has contributed significantly to the academic growth of his students. His work emphasizes the integration of practical applications in computer science, preparing future engineers to excel in a rapidly evolving technological landscape. Under his guidance, the department has seen advancements in curriculum development and research initiatives, reflecting his passion for education and technology.

S. Poorani is currently working as an Assistant Professor in the Department of Computer Technology - UG, Kongu Engineering College, Tamilnadu, India. She has 18 years of teaching experience. She published 22 articles in International journals and conferences. Her area of interest includes data mining, machine learning and deep learning.

Sarah S. has completed B.E in the year 2000 at Madras University in Computer Science and Engineering and received her M.E in Computer Science and Engineering from Anna University in the year 2010. She has around 20 years of teaching experience in Technical Teaching.

Sameer Babu M is currently serving Jamia Millia Islamia Central University as Associate Professor in the Department of Educational Studies. He is also associated with Universitas Pendidikan Indonesia as a Visiting Professor of Education. He has also served as a visiting professor at the UNESCO Chair for Social Pedagogy, the MGU, Warsaw Poland. Earlier he has worked with reputed universities like the University of Kerala, Central University of Rajasthan, Aligarh Muslim University, and Delhi University. He has 11 projects to his credit including ICSSR IMPRESS Major. He was awarded prestigious Shastri Mobility Grant to Canada in 2020.. He has published four patents for innovations and has received Research Awards from the University of Kerala for three consecutive years. He has also published 11 tools, and 26 authored and /or edited books. He also offers one complete MOOC on Swayam platform. He also received the Best E-lecture award from REST. He is a reviewer of many known journals like the British Journal of Educational Psychology, the Canadian Journal of Education, and Asia Pacific Journal of Humanities and Social Sciences.

Sheela Selvakumari is an Associate Professor in the Department of Computer Science at Sri Krishna Arts and Science College, with 19 years of experience. Her research focuses on machine learning, signal processing, and healthcare applications. She holds a Ph.D. in voice disorder classification using optimization techniques. Dr. Selvakumari has authored books, published papers, and holds patents in IoT and wearable medical devices. She is also guiding research scholars and has led funded projects related to voice system classification.

C.V. Suresh Babu is a pioneer in content development. A true entrepreneur, he founded Anniyappa Publications, a company that is highly active in publishing books related to Computer Science and Management. Dr. C.V. Suresh Babu has also ventured into SB Institute, a center for knowledge transfer. He holds a Ph.D. in Engineering Education from the National Institute of Technical Teachers Training & Research in Chennai, along with seven master's degrees in various disciplines such as Engineering, Computer Applications, Management, Commerce, Economics, Psychology, Law, and Education. Additionally, he has UGC-NET/SET qualifications in the fields of Computer Science, Management, Commerce, and Education. Currently, Dr. C.V. Suresh Babu is a Professor in the Department of Information Technology at the School of Computing Science, Hindustan Institute of Technology and Science (Hindustan University) in Padur, Chennai, Tamil Nadu, India. For more information, you can visit his personal blog at https://sites.google.com/view/cvsureshbabu/.

Index

A

C

D

E

N

O

P

Q

R

S

T

U

www.ingramcontent.com/pod-product-compliance
Lightning Source LLC
LaVergne TN
LVHW080609300926
849162LV00005B/1089